THE STRINDBERG READER

THE STRINDBERG READER

A Selection of Writings of

August Strindberg

Compiled, Translated and Edited

by

Arvid Paulson

PHAEDRA, INC., NEW YORK

PHAEDRA, INC., NEW YORK

ACKNOWLEDGMENTS

The translator and the publisher acknowledge with gratitude the permission for inclusion of excerpts and materials, previously published in the following volumes and periodicals:

EIGHT EXPRESSIONIST PLAYS by August Strindberg, translated by Arvid Paulson. Bantam Books, Inc. Copyright, Bantam Books, Inc., 1965.
> The Keys of Heaven. Copyright, Arvid Paulson, 1963.
> A Dream Play. Copyright, Arvid Paulson, 1957.
> The Great Highway. Copyright, Arvid Paulson, 1945; 1955; The American-Scandinavian Foundation, 1954.

LETTERS OF STRINDBERG TO HARRIET BOSSE. By permission of The Universal Library (Grosset and Dunlap), Publishers. Copyright, Arvid Paulson, 1959.

THE NATIVES OF HEMSÖ. Bantam Books, Inc. Copyright Arvid Paulson, 1965.

THE SCAPEGOAT. Bantam Books, Inc. Copyright, Arvid Paulson, 1967.

SHORT STORIES.—For permission to reprint LEONTO-POLIS and VESTMAN'S SEALING ADVENTURE acknowledgement is made to The American-Scandinavian Foundation and Erik J. Friis, Editor of The American-Scandinavian Review, in which they first appeared.

PROBING STRINDBERG'S PSYCHE. By Arvid Paulson.—The American-Scandinavian Review, March, 1965. By permission of Erik J. Friis, Editor, and The American-Scandinavian Foundation.

THE FATHER. A Survey of critical opinion of August Strindberg's tragedy and leading American performances of it during the past half century (1912-1962). By Arvid Paulson.—*Scandinavian Studies*. The American-Scandinavian Foundation-The University of Washington Press. Copyright, The American-Scandinavian Foundation, 1965.

—and—

THE OUTLAW.—To be published by Washington Square Press in a volume of one-act prose plays by August Strindberg in 1968.

LETTERS FROM G. B. SHAW to AUGUST STRINDBERG.—The Royal Library, Stockholm. (These two letters were found in that library by Mr. Sven Åhman, through whose courtesy they are being published here, perhaps for the first time in toto.)

❋   ❋   ❋

I wish to express my special gratitude to Dr. John A. Mish, Chief of the Oriental Division, New York Public Library; Mr. Francis Paar of the N.Y. Public Library Oriental Division, and to Mr. Sven-Erik Hsia, who were of infinite help in checking the Chinese names and words and historical dates appearing in the essay on CHINA.

A.P.

NOTE ON THE TRANSLATOR

Born and educated in Sweden, Arvid Paulson came to America as a young man. After having been a journalist for a few brief years, he went on the stage and quickly distinguished himself as actor, producer and translator of plays. Mr. Paulson's mastery of both Swedish and English, his close association with the theatre, having acted both in Swedish and English, and his lifelong devotion to Scandinavian literature, qualify him perhaps better than anyone in the world for the task of translating Strindberg. Having translated the greater part of Strindberg's many plays, SEVEN PLAYS BY AUGUST STRINDBERG and EIGHT EXPRESSIONIST PLAYS BY AUGUST STRINDBERG have been published by Bantam, and LETTERS OF STRINDBERG TO HARRIET BOSSE by The Universal Library (Grosset and Dunlap). Bantam has also brought out LAST PLAYS OF HENRIK IBSEN in Mr. Paulson's translation. In 1960 his translations of MISS JULIE and THE STRONGER were presented on television by The Play of the Week. In 1962 he was invited by The Library of Congress to present a program of readings from his translations of Strindberg's plays, novels, short stories and letters.

Mr. Paulson has been decorated by the King of Sweden for his efforts in strengthening the cultural relations between the United States and his native country, and in particular for his authoritative translations of August Strindberg's works.

In 1964 he was awarded the Gold Medal of the Royal Swedish Academy of Letters for his translations of Strindberg and other Swedish authors—the first time this medal has been awarded for translations of Swedish literature into a foreign language.

DR. AMANDUS JOHNSON, professor emeritus of the University of Pennsylvania, is the dean of Scandinavian scholars in America. As historian of the Swedes and their achievements in the United States, he has written many books on the subject. His work "The Swedish Settlements on the Delaware, 1638-1664" is perhaps his most notable contribution to the knowledge and history of the New Sweden colony established in Delaware and Pennsylvania by Queen Christina of Sweden. As the foremost authority of our time on the historical and cultural relations between Sweden and America, he has translated into English numerous Swedish works dealing with important events, accomplishments and personages. Dr. Johnson is also the founder of the American-Swedish Historical Foundation and Museum in Philadelphia as well as of the Swedish Colonial Society. He holds honorary and other degrees from numerous universities here and abroad and is the recipient of several decorations from the King of Sweden, as well as from the Republic of Finland.

CONTENTS

INTRODUCTION

Sweden has produced two geniuses in the realms of literature and the humanities whose contributions to the world stand out among the many of other prophets and spiritual pioneers of the past two centuries, who have had their birth in that land of the midnight sun, paradoxically cold and warmhearted, just below the arctic circle: Emanuel Swedenborg (1688-1772) and August Strindberg (1849-1912). They are without doubt two of the most remarkable personalities of modern times in the western world.

They had much in common. Both were interested in practically every branch of learning: literature, the arts, music, mathematics, astronomy, medicine—in fact, in all the sciences, as well as in religion, including the supernatural and manifestations of the spirit. Both labored unceasingly to discover the meaning of life and death and the hereafter, and their production was enormous.

Swedenborg acquired a position among the world's great long ago. Strindberg has grown in stature with the years and is only now coming universally into his own, thanks to translations not merely of his dramatic works but of his novels, short stories and his other literary contributions. As Eugene O'Neill and others have witnessed, he is without peer not alone in his native Sweden but in the world. Shaw stood in awe of Strindberg's genius. Ahead of his time as Strindberg was, the present generation in every civilized country throughout the world is rediscovering the magic of his dramas. Many eloquent dramatic works hitherto untranslated into most languages are now being prepared for publication, among them his Swedish and world historical dramas. In France, for instance, C.-G. Bjurström is editing an imposing series of his works, translated by himself and a host of select scholars, authors and actors. Similarly he is being rendered into Italian, Greek, Polish, Japanese, Chinese, German and many other languages. Some of his plays have even been translated into esperanto. A number of his dramatic works were first produced abroad: in Denmark, Finland and Germany, before being given in Sweden.

Indeed, Strindberg had his greatest vogue in pre-Hitler Germany, where in the 1880's many different translations of his dramas and novels appeared. At about the same time a number of French versions were brought out in Paris; and Strindberg contributed numerous articles to French periodicals also. During Hitler's regime his writings were confiscated and burned in Germany, but his plays are now acted there again and all his works are being read widely.

As a youth August Strindberg was pietistically religious. Through a friend he then became acquainted with the writings of the noted American theologian and Unitarian clergyman Theodore Parker (1810-60), whose philosophy at times bordered on agnosticism. Having been torn by doubts about the tenets and dogmas forced upon him in church and school and in his home, Parker's teachings made a deep impression upon him. He read his tracts avidly, and they nurtured his doubts. He became a rebel. And a rebel he remained throughout his life, vacillating between belief and unbelief, and for a short time turned from agnosticism to outright atheism. Yet even in his atheism he was religious. Pursued by doubt until toward the last days of his life, he embraced the cross on his death-bed—the cross he had had to bear since he was born—as his hope on the journey to the beyond. But in plays such as A DREAM PLAY, THE GHOST SONATA and THE GREAT HIGHWAY one finds strong influences of philosophers like Swedenborg, Schopenhauer, von Hartmann and Buddha. His search for an anchorage of his restless spirit knew no bounds. He was a deeply tormented soul, yet found peace at least in death.

His rebellion was brought about by much of what he witnessed, experienced, and had had to endure in his early life during an era when social concern, democratic ideals and burgeoning change were only just beginning to raise their heads. He remonstrated against many traditional, hidebound customs and beliefs; hence he stood most of the time alone. Yet he was not alone. Although continually surrounded by a sea of troublous antagonists, he stood steadfast, true to his conscience and convictions, like a rock in a turbulent ocean. At one period he turned toward radicalism and became spokesman for the 'common people'; at another he was close to socialism in his views.

In fact, he became—through the sentiments and opinions which he expressed in his writings—the precursor of some of the more significant social and religious reforms in Sweden.

Strindberg was an accomplished linguist and also a musician. He studied a dozen or more languages, including Chinese, Hebrew and Sanskrit; and some of his works were originally written by him in French and German and later translated into Swedish.

He tried his hand at many occupations. He studied to be a doctor, but fortunately lost interest in medicine after assisting his teacher, Dr. Lamm, in performing autopsies. He was a teacher in a public school, then attempted to be an actor but failed, being by nature timid, and hampered by indistinct speech when he was young. He tried journalism and was for a time a reporter on *Dagens Nyheter* (The Daily News) and other newspapers. He also founded and edited an insurance periodical which had a very brief life span. He proved himself an outstanding art critic and wrote articles which showed remarkable insight and discernment. In 1880-82 he wrote, in collaboration with Claes Lundin, *Gamla Stockholm* (Old Stockholm), a voluminous work about the Swedish capital and its history; in 1881-82 he wrote a history of the Swedish people, a work in two volumes; and between 1882 and 1891 he completed a work in three volumes entitled *Swedish Destinies and Adventures*. Much in these works was devoted to the cultural history of Sweden, and they were written from an independent and liberal point of view, frequently fictionalizing events and incidents. In spite of their being severely criticized by history experts and other critics (and when was Strindberg not taken to task by the critics of his day!), they remain absorbing in interest and are fascinatingly told.

In view of Strindberg's enormous production of plays, novels, short stories, historical works, essays, poetry and other writings, it is evident that only a small fraction of these could be represented in a Reader. No two Strindberg specialists would select the same material as a sample of the Swedish author's works, although they might agree with certain choices. I feel that Arvid Paulson has done a fine job and made a good selection.

That Strindberg is at long last being recognized in America is primarily due to the efforts of Arvid Paulson. This Reader will do much to make Strindberg better known in the United States and other English-speaking countries. Even in Sweden there exists no similar anthology, and it seems likely that many in that country will look forward to seeing this book which gives a general view of the great author's limitless interests and scope. Until a few years ago only a small number of American intellectuals, and those who possessed a knowledge of the Swedish language or had read or seen his plays in a foreign language at home or abroad, knew much about Strindberg; and even these few will find items here which may be unknown to them.

Anyone familiar with Swedish and English can translate a treatise or similar paper. But to translate a book word for word, i.e. literally, is inimical to its author, in the case of a work of art. The novel HEMSÖBORNA is the most widely read of all Strindberg's works. It has been read by every Swedish adult at least once. Its title can be translated in three ways: The Inhabitants of Hemsö; The Dwellers of Hemsö (perhaps the most literal—*att bo:* to dwell, to live in) ; or, as The Natives of Hemsö. The latter title gives the spirit of the novel better than the other two. It refers to the people who are part of the island, who were born there—not to persons living there who may have come from other parts of the country. "It takes a poet to translate a poet", as a famous author once said. It is this ability not only to transfer the meaning of a poem or other literary work from one language to another but to instill the spirit of the author, that has made Arvid Paulson the foremost translator and interpreter of Scandinavian literature today.

Philadelphia, Pennsylvania

AMANDUS JOHNSON

TRANSLATOR'S FOREWORD

To compile a Strindberg Reader, sufficiently inclusive to conform with everyone's notion as to which of the great Swedish author's writings such a volume should contain, is no easy matter. Because no such Reader exists today, and since there is such an unusual abundance of topics among Strindberg's enormous production from which to choose—much of it virtually unknown to the English-speaking public—it seems permissible to make selections more or less at random. I have been guided, however, by the thought that a first Reader should contain selections with an appeal for the greatest number of readers, as well as material which has hitherto remained untranslated and therefore not been within reach of most persons.

Strindberg's international fame rests principally upon his stature as dramatist, while his noteworthy literary contributions in the realms of the novel, the short story and as an essayist, historian, scientist, poet and letter writer have been overlooked or lost sight of mainly for lack of adequate, authoritative translations. Moreover few are acquainted with the fact that he, while a librarian at The Royal Library in Stockholm, collated and arranged its rich and valuable Chinese and Japanese collections of rare and priceless manuscripts from ancient times. As a result he became an accomplished amateur sinologist; and during his more than seven years of employment at this library (1874-82) he wrote extensively on topics which he had unearthed during his researches. Some of the results of his investigations of Swedish relations with China and the Tataric countries he embodied in a lengthy historical essay, *Les Relations de la Suède avec la Chine et les Pays tatares,* which in 1879 was read at the *Académie des Inscriptions et des Belles Lettres* in Paris. In view of the interest centered on China today, I have included the historical essay on that country, first published in the literary periodical FRAMTIDEN (The Future) in Stockholm, 1877. SHAKE-SPEARE'S OUTLOOK ON LIFE and Strindberg's MEM-ORANDUM TO THE MEMBERS OF THE INTIMATE THEATRE, both written in 1908, are the two literary and theatre essays I have chosen. Among the plays, which I have included, THE DANCE OF DEATH (Parts I-II) is undoubtedly the best known to English-speaking readers and theatregoers. SWANWHITE, a medieval fantasy, to which Sibelius wrote incidental music, reveals a different Strindberg from the conception commonly held of him. STORMCLOUDS depicts Strindberg's withdrawal from life and his resignation of mind and soul during his final years, following his divorce from his third wife, the distinguished actress Harriet Bosse, who appears in this play in the guise of *Gerda*. THE BLACK GLOVE, first produced in the provinces in 1909 with the author's daughter Greta in the rôle of the young lady (Mrs. Hart), was considered by Strindberg one of his finest efforts. When George Bernard Shaw made a fervent plea for a production of LUCKY PER'S JOURNEY in London Strindberg stubbornly refused, maintaining that THE BLACK GLOVE was a far superior play and should be produced in England before any of his other plays were seen there. I have obtained Shaw's letters to Strindberg*) and have included them in this volume because of the light they throw on the influence the Swedish author exerted on his contemporaries in the literary field.

I have included only two of Strindberg's poems in this volume: SATURDAY EVE and THE ESPLANADE SYSTEM, the latter freely translated. In addition, it contains poetic excerpts from four of his plays: THE OUTLAW, THE KEYS OF HEAVEN, A DREAM PLAY, and THE GREAT HIGHWAY. I have also felt it pertinent to embody in it excerpts from Strindberg's letters to Harriet Bosse; and finally I have included the previously mentioned letters from George Bernard Shaw to Strindberg and, as well, excerpts from an article on Strindberg's psyche, together with a survey of critical opinion of his drama THE FATHER, as produced on the American stage during the half century 1912-1962.

In brief, there are represented here merely a small part of the fifty-five volumes of his collected works and the astonishingly huge number of letters he wrote in his life time. Yet I confidently hope that even this modest gleaning, this first cross-section of his literary production, will help to make the scope and breadth and genius of this remarkable literary giant somewhat better known and understood by readers in English-speaking countries.

ARVID PAULSON

---

*) Shaw had gone to Stockholm in the summer of 1908 for the purpose of meeting Strindberg, for whom he had acquired an unbounded admiration after reading some of his plays in German. The two letters from Shaw were discovered in the Royal Library in Stockholm by the New York correspondent of DAGENS NYHETER. Mr. Sven Åhman through whose courtesy and that of the Royal Library they appear in this volume.   A.P

SHORT STORIES

A SNOB

(1877)

This particular young man had the misfortune to be the son of a highly placed government official, who was also very rich. At the same time he bore a name which—while it was not to be found in the Almanac de Gotha—nevertheless possessed a challenging sound that awakened so much the greater an annoyance in people because of the foreign way it was spelled, causing it to be pronounced wrongly. It had a couple of letters too many.

Furthermore, he had been endowed by nature with an attractive appearance, for which he showed his gratitude by grooming himself well. He liked nice clothes and provided himself with new ones every six months, had them properly brushed every morning, and could never persuade himself to attend a lecture without starched collar and cuffs. Whenever he went out in inclement weather, he did not stuff his trouserlegs inside his boots; he put on galoshes. As his eyesight was bad, he used a monocle; he thought himself too young to use eyeglasses.

This envied and bitingly criticized young man had his upbringing to thank for all his ill-luck and misadventures while at university, and his story should serve as a warning to both parents and guardians.

In keeping with his father's wish, he was enrolled in the fraternity of his father's province, despite the fact that he had been graduated from a preparatory school in the capital. When he made his entrance into this fraternity, he found himself in the company of six foot tall, broadshouldered students from his father's province, on whom he had never before set eyes and who spoke in a tongue that to him sounded strange. They regarded his fine, expensive clothes with suspicious eyes. At first nobody had the courage to sit down and drink with him and call him by his first name. They took his modesty and reserved manner for arrogance. Finally one of the older students pro-

3

posed that they all drink a general toast of friendship with the "gutte snipe"—an appellation generally given to them who hailed from the capital in those days.

But as the victim had made up his mind not to imbibe to excess, he refused to drain his glass after each and every toast, and this brought forth a storm of displeasure and disaffection.

He tried to make friends with some of his own age, but they were too busily engaged in forming more profitable acquaintanceships with the older men.

His second visit at the fraternity house turned out even worse.

He was unable to participate in a cavalry battle because his monocle had been crushed during the playing of the amusing game "spänna kyrka". The cavalry battle was acted out in this manner: the students divided themselves into two groups; then—attired in armor and helmet, and with swords borrowed from the fraternity's theatrical wardrobe—they seated themselves astride the chairs, and after a general trot around the room, it ended in a charge to the accompaniment of the most fierce trumpet calls. The broken, battered chairs were then written down as fraternity expenditures under the item of *Theatre*.

At the next fraternity gathering, a young rhymster read a doggerel entitled *The Snob*. It was greeted with general jubilation. In this poem our unfortunate young man was described from top to toe: his trousers, his watch chain, cuffs, galoshes, his bad eyesight, his impeccably clean handkerchiefs, his father, his mother.

From that moment, the snob paid no more visits to the fraternity house. Instead he sought out his old comrades from his preparatory school in Stockholm.

Strange rumors began to circulate. One person had seen him at Gästis eating with his fork, another one had heard him refuse to drink four glasses of schnapps at the smörgåsbord; still another had seen him riding horseback on the road to Stockholm. He regularly went to lectures and took private tutoring courses. He was, consequently, a blockhead, and you had only to look at him to know that he was.

One morning the unfortunate young man was awakened by a fraternity brother of exceptional dimensions, who let out an oath to the effect that he simply had to lend him some money. The young man's protests were to no avail, for in his hand he held a registered letter, which he, out of courtesy, had removed from the letter box to give to his young fraternity brother; he had, in fact, already opened it and, in brotherly fashion, divided the money it contained, in two equal parts. He swore, however, that he had not read the letter.

When the addressee declared his displeasure with his visitor's having opened the letters, he was charged with insulting behavior at the next election of junior members. As a result he found himself unable to go to the fraternity's reading room, as he would always be met by invectives and insidious, provocative whisperings there.

The upshot of all this was that the young man and some of his other unfortunate comrades rented quarters of their own, where they could read their newspapers and also play cards. This turned out to be the height of imprudence, for thereby the little town had been given something to gossip about.

There were clandestine rumors of secret orgies, of immoral behavior; and if in the past people had merely looked down upon all better-than-average dressed students, they now began to despise them.

His sister was about to leave for Lausanne, where she was to stay at a *pension;* and as she could not take along her pretty little greyhound, she left it in her brother's care.

Never had any visiting royal personage created such a sensation as that poor dog did. People lined up at the edges of the sidewalks, loudly roaring with laughter; they sicked bigger dogs onto the poor little creature; and it even happened that someone gave him a blow with a stick in passing. When the thermometer dropped to 20° Centigrade and the dog started to feel the cold, he was pampered with a woolen blanket for covering. This unnecessary novelty was something unheard of and caused general indignation. A cry went up: "A dog with a horse blanket!" It was common belief, namely, that such blankets were only used for horses.

But the dog had to be sent back home, after having first been treated at a rathskeller to lumps of sugar, dipped in cognac; and that had made him sick.

A devoted relative had had the temerity to present the young man with a very fine walking stick, made from the fiber of a palm leaf; and he had become quite attached to it, so he decided to affix a nameplate of silver on the knob. This unnecessary luxury cost a whole *riksdaler,* or four toddies, as his fraternity brothers would have calculated it. But the silversmith, either from vanity or care-

5

lessness, had stamped it with a control mark, and this turned out to be a source of much annoyance and indignity to him. One of his cronies discovered the secret one evening while he was searching for his own Bengal cane; and word of it was spread about like fire, with everybody asking: "Have you seen the young dandy's walking stick?"

The stick was a conversation piece for more than a week. It was kicked about and tortured and thrown hither and thither in every restaurant vestibule until the varnish was rubbed off, the nameplate was buckled, and yet the cane survived because it was a good, solid cane—and that was just what was the young man's misfortune.

One day it disappeared. Its owner hunted in vain for it on the shelf where he kept his galoshes, and behind which he was in the habit of placing it. He advertised his loss by putting up a notice outside the house, offering a quite generous reward to the finder. The placard attracted people galore; they gathered in droves outside the house, making jesting, satirical remarks about the advertisement, laughing boisterously, and adding sardonic comments which they scribbled on the placard.

One morning the owner of the stick took a walk along the edge of the river nearby. He noticed the grass on the ground had been uprooted, the sod had been trampled up, as if by grazing cattle. But no cattle were out to pasture, and there were clear tracks of human feet in the moist turf. There—in the grass—he saw something shining. . . . It was the fatal silver name-plate, and close by it lay the battered and trampled walking stick—but crooked as a corkscrew, yet not broken, and that was the reason the sod was so uprooted. That it could not have been a thief who had taken the stick, the still remaining silver name-plate testified to. Then—who could have taken it?

For four long years this young man, whom Nature had endowed so lavishly with its gifts, dragged on his existence like an exile or outlaw in the little university town. He was not really a student, although he was matriculated as one; he never felt he had the courage to attend either the glee club rehearsals or the fraternity meetings, or inaugurals, or receptions. Nor did he go to dances or any public performances, as he was always the victim of insults. To his fraternity brothers he was never anything but stupid, arrogant, shallow, superficial and dissolute—in short, a snob! And in reality he was nothing of the sort!

After four boring, tedious years, he finished by taking his bachelor of law degree with flying colors.

And do you know what people said then?

They said: "Pooh!"

AN ATTEMPT AT REFORM
(1884)

She had noticed with repugnance how girls were brought up to serve as housekeepers for prospective husbands. And so she had taken up a profession which could provide for her under no matter what conditions of life. She had learned how to make artificial flowers.

He, on the other hand, had been distressed to see how girls sat waiting to be taken care of by their husbands-to-be; for he was looking for a free, independent woman to marry—a woman who could earn her own living, someone he could look upon as an equal and who would be a companion for life, and not a mere housekeeper.

And then the inevitable happened: they met. He was an artist—a painter, and she made artificial flowers, as mentioned before. And it was in Paris where they had been introduced to these new-fangled ideas.

It was a chaste, beautiful marriage. The two lived in three rooms in Passy. He had a room of his own at one end of the flat and she had hers at the other end; and the room in the middle served as their studio. They were not to share the same bed—that would be nothing short of obscenity, an indecent beastliness which had not the slightest counterpart in nature and which only led to excesses and mischief. And, of all things—think of it!—having to undress in the same room! Phew! No, each one to his own room—and then a neutralized common room, the studio. No maid, for they were both to share the kitchen chores; they would only have a woman to come in mornings and evenings.

The whole thing was well figured out and it had logic in it.

—"But when you get children—what then?" demurred those who had their doubts about such an arrangement.

—"We are not going to have any children!"

Fine! They were not to have children!

8

Everything went along beautifully! He went to the market in the morning and did the buying. Then he made the coffee. She swept, made the beds, and did the dusting and cleaning up. After that they started to work.

When tired of working, they chatted for a while, made suggestions to each other, and had a thoroughly enjoyable time. And when dinner-time approached, he started a fire in the stove, and she washed and cleaned the vegetables. He kept an eye on the beef broth while she ran down to the grocer's; and after that she set the table, while he dished up the meal.

Yet they did not live like brother and sister. They bid goodnight to each other at night, and when that was done, they went to their respective rooms. But then there would come a knock at her door, and she would call out: "Come in!" The bed was narrow, however, but there never was anything out-of-the-way and they each woke up in their own bed in the morning. And then there would come a knock on the wall.

—"Good morning, my little girl! How do you feel this morning?"
—"Oh, I feel fine! How do you feel?"

It was always a new experience when they met in the mornings, and it never seemed anything else.

Evenings they would sometimes go out together and would then meet with some of their countrymen at Syrach's. And she never let herself be affected by tobacco smoke, and she never in any way embarrassed him.

It was an ideal marriage, everybody thought, and they had never seen a couple that was so congenial and happy.

But the girl had parents, and they lived far away. And they kept writing, always inquiring whether Lisen would not soon be expecting; for they were yearning to have a grandchild. Lisen should remember, they said, that marriage was made for the sake of the children and not for the sake of the parents. But Lisen thought this an oldfashioned view. Retorting to this, Mamma asked whether it was the purpose of these newfangled ideas to root out mankind. This was a thought that had not occurred to Lisen, but she did not let it perturb her. She was happy, and so was her husband; and the world was envious because it had at long last seen a happy marriage.

And they certainly showed that they enjoyed their happiness. Neither one lorded it over the other one; and expenses were paid out of their common purse. One time he earned more, another time, she; and that equalized matters.

And when they celebrated a birthday—then their old woman would come in and wake her with a bouquet of flowers and a little note with flowers painted on it, and the note would read: "Congratulations to Mrs. Flowerbud from her dabble-daub husband, who requests her presence at a light but luscious breakfast in his room—without delay!" And with this there came a knock on the wall, and Mrs. Flowerbud hastily put on her morning wrapper, knocked at her husband's door and was greeted with a "Come in!" And then they breakfasted in bed, in his bed, and that day the old woman stayed with them the whole forenoon. It was delightful!

And this kind of life went on for a couple of years, and they never tired of it. And all the prophesying of the prognosticators turned out to be wrong. For theirs was the ideal marriage.

But then it came about that the wife was suddenly taken sick. *She* thought the wallpaper had something to do with her illness, and *he* suspected it came from microbes. Yes—it must be caused by microbes!

But something was radically wrong, definitely wrong. She was not herself at all. They wondered whether it could be a cold. But then Mrs. Flowerbud began to grow decidedly obese. Could it be that she had developed a growth of the sort, of which they had read so much lately. Yes, it must be a growth. And so she went to a physician. And when she came home, she broke into tears. Yes, it was indeed a growth—but the kind that eventually would seek daylight and blossom and, in time, go to seed, that also.

The husband did not weep, however. He thought it was just fine; and the rascal even went about boasting of it whenever he visited Syrach's. But his wife wept more tears. What would become of their position in relation to each other? From now on she would not be able to earn anything, and she would have to eat his bread. And then they would have to have a maid. Oh, those maids!

All their painstaking efforts, all their precautions and prudence and foresight had been wrecked by force of the inevitable.

But her mother-in-law wrote enthusiastic letters of congratulation, repeating over and over again that marriage was a divine institution, made for the purpose of having children and that the gratification of the parents was only of secondary importance.

10

Hugo, the husband, swore it would not matter in the least whether she earned anything or not. Wasn't the help she would give him by slaving for his child sufficient; and wasn't that worthy of payment also? She contributed her share. But for a long time the thought of being supported by her husband rankled in her. But when the little one arrived, she forgot all about that. And she remained his wife and companion as in the past, but more than that, she became his child's mother—and that, he thought, was the very best of all.

THE STRONGER ONE
(1885; publ. 1886)

In Geneva lives a Mme. X., who publishes a newspaper called *The United States of Europe*. The idea of a European federal republic is an inheritance from the Saint-Simonists; and Napoleon III, who was a socialist before becoming emperor, had a United Europe on his program. After being married to Eugénie Maria de Montijo, who was the stronger of the two, he changed his political program.

Mme. X. sticks to her program, however. She was married to an elderly Saint-Simonist. The marriage was childless. Mme. X., who was an idealist, looked upon housekeeping as something base. The husband—who was also a litterateur—cooked their meals and looked after the ménage. He did not consider it to be below his dignity. But people laughed at him and thought him ludicrous.

But what was ludicrous about it was not that he did chores that are ordinarily performed by women; it was the fact that he alone did them. Had they both done these tasks, neither of them would have appeared ridiculous.

The husband is now said to be dead, although some say he is living in America. It seems, consequently, as if their marriage turned out to be no marriage at all; and, since they had no children, it was in actuality not a marriage.

Their story, only incompletely known, gives free play to a construction novel, and the subject lends itself to all manner of partisan interpretation. I have in vain tried to get more information but have received none.

Did he find his position untenable? Did he break down under the ridicule? Did she consider herself humiliated for having to live off him and for having to eat his bread?

Who knows?

On the occasion of Victor Hugo's funeral, a lone carriage stood

12

waiting at Porte-Maillot, ready to fall in and take its place in the funeral procession. It was a one-horse vehicle of simple, poverty-stricken appearance, the kind that is generally used to carry away a drunkard, or a man stricken ill on the street. On the coachman's box was erected a sort of obelisk, draped in black and decorated with a wreath of spruce and flowers, in the center of which a printed poetic tribute to Victor Hugo was placed.

Inside the closed carriage sat two elderly women and a man. The man was seated on the rear seat. The women held a large banner, and they let the bunting flutter freely in the wind. On it was painted a landscape, and there could be seen representatives of all the peoples of the world, all stretching out their hands to one another. Above this scene were printed in gold the words: La République Universelle, and underneath was a poem of Hugo's, dedicated to such a united world organization.

All the onlookers, those dressed in a shabby blouse as well as those in redingote; those who wore decorations and those who had none; women as well as men, halted dutifully to brand this spectacle with an outburst of laughter. And they who were not inclined to laugh, did so nevertheless, in order to save their honor and their intelligence.

But the two women held their banner high, adding now and then an earnest, explanatory remark in a friendly voice, without any sign of either ill-will or rancor, aggressiveness or attempt at persuasion.

Were they unaware of the laughter? Oh no, they could not fail either to see or hear it. But unquestionably they had not expected anything else, and therefore they were neither surprised nor did it arouse their anger. They had fixed within them the ideal demands upon the future—but from their own generation they seemed neither to demand nor expect anything whatsoever.

But the man on the rear seat—he saw and heard and felt the laughter; and it caused him to turn and twist like a sinner in the stocks. Why did he act the coward?

My thoughts went to Mme. X. Could it have been she who held the banner that time? And could it have been her husband who tried to be unseen?

And from these two my thoughts went to Napoleon III. What if he had lived today and had seen the utopia of his youth fluttering from a pole during the funeral procession carrying the remains of the author of *Napoleon the Insignificant?* And suppose, if Eugénie de Montijo had come down from Avenue de la Grande Armée and met Mme. X. in the closed carriage (in case it was Mme. X.). . . .

"Howdoyoudo," she would have said, "you have stolen my Louis' idea, that's what you have done!"

And Mme. X. would have answered:

"Well, that poor creature of a husband of yours, he hasn't the courage to carry the banner! He does not dare—because of you —and so I have to do it. Look at this poor wretch of a man, who is sitting there on the seat, shaking from top to toe. Fine heroes, these men are! And yet they talk about the weaker sex!"

"That's something I never heard Louis say. He knew well enough the history books ought to be written this way: Eugénie I, 1853-1870, instead of Napoleon III, 1852-1870."

"And yet they refuse to give us the right to vote!"

"What's the use of having the voting right when one has absolute veto power? The Emperor was the least important one in the whole empire. He had neither a vote nor veto power. I did, at any rate."

"Yes, it was too bad that you did have it—that time!"

"For good or for bad, whether man or woman, when all is said and done, it is the stronger one who carries the day!"

"For the present, *I* am the stronger!" says Mme. X., waving her banner.

And with that, the police calls out:

"La République Universelle! Move into place!"

And the Universal Republic drove up between a rowing club and a singing society, which had been registered under the category of sport.

But the Empress's name is not called out, for she is in Chiselhurst, busy receiving Bonapartisans who are agitating for the Third Empire.

MISMATED

(1885; publ. 1886)

For three years I met them almost every day of the week at noon on my way home from the library.

The first year he was straight as a ramrod and lithe as a young lieutenant—which is exactly what he was. She danced ahead at his side and turned her head on the bias to be able to look into his sunken eyes.

He was gradually growing paler, while she retained her pink complexion.

The third year he came alone. His neck seemed to have been elongated, and his chin was beginning to sag. His cheeks looked as if they were pasted onto his cheekbones, and his eyes were framed with black borders. When he appeared in uniform, the sword-belt hung down on the spear-side, and the yellow braid on his trousers, which flapped about his emaciated legs, signified his attachment to the general staff.

She would occasionally come alone. Her step was light and dancing as before, but her face had now a hard, discontented look. Her nostrils were extended as though they scented a prey, and her eyes were stalking across the street toward the opposite sidewalk, as if hungering for satisfaction.

The fourth year he no longer came.

"Did you hear that Captain X. is dead?" a friend asked me one day.

"No—I don't know Captain X.," I answered him.

"Oh, he was a young man who had a most promising career ahead of him. You must have come across him, for he lived on the same street as you."

"Ah! Was he on the general staff—and did he have a beautiful young wife?" I asked.

"Exactly!"

15

"What did he die of?"

"Well—that is the big question!—Did you ever see DIVOR-ÇONS?"

"No."

"Then read it!" my friend suggested.

"It's about a man and a woman happily mated, isn't it?"

"No—unhappily mismated!!"

CHEATED

(1885; publ. 1886)

When the fish was spawning and the male birds were beginning to sing, the children of mankind went to their pairing grounds to play their game. The mothers decked out their young females to attract the males, the seamstresses put padding in the waist; and the tailors did likewise in the men's jackets and other wearing apparel. And so they went out into Nature to choose a fitting environment for the natural act, for which preparations had now been made.

The scene is a resort on the seacoast; and to this place came the wife of a wholesale dealer. To it came also a lieutenant with his uniform and debts. One evening, when the midges were waltzing in the air and the cats were miaowing, the girls were dancing in the ballroom of the Casino, and they had scissored out the upper parts of their gowns, cutting them low, and had had the shades pulled down in order to be in the full glare of the light. And in a window-splay the lieutenant leaned close to the wholesale dealer's daughter and asked with his eyes:

"Will you pay my debts for me?" But with his lips he asked the question: "Will you love me in fair weather and foul?"

And the wholesale dealer's daughter replied with her eyes: "Yes, if you will make me your countess and introduce me into high society; if you will see that papa gets a chance to play cards with your generals and that mama becomes an intimate of your nobility; if you will provide for me for the rest of my days and let me enjoy life."

Yes, he was willing, and so the deal was consummated.

Two years had passed. Apathetic and bored, they were sitting in their dressing-gowns, exchanging a few plain words of truth.

"Padding!" he said, pointing to her dress which, puffed up, was hanging on the arm of a chair.

17

"Padding!" said she in return, pointing with her slipper to his tunic which dangled over by the towel rack.

He pulled the dressing-gown around him and made no reply.

Two years later, the wholesale dealer went into bankruptcy. That made it impossible for him to think of playing cards in the future with the generals, as he had been promised, and the countesses promptly cut off associating with his wife. The daughter was received with less warmth, and the lieutenant cultivated a taste for home life, especially since the subsidies from the father-in-law had now ceased. One day, after having been unusually truthful to his wife, she decided it was time to go into details.

"You are not so polite any more after I turned out to be poor", she said.

"I was never polite before either, for that matter", was his answer, "so it isn't only your poverty that is to blame. . . ."

"Yes, but you used to be more polite to papa."

"Y-e-s, because that was the only thing he had in his favor—being rich. Now that he has lost this respectable asset, I see no reason why I should show him any excessive respectfulness."

"You admit then, quite unashamedly, that you married me for my money?"

"Certainly! I think it's a fine thing to admit ones own—motives."

"And you are not ashamed to say this to me?"

"Oh yes, I am, but you are not trying to tell me that you took me because you loved me? I am inclined to believe that you paid the paltry ten thousand I was in debt for in order to get the title of countess. It was a cheap price. Dickson had to pay a couple of hundred thousand to become a simple nobleman, and L. O. Smith paid sixty thousand to get the Order of Vasa. I haven't swindled you on the transaction, for you are still a countess; but you have cheated me for you baited me with a rich father-in-law, and now I find myself having a poor one! Padding—padding from beginning to end!"

"Yes, but I didn't marry for money, at least!"

"No, but for a title, and. . . . Oh, but it doesn't matter. . . ."

"You may as well speak out! Anyone who dares to destroy a poor woman's money, has the audacity to do anything!"

"Now listen to me, my little chick. . . ."

"I am not a chick!"

"Let's see! You brought with you ten thousand crowns. But do you know how much I have paid out during these four years, do you? Forty thousand! Your father has given us five thousand. How much of your poor husband's money have you then squandered?"

"You ought to be ashamed of yourself! Perhaps you think the wife ought to support her husband too?"

"No—but she shouldn't say that the husband has wasted her money, when they both have had the benefit of it! And, besides, you keep talking about *your* money! From where did that money come? Did you work for it? You should not talk about money—for that's what you all marry for!"

"What you mean to say is that you are keeping me! Just as if I were your mistress!"

"Since you seem to perceive it yourself, I don't have to say it for you. However, that is a good thing, and now you may as well hear the whole truth. For, after what has happened, we shall have to change our mode of living. Wouldn't you like to take advantage of this opportunity and set yourself free, emancipate yourself from living on charity?"

"Yes, I certainly would!"

"Then do it! Do some work!"

"I don't know how to work!"

"Do whatever you can do! Look after my home!"

"I wouldn't call that work!"

"You are right! And so nothing remains but to continue to do nothing. Society has entrusted that rôle to you!"

"A fine rôle, indeed!"

"You realize that now, do you?"

"Oh yes, I realize it now. I am condemned to live on a man's charity for the rest of my days! When my father could no longer support me, my mother dragged me out into the market places to find someone else who could feed and take care of me."

"And so she discovered me. By so doing, your father's credit rose, and I assume I have brought back to him many times over what he had paid out for me. That is the way matters stand. Now—what do you really think we ought to do about it?"

"Nothing!"

"No, I really don't see that there is anything that we can do about it. For all through it, the whole thing is hollow—padded! Nothing but padding—all of it!"

The lieutenant became cross and irritable and his wife became miserable. After two years they were divorced. The lieutenant was ordered by the court to pay for her support as long as she lived.

"Things like that are expensive", said his Captain one evening while they were dining at a restaurant.

"Any genuine article is expensive, but when it costs as much as that, one should have the right to take it on approval," finished the lieutenant.

LIKE TURTLE DOVES
(1885; publ. 1886)

They loved each other. Of that there could be no question. And their love was true, healthy love—the kind that has the spontaneity and naivité of youth and that transcends all calculations on common interests and identical thinking.

After a year of love he suffered a stroke of apoplexy. He was a musician and she was a singer.

And so they went to Lysekil, where he was to have the benefit of saltwater bathing.

They took in at the Casino. She accompanied him on his daily walks, sauntering by his side, step by step, like an old woman. She became his other crutch. She was young, and her blood was always at the boiling point. She observed how the young people amused themselves and saw them dancing.

For two years she acted as his nurse. The world felt sorry for her, but no one was willing to help her.

For the third year they returned to Lysekil. One evening, while she was sitting in her beloved invalid's room and through the window saw the Casino ballroom all lighted up, and naval officers dancing with young girls and married ladies, and heard the lively, enticing tunes from the piano, she felt a burning desire to take part in the frolic. Her whole youthful spirit suddenly rose up in rebellion against the sick-room, against being fettered to it. She got up and said:

"Let me go down and dance just one dance! Do you mind if I do?"

"I can't say it will make me happy—but go."

And she went.

He lay there alone, and he couldn't sleep. The bedsheets burned as they wrapped themselves around his body, and he tried to get up and go down to the ballroom, but he couldn't.

In the morning she came back up to him, her cheeks flushed, and with eyes flashing, and brimming with good cheer.

21

He was glad to see her, but he was hurt.

The following evening, after they had dined, she remained down below, while he trudged upstairs and went to bed. He lay awake and he heard her sing all their favorite songs for her newfound friends.

The evening after that he stayed below, for he thought he would find it diverting. But it turned out to be a quiet evening; everybody seemed reserved and rigid. He fought against dozing off, but he refused to leave. Finally he had to.

He got up and said goodnight. And with that he turned to his wife.

"I promised I would sing for them tonight," she said.

He was ashamed to ask her to come upstairs with him. And so he left by himself.

When he had come up to his room, he heard a waltz being played on the piano, and through the window he saw his wife floating past in a gentleman's close embrace, tightly pressed to him, her hand resting upon his shoulder.

Well, what of it? She was dancing with a gentleman. Yes—but she had told him that she was going to sing.

A week later he saw two shadowy figures in the garden behind a hedge of jasmin. He recognized one of them, for he knew every line and curve of her body. And he saw the two embrace, as they had done when they were dancing, and they exchanged kisses. Well, what of it? They kissed. But she had vowed to kiss only him. Why should one promise something which one cannot keep!

Soon after, the musician died, and the world passed its judgment. The dead man was exonerated, but the survivor was condemned and judged guilty. Unfortunately, the sentence was passed without any previous trial. Unfortunately, no inquiry could be made after one of the parties had passed away.

And so, if there must be a judgment, the sentence has to be postponed to a future time and generation, which will be more understanding, more comprehending.

And he who refuses to wait for such a time, may consult the Scriptures. The tale of Tobias is not too farfetched, although it is apocryphal; the verses about Asra suffer from being written in poetry; and *The Warning of a Friend of Youth* has the fault of being much too moralizing.

HIS POEM
(1885; publ. 1886)

He goes to stag parties because he has a mean wife.

An ugly, nasty little man, always itching for a quarrel and who revels in the legislated injustices against women.

To hear him during the nocturnal hours, or in the wee hours of the morning, when the wine draws down the shade over the present and puts the past under a spotlight, is something quite extraordinary.

Not long ago he sat on the edge of the bed at the home of his friend the actor and talked about his wife. He conjured forth scenes from the past, from the gilded engagement days, from the early days of his marriage. And the present and the past merged into one: he possessed the most beautiful woman in the whole world, the best, the most intelligent and the most capable one. She was a masterpiece. He confessed he had been spiteful and unjust to her and that he was far from worthy of being her husband.

As he put on his overcoat and downed the last drink, he suddenly became serious.

"She has one fault, however—she, like everybody else! For we all have our faults", he said. "She doesn't approve of my staying out nights."

"Why *do* you stay out nights?" put in a young bachelor.

"Why? You ask why I stay out nights?"

The mental window shade seemed to be raised, letting the daylight pour in to illuminate every nook and corner of the man's misery. And by the rigid, benumbed facial muscles and the twitching nerves around the eyes, it could plainly be seen that he had engaged far too long in the cult of staring in adoration at a Gorgon.

"But she is a nice woman, nevertheless," he ended by saying; and with that he staggered out.

Nevertheless! H'm!

"Max Nordau likens woman to a poem by an intoxicated man", remarked the young bachelor. "But when will we hear a poem in praise of men by a woman?"

"When a woman can learn to love a man!" broke in another who looked somewhat done up. "But I'm afraid that's a long way off! To love is essentially a man's attribute; to be loved, a woman's prerogative."

"The man gives; the woman takes. It is more blessed to give than to take—but it is also more stupid!" came from another one.

"That silly fool who left just now—he is continually poetizing! But when daylight sets in and he is sober—then his inspiration is gone, and his poetry turns into nothing but prose. Now do you understand why he is away from home nights?"

THEIR BUSINESS ARRANGEMENT
(1885; publ. 1886)

Whether she loved him or not was not easy to tell, for it was he who proposed, and she was dying to get married. But he was in love with her. If it was because of her beauty, her virtues, her little idiosyncracies or her common sense, he could not tell; all he knew was that he loved her.

So he started his courtship pilgrimages to her home in the evenings. And to prepare for their future wedded life, they went to the theatre, to concerts, and to dances.

One evening, when they had succeeded in capturing the drawing-room sofa for themselves, and she was sitting with her tresses nestling against his English shirtfront, she suddenly asked him:

"Robert, do you love me?"

"What a question!"

"Then you won't be angry if I ask you another question, will you?"

"Angry? Why. . . ."

"Did you know that I will have a dowry when I marry?"

"No."

"Yes, I have an income of four thousand a year. Half of it comes from Jockum's pin factory, half of it from Bobb's zinc mines."

"I am not interested in that? I am not in love with you for the sake of your money! I didn't even know you would have an income!"

"Yes, I know it makes no difference to you. But all men are not like you, Robert."

"Well—but exactly what are you driving at?"

"Well, you see, I belong to the Society for Woman's Proprietary Rights, and I would like to set an example to the world. For that reason we must enter into an agreement that will ensure that this income remains my own. One never knows what may happen in the future.—Wouldn't you like to become a member of the society, too?"

25

"No, my dear little darling", was Robert's reply, "I do not. For the right kind of marriage should be founded on mutual rights and mutual obligations. If a married woman is to have proprietary rights, then the husband should possess the same rights. This is something the law has properly taken into consideration, and that is why we have the provision for the marriage settlement."

"The marriage settlement? What is that?"

"That's something you ought to have found out about before you run ahead and try to change the law! I'll tell you what it is. It is an unimportant statute which provides for each one of the marriage partners to retain his or her own property."

"Yes, but we are talking about a married woman's right to her own property."

"Exactly, so we are! But that includes the husband's right to his property. If you wish, we can arrange to make a marriage settlement. . . ."

"H'm. That's something I hadn't thought about!"

"Yes, my darling, but you should always think before you jump. I have my little income, and you have yours! We each keep our own! Don't you think that's the proper way? Don't you?"

"Certainly! Of course!"

And so they became husband and wife with a marriage settlement.

Mr. Robert thought it was a little petty of his betrothed to bring money matters into their relationship, as he himself had never broached that subject. Nevertheless he was in a happy frame of mind when he drove home to his estate in the country with his young wife.

A year passed, and they had a little one. Mr. Robert's farm property was sufficiently large to take care of wife and children, but was not large enough to defray the expense of both a greenhouse for palms, and for carriages. However, the wife was ailing after childbirth and was unable to go out. The Baron at Rockelsta had a greenhouse for palms, inside which the Baroness would take her walks. Mr. Robert was given a hint that he ought to build a similar greenhouse. That was something he could not afford, for it would cost six thousand— which was all that the farm yielded in a year. But in the end he was forced to do it, since his wife's doctor had prescribed it. Mr. Robert cursed the new tyrant in his home and argued that he might as well have prescribed a trip to Africa, or a castle, or a painting by Meissonier. These reflections he made to himself, just as he meditated on the fact that the household budget had not been augmented by his wife's income. However, he did all this silently, secretly.

And the wife got her greenhouse with palms, although hers cost only three thousand. But the palms turned out to be not so good for her health, and in the autumn she came down with an attack of migraine. The doctor promptly declared that the country air was not good for her and that they should spend the winters in the city.

That he couldn't possibly do, as he would then be unable to give his farm the attention that it required; and besides, he could not afford to keep a home in the city as well.

He could not afford it!—

No, he could not. But she ought to be able to—she who did nothing but clip coupons.—

Oh—so he was after her paltry little income!—

No, he was not. He simply did not want her to build greenhouses for palms for him. He did not want her to keep an apartment for him. And he could not understand why. . . .

What couldn't he understand?

Oh well, what did it matter. . . .

Oh yes, it most certainly did matter! It was her money he was after!

Not at all—it was she who was after *his* money—for during their marriage he had not seen the slightest sign of her money, despite the fact they had made a marriage settlement—which was what she wanted.

Oho, he meant that she was to support him!

Far from it! He merely thought that they were to pay for the upkeep of the property and the household expenses jointly, so that she would be able to indulge in the pleasure of not having to eat his bread.—For that was what she wanted, wasn't it?

Well, perhaps it was. . . . Yes, of course, it was. He was right— she would write to papa and ask him about her dividends.

She wrote to papa. After corresponding back and forth, her father expressed regrets that she had married a wretch like her husband, who could not support wife and children by himself but had to get help from his wife after squandering her money. In the end the father came through with three thousand crowns. There had been a slump in business, factory production had slowed down, and the company shares had not yielded any great returns.

27

Now they had to settle in Stockholm, and it was she who furnished the wherewithal. This was something Mr. Robert's cash ledger found it difficult to adapt itself to, as keeping house in the country cost six thousand a year. Of this amount, the wife was supposed to pay half—but there was no need of being too punctilious or particular about that!

The following year there were no dividends, for the factory operations were practically at a standstill. She was now obliged to eat the bread of the husband. It was a bitter experience, a dreadfully bitter experience for her. The husband never made any allusion to it, but she said so much the more. She protested morning, noon and night, and she softened her hard bread with her tears of humiliation.

But nothing dries quicker than tears, and the wife soon was happy again and did not feel much more unhappy the following year when she learned that both her father's companies had crashed.

And so they went to live in Stockholm for the winter, and there every sign of her tears was eradicated.

In the spring Mr. Robert was taken ill and died. He died much faster than the ending of a short story should allow. Now came administrator and executors and took an inventory; and when they had finished their task they arrived at the conclusion that—thanks to the marriage settlement—there was nothing for the wife to inherit. And the farm was sold, and so were the furnishings, the proceeds were turned over to the administrator of the Guardianship of Infants, and the widow had to go back home to her papa.

And papa flew into a rage. "Damned ideas!" he sputtered.

"Yes," acquiesced the widow, "there is certainly something wrong with our laws! Isn't that what I have always said: Yes, then it is far better for a woman to have proprietary rights!"

The person who related this anecdote meant that a husband's proprietary rights were even better; but as it was a man who made this remark, his opinion does not count for very much.

IDEALS TO SUIT THE CIRCUMSTANCES
(1885; publ. 1886)

In our idealistic times, the ideal demands from life are tremendously on the increase. I take it for granted that it is because the belief in a life after this is on the wane and that people therefore wish to live the only life they have as fully as they possibly can.

Thus a young girl of twenty emphatically declared that she was not going to marry because the laws of her country appertaining to critical childbirth, permits the mother's life to be sacrificed if the child can be saved. A voluminous tome of sermons could be written on this subject—primarily about the law, the ancient Christian law, which puts mankind as a whole above the individual, but also about the young woman, the atheistic, darwinian young woman who places the individual above the race.

When Gamahut, a notorious murderer, was guillotined last winter in Paris, an atheistic newspaper declared that it was unjust to take the life of a young, virile man in retribution and as an indemnification for the life of an aged woman.

Consequently the atheists have not adjusted their morality to conform with their philosophy.

Is it necessary to bring children into the world? That is what the atheists-malthusians ask.

As far as Nature is concerned, it is not at all necessary, for if the six races of human beings should die out, it would be as immaterial as when the five thousand species of ammonites were extinguished. But in order to sustain the atheist woman in her joy of life, it is a necessity for her to have children, for it gives her enjoyment as well as being good for her health.

That women can die during child birth is no reason for doing away with marriage. To grieve over such a possibility is as unwar-

29

ranted as when the familiar card players, in the middle of their playing, interrupted the game to weep over the death of Homer. And it is quite as dangerous to walk across the street because a tile might come hurtling down from the roof.

There is as yet no law against a roof being tiled, despite the fact that the tiles may be a danger to life, just as chimneys, bolting horses, seashores and sailboats, and especially locomotives and firearms.

A married couple had two children. The children died of typhus. After that they had no more children, but instead the wife got herself two dogs. She lived for these two dogs and for her household, which included her husband. She never felt that the children should have been unborn, although they had brought her sorrow, for they had also given her joy—as long as it lasted. And she does not recommend dogs instead of children, for she knows that the dogs, too, will be dead in a few years.

This woman is a Christian and an idealist, but her ideal demands from life are less than those of the realists.

HIS MAID
or
DEBIT AND CREDIT
(1885; publ. 1886)

Mr. Blackwood was a dockyard superintendent in Brooklyn. He had married Miss Danckward, who brought with her as dowry a heap of modern views. In order not to have to see his beloved wife performing the chores of a servant girl, Mr. Blackwood had established himself with his wife in a boardinghouse.

The wife, having nothing to do, spent her days playing the piano and playing billiards, and half of her nights discussing the woman question and drinking grog.

The husband had a salary of five thousand dollars a year, which he regularly deposited with his wife to be administered by her. She herself was given five hundred dollars in pin money, which she had the sole use of.

Then they had a child. A nursemaid was engaged and she under-took the precious job of substituting for the mother, and for this she was paid one hundred dollars.

They had two more children. And they grew up and the two eldest began going to school. But the wife was bored, and still she had nothing to do.

One day she came inebriated to the breakfast table.

The husband took the liberty to remind her that it was unbecoming and improper.

The wife became hysterical and was put to bed; and all her women friends waited upon her and brought her flowers.

"Why do you drink, my dear?" asked the husband in as gentle a tone as he could. "Are you grieving over something?"

"Indeed! I have every reason to grieve—my life is a failure!"

"A failure? How? You have born three children, and you could use your time to bring them up, couldn't you?"

"I am not made to have children!"

"H'm, h'm! You are not made to have children, you say. Then you should try to adapt yourself to having them. It is a service to society, and it is a glorious and honorable task—far loftier than being a superintendent of a dockyard."

"Yes—if I were free. . . ."

"You are much freer than I am. I am at your beck and call— under your supervision. You make the decisions about spending my income. You have five hundred dollars in pin money that you can dispose of as you see fit—but I have no pin money. I must ask for money from your cash box for every little expense; in other words, come begging to you whenever I need money for tobacco. Haven't you more freedom than I have?"

The wife made no answer but tried to think.

The upshot of it was that they decided they were to try house-keeping, and they started to keep house.

"Dear Friend", Mrs. Blackwood wrote to one of her intimates some time later, "I suffer and am tired to death. But I wish to suffer to the very end, for life has nothing more that it can offer to a miserable woman who has nothing to live for. I want to show the world that I am not one to live on a man's charity, and therefore I am going to work—to work myself to death. . . ."

On the first day after her decision, she got up at nine in the morning and tidied up her husband's room. That done, she discharged the cook, and at eleven she went out to do the marketing.

When her husband came home for lunch at one o'clock, the meal was not ready. She blamed it on the maid.

The wife was terribly tired and wept. The husband didn't have the heart to complain. He ate a burned cutlet and went back to his work. But he added: "Don't tire yourself out, my dearest!"

In the evening she was so exhausted that she had to stay home from a party, and she went to bed at ten o'clock.

The following morning, when Mr. Blackwood was about to greet her with a *good morning,* he was surprised to see how blooming his wife looked.

"Did you sleep well, my dear?" he asked her.

"Why do you ask?" retorted Mrs. Blackwood.

"You have such a healthy color today, it seems to me."

"Do I look—so—so healthy?"

"You do. A little something to occupy yourself with will be good for you, I think."

"A little something! You call that little, do you? I just wonder what you would call a lot, then!"

"Now, now. . . . I didn't mean anything by that!"

"Oh yes, you meant that I don't do enough work, and yet I have been working like a slave, have tidied up your room, and been standing bent over the kitchen stove. Perhaps you will also deny that I am your slavey?"

When the husband left, he told the maid: "I would like you to get up at seven and tidy up my room so that my wife doesn't have to do it for you."

When Mr. Blackwood came home in the evening, he was in a very good humor, but his wife was in a very bad humor.

"Why don't you want me to tidy up your room?" she demanded.

"Simply because I do not want you to be a servant to me."

"Why don't you?" she asked.

"Because it makes me feel bad!"

"It doesn't seem to make you feel bad that I cook your meals for you and look after your children!"

That caused him to reflect.

On his way to Brooklyn on the streetcar he thought hither and thither.

When he arrived home in the evening, he had been thinking a good deal.

"Listen, my dear", he said. "I have reflected over your position in this house, and under no circumstances do I want you to be my maid. Therefore I have thought like this. I will be your boarder and will pay for my board. Then you will be the master of the house and I shall simply be coming here to eat, as a paying guest."

"What do you mean?" asked the wife somewhat uneasily.

"Exactly what I say. Let us pretend you are keeping a boarding-house and that I am getting my room and board here. Let us pretend only."

"Well, let's hear. . . . How much will you pay?"

"I shall, of course, pay you sufficiently well, so that you won't think I am in any way indebted to you. In that way my position will be more pleasant, for then I shan't be receiving anything on charity."

"On charity?"

33

"Yes, you throw halfcooked food at me and continuously keep saying that you are slaving for me—in short, that you are working for me for nothing."

"Well, what are you driving at?"

"Would you consider three dollars a day sufficient payment for my board and room? I can get board and room in a boardinghouse for two dollars."

"Three dollars should be enough," the wife thought.

"Very well. That should add up to just about one thousand dollars per year.—Here is the money in advance."

He put a sheet of paper on the table.

"Here you see the itemized bill", he said.

Rent	500 dollars.
Wages to the nursemaid	100 dollars.
Wages to the cook	150 dollars.
Board and lodging for Mrs. B.	500 dollars.
Clothing for Mrs. B.	500 dollars.
Board and lodging for the maid	300 dollars.
Board and lodging for the cook	300 dollars.
Board and lodging for the children	700 dollars.
Clothing for the children	500 dollars.
Wood, light, extra help	500 dollars.
Total.	4050 dollars.

"We divide this by two," he continued, "since we share expenses equally, and two thousand twenty-five dollars remains. Deduct from that one thousand, and give me one thousand twenty-five dollars. If you have the money about you, so much the better."

"Share expenses!" was all that the wife could stutter forth. "You want me to pay you?"

"Why certainly!—if we are to be on equal terms. I pay half your keep and half of the children's. Or do you expect me to pay the whole thing—four thousand fifty dollars? Very well, I'll pay you four thousand fifty plus one thousand for my board and room. But at the same time I pay separately the rent, provisions, light, wood and all the other expenses. What do I get in return for what I pay for board and room? My meals. My meals for four thousand fifty dollars! And if I should now deduct half of that amount—in other words, what I am obliged to pay you, two thousand twenty five dollars—then two thousand twenty-five dollars remains as payment for the food I get. But as I now pay the cook separately for fixing the meals, then why should I pay two thousand twenty-five for my meals and in addition to that an extra thousand.

"I just don't understand!"

"Nor do I! But I know one thing: that I owe you nothing as long as I pay for your subsistence as well as the children's, and for that of your servants—who do your work for you, and which you look upon as equally important with mine, or even more so. And even if it were worth more, you still receive five hundred dollars extra for that, excluding the household expenses—while I take out nothing," Mr. Blackwood summed up.

"I repeat—I don't follow your calculations at all!"

"Nor do I!" admitted the husband. "So perhaps we had best forget about the board and room business. I think that might be best! And drawing up a debit and credit plan also! But if you are interested in hearing how your current account stands, here it is:

To Mrs. Blackwood for help in the house for Mrs. Blackwood's cook and nursemaid:

For board and lodging .... 1000 dollars.
Clothing .... 500 dollars.
Entertainment .... 100 dollars.
Cash (pin money) .... 500 dollars.
The maids who perform her work .... 850 dollars.
                                         ─────────────
                        Total: 4750 dollars.

Paid:
                    Mr. Blackwood,
                    Dockyard superintendent.

"Oh, this is outrageous! To come with bills to one's wife!"

"Counter bills, my dear! And you don't have to pay them either, since I pay all the bills."

The wife crumpled the paper together and said:

"Do you expect me to pay for your children's education also?"

"No, I'll do that, and I'll pay for the education of *your* children as well. I alone! But you—you don't pay a cent for mine. Is that equality, eh? But I'll deduct the keep of my children and the maids. You'll then still get two thousand one hundred dollars for helping my maids in the house. Do you want to calculate some more?"

The wife didn't care to calculate any more—never any more!

35

IT ISN'T ENOUGH!
(1885; publ. 1886)

Madame St. Brie keeps a family *pension* in Passy. She is a widow, forty-eight years old, and has three sons. The eldest one is twenty-eight and married; another one is twenty-six and married; and the third is twenty-four and unmarried; he is an artist. Her husband was a physician. He died, after having been decorated, two years ago.

She has a small annuity, enough to support her, but the son who is an artist has to have money for studio, paint, canvas, models, and absinthe. That is why she keeps a *pension,* but another reason is that she loves to see people about her.

The two eldest sons never come to see her. The daughters-in-law have alienated them from their mother. All through her married life she has lived for her children; they have been her only interest. Now that they have flown from the nest, she is left alone with her youngest, and he is never at home. She still may be able to live another twenty or thirty years—but she has no one to live for any more. And she can't live for herself alone, for she was born and reared to be a mother and to live for others.

Charles, the artist, has been squeezing a good deal of money out of her this April, for he has plans to exhibit at the *Salon* for the first time and is now anxiously waiting to hear from the jury.

This morning Monsieur Charles came down to the breakfast table, his face a light yellow with a tint of umber under his eyes, making them look as if they had been greased with green machine oil. A light dew of cold perspiration lay settled at the top of his brow, and an odious breath came from his mouth.

"Where were you last night, Charles dear?" asks the mother while she places half a dozen oysters on his plate.

"What business is that of yours?" is Charles' reply, while he sniffs of the oysters. "Portuguese! Phew!"

36

"I thought I was giving you something special," said the mother.

"I don't want you to put yourself out for me", Monsieur Charles tells her. "You plague the life out of me, and if you continue in this way, I'll move, so help me Beelzebub!"

The mother turns to one of her guests, a young mother with her two little boys sitting on either side of her.

"One certainly gets a lot of joy out of one's children these days, I'll tell you. Two have left their home for ever, and Charles is my last one. Do you think he treats his mother the way he should?"

"No, I do not," answers her the young woman.

Monsieur Charles gets up, red in the face, as red as his thinned blood allows him to be, and roars out:

"Goodbye! I'll send someone to pick up my belongings after breakfast!"

The two exchange some verbal blows, and Monsieur Charles leaves.

The mother breaks into tears.

When breakfast is over, a moving man arrives to collect her son's belongings.

Crying, the mother gathers together her Charles' drawing and painting materials. She empties the bureau drawers and puts his linen in a knapsack. She removes his paintings from the wall and has the maid beat and brush his clothes. And after that the room stands empty.

All her fledgings are now gone; they have abandoned the nest. What is she now to live for? For whom is she now to tear her heart out in the years to come—perhaps as many as thirty, a whole generation?

"It is the law of nature, dear Madame St. Brie", the young mother says. "And we should not bring up our children and educate them for ourselves alone. Just as we abandoned our parents, so our children will abandon us. We ask too much from life, and it gives us so little in return."

"But what shall we do when our children have all left us?" the deserted mother protests.

"Work for ourselves, I imagine", is the young woman's answer.

"It is not enough. I can't live for myself alone. I must have someone—I must have someone. . . ."

And now the widow sits there alone, sorrowing. With all the

goodness she possesses within her, she now takes to her heart the young mother's two little boys. She plays games with them, reads with them, plays domino with them, and when they are ailing she takes care of them. And so she has something to live for—for a whole month!

And when the month is up, they depart. She stands on the steps when they drive away in a carriage; and when it rolls down the avenue, she remains standing there, gazing after them as if they had taken with them another piece of her heart. But her heart is like the liver of Prometheus: it grows back again after being devoured by the vulture.

And soon she gets a new paying guest—a man who keeps travelling about in order to drive away a great sorrow. And so he encounters the widow with her wounded mother's heart. And he is given his piece of it, which he in turn devours, and then he, too, drives away in a carriage after a time, giving to each one of the maids a louis d'or for the heart he had been gnawing at. But to the widow he gives nothing, for it would not be proper. Oh yes—it is true, he did open his heart to her and gave her as a souvenir a share of his own sorrow; and this she accepted and added to her collection.

But how stupid it is to live for others. It is not enough, and it will not last.

OUR UNNATURAL NATURE
(1885; publ. 1886)

The cutter sped forward in a stiff breeze through the outermost skerries, and the sea lay open, illuminated by the afternoon sun.

The doctor searched for words to express his rapture, for he was born far away from the sea and had only had a glimpse of it from the deck of a steamer a few times.

After the lieutenant had shifted the tiller and headed for the beacon of Landsort, he ordered Swedish *punsch* and cigars.

The silence, the solitude, and the absence of objects to which the eye could attach itself, put them in the humor of being communicative; and although the two childhood friends had chatted three days in a row about both the past and the present, there seemed to be no end of conversational topics that they had not touched upon.

"Life on the sea must be a glorious life to lead," the doctor remarked while his eye flitted across the horizon.

"Yes, when you sit like this, in pleasant company, and when you are your own master," said the lieutenant. "But on board ship, in the service, God help us! First of all, you are shut off, isolated. The ship is a cage, you must remember, and the horizon—once you have become accustomed to looking at it—narrows down and gradually gets to be confining; the blue streak, behind which we—when we are young—dream that something mysterious exists, turns into a gray stone wall. Imagine yourself in a cage in the middle of a prison yard. If you have an enemy on board—then you will surely be aware of being alive . . . ."

"Nonetheless, it is a healthy life."

"Healthy! Yes, so it might seem. But the mind does not get healthy when your brain receives no impressions from outside. And to be gazing at nothing dulls the brain eventually. But there is also a seamy side to the life of a sailor, more than one as a matter of fact, and it is anything but a healthy side."

The lieutenant's countenance darkened and he gave a glance toward the bow to see whether the crewmen were far enough away to be out of reach of his voice.

"You must keep in mind that the sailor lives a life like that of a monk or a prisoner. He is isolated from the opposite sex."

"Oh, but you are certainly not so very isolated when you come ashore," broke in the doctor.

"No—but before we come ashore! One month, two months at sea! Much of the time without anything to occupy yourself with. Then your thoughts take off in different directions and your willpower finds its own outlet, pushes aside accepted notions of morality, honor and all that. I have seen strange things being done at sea."

"I admit I have heard it said that sailors are a reckless lot," the doctor broke in.

"I feel sorry for those who are married, for, you see, that poem about the sailor's wife sitting sorrowing at her window—that is, after all, only a poem. But the husband, the married man—he is not keen about dissipating or carousing when he gets ashore. So you may be sure he gets enjoyment out of the money he makes! Yes, indeed! For the general state of affairs is this: the wife is consoled long before the husband comes home! But, you see—there is still another side to it—what is commonly called the shady side—and that is those outbursts of passion brought on by nature in vengeance against itself—outbursts which to us seem horrible and shocking for the reason that we are at a loss to explain them when we first encounter them, and for which we hold the individual to be punishable, despite the fact that he is himself a victim," the lieutenant expostulated.

"So-o? You have such goings-on aboard ship also? We hear so little about that sort of thing, despite the fact that it is one of the strangest phenomena of the times," commented the doctor.

"You don't consider it to be a crime, then?" asked the lieutenant with a degree of eagerness, puffing at his cigar.

"Crime? What is crime? Things that are brought before a court by a plaintiff or a prosecutor? It may be a crime committed by nature, as in those cases where the sex of a newborn child remains undecided long after birth. Such cases do exist, as can be proved by the advertisements you sometimes see, announcing a change of the given name. Nature has its whims, and civilization and culture aid and abet it. Still, people should by this time be so enlightened that they do not exact punishment for defects or frailties."

"So-o, is that what you think? I am glad to hear someone speak a sane word in the midst of the general furor," interpolated the lieutenant.

"Oh, I am quite convinced on that score. In France, there have already been propositions in both chambers about changing the law and eliminating the paragraph dealing with the alleged crime."

"You don't say! And here they walk about like lepers, being constantly preyed upon by a consuming anxiety of being suspected or discovered. Let me tell you of a case I have witnessed with my own eyes; then you can judge whether it is a vice, depravity, or simply a phenomenon, the source of which we do not know," the lieutenant continued.

"It makes no difference to me what it is called; for monks and for men of the sea it is an occupational disease. The phenomenon is just as interesting as when nature produces human phoetus with a calf's head, or with three arms," the doctor added.

"A little more unusual than that, I should think, especially since it appears as something of a physical nature, accompanied by all the symptoms that manifest an innocent infatuation between a male and a female." said the lieutenant.

"Innocent? H'm!"

"Yes, yes, innocent!" the lieutenant reiterated. "I know that such a relationship can be innocent."

"Yes?—Well—perhaps for a time. *You* are rebuffed, or *she* dare not! . . . . We know—it's the old story! But continue your. . . ." the doctor urged.

They took a sip or two of their *punsch* and lit another cigar.

"Do you know what the highest officer on a flagship is?" started the lieutenant, putting the tiller in the taffrail. He is a tin god. He is there on board the ship—but you never see him. He is not the actual commanding officer; for that is the officer next in command. And still he is above the commanding officer. Seamen habitually call the skipper "the old man," just as farmers speak of a thunderstorm as "God Father." The second in command is called "the old man" on a warship; the admiral is given no such name. He sits in his cabin suite, locked in there, unavailable to all except to the second

41

in command; eats alone every day of the week, except one, when he accepts an invitation to dine with the officers. He never rebukes or reprimands, he never rewards or punishes, he never gives orders. What he does do, his second in command is the only one who knows. If he ever comes out on deck, he never goes closer to the bow than the mizzen mast.

A ship is the most perfect of all social communities, yet in its organization it is a thousand years behind its time. With women aboard it would not have been perfect." The lieutenant continued: "Very well. I made my first voyage as a cadet on the frigate *THOR*. Life aboard ship was not what I as a schoolboy dreamed it would be when I enviously gazed at the naval cadet's coquettish uniform jacket and poniard. It was something quite different; something very bleak and bitter, and very ugly. Above all, it was exceedingly unpoetic.

One day I had been given the watch on board and was standing at the helm, a most responsible assignment. I stared afore through rigging, rope and tackling over and beyond the crew on deck, trying to keep my thoughts undistracted and fixed upon nothing but the course of the ship. But partly because I was anxious about my urgent and serious task, since I held the fate of all on board the ship in my hand; partly because I had a vague, nervous feeling that someone's eyes were fixed on me, I forgot myself. The tackling screeched, the bowsprit yawed, and the wind began to touch the flying-jib so that it fluttered gently. Just then the flag officer who had been standing at my side—cried out: "Hold on there!" At the same moment my hands were violently jerked from the steering-wheel and I was given a shove that catapulted me onto the deck. I tumbled forward like a mitten thrown away and to my astonishment found myself lying at the feet of none other than the admiral himself. I looked up and saw a grayish yellow face, resembling nothing so much as that of a prosperous wholesale dealer. The mouth was cut sharply and was framed by a pair of deeply grooved furrows which gave him an expression of hardness. This impression, however, was mitigated by a pair of blond side-burns. He looked as if he would have liked to throw me overboard, but he said nothing. He gazed at me as though he wondered whether he could allow himself to address a creep such as I. Finally his severe features relaxed and he looked at me as though I were a little child. "What is your name, cadet?" he inquired. I told him my name. "And who is your father?"—"He is dead," I answered. "He was a lieutenant colonel in the Corps of Fortification."—"Oh! I knew your father. We were childhood friends and I thought very highly of him.—Go back to your post and keep your thoughts together." I returned to the steering-wheel and exerted myself to the utmost to be attentive to my duty. But the admiral kept pacing back and forth, and I could feel his eyes upon me. When I had finished my watch and I came down into the cadets' messroom, I was surrounded by my comrades and I was asked what the Chief had said to me.

When they learned that he had known my father, the younger ones looked up to me with a certain respect; but the older cadets had a knowing look on their faces. At that time I could not understand why.

A few days after that episode, some of my fellow-cadets and I sat on deck, splicing rope. We talked about one thing and another. Having always been of a highly nervous temperament and sensitive as a compass needle, I felt somewhat ill at ease, as though I were being probed by someone's gaze. I turned around several times trying to discover whose eyes might be following me so persistently and stubbornly. At last my gaze stopped at a little round window in the Chief's outer cabin. There I saw the two slanting furrows around his mouth; his eyes had quickly withdrawn behind the curtain. This disturbed me without my being able to say why it did. Two days later I was summoned in the evening to the Chief's quarters. It was an elegantly furnished room with bookshelves, paintings, photographs and a small organ. The second officer was sitting there with the Chief. He held his cap in his hand and looked uncomfortable.

"Captain," the Chief commenced in an unnaturally easy tone, "this young man is the son of a dead childhood friend of mine, who at one time did me an invaluable service. I have always felt indebted to this young man's noble father and I would like to look after his son. I want to take charge of his education as long as he is on board this ship.—Would you like to be my disciple?" he added, turning to me.

Overcome by an opportunity such as this, offered me by my late father's friend, I could only stutter forth some indistinguishable words of gratitude.

He then beckoned me to sit down, and gave a sign to the second officer that the interview was over.

We were now alone. Something in his manner made me feel disturbed; but I couldn't tell exactly what it was. He was no longer the Chief, the idol. He was someone else. He was abashed and embarrassed in his manner, and self-conscious in his speech.

At first he did not look me in the eye.

"Are you good at mathematics, my boy?" he began.

"Not especially," I answered him.

"You can solve equations of the second degree, can you?"

"Yes, I know equations fairly well, sir."

"Well—then let us go on to logarithms. You see, a sailor without logarithm is like a ship without compass," he remarked.

He got up and took down the tables of logarithms from the bookshelf, pushed a chair over to the table and brought out paper and pen.

After having talked hither and thither about index and mantissa which, I realized later, he confused with each other, he put away the pen.

"Well," he interrupted, "how do you like it on board?"

"Very well, admiral," I replied.

"And your fellow cadets?"

"One does not talk about one's comrades, sir," I blurted out before having taken time to realize what a reproof my answer implied.

"I like your answer, my boy," he said, looking at me with the kind of expression older persons assume to the young when they allow them to take unusual liberties.

"Would you like to have a glass of *punsch*?" he asked. "It's damp in here."

To refuse was impossible, as I was not an abstainer. But suddenly I was gripped by an inexplicable fear. Suppose someone should come in and see the Chief drinking with a cadet! The situation was awkward. Have you ever had the feeling of being abashed and ashamed on someone else's behalf? I was concerned on his account.

The Chief opened a cabinet and took out glasses and a decanter, which he carried into his cabin.

"Come inside," he said.

My uneasiness grew still more. The situation was so false, so contrary to all conventions, and my idolized Chief fell hopelessly.

Inside the cabin, he seated himself opposite me, gazing at me like the giant as he was about to devour Tom Thumb.

"You are a fine boy," he said, emptying his glass, but without

44

clinking it with me," and you have an appearance that will be of advantage to you in your career. Do you know that you are good looking?"

I could feel my face getting red and didn't know what was in his mind. But I noticed on his face a strange expression I had not seen before, and his eyes fluttered like gas flames.

"Have you ever had any amorous experiences?" he suddenly asked. And his eyes took on a glowing sheen.

I didn't know what to answer, for as he was my father's friend, I had respect for him.

He rose and began to pace up and down the cabin floor.

"You should have been my son, my boy!" he finally uttered. "That's what you should have been!"

I knew he was not married and I could understand to a certain degree the old bachelor's outburst of loneliness.

At that moment a bugle call blew to mess and I had to leave.

"Tomorrow evening—at the same time," he said.

And I saluted him and went.

My evening lessons continued for some time after that. He grew more and more intimate in his manner. At times his attentions embarrassed me indescribably. If ever I was intentionally late in arriving, he seemed distressed.

"You are getting tired of me," he would then say, "I am old and a bore! Am I not?"

Then I was seized with compassion for the poor lonely man, whose exalted rank prohibited him from seeking intimate companionship.

We finally reached Havana, and I was given permission to go ashore. But first the Chief extracted a promise from me not to accompany my fellow-cadets to any places of ill-fame. He made me promise this on my honor. When I returned on board ship, he asked me whether I had been together with any girls. I answered, as was the truth, that I had not.

"That's right, my boy," he said, "watch out for women! Be careful of them!"

And so we set sail again.

One evening—an evening I shall never forget—we were ashore, climbing the mountains of Madeira, and the weather was hot as in a greenhouse. We went dressed only in shirts and duck trousers, and the sea had lain dead calm for four days.

At about eight that evening, I came to the Chief's cabin, fully

45

dressed in my uniform. He was frightfully agitated and could scarcely speak.

"This heat is unbearable," he sighed. "Take off your uniform!" Well, I had no objection, although it was completely contrary to all regulations as well as ordinary etiquette.

He seated himself beside me, somewhat behind me. I felt his hot breath on my neck, experienced a strange apprehension, felt sick at heart in a way I can't even describe.

We were at work on trigonometry, and I sat huddled over the paper. I became drowsy, and to keep awake I forced myself to sit erect, throwing my head back. As I did so, my eyes fell on a mirror hanging directly opposite me. What I saw in it filled me with such horror as if I had suddenly seen nature turned inside out, showing me its wrong side—as if the sun had turned blue and the sky yellow, the trees red, or the moon shooting flashes of lightning. His face lay directly over my shoulder and his eyes went searching underneath the open collar of my shirt. I think I must have given a shriek; I tried to jump up from my seat, but was held down by a pair of arms and felt a kiss pressed on my lips—a kiss like that from the sharp tongue of a bull; and across my face I felt a breathless puffing and panting as if I were being licked by a seal.

When I at last came out on deck, I had to take hold of the gunwale to keep from falling, for my legs were trembling. Life, nature, everything lay black before me. I had witnessed a revelation of the ugly in the world, had had a glimpse of the evilness in it.

"And with that the acquaintanceship was at an end!" the doctor concluded stoically.

"No, not entirely. Do you know what he did afterwards? He wrote letters to me. I read only one of them. It was a love letter. He was in love with me!"

"As Socrates was in love with Alcibiades! Do you think you have made a discovery? And do you think it is only isolation or over-civilization that are the sources of such phenomena, do you? They exist among savages; yes, even among animals. It seems to me we ought to shut our eyes to such whims of nature; at least we ought not to punish the innocent, as I remarked before. If you care to listen to another story on the same subject, I'll tell you one?"

"Yes, but let us first have something to eat; I see the table is set down below."

He called to one of the crew to take the helm, and then they went inside, into the cabin.

The conversation turned to another subject, but somehow the two always came back to their original topic.

"Do you recall the time you went to school," the doctor started, and how you formed friendships with those of your own age, do you? You always went home from school together, always sought each other out when you had a free moment, shared each other's opinions and whatever allowance you had. Yes—there were times when you were downright jealous of your friend, if you found that he neglected you for someone else. Am I not right?'

"Yes—but that was friendship!"

"Yes, so it was! But that is the way love between the opposite sexes begins. It generally takes quite a while before either he or she feels the need of bodily contact through either a kiss or a caress. Friendship between girls, on the other hand, finds its expression in kissing and embracing. This is done entirely innocently, no question about that, but the symptoms resemble very much those of what we call love. They are as innocent as the compulsive feeling which makes parents take their children into their arms to kiss and embrace them. Can you then tell me what is pure and what is not pure, carnal or spiritual? It is not easy to do that, for the parents' love for their children produces an irresistible need to express itself by touching their bodies. Yet such manifestation is above all suspicion of being in any way sensual. But—let a poor family live together in one room, with father and daughters sleeping in the same bed—and, when the girls are fullgrown, it *m a y* happen that the nature of their feelings changes. In such a case it is the outer circumstances that are at work, just as cases of bestiality most frequently occur among shepherds and cavalrymen. And don't tell me this is in any way a new, unnatural behavior that we witness; it is the same nature which, for lack of other outlets, like the tissues of the body, opens up and forms a fistula when the discharge passages are closed by disease. That's that! —Now you'll hear my story.—He was slight, and of no consequence, and the girls passed him by because they saw nothing promising in him, either as a lover or protector. This developed in him a lack of faith, a disbelief, in himself and an animus toward the opposite sex. As he grew older and started to go to girls, he discovered—what the rest of us considered to be quite natural—that the girls had to be

47

paid. This was a shock to him. Why should one of the parties be paid and not the other one, since they had both enjoyed the pleasure. After that he tried a little mild relationship with a seamstress. She liked him, and she made no charge. But after a while she began to be troubled by strange dreams, which soon were to bother him also. One day she dreamed that he invited her to the theatre; another time that he presented her with a pair of gloves; the third time, that he paid her rent for her. My friend was not especially versed in the unriddling of dreams, for the reason that he was poor, and so the girl's dreams remained unfulfilled. The friend felt it was sufficient that he had paid for all their meals together, when she had paid for none of them—but this he didn't say out loud. However, she grew tired of living on dreams, and so she bestowed her love upon a book-keeper who had the means to make her dreams come true. This made my friend bitter and turned him against women, whom he had found to be such materialists and who could not love merely for the sake of love. Despite his rebuffs he fell in love again. When the question of marriage was broached, he went to the father. The father, of course, inquired about his economic situation.

"Oho, so one has to pay here, too?" he thought. "Always one has to pay, all the way up!"

But he was in love, and so he decided to go through with the business deal. He was a teacher of calisthenics and swimming. I suppose by now you begin to get the drift of my story.—He married. After the first child had come, he discovered that his wife had talents for "greater and more exalted tasks" and that she had no desire to have another child. The result: a stormladen atmosphere! And after that, a semi-calm set in. Sometimes he found it hard to take, having to pay in return for nothing, but it was too late to do anything about it. His celibacy went on for fifteen years, and the wife snatched every opportunity she could get to emphasize and make clear her position.

"I am the mother of your child, and that is my position in this house."

But, frankly, she was not a mother to her child, for she was constantly running to bible meetings and pursuing other exalted activities which stood in the way of her duties as a mother. And that made her forget she was his wife. Oh well! After fifteen years of this, there was a violent storm one day at his swimming school. My friend had exposed himself to what Darwin would have called geneagenetic varia-

48

tion. An analysis of his fifteen years of celibacy would prove material for a Russian novel. I myself wouldn't be capable of doing the analysing. The stormy scene resulted in a secret police inquiry—exoneration—and a new child in their marriage. And that is how their marriage was saved. There you have two factors that contributed: on the one side, occupational disease, or a ready opportunity; and, on the opposite side, a lack of opportunity.

"Yes, but there was still a third factor,' the lieutenant added.

"What, then?" the doctor asked.

"His lack of means as a young man," answered the lieutenant.

"In that case you can add a fourth factor," interpolated the doctor.

"What is that?" queried the lieutenant.

"The high wages of labor."

"Huh! Let's go out on deck now," the lieutenant said. "This is getting to be gruesome, once you begin to delve too deeply into the subject."

"Yes, you are right, but there is a time for everything. Do you know that the university in Dijon last year offered a prize of ten thousand francs to whomever could satisfactorily answer the question: "Why are we not allowed to write as we speak?""

"Well, who won the award?"

"A fellow in Växjö. He reasoned that if he were to write the way he spoke, he would land in prison."

"You are mad!"

"Why, look at the moon! She is out!" the doctor exclaimed as they came out on deck.

"Why do you say *s h e* ? Don't you know that the moon is masculine?" the lieutenant quipped.

"Well, perhaps in Stockholm—but in Greece she is feminine."

"Oh well, but then the Greeks never made much distinction between the sexes. And do you know why?"

"I assume it had something to do with their religious belief? Zeus was attracted to Ganymede, wasn't he? And the Greeks were a great and cultured people, who showed respect for their religion!"

VESTMAN'S SEALING ADVENTURE
(1888)

Erik Vestman of the Nether Farm Isle in the Stockholm archipelago had once shipped on a schooner that sailed regularly on the
Norway run, and had been as far north as the Lofoten Islands.
There he had come to know whaling men and had learned quite
a few things about their method of catching whales with harpoons.
And so, when he came back home to his little island, the thought
occurred to him that when he again went seal hunting in his home
waters he ought to put to use what he had learned; for the catch
had been continually diminishing because of the frightening effect
that the loud reports of the rifles had upon the timid creatures. So
he set to work in the following less-than-well-considered manner,
which ended in a way that neither he nor anyone else could have
anticipated. And what he did led to an adventure of which the legend
still lives in the skerries.

One evening late in the spring, Vestman set out in a flat-bottomed
boat, taking a boy along with him, and headed for the outer skerries,
where the seals were in the habit of clambering up on the shore to
sun themselves. For this remarkable undertaking he had brought
with him fishing tackle, consisting of a board attached parallel with
the boat, through which a line with hooks could be payed out. This
contraption was ordinarily used for the purpose of hooking otters
and dragging them out of mountain crevices; and Vestman had now,
whaler fashion, secured the running line to a windlass at the bow
of the boat. How he was to approach the shy, frightened animals
and get close enough to capture them with his makeshift harpoon
was something neither he nor anyone else knew. But then, as his
friends would say, one can in a pinch set nets in a water barrel.
However, Vestman had planned his strategy this way: the boy was
to go after the seals from landward with the rifle, and Vestman him-

self was to steal in between the ice floes and from there go after the fleeing beasts, which would be unable to move too quickly upon the rough, uneven drift ice that had formed into a pack close to the shore.

He had put the boy ashore just before the sun had gone down, and now he was sculling the boat, a pair of woolen socks wound about the loom of the oar in order not to make any sound; so that he would not be seen, he had pulled a white shirt over his clothes. And, protected by the rocks and the pack ice, he came to an embankment where a cleft indicated that the seals had come up at that spot and consequently had to take the same way out, for there was no hole in the ice near the shore.

Well hidden, Vestman sat still, holding the hook high, ready to attack. He sat there so long that his fingers became cold as ice, and he began to wonder whether the old way of hunting with rifle and using leaden bullets was not the simpler and better way, after all. The seals were there—there could be no mistake about that—he had heard them bark; but why they had picked just this dangerous spot for getting into the water, that was the big question.

Bang! A loud report came from behind the pine trees on the islet, and he heard a peeping and a whistling in the air and a splash in the water like the sound made by people running about the floor in their bare feet. Before Vestman had time to grasp how foolish and stupid the whole thing really was, a hairy head shot out through the opening, then rose and plunged into the sea—and the seal was hooked in its fleshiest part. Out went the line in a jiffy, and the boat was given a jerk and quivered so violently that the hunter fell to the bottom, near the back of the boat; and, then, off it went at full speed out to sea! And what a sea trip it was! At first Vestman thought it was something new and full of fun. He mused over what a splendid hunting tale he would now be able to tell; and he was confident that he already had his booty safely in hand. But then he suddenly came to realize that the rocky islets were flying past his eyes and his own little house was disappearing.

"Good-by for a little while," he thought, giving a nod to the shore. "I won't be gone very long!" The boat was wrenched and jerked from side to side, but Vestman felt there was no cause for worry until he found himself beyond the outer skerries and no longer could sight land.

There the sea was running quite high, and the sun seemed to have

51

gone down, and all about him was a circle of total darkness. "At worst, if he takes me much farther I'll cut the line," Vestman thought to himself. And, then, off it went again! But now the punt started to wind and sway and wriggle hither and thither; the waves were pounding it and it began to dip its nose.

"Only a little farther," thought Vestman, who was disinclined to let go of his assured booty and was aching to prevent such a promising beginning from coming to a sorry and inglorious end.

The waves grew higher and the stars were lighted. He could still see the axe which lay close to the bow of the boat; the axe was his final hope if he decided he could venture no further.

"Keep on going, old man! If I know you aright, you'll soon be tired out," muttered the hunter, now frozen stiff and yearning to get to the oars so that he could get warmed up.

At that very moment he felt his feet getting wet and heard the boat scraping against something. "Cut the line!" he commanded himself, and stood up to start for the bow, meaning to pick up the axe and cut the line. But he instantly sat down again, for the moment he left his place aft, the seal pulled the nose of the boat down below the surface of the sea.

After several fruitless attempts to crawl forward to the bow, he realized the necessity of sitting still; he was at the mercy of the seal, and the creature could decide at whim whether Vestman would survive and get back home.

By this time it had ceased to be amusing, and a quiet seriousness had settled upon the downhearted seal hunter. To give himself more courage than he actually had, he grabbed an oar, put it out aft and made believe he was steering the punt. But that was just what he didn't do, for the steering was done by the seal; and he continued to set the course straight out to sea.

"If I ever get out of this, then by Beelzebub, I'll . . ." The seal performed a few snakelike turns and twists, and Vestman's diabolical oath was left unfinished, for the oar had to be taken in and the bailer brought out, in order to clear the boat of water.

After he had scooped out the water, he put the oar out again, and immediately he felt himself more at ease, exactly as if he were really steering the punt. By now the stars had gone to sleep, and rain, mixed with snow, began to fall. Soon Vestman could see the axe no more, for he found himself enveloped in a gray haze wherever he

52

looked. And the boat kept shooting forward . . . forward . . . but the wind seemed to be shifting, for the waves were now driving broad on the bow; and the wind kept veering ever so often.

Now he was really frightened! And while he was using the bailer again, his thoughts went to his wife and children, to house and home and tackle and other belongings, and finally to eternity—which certainly did not seem to be very far off! He thought about the fact that he had not been to church for . . . well, he couldn't remember for how many years; he hadn't been there since the year the cholera was rampant! And that he hadn't been to communion. . . . Now the lee side of the boat was scraping against drift ice. . . . "Lord Jesus! . . . I'm a poor, sinful creature!" He had forgot about things of that sort. . . . "Our Father Who art in Heaven . . . Thy will be done . . . on earth as it is in Heaven. . . . I don't even remember the Lord's Prayer any more!"

How long the hours seemed—and how many of them! It wouldn't be long before he would be all the way to the Åland Islands with this kind of wind. But if he should come up against drift ice, then he would have to follow along all the way down to Gotland, or land somewhere in the Gulf of Finland But before he arrived there, he would have frozen to death. . . .

He huddled in the bottom of the boat to seek protection from the cold blasts; and when he had sunk down to his knees, the whole of the Lord's Prayer came back to him and he repeated it at least twenty times. And every time he came to "Amen," he made a notch on the gunwale of the boat with his jackknife. And when he heard his own voice, he felt more at ease, for it was like talking to someone, and as if someone were talking to him . . . and the words brought back memories of a flock of people gathered in church . . . and he saw them before him now, consoling him, reproaching him. He saw the Geling boys—together with whom he had recently been out to sea and fished up coal from the cargo of a brig that had met with disaster and foundered out there. This was not completely honest—but it might be defended. He saw. . . . Now there was a tugging on the line at the bow! "Lord Jesus! Son of God! If I ever come out of this alive, I promise . . . I promise to give a new chandelier with seven branches—all of it of pure silver—even if I have to take all I have saved for my children . . . I promise to give a silver chandelier to the church . . . of pure silver! . . . The Lord bless us and keep us, the Lord make His face to shine upon us and give us peace. . . ."

Through the mist could be seen a light dead ahead—a penetrating light, but blurred—like a lantern with panes made of horn.

"It's the beacon at Hangö—it's the coast of Finland!" Vestman thought to himself. "I might have known . . . we have been on our way for twelve hours . . . they seem like a whole week!" Again there was a crash under the boat, and it came to a standstill so abruptly that Vestman was thrown forward to the floor of the boat. After that there was neither sound nor movement. Vestman wondered how far it might be to the lighthouse. About eight—nine—miles? But he was unable to move, neither here nor there! He was now worse off than ever, for at the slightest motion he made the boat rock.

Vestman sat still in his place and he waited for the sun to come up and to see the dawning in the east; and he was freezing. And he prayed to God, and he promised, and made all kinds of vows about the silver chandelier, which would cost him no less than two hundred *riksdaler* and would be made of the finest silver, have seven branches, and be adorned with all sorts of elegant embellishments on the candleholders! And suspended from it would hang a fishing line with bullets attached, and whenever people saw it, they would say: "That, you see—that is the fulfillment of the promise made by Erik Vestman of the Nether Farm—because our Lord, in His grace and compassion, rescued him when he was in such dire peril in the year 1859!" Over and over again he repeated these words, "God saved him by His grace and love and charity," until he finally began to believe his own words; and, in his overflowing gratitude for the merciful help from above, he recited the first words of the hymn "Thanks be to Thee, and praise, O Father dear!" God had saved him, there was no doubt of that, since the chandelier gave testimony to it, and people said—people would be saying—they hadn't said so yet, for. . . . The beacon suddenly went out! . . . "Lord Jesus! who walked upon the water and bade the waves be still!" Why, now the sea was becalmed . . . the waves had already quieted down some time before . . . it was now absolutely calm, and it seemed so strange because here was the open sea, and it had been infernally wrought up not so very long ago . . . last evening, last night . . . for now morning was drawing near, it could not be very far away, since he now felt the cold so frightfully in his feet, and he was hungry; but soon he would be drinking some hot coffee . . . very soon . . . if only the pilot boat would come. . . . which it must do, because some sailing vessels, which had been cruising in the outer roadstead, were expected at sunset . . . but why . . . why the dev . . . why in all the world had they put out the light in the beacon just at this moment . . . perhaps it was daylight already, even though it could not be seen, owing to the mist . . . no doubt that was the reason . . . that is, unless the Russian government had different rules and regulations for their lighthouse service. . . . Oh yes, now it came back to him as if in a dream . . . the Russians used a different calendar, of course . . . the old calendar, which is thirteen days ahead of our time, or behind it . . . it doesn't matter which, for there must be a difference in time, of course; and, to be sure, there always was, for the Finnish ships invariably arrived one hour later than they had telegraphed they would arrive—yes, that is exactly the reason they put out the light in the lighthouse one hour before dawn; therefore, the sun will rise one hour from now. And now he began to realize why he was freezing so terribly: for that is what all who have had the rickets or malaria do when the sun is coming up. . . . But the seal . . . the seal was absolutely still, and the wind had quieted down . . . perhaps it had exhausted itself and fled. . . . "I have to investigate and find out—at any rate, to sit here unnecessarily is more than the dev . . ."

Vestman stared in the direction of the bow and gradually became aware of the outlines of something jagged and sharpedged and murky —like a great many masts and tackle rising out of the darkness. "In the name of Jesus! If it's the Russian navy, they'll shoot me for smuggling and send me to Siberia! And what an enormous lot of them! Father in Heaven! There's a whole forest of them!"

He got up and straightened his legs! The boat merely rolled a bit to the sides, but it didn't dip its nose any more. He prudently stepped over the sharp-edged axe and the knives near the bow, noticed that the line was strained like a telephone wire, got out of the boat, noticed footprints on the ground, and stubbed his toe against a stone. He was on land! And he saw fir trees!

"It that you, father," piped a voice from behind a juniper bush. He knew the voice well.

"Ludvig, my son! How the devil did you get here?"

"I wondered what had happened to you, father!"

Vestman rubbed his eyes.

"Tell me—do you know what time of the day it is?"

55

"I guess it must be going on eight, and you must have been gone at least a whole hour! And I see you have the seal with you, haven't you?"

On the rocks lay the animal with the big otter hook imbedded in its back, dead, dead as could be, after having made a trip to sea, turning back because of the high waves.

And to this day the adventure is related as the strangest ever to have happened in the skerries, next to the weird tale of the sea serpent. And he who refuses to put any credence in it can go to the church on Nether Farm Isle and look at the little chandelier hanging there underneath the organ loft in eternal remembrance of the blessed rescue of the late government pilot Vestman from a most unprecedented and fantastic danger at sea, when he—in the face of death —promised the Lord to donate this chandelier of pewter for the blessing and edification of the congregation.

LEONTOPOLIS
(1905)

A caravan was encamped on a height east of the ancient city of Heliopolis. It numbered a great many people, all Hebrews, and they had traveled on camels and donkeys from Palestine through the desert—the same desert the children of Israel had traversed more than a thousand years before.

In the dusk of the evening, by the mellow light of the moon, the campfires could be seen by the hundreds. Seated by them were the women with their youngest offspring. The men were busy carrying water. Never before had the desert seen so many little children; and as they were now being prepared for the night's sleep, the camp echoed with the cries of the little ones. It was like one huge, enormous nursery, but when the bathing of the little babes was done with and they had been tucked in at the breast of their mothers, the crying subsided, little by little, and it grew quite still in the camp.

Underneath a sycamore tree sat a woman suckling her newborn. Beside her stood a man, Hebraic of feature, and placed a fagot of wild broom before his donkey. When he had finished this chore he took a few steps forward on the hillock and gave a searching look toward the north.

A stranger, who, to judge by his attire, was a Roman, came by. He scrutinized the woman with the little baby, as if he were taking inventory of them.

The Hebrew showed signs of anxiety and, in order to hide his feelings, started a conversation with the Roman.

"Tell me, wanderer," he asked, "is that the City of the Sun— over there in the west?"

"You are looking straight at it," the Roman answered.

"Then this is Beth Semes? . . ."

57

"Heliopolis—where Greeks and Romans have gathered their wisdom . . . Plato himself has been here . . ."

"Can you see Leontopolis from here also?" asked the Jew.

"You can see the towers of the temple two miles north from here."

"This is the land of Goshen, then, that our Father Abraham visited and that was given to Jacob", said the Hebrew, turning to his wife, who acknowledged his words with a mere bow of the head.

Then he said to the Roman: "Israel wandered out of Egypt into Canaan, but after the captivity in Babylon some of the Jews came back and settled here. This you know, of course . . . ?"

"Vaguely. I have heard something about it. And now the Israelites have multiplied into many thousands of souls . . . . They have even built a temple of their own. It's the very one you see there in the distance. Did you know that?" asked the Roman.

"I knew that they had, yes. But this is now a Roman land, isn't it?" the Hebrew retorted.

"So it is!" replied the Roman.

"The Romans are everywhere: Syria, Canaan, Greece, Egypt . . . ."

"And Germania, Gaul, Britannia . . . . The world belongs to the Romans—as it was prophesied by the Sibyl of Cumae!" said the Roman with pride.

"So far, yes! But the world shall be saved through Israel—as God himself has promised our Father Abraham," said the Hebrew.

"That fable I have heard, too," admitted the Roman, "but for the moment it is Rome that holds that promise in her hand. Do you come from Jerusalem?" inquired the Roman.

"I come from the desert, like the rest of these, and have wife and child with me," confessed the Hebrew.

"Children, yes . . . . Why do you drag along so many children with you?" said the Roman with a certain contemptuousness.

The Hebrew stood silent. But as he took it for granted that the Roman knew the reason, and as he had the appearance of a man of good heart, he decided to tell him the truth.

"Because," the Hebrew said, "Herod the Tetrarch has been told by wise men from the East that a king of the Jews has been born in Bethlehem in the land of Judah. In order to escape the dread danger, Herod has all male infants born in that area in recent days, put to death. Just as Pharaoh once killed off our firstborn in this very

58

land . . . . and Moses was saved to lead our people out of the Egyptian bondage."

"Well—but the king—who can he be?" wondered the Roman.

"He is the Messiah, the promised one . . . ." said the Jew humbly.

"Do you think he has been born yet?" asked the Roman with curiosity, mingled with contempt.

"I don't know," came hesitatingly from the Jew.

"I do—he has already been born," the Roman said with conviction, "and he is the one who will rule the world and subjugate all peoples under his scepter!"

"Who is he?" asked the Hebrew.

"The Emperor—Augustus!" said the Roman proudly.

"Is he of Abraham's seed, or of David's House? No—he is not. And has he come with peace, as Isaiah prophesied when he said: 'His Kingdom shall be great, and of peace there shall be no end!' Indeed, the emperor is no man of peace," said the Hebrew with courage.

"Farewell, you child of Israel! . . . You are now a Roman subject. And you have to be satisfied with the salvation Rome can give you. It is the only salvation there is."

The Roman went. The Hebrew came close to his wife.

"Mary," he said.

"Joseph," said she. "Walk softly. The child is sleeping."

Dedicated to Vifvan Shellabarger.

ESSAYS

MEMORANDUM TO THE MEMBERS OF THE
INTIMATE THEATRE
·
SHAKESPEARE'S OUTLOOK ON LIFE
·
CHINA: AN HISTORICAL AND
CULTURAL SURVEY

MEMORANDUM
to
the Members of the
INTIMATE THEATRE
(1908)

MEMORANDUM TO THE MEMBERS OF THE INTIMATE THEATRE

When I now enter upon regular duties at The Intimate Theatre, I greet the personnel with this memorandum, for I cannot make speeches.

I have given this note the name of Memorandum because I am not stating anything that is particularly new but merely wish to recapitulate, or summarize, what I in my little notes at the conclusion of each dress-rehearsal have communicated in the way of instructions, observations, criticism, words of encouragement, advice and admonition.

Soon we shall have worked together a year. We have passed through hardships, which it would be best to forget, even if the remembrance of these prompts us to be cautious. You have been found fault with and criticized, sometimes unjustly, sometimes justly, but you have also been given commendation and praise. The bad days you have taken with the good ones. You have labored, at times without remuneration, at times being paid, and have not disdained to participate in the meanest of tasks, not demanded of you by your contracts.

This your readiness to make sacrifices and your devotion to your tasks has lightened my burden. And the thought of all that I have seen of beauty and talent at your performances, and the goodwill you have shown by accepting my comments, inspires in me the most ardent hopes as I from now on become

Stage Director of The Intimate Theatre.

MEMORANDUM TO THE MEMBERS OF THE INTIMATE THEATRE

The Intimate Theatre: Its essential connotation

When in the 1860's and 1870's a full length play was submitted to The Royal Theatre, its acceptance for production was concommitant upon the following conditions. The play ought preferably to be in five acts, each act consisting of approximately six sheets of paper, or a total of $5 \times 24 = 124$ folio pages. Division into tableaux or *changements* found little favor and was considered a weakness. Each act had to have a beginning, a middle and an end. The ending of each act had to bring applause; this was accomplished by an oratorical figure, and—if the play was written in unrhymed verse—the last two verses had to rhyme. For the benefit of the actor

64

there were scenes in the play of a *tour de force nature,* and monologues [soliloquies] were permitted; these were frequently the culminating point of the play. A prolonged outburst of passion or emotion, a reproof, a punishment, a revealment were almost imperative. One also had to relate an incident: a dream, an anecdote, an event of some kind.

This poetic theory of drama had much in it that was both attractive and justified. It originated after there had been a rebellion in the 1830's against Racine's and Corneille's age old abstractions, and had as its champion Victor Hugo. But like all other forms of art, it degenerated after it had had its day; and in the five-acter any and all themes were brought into play, including the trivial plot or story, or the anecdote. Practical considerations, such as preventing a part of the theatre's large personnel from remaining idle, necessitated that the play contain minor rôles which, however, should not be supernumerary but speaking rôles. This matter of rôles was confounded with characterization, and we have in recent times heard the practical Björnson described as the great creator of rôles.

The fear of more serious and pregnant subject matter brought about an unnecessary stretching out of bagatelles so that the management continually was forced to suggest the elimination of lengthy, long-winded passages. When, about 1870, I had written the five-acter BLOT-SVEN[1] in verseform and read it aloud to my poet friends in Uppsala,[2] I discovered that my drama was nothing but one extended monologue.

Therefore I burned the manuscript (as I did with the original manuscript of *ERIK XIV*). Out of the ash arose the one-acter *THE OUTLAW,* which—aside from its great weaknesses—possesses the merit of adhering to the subject and which, despite its brevity, is also comprehensive. In this I was undoubtedly influenced by Björnson's masterly one-acter *BETWEEN THE BATTLES,* which I found to be ideal as a model. For in the course of time people had grown

---

[1] Blot-Sven, a Swedish king, elected about 1080, when King Inge the Elder was banished because of his Christian zeal. The name Blot-Sven was given him because he himself performed the sacrificial ritual. After ruling for three years, he in turn was deposed and killed by Inge. (Blot—blood sacrifice.)

[2] Strindberg and some of his fellow students had formed a literary circle at the University of Uppsala, in which they discussed one another's poetic efforts. A.P.

65

impatient and had come to expect swift results. Thus the tempo increased.

In *MASTER OLOF* (1st version) I made an attempt, however, to effect a compromise. The poetry was done away with, prose took its place; and instead of the iambic drama that was reminiscent of the opera with its arias and duets (trios, etc.), I made use of polyphony: in other words, a symphony of harmonious sounds, in which all the voices fitted in with one another (the minor characters were treated on an equal basis with the leading ones) and the soloist was unaccompanied [by other voices]. The attempt succeeded, although since then some deletions have had to be made owing to the fact that the people of today found the play to be too long. But in the beginning of the 1880's, the trend of the times began to exert its demands for reform even in the theatre. Zola took up the cudgels against the French comedy with its Brussels carpet, its patent leather shoes and glossy, lacquered motifs, with dialogue reminding one of the questions and answers in the catechism. In 1887, Antoine opened his Théâtre Libre in Paris, and *THÉRÈSE RAQUIN*—although merely the adaptation of a novel—set the pattern for the day. Here was exhibited the powerful *motif* and the concentrated form which bespoke the new modernity; yet the unity of time was not observed [in it] and the curtain effect remained.

It was after this that I wrote my three dramas *MISS JULIE, THE FATHER* and *CREDITORS. MISS JULIE*, to which I wrote a now well-known introduction, was given by Antoine, but not until 1893,[3] after it had been first presented at the University Students' Association in Copenhagen in 1889.[4] In the spring of 1894[5] *CREDITORS* was given at the Théâtre de l'Oeuvre in Paris, and in the same year *THE FATHER* was also presented at that theatre (with Philippe Garnier in the title rôle). But in 1889 [Die] Freie Bühne had opened in Berlin, and already before 1894 all these three plays had been given there, *MISS JULIE* preceded by a lecture by Paul Schlenter, the present director of the Hofburg Theatre in Vienna. Rosa Bertens, Emanuel Reicher, Rittner and Jarno acted the leading rôles, and Sigismund Lautenburg, director of the Residenztheater, had *CREDITORS* presented one hundred

[3] 16 January, 1893.
[4] 14 March, 1889.
[5] 21 June, 1894.

66

times there. Then a certain silence set in, and theatre fell well-nigh into the same old rut again, until Reinhardt at the beginning of the new century opened his Kleines Theater in Berlin. There I was represented in its early days by the long one-acter THE *BOND*, together with *MISS JULIE* (acted by Gertrud Eysoldt) and *CRIMES AND CRIMES*. Last year (1907) Reinhardt went all the way and opened the Kammerspielhaus, the name of which implies an intimate program; the chamber music idea carried over into the drama: the intimate procedure, the significant *motif*, the highly finished treatment. Last fall (1907) the Hebbeltheater opened with much the same intent and principles, and throughout Germany theatres with the name Intimate Theatre have sprung up.

One of the last days in November, 1907, August Falck opened his Intimate Theatre in Stockholm, and as a result I was given an opportunity and incentive to follow its efforts on the stage in all their details. Through this, memories from my forty years of association with the theatre were awakened, observations I had made in the past were re-examined, old experiments were repeated, and my re-awakened interest gave me the impulse to write this *Memorandum*. If one should now ask what an Intimate Theatre has as its function and what is meant by the term *chamber plays*, I shall answer as follows: In drama we are in search of the powerful, meaningful *motif*, but within bounds. In the treatment of it we wish to avoid everything touching on vanity, any calculated effects, scenes that beg for applause, *tour de force rôles,* monologues. The author must be bound by no definite form, for the form is conditioned by the plot and subject matter. Thus, [there must be] freedom of treatment, bound only by the unity of conception and a feeling for style.

When director Falck broke away from the long-drawn out performances that lasted close to midnight, he broke not only with the classical theatre but with the retail sale of alcoholic beverages. This took courage, for the retail sale of liquor generally paid at least half the rent for the larger theatres. But in the wake of this combination of theatrical art and alcohol followed the long intermissions, the duration of which was dependent upon the restaurateur and controlled by the stage manager.

The inconveniences of allowing an audience to slip out to consume intoxicating beverages during the progress of a performance are too well known. The atmosphere is either dissipated by conversation or

67

the enraptured mind is dulled and tends to make conscious that of which it ought to remain oblivious. The illusion which the drama might provide, can not be kept alive, and instead the half awake spectator becomes engaged in banal reflections, or occupies himself with reading the evening newspaper, or chats with acquaintances whom he meets at the bar about one thing or another, and is distracted—and the plot and action of the play are forgotten. When the spectator returns to his seat, he is in a wildly different state of mind, in vain trying to catch up with what he has seen in the preceding act.

For many this system degenerated as well into [the habit of] folding chairs at tables [as a means of reserving tables] before the play began. In this way, the play was treated as an entre-act; indeed, there were those who stayed away for an act, if they found the shag sofa in the bar especially comfortable, and too irresistible to leave.

The economy of the Intimate Theatre suffered from this break [with the status quo] although the theatre gained in other respects. The attention of the audience was in turn undividedly directed to the stage, and in return the public had the opportunity to go out to supper afterwards and in comfort discuss what it had heard and seen.

We decided upon small premises because we wished that every voice should be heard to the last row without having to resort to screaming. There are, namely, theatres so large that the actor has to force his voice when speaking. This causes the actor's intonation to sound false and makes it necessary for him to bellow and blare out his declaration of love, to entrust a confidence to someone with the loudness of a gunshot, to whisper forth the secrets of his heart at the top of his voice—all of it as if the actors were angry, or in a hurry to get off the stage.

We obtained the small premises, and after we had toned down the actors' voices, we gradually advanced toward our goal, meantime realizing we had a long struggle ahead.

The art of acting is the most difficult and also the easiest of all arts. But, like beauty, it is wellnigh impossible to define. It is not an art of pretending, for the great artist does not pretend: he is true, sincere, and does not rely on make-up. But the low comedian uses every conceivable means to disguise himself with make-up and costume. And acting is not imitation, for the bad actor frequently possesses a demoniacal gift for imitating well-known persons, while the true artist may lack that very gift. The actor is in no way a medium for the author except in a certain degree, and with reservations. Esthetically speaking, acting is not accepted as one of the independent arts but as an appendant art. It can, for instance, not exist by itself without the author's text. An actor can not do without the author, but an author can, if need be, dispense with the actor. I have never witnessed the second part of Goethe's *FAUST,* have never seen Schiller's *DON CARLOS,* nor Shakespeare's *THE TEMPEST*—but I have nonetheless seen them when I have read them. And there are worthy plays which ought not to be performed, which can not suffer the footlights. On the other hand, there are bad plays that have to be acted in order to have life infused into them; they have to be complemented and ennobled by the actor's art. The author generally is aware of what he owes to the actor, and usually manifests his gratitude. The same is true of the superior actor in his relationship to the author. I would like to see that they appreciated each other since their obligations are mutual; and if the question of who is indebted to whom were never brought up, they would have respect for each other. But it is often brought up by conceited fools and by stars when they happen to infuse life into a failing [yet] deserving play. To them the author is a necessary evil, or one who [simply] supplies the text, since the play must contain dialogue.

At the Intimate Theatre I have never heard this question raised, and I hope I never shall. I have seen actors develop characters out of my rôles that made them superior to my original conception of them, and I have publicly acknowledged this.

The art of acting is seemingly the easiest of arts, for every human being can by nature speak, walk, stand, gesture, and change expression. But that is merely being oneself, and it does not take long to realize that this has nothing to do with the art of acting, for if he should be given a rôle to learn and then perform it on the stage, it will soon be noticed that the ablest, the strongest and most profound and penetrating personality can turn out to be a fiasco, while a quite ordinary person immediately may be at home in the rôle. Some show themselves to be born with a propensity for reproducing [a character], others are not endowed with that gift. Yet it is always difficult to judge a beginner, for the talent may exist without being immediately discernible; and great talents have frequently had a very mediocre beginning. Therefore the producer and the stage director must be prudent in their judgment whenever they hold the fate of a young man or woman in their hands. They must test and observe, exercise patience and defer their judgment until later.

It is difficult to determine what qualifications and attributes are required to make an actor, but I shall try to mention a few. Firstly, he must give undivided attention to his rôle: in brief, he must be able to concentrate with all his mind upon it and not allow himself to be distracted. Anyone who plays an instrument knows what it means to let one's thoughts stray. The notes disappear, one's fingers [begin to] rove, and touch the wrong key, and one becomes confused, even though one is familiar with the score. Secondly, another essential is no doubt having imagination, or the ability to fathom the character and the situation so vividly that it takes shape. I assume that the artist goes into a kind of trance, becomes oblivious of himself, and in the end develops into the character he is to personify. It has a relationship to sleepwalking, yet is not exactly the same. If the actor is disturbed while in this state, or if he is awakened to consciousness, he becomes confused, is lost. That is why I have always hesitated to interrupt a scene during rehearsal. I have observed how an actor suffers anguish when he is waked. He stands as if flustered and it requires time for him to get back into his [particular] state of sleepwalking again, to recapture the atmosphere, the feeling and vocal intonation.

No art is so dependent upon the other arts as is the actor's. He cannot isolate his work [of art], exhibit it, and say: This is mine! For if he receives no support from his co-players, if he fails to establish rapport with them, he becomes upset, disorganized, is forced into false inflections; and even if he himself does his own rôle as well as he can under the circumstances, the total effect will be out of focus. Each actor is dependent upon the actor who plays opposite him. I have seen some extremely selfish individuals who have treated their fellow-actors as subordinates and rivals, erased them, so to speak, in order to exhibit themselves and outshine their colleagues.

For this reason the spirit within a theatre, i.e., a beneficial relationship, is of the greatest importance for the full realization and effective presentation of a play. One has to [learn both how to] dominate and how to subordinate oneself, to co-ordinate, how to fit in, —and above all, how to be part of the ensemble. This is a good deal to ask of people, especially in a field where each one is driven by a praiseworthy ambition to be in the spotlight, to gain recognition, and to receive well-earned applause by honest means.

As soon as the actor has a vivid picture of the character and scene [or scenes in which he is to act] his next task is to memorize his rôle. This begins with the spoken word, and this, I believe, is the most important thing in the art of acting. When the correct intonation has been achieved, gestures, facial expression, posture, and position will follow instinctively, if the actor possesses the gift of imagination. If the actor is lacking in the latter, one is confronted with the spectacle of seeing arms and hands dangling like lifeless objects; the torso is as if dead; and all that you see is a talking head on a body without life. This is often typical of the beginner. The word, the spoken word, has not had the power sufficiently to penetrate and co-ordinate all the vital appendages of the body; and there is a break in the conduit. But contacts can also be created so that muscles that are not intended to be used, begin to flounder and move: the fingers pluck nervously, the feet continuously seek new positions without coming to rest. The actor, in short, is nervous and in turn makes the audience restless. For this reason it is not unessential that the actor keep his body in sound health in order to have it under control. Nowadays I am most generally inclined to place the spoken word first, for a good voice is of prime importance. A scene may be performed in darkness and still be made enjoyable, as long as it is well spoken.

To Speak Well

The first requisite for this is to speak slowly. The beginner has no idea how very slowly one both can and should speak on the stage. As a young aspiring actor I watched our foremost actor of conversation pieces and half audibly I repeated his speeches [in the play]. It was a surprise to me, for no one could have persuaded me to think that anyone could speak so slowly without making it sound like preaching.

The Tone of the Voice

The tone must be formed in the larynx, which with its vocal cords is solely created for this purpose. But vowels and consonants are shaped with the mouth: tongue, lips, teeth.

Only when one whispers, does one speak solely with the mouth; and conversation in a room is usually a kind of whisper or subdued chatter. When two persons are talking, consonants especially are left out, for in such intimate conversation one can almost read by the lips and by the expression of the eyes what is being said.

On the stage it is different. There one is a public speaker, whether one wishes to be or not. There the larynx must function, and there every syllable must be pronounced.

If every sound is heard, especially the consonants, and if one phrases distinctly and correctly, even the weakest voice may be heard and understood. Rachel[6] had a very weak voice, yet she could be heard throughout the Comédie Française by its audience of one thousand.

The most common error is to speak too fast, and carelessly. For example: "De gå för fott!" instead of "Det går för fort!";[7] "svåt" instead of *svårt;* "teaten" instead of *teatern.*[8] The actor need not be coached (in his rôle) by anyone; he need only pay attention to [his speech] himself, learn to speak his rôle slowly and, in the beginning, pedantically listen to the sound of his voice to learn how closely he has approached the correct intonation and that all the syllables are enunciated clearly. After that, the tempo will increase by itself, and when he then speaks the words at a normal or more rapid pace, his delivery will sound quite natural and not at all pedantic.

But first and last, the tone must come from the larynx, and the sounds must be given shape by the mouth.

An actor who speaks well is always acceptable to an audience, even if he is an actor of moderate ability. He is never a failure, he never ruins (a play), is offered [engagements and] rôles and has a chance of advancing in his chosen profession. If, on the other hand, he possesses a beautiful voice and falls in love with it—then he frequently stops short of progress and may be on the road to oblivion. That, too, is one of the dangers! Therefore, let everyone be heard on the stage—and no mumbling! Inadequate speech and pronunciation have their origin at minor theatres, where rôles are swallowed and hastily digested, only half-way done, and where no stage director of authority and knowledge is at the helm.

It is of advantage to the actor that he seek out his natural voice register and that he place the voice correctly. Having once developed

---

6 Rachel (1821-58).

7 It goes too fast!

8 Svårt-hard; sad; difficult.-Teatern.-the theatre.

his register, his voice is best and most appealing in that position; he is always at home with it and is never at a loss as to how to use it.

There are, however, strange exceptions. I know one actress who is never allowed to use her beautiful, enchanting alto register because she cannot be heard, and so she has to screw herself up into a shrieking soprano. When the voice wabbles, it results in distortion; and false or off-key tones are disturbing because they can produce an atmosphere that would be alien to the scene.

To speak so that it sounds "like theatre" is a matter that should be especially observed and guarded against. Actors who are guilty of such speech produce tones that have no relation to their rôles; they trail along at the side like unharnessed horses that do no pulling—"one can see the rôle script hovering in the air." I mean that it sounds as if the actor were reading from a book and it indicates that the artist is not yet at home with the rôle, and that it is [not part of him, but superficially] an appendage.

Faulty pronunciation is often replaced by screaming, but—strange to say—the dialogue is then not heard. At a dress rehearsal I once observed a famed actor who was attempting to characterize the raging person he wished to portray by bellowing throughout [the play]. He drowned out his own characterization.

The beginner frequently masks his timidity by shrieking, and one wonders why he is in such a rage—for that is the way it sounds and the way it looks, since shrieking produces all the symptoms of anger.

On the other hand, I have—from the fourth balcony of the old Opera—heard an actress who spoke in a whisper from the big stage in such a manner that not a single word was lost. She had learned to speak, had taught herself to speak, through strict attentiveness and by critically listening to herself, as well as to capable speakers.

To use a rôle as an exercise in speech, to tear it to shreds, is not a good method. To read it for others (for instruction) can lead to the awkward disadvantage that the intonations of the coach, his individual, peculiar characteristics and facial expressions, perhaps even his mannerisms, are copied, so that the actor's own individuality is suppressed. It is far better to rely upon oneself and to seek to cultivate what is one's own, even if the basic qualities are minor.

For speech exercise, poetry is the more suitable. The verse form permits less carelessness, for the omission of a syllable immediately

73

disrupts the meter and causes it to limp. Also the verse form gives the delivery the poetic touch: it helps to achieve a *legato*—the *legato* which also gives charm to prose. This *legato* which I so often have asked the members of the Intimate Theatre company to observe, signifies: that all the words in a sentence follow closely upon one another, clinging together in a rhythmic movement, in tune with one's breathing. In this manner, the sentences will be more euphonically rounded and come trippingly on the tongue. The essential meaning of the sentence will be given prominence, without sacrificing the unessential. The most valuable resources of the voice and the language are those through which the words form a necklace of pearls instead of being piled in a heap, rattling like peas. In contrast, the beginner's *staccato* resembles spelling letter by letter without adding them together, as if *counting* the words instead of *reading* them—the breathless, short-winded, stammering, stuttering manner of speaking, which eventually ends up in a babble and gabble.

(For the purpose of effect, however, a staccato is, as we know, of importance when a feeling of agitation or anger is to be conveyed.)

How to study a rôle

Though there may be other ways, the most dependable way is no doubt the following: First of all, the play must be read carefully and conscientiously. This used to be done at the initial reading, and I deem it advisable that it be done then. For I have noticed with horror how great artists pick at a rôle as if they were picking the grain from the chaff and leaving the rest [of the play] to its fate, as if it were of no interest to them. I have also observed the consequences of this procedure. They have obtained a wrong impression of their rôles, or they have portrayed them falsely. Because they have no idea of what is being said about them when they are absent from the stage, they fail to know who they really are. In a play it frequently happens, namely, that the other actors describe the characteristics of a person when he or she is off stage, and this character may thereby deceive himself [or herself] by not realizing his [or her] importance [to the play].

I once saw a great artist who made a fiasco of his best scene because he failed to grasp what the scene was about. The audience which had heard [and seen] the preceding scene and had realized the situation, understood the allusions and found it impossible to comprehend what the artist meant, because of the way he acted the scene. He had not read [and studied] the play in its entirety, as an integral whole.

If the character of the leading man in a drama is outlined by the other players in the exposé, the actor is, of course, expected to live up to this characterization and satisfactorily correspond to the description. Consequently he must be cognizant of it, or he will give a false portrayal, which will not only be incomprehensible but could easily become ludicrous. I have been told that the following scene once took place at a rehearsal: *The Leading Actor*: Why doesn't he come? Must I wait for him much longer? *A Voice* (Off stage.) He can't come—he died in the last act. *The Leading Actor*: He died, did he? Well—that's another matter!

In analyzing and studying a rôle, one can go to the extreme and perceive in advance the unfoldment of the character. In the hands of a vain artist this can easily lead to (the use of) tricks. A play can be rehearsed too long and thus lose its freshness [and spontaneity]. Acting is a creative art. It is hardworking play, but not [some kind of] drill, and not philosophy. A touch of carelessness does not matter, for it makes room for improvisation; and I have seen rôles so overloaded with technique that they have been mutilated, aborted.

The terms *character, characterization, to portray a character* have so frequently been misused that I must dwell upon them a moment in order to clarify them.

The actor, most often the special favorite of the audience, who [merely] acts himself—and who therefore must be the possessor of a sympathetic personality, since he is the favorite—generally sacrifices the rôle and simply presents himself without any attempt at personifying the character by making up to look the part. This is one way—and it may succeed for a time. He does not personify the character but presents some other character that is pleasing and interesting.

The character actor, on the other hand, rubs out his own personality, creeps into his rôle hide and hair, and becomes the character he intends to be. And in that *genre* I have seen regular wizards that I have admired. But the character actor can easily be led to create types that he transforms into caricatures. Character is naturally the essential of a human being's inner life, his inclinations, passions,

75

weaknesses. If the character actor holds up the exterior [physical] unessentials or seeks to express the characteristically spiritual in the rôle by superficial means, he is getting close to caricature. And instead of creating a character, he merely grimaces. A character is often confused with a type or an eccentric and demanding what has been called consistency in portrayal. But there are also inconsistent characters—characters that are weak, characterless, disjointed, tattered, fickle and capricious.

In order to illustrate this, I would like to refer to my latest Blue Book.[9] I have there pointed out how Shakespeare draws human beings in all their facets—in contrast to Molière who actually produces types shorn of life and limb (*The Miser, The Hypocrite (Tartuffe), The Misanthrope,* etc.)

How to listen on the stage: silent acting

Whoever is not engaged in speaking but is listening to what is being said by another actor must be actually listening [be all ear]. He must not seem bored, even if he has heard a hundred times what the actor is saying. His facial expression must not give the impression that he is waiting for his cue to speak or that he is impatiently anticipating the moment when the other actor will come to the end of his speech and he himself can take over the dialogue.

There are actors who shut their eyes and look as if they were memorizing their next speech, which they are already chewing on in order to have it ready. There are others who use the interim to count the number of spectators in the audience, while still others engage in a casual flirtation with the audience and express with eyes and shoulders and forefoot: "Listen to how stupidly he talks! Just wait till my turn comes! Keep reeling off—it will soon be my turn to talk—and then you'll see!"

Still others try to give the appearance of being interested and assume a listening attitude. But they only manage to take on a spurious expression, or they keep drumming with their fingers and moving their lips as if they were giving their attention to every single word being spoken.

Whoever listens silently must not get out of his rôle. On the contrary, his face must reflect what the other actor says, and it is

---

[9] The Blue Books, I-V,

76

imperative that an audience sees what impression his words make. This sounds simple enough and is, of course, elementary, but it is very difficult—as difficult as to listen to a story or an anecdote you have heard repeatedly, and feign interest in hearing it again. Nonetheless, I have in *MISS JULIE* witnessed master performances in the art of listening and in pantomime. I have seen Jean listening to Miss Julie's long description of her life as though he were hearing it for the first time, despite the fact that he had heard it 150 times. And in the same play I have seen the cook [Kristin] listening to Miss Julie's death fantasies of an imaginary future with such concentration that I felt forced to applaud the actress. Finally I wish to make the comment that it is exactly as listener that the selfish, malicious actor finds his opportunity to rub out or to play down his rival. Through a cleverly calculated absentmindedness, by making himself indifferent and apathetic, by turning his back on the other actor, or making a skeptical, impatient expression, he can distract the interest from the actor who is speaking, erase his words and his person, and force the attention upon himself. But the actor who is speaking, must not lose his temper or composure. He should simply resort to the tactics of his *vis-à-vis,* make his acting conform to *his* tactics, and if need be take the first step and with quiet, fitting contempt unmask him in such a way that the audience has the illusion that it is part of the play, and thus save the situation.

Placement on stage

In most cases entrances and exits are indicated in the play manuscript, together with the manner in which they are to be made. But frequently the author has neglected this phase of stage direction. In that case it becomes the stage director's task to attend to this matter. But to lay out a complete plan of positions, deployment and attack is by competent experts considered impossible. This part of the staging comes gradually and naturally during the course of rehearsals. However, when the most favorable arrangement has been attained, one must abide by that and use the entrances and exits that have been mapped out, in order to avoid collision and ludicrous, embarrassing conflicts and encounters. Most frequently the more important scenes are acted down stage, for the purpose of being clearly heard and seen; yet the opposite may sometimes be more effective. Explanations and settlements are made eye to eye. I generally designate that lengthy disentanglements and analyses take place across a table with a chair on either side. The table both separates and brings together the antagonists; it also offers the actors an opportunity to use easy, natural gestures, gives support and repose to arms and hands. The chairs should not be too low lest they cramp and foreshorten the body, making it difficult to speak. To seat oneself gracefully on a chair, and to rise from it demands thought. A gentleman must give attention to his trouserlegs that they fall gracefully and cover the footwear and do not pull up and show too much of the ankle. Furthermore, the knee should not exhibit a sharp, angular profile, and the calf [of the leg] should not meet the foot in a set square. The actor should be well shod [on the stage and his footwear should conform to the rôle he is playing], for the eyes of the parquet [orchestra] are in an even line with the actor's foot.

In some theatres there prevails an arrangement according to which the placement of the actors is dependent upon rank. There the leading actors always take precedence of the younger ones, notwithstanding the importance of their respective rôles. Such procedure we are doing away with. Any situation concerning precedence should be determined by the importance of the rôle.

The habit of placing all the actors in a row down stage just before the fall of the curtain of the final act is a custom surviving from the old German farce and is [a way of] begging for applause. Like all such vanity, this is banished in our theatre, even though I saw it as recently as at a revival of [Ibsen's] The League of Youth.

Mannerisms

When an actor has discovered a certain way of expressing the more common sensations and sensibilities, and in this manner has made a success, it becomes a temptation for him to use this means in and out of season, partly because it is convenient, partly because it has proved useful in achieving success. This, however, is mere mannerism. The public will tolerate it from a favorite as long as it has to, but the critics will tire of it sooner and utter the fatal word that dooms it. To give but a few examples. There is an artist who forgets and constantly leaves his mouth wide open. This expression he first used in a farce, where it fitted; but when employed in dramas of quality, it is out of place. A wide open mouth and hanging chin are the comic's habitual way of looking stupid, in order to flatter the

78

audience, but there is also a touch of sarcasm in it that says: "I am not so stupid as I look. Perhaps you are the fool [and not I]!" With time the gaping mouth became a collection bag for applause. Here was not only mannerism but a lack of feeling for style. Farcical mimicry does not belong in a drama or tragedy. Another artist has the habit of plucking invisible burls from her sleeve. When she does this with downcast eyes, it implies something insidious, treacherous, and it might be employed once a year, but not every day. Still another actor will shrug his shoulders—no doubt to annoy his confrères on the stage and to gain favor with the audience, trying to appear as number one. Another one regards his legs. Still another receives his cue openmouthed, awaiting the end of his opposite's harangue with a frozen face, distorted by impatience [to speak], instead of reflecting what the other actor unveils in his speech, by continually changing facial expression.

When some years ago a great actress hit upon the idea of laying the back of her head against her shoulder and putting her chin in the air, it was effective because it was something of a novelty at that time. But when this pose began to make the rounds of all the theatres, it grew tiresome, especially when it was used without motivation. In my youth, Mrs. Heiberg's[10] handkerchief was the talk of the town—a mannerism that no doubt had its origin in Paris. This, in fact, indicated double-dealing in that the hands tore the handkerchief to tatters while a smile played on the countenance. Such exhibitions we today call affectation. The same can be said about the agonized father in KABALE UND LIEBE[11] when he, with a smile on his face, tightens the strings of his violin until they snap. —At one time women on the stage performed with their eyelids. This was an affectation that was borrowed from a sculptor's plaque of a famous demimonde.

Vocal resources also are often misused as mannerisms. An actor discovers he has a beautiful voice and soon he is tempted to speak his lines as concert arias in order to show off; another one has found he can more easily move [his audience] by using a funereal voice, and so he adopts that register; others again break out into laughter without rhyme or reason, or exhibit a sphinx-like smile.

[10] Undoubtedly Johanne Luise Heiberg (1812-90), a Danish actress who appeared in several Schiller dramas.
[11] By Johann Christoph Friedrich von Schiller (1759-1805).

Any use of effects without cause or motivation is affectation: "artistic" pauses that serve no purpose, false exits, sudden movements, floundering, sprawling, arm movements, flirtations with the audience, weeping without reason.

Playing Oneself (or Exhibiting One's Own Personality)

A person with a rich, winsome personality always adds something to his rôle if his own individuality permeates it, and he is seen with pleasure even though he does not give the rôle its rightful character. If this actor is permitted to choose his rôles, everything may go well throughout his career despite the fact that he is the same in every rôle and that he simply presents himself. But the reason for his success lies in his limitation; and if he should go beyond the limits of his talent, his shortcomings would soon be visible.

The truly great actor gives a complete rendition of his rôle, yet ennobling and magnifying it through his personal quality. And the true actor is able to perform all rôles, and he does them with enjoyment, although in a greater or lesser degree.

The actor who opens the play and speaks the first line, ought to allot himself a moment's meditation and concentrate on the action and the mood so that he from the very first is one with his rôle. And the actor who has thus been given the key note answers in the same key and should retain it. If Actor 1 fails to set the right tone, Actor 2 must try to establish it.

A drama should always begin with slowly and distinctly spoken speeches. The audience is not yet ready to hear and to grasp keenly; and until the characters and the exposé have been made clear, it is impossible to comprehend the plot and action of the play. A common error is that the actor who opens the play enters speaking "in the air," or in every direction. This is reminiscent of the novice and it sounds "like acting, or theatre": a wavering, indetermined seeking after the correct tone; and this confuses the person who enters next or who has to take up the dialogue.

If a word, and especially a name, should be lost in the exposition, the audience will be unable to differentiate between the persons in the play and will get them confused with one another. Because the auditorium is darkened, the playgoer will be unable to consult the program [until the intermission]. When an actor is about to make an entrance, he should wait in the wings for his cue and listen to the tone of voice used by those on the stage, and not rush on the stage bringing with him a wildly different mood—something that frequently occurs.

When the exposition—which helps to inform the audience—has been introduced at an exaggeratedly slow pace, those on the stage must seek the correct tempo of the action in order not to drift into a sluggish, dilatory tempo that will put the audience to sleep. However, there must be no racing forward with such speed that the plot is missed.

When an actor is about to make an exit, he must prepare for it by a *ritardando* [slowing down in speech], and not take a bounding leap as he exits, or run out, so that he cuts off rather than finishes, [as he should]—in preparation for the next scene. This, of course, does not refer to such instances as where directions demand otherwise. When the curtain is about to fall at the end of an act a more careful exit is necessary; and toward the fall of the final curtain, dialogue exchange, position, gestures, facial expression, carriage and [general] attitude should be slowed down to indicate the end of the play. In a word, the audience must realize in advance that the play is nearing the end so that the fall of the curtain will not come as a surprise and the spectators remain seated, expecting still more.

The actor should be the master of his rôle and not let himself become its tool. This implies that he must not let himself be carried away or be intoxicated by the dialogue so that he loses his head. He must keep a clear mind and not run away with the part at full speed; and this [mastering the rôle] he can only do when he has transmitted the rôle from his memorizing of it to his imagination, physically expressed in performance. Then the rôle will be rooted in the soul, and his conscience will stand guard over it. A rôle that has not penetrated any further than the memory will have a hollow ring [to it] or no ring at all, and will appear false. The danger in this respect is too much consciousness of oneself—which will turn into cold calculation, premeditated effects, stress of words, exaggeration, blatant attempts to attract attention, etc.

The actor must also be strong enough to remain unaffected by his co-actors so that he will not be persuaded to fall into the same key or pitch of voice. A weakness, whether temporary or not, may tempt an actor to adapt himself to the actor with whom he speaks, so that he lets go of his hold on the rôle and commences to speak in different

81

keys, according to the tone set by the actor with whom he is exchanging dialogue.

Whoever acts the leading rôle ought never to allow himself to be distracted while off stage by reading or engaging in conversation, for both those on stage and in the audience are concerned with his person. It is as if he were still present before them; and it is he who holds the invisible threads to the mood and atmosphere. For this reason he should also pay particular attention to his exits so that he take nothing along with him when he goes off stage and thereby leave a vacuum after himself, tearing down what has just been built up and presented.

It is the duty of every actor to watch his own entrances. While waiting in the wings, he must still bear in mind that he is part of the play and he has then the opportunity to regain the correct tone and tempo.

We at the Intimate Theatre seek to avoid all that is stilted. However, on the other hand, we must also guard against stooping to what is banal. Simplicity—but nothing that is commonplace; ease—but nothing that is careless, slovenly or slipshod. The actor—even on our little stage—must always keep in mind that he is not acting for himself up there on that limited space and must remember that there are 150 persons seated out in the auditorum and that these have the right both to see and to hear. For that reason the rôle cannot be given in a prattling tone of voice; it must be spoken in a [somewhat] amplified voice, just as a public speaker has to raise his voice and phrase [with care] in order to be heard and understood.

Therefore the actor must at all times keep in mind the audience, even when the most intimate scene is given—but without acting *for* or *with* the audience. He must not ogle the spectators or deliver his speeches to the audience but to his vis-à-vis on the stage. However, this must not be done so confidentially that the audience is excluded [from hearing]. Every attempt to "dedicate" a speech to the audience or to take it into his confidence, to make up to and court its favor, should be banned. The actor who underscores and draws attention to a speech of his, can easily annoy the audience. It wants to understand what is being said without any extra help, and it is not asking for intelligence or instruction. The rôle itself determines when the actor should resort to glances or use his eyes for expression. Misusing the eyes has by the Germans been called *"mit den Augen arbeiten."* A declaration of love should always be addressed to the object and consequently must be made face to face, and not to the audience. Turning one's back to the audience may be permissible if there is motivation for it in the rôle; but it must not be abused in scenes of important settlements or revealments, where it is of moment that the facial expression be seen.

A certain self-confidence is expected from the actor—and self-assurance makes an impression—but vanity and blatant over-confidence rub an audience the wrong way. Exceptions are tolerated in the case of favorites—who may do whatever they please without criticism— at least for a time!

An actor is really an illusionist. He must give the illusion of being a different character from what he is. If he possesses a strong, powerful personality, this will make an impression and serve as a positive gain. This is what makes the great actor. It is this *plus* which is difficult to define, and which can not be learned or taught—a general heightening of the imagination, observation, feeling, taste, self-discipline. He is like other actors, he possesses no fresh, unusual attributes—he simply possesses all required attributes in a higher measure.

While at home, he reads and meditates, but I have been told that it is not until he rehearses with the company that his rôle begins to take shape, and no doubt that is so. But if the play is a serious one, the rehearsal must be conducted in that spirit. If the play is a comedy or farce, it will be amusing—yet it will entail work. There are important theatres where tragedies are presented as a variety show; they have even been known to have been parodied [burlesqued]—a fate entirely undeserved. Such a tasteless note ruins the performance; and malice, frivolousness and recklessness can thus spoil a play.

The stage director, just as the orchestra conductor, is not generally a popular person because it is his duty to correct and make suggestions. He is the schoolmaster, even for seasoned artists, and he is often answered back by them. Experience has taught me that the artist may be right without the stage director being in the wrong; for a thing may, in doubtful cases, be seen from different angles. But for the sake of maintaining peace in the company, it is better for the actor to adjust himself to the view of the stage director—for one must do either one thing or another, since a thing can not be done two different ways at the same time. And the stage director is usually the only one who thoroughly knows the play and its entire action, its counterplots, and all its characters. Therefore he is the one best qualified, and for that reason should have the deciding voice. Even though he should not be an actor and unable to play the rôle himself, he will nevertheless know how the part should be acted. The artist may explain to the director his conception of the rôle, and motivate it, but he must not be challenging [and reject suggestions] in an unkindly manner, or try to browbeat the director. Such tactics lead to strained relations and only [serve to] bring about enmity. It causes lack of interest, and constraint from which the performance as a whole will suffer.

As author I have at dress rehearsals on many occasions seen actors interpreting characters quite differently from what I intended them to be. If, in such instances, the portrayals have proved to be consequentially thought out and acted; and if they have not done damage to the play, I have not suggested that the characterizations be changed but have permitted the actors to retain their creations. It is of greater benefit to allow them to carry through their own conceptions rather than to tear apart what has been created—as long as it is a complete characterization and is tenable. The author should best be able to know and judge his play and what his intentions are. On the other hand, he may have been away from his play so long that he has forgotten its details, and by questioning their interpretations, the author may thus do the actors—who have a fresh conception of it— an injustice. In such a case, it is the author's duty to acknowledge that he has been in the wrong. And as author, I have seen actors who have made more of a loosely drawn part than I could have imagined possible. It has even happened that I at the end of a dress rehearsal have had to admit: This is in reality not my creation, but it is quite as good [as mine] and in certain places better—though perhaps in other places not as good. That is the reason I have come to the conclusion that it is best to give the artist as much freedom as possible in the performance of his task; else he will remain an apprentice all his life.

I have seen subjective stage directors who have drilled and threshed a play to pieces; and I have seen others who have attempted to force upon all the members of a company—men and women, young and old, all artists—their own intonations, mannerisms, even their own frail voices. I have seen some go so far as to teach tricks and affectations. Such things we will have nothing to do with.

As far as make-up and dress are concerned, the actor generally has a better idea of such things and ought to be given a certain freedom in such matters. However, if an obvious, flagrant error (in choice) has been committed, the director must, of course, request that it be corrected. If the error is unmistakably glaring, he must indeed insist upon its correction.

In delicate, fragile plays, especially in period plays, the director alone must be the arbiter and choose the color scheme in order that there be no clashing of colors and that the total effect be consistent and compatible, harmonizing with the ensemble, as well as the *décor*.

Nonetheless it may be to his advantage to confer with actors in the leading rôles and accept their advice when it is constructive and convincing.

The public favorite is a curious yet not uncommon phenomenon. He [or she] is generally not the great talent, the adornment of the Theatre, its acknowledged first artist, the unrivalled actor; he can be a quite ordinary talent. An insignificant person with something about him that attracts and pleases may quickly be launched on a career by a clique and praised to the skies by friends among the critics. Sympathetic rôles of a nature not too complicated will be chosen for him. He will frequently be forced upon a goodnatured public that is flattered by seeing its attentions rewarded, or by being fawned over, by a great stage figure. This type of actor plays upon his own Godgiven attractions—a pair of beautiful eyes, a few ringing tones in his voice, engaging gestures, a challenging expression. He does not play upon personality—for he possesses none. He performs a sort of anti-spiritualistic séance, in which all the tricks are visible—for the simple reason that they cannot be concealed. On occasion these may assume undue proportions and he may—for instance, at some grandiose festivity—be proclaimed as "great", and as an illusionist give the illusion of having talent. For such a person the art of the stage is a form of higher coquetry and the auditorium actually a drawingroom, where social triumphs are celebrated as stage triumphs.

For eight years I followed such a meteoric career. The first

85

year I was asked to give my opinion of this actor; and—although recognizing his indigenous, embryonic aptitude and outwitted by his animation and the buoyancy of his movements—I nevertheless could not yield before a talent that I felt he did not possess. However, I hoped that in time something of worth would develop in him—and so I encouraged him. What I saw later was discouraging. I was able to hear nothing, although I imagined I did hear. And what I saw was unreal, vague, faltering—an image projected upon vapor. Yet I was confused, since both the critics and the public praised him to the skies. So I refrained from giving voice to what I actually thought for fear that I might be in error.

His next task was a rôle, serious and demanding in caliber. But I noted no seriousness, could not observe a single expression or gesture that was true. Underneath all, I saw an ingratiating personality which played up to the audience and begged for its favor—and succeeded. When I spoke out in plain words and called his performance false throughout, I was voted down—and so I remained away for seven years. Meantime his reputation had increased enormously. The favorite had risen to greatness, had become a celebrity, and his victory march had left a wake of bloody victims, mowing down the great as well as the lowly.

However, with his forward march there was an undercurrent of criticism and opposition, so that the applause was never undivided. Occasionally the opposition would break out and say: "This is a case of lack of talent—it is sheer nothing! "This had the effect of inciting the favorite's friends to increase still more their efforts in his behalf—and before long the culmination point had been reached. Then I felt I just had to go and take a look at the miracle. I went with an open mind, ready to admire, prepared if need be to be lenient and make allowances—which I thought would be unnecessary. Eight years later, I saw an actor lacking in voice, resembling a tenor with a faded, rusty voice, devoid of anything that might be called soulfulness. The man had no feeling whatsoever, was uninteresting, lifeless, talentless.

It was a sheer nonentity I saw! There was nothing in him that could be corrected, much less improved, nothing that could be built upon. And despite this, he was a success! The public still saw its favorite as he once had appeared but no longer did; it heard a voice that no longer existed. This phenomenon can only be explained as a hypnotic séance at which weakminded persons can be made to see and hear anything whatsoever, but at which also the public reciprocates by giving their favorite the impression of being a great star. It can not be called planned deception. This so much the less because the favorite is living in constant fear of waking up from his intoxication and of losing the ability to create an illusion and is plagued by doubt as to whether he really possesses talent or not. In moments of deepest dejection, his doubt grows into certainty and may then turn into scorn for his art and profession, as well as for the public, which allows itself to be deceived.

The mutual awakening is frightening, makes him panic-stricken. But the actor who has misused the stage for private exhibition of his vanity and who has sacrificed his good name and conscience for momentary favor can expect no other reward, even though one sincerely may feel pity for him. What is most incomprehensible about this phenomenon is, however, that those who have been duped, interpret their favorite's faults as merits, and his ineptitude as perfection; and when finally his few undeniable attributes: his natural charm, his slender figure, his handsome face and youth have disappeared, then his infatuated admirers still continue to see— what no longer is there. It reminds one of nothing so much as the distorting af a person's vision, the practising of sorcery; and on the distaff side the favorites often take on the appearance of witches in their old age.

The Producer.

The most important attributes of the producer should be the taste and acumen to choose a repertory and discernment and good judgment in the distribution of rôles. To read a play is almost like reading a score. It is a difficult task and I know of few who have that ability, although many profess to have it. The very arrangement of the text, making the eye rove from the name of the character to the dialogue requires concentration. The seemingly unimportant exposition must be labored through and carefully impressed upon the actor, since it contains the warp on which the weaving is superimposed. Parenthetical directions also tend to delay and distract. Even today, when I read Shakespeare, I find it necessary to scribble annotations in order to differentiate between the many characters, and especially the divers lesser characters. I continuously have to consult the list of *dramatis personae* and go back to the first act in order to refresh my mind as to what was said there. A play must be read through at least twice so that one may get a clear idea of what it is about; and in order to be able to assign the rôles, one must read it with scrupulous concentration a number of times. Usually it is only the author (or the translator) and the producer who are thoroughly familiar with the play. Therefore they are the ones most competent to assign the parts. But the producer (or stage director) holds his position primarily because he undoubtedly likes to feel his authority in the assignment of the rôles, and for this reason he is averse to taking advice. Thus the play is often badly cast. But there are other reasons that are responsible for a play being cast badly. Personal considerations, favoritism, antipathy, partiality may contribute to this procedure.

The producer who knows his company—the mentality, ability and limitations of each actor—will immediately see at the first reading of the play whom to choose for each part. But there are producers who have not seen all the plays they have produced and therefore are not familiar with all his actors. In such a case, the casting will be haphazard, with the result that the play will suffer and the artists will be uneasy or indifferent in parts not to their liking.

But even the conscientious producer will experience difficulties in assigning the rôles. For he must consider not only his theatre and the play but the actor—and all at the same time. He must be on guard that the theatre not be without one of its main-stays, leaving him or her idle, to become forgotten by the public. Sometimes he may be forced for economic reasons to keep the public favorite in the limelight because he or she has a drawing power at the box office, rather than to attempt using a fresh, gifted, promising talent. If the producer is also a stage director, his theatre may be ably managed. But if the producer as well has to take part in the repertory as an actor, this should only be done if the theatre is a minor one. In a larger establishment it might be disastrous.

When it comes to choosing plays, the producer has not the freedom of choice that the actors in the company and the playwright may imagine. In order to satisfy the current taste, economic conditions and public opinion, he is frequently forced to choose a play that people can be expected to patronize, even if it is valueless. How far he can go in catering to bad taste depends upon his artistic integrity, his financial position, and upon the traditional policy of his theatre. If the offerings habitually have been good, i.e. serious dramas, the public will object to seeing comedies and farces there, although it will tolerate such plays at another theatre.

Authors are often surprised when a truly good play of theirs is rejected. But the reason for the refusal may partly be that a similar plot has just been seen at the same theatre, or in some other theatre, so that the theme has become hackneyed and people therefore no longer care to see that type of fare; partly because the play, despite its being written with technical skill, may be boring, or painful, or impossible to cast, or too costly to produce. To take an example from among classical dramas: *KING LEAR*. This is a play that all theatres would like to give as frequently as possible. It is interesting, exciting and well written. But how many theatres have in their company a seasoned talent with the power of a giant such as the drama requires?

However, it may prove risky to let public taste dictate one's choice of plays, for taste changes continually, and often without warning. At one period there may be a craze for uniforms on the stage. This may prove successful for a couple of seasons; and then the producer buys an expensive military play without having seen it performed elsewhere. It entails a costly production—and the play is a fiasco! The public's taste has suddenly changed.

It is not easy to be adviser to a producer. The only guide to follow in seeking to fathom and evaluate the public's taste is no doubt to be found in the issues of the day and in contemporary literature— whatever presently occupies people's minds. But one fine day people grow tired of the discussions and want to talk about something entirely different. They want to forget the painful controversies and long for something more peaceful. That explains why an idyl such as *ABBÉ CONSTANTIN* could prove so timely and opportune in the midst of the *Nora* battle.[12] *LIFE IN THE COUNTRY*[13] is used even today as a lightning rod, whenever the occasion demands it. *OLD HEIDELBERG* became on oasis in the theatrical desert journey, and *DON CAESAR* has always proved useful as a makeshift when one wishes to put an end to unpleasant contentions. But

---

[12] Refers to Ibsen's *A DOLL'S HOUSE*.
[13] Probably the dramatization of Fritz Reuter's famous novel.

one has to be a weather prophet in order to know when the discussion is ripe for a conclusion so that one does not take a fall and come tumbling down.

The producer must also be able to sense when the public is in a mood to accept a classical repertory. A theatre subsidized by public funds should feel a responsibility occasionally to present a classical drama. To be able to enjoy fully such a play demands an earnest will, a semblance of culture and the ability to apprehend it from the historical point of view. To enjoy completely such a drama requires knowledge: one must have the prerequisites for fathoming its intentions when it refers to things presumed to be known. One must, for instance, be familiar with the story of *Antigone,* have an idea who she was, before going to see this tragedy.

One hears that the classics are boring. But one ought to peruse them, and it should be of benefit to the generation now growing up to do so. There are things that one *need* not see but *should* see—just as one visits foreign cities, museums and cathedrals.

However, there are among the classical repertory plays that will hold one's interest throughout the ages and whose characters should evoke compassion, even without make-up or costume. [Prince] *Hamlet* remains forever an enigma, and his fate moves us. Parts I and II of *FAUST* should be seen now and then—but not Part I alone, for it has been worn out as opera text. *DON CARLOS, MARY STUART, THE MAID OF ORLÉANS* have not become dated, and Schiller's severe, cleancut style and his characterizations, although occasionally pedantic, give a firm, disciplined stature to his dramas. Molière has his share of admirers, although I have never cared for him. Oehlenschläger's *AXEL AND VALBORG* did not find favor with our unfeeling generation, but it will have its day. *HÅKON JARL,* and *ALADDIN,* are still waiting for their day of resurrection. Holberg's *JEPPE PAA BJERGET* and *ERASMUS MONTANUS* may well be augmented by *BARSELSTUEN, DEN STUNDESLÖSE* and others. Among Calderon's works one need only know *LIFE IS A DREAM,* although he no doubt has others that are worth playing. Whether it would pay us to attempt Corneille and Racine, I do not know, but their wines do not seem able to stand being exported or re-tapped (translated). The Germans have dug up Kleist and Hebbel, but to me they remain fossils, as Lessing does. But let us clear up what the concept *classic* means. It is not only a great literary name or the fact that he or she has been dead for many years that makes a work worthy and superior. Goethe was both theatrical producer and actor, but his sense of form failed him when he constructed his dramas. *EGMONT* is not a classic, if by that you mean a superbly fine play. It wavers in its form and is put together haphazardly. Nonetheless there is a demand for it because it gives us an opportunity to hear Beethoven's overture—just as one shouts for *ANTIGONE* because of Mendelsohn's cho ses (incidental music). *CLAVIGO* is hopeless, reminiscent of the novel; *STELLA* depends on incidents just as *GESCHWISTER* does. But *GOETZ,* with all its apparent lack of form, is severe in conception, and despite its 56 scenes, it holds together, is interesting and alive. However, it is primarily for Germans. *TASSO* is beautiful, intelligent and captivating but loses in translation. It is doubtful whether it will ever reach the greater mass of the theatre public, which feels itself a stranger before poets and artists on the stage.

Blindly to admire everything that is written by great names brings with it the danger that one might come to value the inferior and develop a taste for it. Goethe himself admired his comedies *DER BÜRGER-GENERAL,* and *GROSS-KOPHTA,* but later generations have called them both rubbish. Several of Shakespeare's comedies are in the same class, and the great classicist had a fiasco here a few years ago when a comedy that in past times had been admired, was completely exposed for what it is.[15]

A Few Words to the Beginner

Many choose the theatre as their profession because they find it amusing, others because they find it an interesting profession. The former entertain the delusion that the life lived back stage is one of exuberance and artistically carefree and easy. But that is an error. It is a hard, stern, demanding life, full of work. Rehearsals are carried on during the forenoon, and in the evening there is the performance, with making up, dressing and playing. The actors' day is not over until close to midnight. During the actor's free time—which at some theatres is nil—he must memorize his rôle and visit the tailor and the wardrobe mistress. The actor who is part of the re-

---

[15] See: Letters of Strindberg to Harriet Bosse, p. 152, 153. Universal Library (Grosset and Dunlap).

pertory, is scarcely ever free during the season. For him there is no enjoyment, no distraction; he has hardly any home life—if he on the whole has a home of his own. He can accept no evening invitations—or rather, no invitations after the performance, for then his work will suffer the following day. He dare accept no invitations for dinner, simply because he has to play at night: a couple of glasses of wine could deaden his memory, or intoxicate him—and that might lead to the curtain being rung down, perhaps forever.

But in addition there are other things to think of! He is forever going about with rôles in his head. He is never at rest. Even if a play is being given a number of times consecutively and the work then becomes easier, a case of sickness may suddenly cause the repertory to be changed at six in the evening. Then another play must be conjured forth in haste and substituted. This is not likely to give the actor much peace of mind, aside from the natural anxiety which always precedes an appearance before an audience, which every night is a different one, changeable, fickle, capricious, sometimes noisy and disorderly, with no respect for even the best of acting, and sometimes unresponsive.

Finally—as an author—the thought has not escaped me that, when an actor has to appear in a harrowing tragedy—and especially when it is given consecutively, over and over again—it must be both wearing and wearisome. This may be said to be simulated torture, but imaginary sufferings are quite as hard to bear as real ones; and the tears that are shed on the stage are in reality just as bitter and heartfelt as tears shed anywhere else.

In days of prosperity and good fortune the actor is an object of envy. But success soon evaporates and can be followed by defeat, erasing in one evening the memory of everything he had done before that was great and beautiful. All that is forgotten, is no longer spoken of, is obliterated. That is how fragile such fame and honors are. And later comes the fatal moment when the young man and the young woman must leave youth behind them. If they had nothing left but the charm of youth, it would mean the end of a career; if there were something more than that, it would mean being moved a peg ahead—into another age class. The time for the character rôles would have arrived.

But youthfulness need not disappear so swiftly. It can be retained, although with sacrifice. Fasting and severe abstainment, going to bed hungry, standing rigid like a stylite [pillar-saint] in the middle of the floor after eating, never giving pleasure to either palate or heart with a glass of wine. For a time, the body retains its youthfulness—but suddenly the nerves begin to rebel, and the voice is dimmed for lack of nourishment. Then the physician is called in and prescribes—everything that will help to put on weight, and thus attempt to counteract and hinder the actor from retaining his youth. That is the insoluble dilemma!

But even if everything in this respect should turn out well, there are so many other thorns on the path of the acting profession. The public may tire of even the best of actors; new actors come into the limelight by using new methods, sometimes merely by using new tricks; the artist may fall out of favor, or for some unexplainable reason draw the hatred of both the public and the critics. Should he tangle with his producer, he can easily be lost, for in that case he will be given meager rôles and be on the downgrade. If he should become sick, or if his memory starts to fail him, he is done for. And so on, *ad infinitum.*

I have brought out all these things in order to discourage those who choose the acting profession because they find the theatre and its life amusing. They who choose the stage because of a true interest in the theatre, who are willing to suffer and who take delight in reincarnating themselves in, and living the lives of, many human characters on the stage, they will not allow themselves to be frightened or deterred. They go where their talent and intellect attract them, through fire and water, and they are not seeking false honors but find inspiration in their work, whether it brings them reward or not, happiness or no happiness. The stage is their world and their home. The work of art that they produce can not be shown in shopwindows or in museums. It is for the moment, and limited to the place of performance, it is passing, transient, disappears in the sunlight—like an undeveloped lantern slide, leaving in the end only a memory which, however, can easily be erased by time and by other, more powerful memories.

This is something that those, who are called, know; yet they do their task—and then die!

THE BEGINNER

The beginner must, of course, begin at the beginning: that is why he is given the minor rôles, most generally the announcing rôles.

I must at the very outset make it plain that the playwright does not write announcing rôles for no reason. A person of some importance is to make his entrance, and his entrance must be prepared in order that it be effective; and the audience will be plagued by uncertainty, not knowing who that character may be when he sees him enter. For this reason, the beginner must not disdain such an announcing rôle; and he must also be familiar with the character which he announces, his importance in the play, the ensuing situation, and whether this scene will be one of tranquility or one that is heated and fiery, whether a decisive one or not. And whatever the mood is to be, it must be reflected in the announcer's tone of voice and tempo.

But there is still another reason why the novice should not carelessly dispose of a minor rôle such as this. It is not impossible that the producer or the director is standing in the wings, observing. If one of the novice's principals should detect a natural gesture or a correct intonation, or if he should notice a voice of fine quality, a personality of charm, and if he finds that the novice shows a serious disposition and effort and is without vanity—then the young aspirant's fortune may be made. For I have seen incidents of this sort when a talent has been discovered in the rôle of a servant, a footman, a voice in a mob scene, a herald, a soldier.

On the other hand, the beginner must be wary of overacting. He must not aggressively push himself forward in a minor rôle, must not try to attract unnecessary attention to himself, or consider himself superior to the rôle and look down on it with disdain or contempt.

I myself was once a novice in the theatre. It is not pleasant to have to loll about in the wings for three hours, waiting to make an entrance in the fifth act. But the time can be spent usefully and fairly agreeably if one watches the players, listening and observing, observing and listening to how different their performances are night after night, how different the audiences are, how differently they react toward the actors. That is the school and the place for study, particularly if the novice has an opportunity to see the same rôle played by different actors; then he can discern how different conceptions and interpretations of the same rôle can be.

To read a great many books on the art of acting is something I wish to advise against. One's studies should be carried on through the observation of living human beings in everyday life, at rehearsals, and at performances. Anyone born with the gifts of speech and expression thinks that the art of acting is easy, while anyone with talent not yet trained finds it difficult; the introvert, held back and repressed, finds it well-nigh insurmountable—for there are people who by nature are uncommunicative and reserved, who lack the qualities that the stage demands.

TO THE PERSONNEL OF THE INTIMATE THEATRE:

When we are now rehearsing a new play, *The Father,* I take this opportunity to express my wishes concerning the pronunciation of the Swedish language on the stage.

As we do not present farcical or low comedy fare, the language must on that account be treated with respect so that it will not lose its capability as a means of expression through careless enunciation.

All letters [and syllables] shall from the outset be pronounced distinctly. Afterward they are glided over, yet without slurring them. . . . The consonants must be given special attention. . . . In general, dialogue is spoken at too brisk a pace in our theatre. Even though it is small and intimate, there are one hundred and fifty persons seated in the auditorium, and they have paid for the right to hear. The actor can only be understood when he enunciates slowly and distinctly every letter [and syllable]. [This is accomplished by *phrasing,* or tonal interpunctuation, i.e. by the stressing of the more important words, and putting no stress on words of lesser importance, in addition to a proper distribution of the phrase; by shading and gradation, i.e. by bearing in mind to raise or lower the inflection of the voice: *accelerando* (speeding up) and *ritardando* (repressing), pausing, and by the use of *legato* and *staccato.*]

In order to speak slowly and well, one ought generally to bind together all the elements and words of the sentence (*legato*), but in such a way that the interpunctuations are heard [but] faintly. *Staccato* is used only where the rôle [explicitly] demands it.

During the first rehearsals, which are [actually] conversation [and speech] practice, the rôles must be spoken leisurely. Later on, when the tempo is increased, the delivery will yet be distinct since all the letters [and syllables] will be heard, having been carefully [and properly] practiced [during the early rehearsals].

In general, one should use chest tones in speaking. One should not speak with the mouth alone, for by using only the mouth a whisper is produced.

To speak well—and that is the principal requirement for the stage—no instruction is needed. All that is necessary is to watch oneself and the actor playing opposite one, to listen to oneself, and to think of what one says.

Having seen so much acting talent, an abundance [of it] almost, at The Intimate Theatre, one is also forced to regret that—on the part of a number of you—the art of speaking has been neglected.

For this reason I wish to call attention in time to this deficiency, so that we may aim for perfection, even if we should not attain it.

26 July, 1908.

The Stage Director.

SHAKESPEARE'S OUTLOOK ON LIFE

Was Shakespeare a pessimist?

Yes, at times, not always, much as the rest of us. In his **KING LEAR** he says when he is dying:

ACT V: SCENE 3

Vex not his ghost: O, let him pass!
he hates him much
that would upon the rack of this tough world
stretch him out longer.

Rack!

And in **HAMLET** he says:

ACT III: SCENE 1

To die . . . 'tis a consummation
devoutly to be wished . . .
. . . who would fardels bear,
to grunt and sweat under *a weary life,*
but that the dread of something after death
. . . puzzles the will. . . .

ACT V: SCENE 2

Or when he exhorts Horatio to live and "in this harsh world draw thy breath in pain".

In **THE TEMPEST** he goes yet further and, like the Buddhists, doubts the reality of life:

ACT IV: SCENE 1

. . . we are such stuff
as dreams are made on, and our little life
is rounded with a sleep. . . .

In MACBETH his pessimism is expressed even more strongly:

ACT V: SCENE 5

Life's but a walking shadow

. . . .

. . . it is a tale
told by an idiot, full of sound and fury,
signifying nothing.

In TIMON OF ATHENS he expresses a hatred, or contempt,
for humanity that is reminiscent of Schopenhauer or Hartmann:

ACT V: SCENE 4

Commend me to them (the Athenians)
and tell them that, to ease them of their griefs,
in life's uncertain voyage. . . .

. . . .

I have a tree, which grows here in my close

. . . .

Tell Athens, in the sequence of degree,
from high to low throughout, that whoso please
to stop affliction, let him take his haste,
come hither, ere my tree hath felt the axe,
and hang himself.

And Timon's epitaph [upon his gravestone], written by himself,
ends in this manner:

ACT V: SCENE 4

A plague consume you wicked caitiffs left!
Here lie I, Timon, who, alive, all living men did hate.

Was Shakespeare a freethinker or atheist?

No, he was a Christian of faith, with moments of the most profound doubts and agony, when God had hidden himself from him.
In RICHARD III, which Shakespeare wrote at the age of thirty—
an early work of his, consequently, as he began writing his historical
plays at twenty-eight—he has Richmond, the noble hero of that
drama, speak the following lines:

ACT V: SCENE 3

God and our good cause fight upon our side;

the prayers of holy saints and wronged souls,
like high-rear'd bulwarks, stand before our faces. . . .

And, speaking of Richard, he says:

ACT V: SCENE 3

One that hath ever been God's enemy:
then, if you fight against God's enemy,
God will in justice ward you as his soldiers;
. . . .
God and Saint George! Richmond and victory!

And when Richard the Evil has fallen, Richmond concludes the
drama by giving thanks, in a prayer to God, for the final end to the
thirty year War of the Roses.

ACT V: SCENE 5

O, now let Richmond and Elizabeth
. . . .
by God's fair ordinance conjoin together!
And let their heirs, God, if they will be so,
enrich the time to come with smooth-faced peace . . .
with smiling plenty and fair prosperous days!
Abate the edge of traitors, gracious Lord. . . .
God say amen!

At the age of thirty-eight, we rediscover the poet in HAMLET.
In Act I he expresses belief in the apparition of his father, for he
adjures Marcellus to confute Horatio's doubts.

ACT I: SCENE 1

Marcellus:

Horatio says 't is but our fantasy,
and will not let belief take hold of him
touching this dreaded sight. . . .

Then Horatio sees the Ghost and is convinced:

ACT I: SCENE 2

As I do live, my honour'd Lord, 't is true!

And Hamlet also sees the shadowy vision of his dead father:

100

ACT I: SCENE 4

Angels and ministers of grace defend us!

This is the true Shakespeare, for he was undoubtedly well enough acquainted with Saxo [Grammaticus] to know that the characters in this drama were pagans of prehistoric times.

Then Hamlet's father, coming directly from Purgatory, gives voice to these words:

ACT I: SCENE 5

My hour is almost come
when I to sulphurous and tormenting flames
must render up myself.

This gives proof of Shakespeare's being a Catholic and of his belief in a Purgatory, the existence of which is denied by Protestants. This emotional need of a purifying process by fire before entering the abode of the holy has a certain allurement, and finding the noble hero and excellent man in such a circumstance should prove neither unusual nor surprising to a Catholic. And the father himself sets Hamlet's mind at rest by saying it is a necessary stage of experience which has to be suffered through, even by himself—although he has lived righteously—for the reason that he had been removed from life ahead of his allotted time and therefore had been prevented from atoning for his minor sins and weaknesses.

ACT I: SCENE 5

Doom'd for a certain term to walk the night
and for the day confined to fast in fires,
till the foul crimes done in my days of nature
are burnt and purged away. . . .

It is of no avail to put the blame on the period when the action takes place, for it is in ancient times. Nor can it be ascribed to the time of Shakespeare, for that was an age of impiety; indeed, there have been those who have called Shakespeare a product of the Renaissance (a pagan) and a freethinker apprentice of Giordano Bruno, with no other support [for their theory] than some botanical reflections; but for the moment I cannot recall to mind just where I have read this.

101

Furthermore, Hamlet takes an oath by St. Patrick, the Irish saint, and in addition swears "so help you mercy" (Act I, Sc. 5).

The thirty-eight year old poet has unquestionably been torn by doubts; and for a moment he thinks the apparition is a delusion which, owing to his heaviness of heart, and gloominess, has gotten the better of him.

This all-consuming doubt of God and His goodness is shown in the soliloquy; and whoever has been through a similar experience will attribute Hamlet's weakening to the circumstance that he has lost the anchor—which is God. Such behavior is, namely, characteristic of a godless creature of revenge and convenient absolution.

Yet at the height of agony he implores Ophelia to remember him in her prayers!

And in Act III, Scene 2, Hamlet swears by the Holy Virgin, who was not an object for adoration during the reign of Queen Elizabeth.

In his monologue in Act IV he shows that he is at least no materialist:

ACT IV: SCENE 4

. . . What is a man,
if his chief good and market of his time
be but to sleep and feed?—A beast, no more!

In Act V Hamlet's godless doubts have been done away with, and in Scene 2 he preaches:

ACT V: SCENE 2

. . . and that should teach us
there's a divinity that shapes our ends. . . .

But the poet (Hamlet) has likewise discovered the finger of Providence in the details of everyday life (Act V, Sc. 2):

ACT V: SCENE 2

Horatio:
   How was this sealed?
Hamlet:
Why, even in that was heaven ordinant.
I had my father's signet in my purse,
which was the model of that Danish seal. . . .

It was no mere chance, consequently, just as the apparition was no fantasy!

In the same act and scene, Hamlet exclaims anew, after having made his discovery: "There's a special providence in the fall of a sparrow."

ACT V: SCENE 2

That, my good heathens, is Christianity!

Horatio, despite being a Roman, is as pious as Hamlet turned out to be. When Hamlet is dying, he addresses him thus:

ACT V: SCENE 2

[Good night, sweet prince!]
And flights of angels sing thee to thy rest!

A figure somewhat overlooked is Shakespeare's Maid of Orléans[18] in his first drama, Henry VI, Part I. The conception is characteristically orthodox (Roman) Catholic.

In the early part of the play she performs a miracle, of which the others had thought her incapable. In order to maintain contact with the spirits and be able to gaze into the future, she must lead a life of purity. Whether she is seized by some sort of inclination or affection for the Dauphin, I cannot determine, for she is being lied about so frequently in the play. In act V, Scene 3, however, she is being assailed by evil spirits as she becomes sensible that her power is waning. It is not unlikely that here is where she may have lapsed into sin, for she promises the spirits her body and soul and all, if they will help her. But:

ACT V: SCENE 3

My ancient incantations are too weak
and hell too strong for me to buckle with. . . .

This rejoinder indicates the English conception of the witch, who—for such very reasons—was condemned to die by burning.

In Act V, Scene 4, she clears her name and defends herself in a speech, in which she says she is of royal birth and that she—because of being a chaste and saintly maiden—had been inspired by heaven and chosen to work a host of miracles upon earth.

---

[18] Joan La Pucelle (Joan of Arc).

103

But you that are polluted with your lusts
. . . .
you judge it straight a thing impossible
to compass wonders but by help of devils.

As much as we can learn from the mendacious history of the world, Jeanne d'Arc was a divinely inspired seeress, who adhered to her mission to see the King crowned in Rheims. But when she allowed herself to be persuaded to go further, she was seized with conflict within herself, met with misfortune, and fell. This is tragedy, and this Schiller has understood. Shakespeare was young when he undertook to fashion the difficult character, and carelessly did the final scenes by halves, where she says she is with child and fabricates a story of having several lovers, in order to escape being burned at the stake. But Shakespeare is no Protestant, for the Protestant verdict is quite harsh, labelling her a fraud, an impostor.

The most convincing indication of Shakespeare's Catholicism is his depiction of Cardinal Wolsey in HENRY VIII, who was England's king of reformation. But this drama deals only with his first divorce, his second marriage, and the birth of Elizabeth. Cardinal Wolsey is a rogue, not because he is a Catholic but because he was a rogue and a mischiefmaker. The other cardinal, Campeius, is sympathetic and has dignity, and allies himself with Henry, although he is being accused of supporting Wolsey's scheming at the Vatican.

Henry makes an attack against Rome [and the Pope] only once, and that rather mildly, and we know that Henry remained a Catholic even after the separation from the Pope; for it was Rome he wanted to be free from, and not from the Catholic Church. Soon after, Bloody Mary brought back Catholicism; and Elizabeth—during whose reign Shakespeare throve—preserved the Roman [Catholic] liturgy and dogmas (through the thirty-nine articles), to the great indignation of the Protestants. And Shakespeare frequently holds up the Protestants (Puritans) to ridicule.

It matters little to what denomination or religion Shakespeare belonged, but it is of importance that he be freed of being called an atheist, since he was neither godless nor impious. This [is addressed] to the neo-pagans who have stolen Shakespeare, just as they have stolen Goethe. Schiller they could not steal; therefore they were contented with ignoring or degrading him!

CHINA
(1877)
Some aspects in the light of history

If the discovery of America has brought about no other advantages to mankind, the gigantic political-economic experiments which have been made from time to time in the new world, and the social problems which have been solved, have provided popular science with the greatest and most valuable contributions. The conquest of Mexico still appears to be almost a miracle. A small band of adventurers subjugates a flourishing nation, whose culture might well be compared with that of the invaders. The rooting out or forcing aside of the North-American Indian tribes has proven the superiority of the educated agriculturist over the physically stronger nomad-hunter, who was gradually exterminated as the colonists' axe went forward through the forests and frightened away game and wild life, thus depriving the Indian of his subsistence. In recent years, following the abolition of the negro slavery, the "black question" in the United States' domestic politics has been to a certain degree pushed aside by the "yellow peril", i.e. the question as to what measures should be taken through legislation with regard to the Chinese immigration. This question, which now demands to be solved, is of a more far-reaching nature, as it is rooted in one of the gravest problems of our time: the labor question.

The right of the stronger, disputed and controverted in theory, has always been accepted as incontrovertible in actuality. While the Americans dealt unjustly with the Indian, forcing his extirpation, they—from humane considerations, political or other motives—gave the negro the rights of citizenship. However, the black man's fate will undoubtedly turn out to be that he, like the Indian, will in time be wiped out, for he is, by his very nature, an aborigine. In the case of the Chinese, the situation is different. *He* is a civilized being, although in the present emotional atmosphere he is

105

branded a "heathen"—a word which on the lips of the (California) gold-diggers must have a peculiar sound. Now he appears as a free-booter and competitor on the labor market and, because of his diligence, his "minor needs" (as his frugality is called), can offer his work for a third, even for as little as a fifth, of the currently accepted wage price. He is no stronger than the American, but he husbands his strength and energy and possesses the conquering power of passive resistance. When he does not work, he sleeps; or he an-esthetizes himself through dope, for he knows that mental exertion brings about muscular oxidization. He does not force his way, he advances by creeping; for by forcing himself he will use up his strength. He obeys the laws, for that is the better way; he submits to humiliations because it consumes time to oppose them; he allows himself to be treated like a dog because it engenders compassion, and he makes believe he is completely unaware of Article XV in the Constitution, which reads:

> "The right of the citizens of the United States to vote shall not be denied or abridged by the United States or by any State on account of race, color, or previous condition of servitude."

Thus he has all divine and human laws on his side, and as well the pregnant negro precedent. If anyone should insinuate and charge him with being a heathen he will accept some form of Christianity, or he will point to the Jews, who are still permitted officially to deny Christ, yet nevertheless are granted citizenship rights.

Consequently he is a peril in any Christian country. But he is interesting because he is the means of bringing out an engagement in combat between Asia and Europe within a neutral region. Whether the peril is greater for America shall be left unanswered, since the emigration is going on beyond the boundaries of China into other lands in Asia as well.

Since it is a known fact that "every third human being is Chi-nese", the world's population being approximately 1,000,200,000 and China proper reckoning 400,000,000, it can only be ascribed to the isolation of this immense country that one has not until recent times encountered its natives outside the boundary lines of that realm. In contrast, there is no spot on earth where one cannot find an Englishman, either as businessman or real estate proprietor. And this despite the fact that he belongs to a comparatively small nation of some thirty million souls. According to the latest well-documented statistics, China has not released more than 5,328,000 emigrants who have been distributed among the following colonies: Amur, 20,000; Formosa, 3,000,000; The Philippines, 18,000; Further India, 1,600,000; Malacca, 150,000; The Indian Archipelago 310,-000; America, Australia and Polynesia (together), 230,000 (of which 130,000 emigrated to North-America). A comparatively small number, consequently. As for the Chinese question in California, especially in San Francisco—which among its 210,000 inhabitants has 25,000 Chinese—this ought to be generally known to [Swedish] readers through the travel descriptions of Dixon, Trollope and Watt. Perhaps less known is the yellow man's presence in other areas where he encounters the European. In the north, the 250,000 square miles of the Chinese realm has Russia (Siberia) across its boundary line. In the west, the Osmanli (Turkestan); in the south, England (India Proper) and France (Lower Cochin China), in the east, America; in the south-east, Spain and the Netherlands (The Philippines and the Sunda Isles). That the points of contact with the inhabitants of Europe's 179,000 square miles are not few is consequently an accepted fact, and that the Chinese emigration question takes on far greater proportions if viewed from the shore lines of the Yellow Sea, is evident. Since time immemorial the Russians have had favorable relations with the Chinese. As early as 1712, a Chinese diplomatic mission was dispatched to Moscow and Petersburg. A Chinese author has given a detailed account of this. Since 1644, when the Ming dynasty was overthrown and the Manchu Tartars came to the throne, they have continuously occupied it; and ever since, the strange situation has resulted in the Chinese having taken possession of the homeland of their conquerors in the most bloodless manner. Today the Englishman who passes through Manchuria will find only a lot of idlers among the formerly proud Tatar tribes; and these are debtridden and in the clutches of the Chinese merchants. The proud Mukden, capital of Manchuria, praised in a long, lofty poem by Emperor Kien-Long (1735-1795), is a Chinese city.

It was north of Manchuria that the Chinese were to make contact with the Russians. It was not to hunt for fur-bearing animals that they went so far north through boundless forests and wilder-

107

nesses. It was to pick the ginseng, to pluck the trepang, and to gather an edible species of rockweed. Recently the Russians, however, have forbidden the Chinese entrance to Manchuria, giving as a reason that "the colonies must first gain stability."

The Sakalin Island,[19] which has long been in dispute as a possession, was for an extensive period populated by Chinese. But in 1868, when the Chinese were on the way to mine coal, they were turned away by the Russians. The Russians afterward declared their delight with the island and voiced their intent to establish a penal colony there—for the purpose of mining coal! In the same manner the yellow men were expelled from a coastal island near Vladivostok, where they had been searching for gold. When they rebelled—a rare habit for them—they were promptly routed. This did not stop them from trying their trading fortune in other places. Starting out from the boundary station Kischta, they frequently traveled toward the environs of Siberia—even so far west that our Jenissei travellers encountered Chinese travelling salesmen at roadside inns, far west of Jenissei.

It was a foregone conclusion that the opium smoking yellow man would be better received in the British colonies. After acquiring Burma, they did everything they could to provide the Chinese with a pleasing home. They even set aside an area for a grave-yard, and this before their arrival—a procedure showing how tactful and considerate the opium merchants were. In Burma the Chinese thrived splendidly and devoted themselves to mining and the mineral industry, as well as trading. In Singapore, which was first settled by the British in 1819, the number of Chinese grew to such an extent— while the Malayan population decreased—that it serves as a spectacular example of how a more tenacious race can drive out a weaker one, a situation to which the rulers of the land raised no objection. It seems that the British felt not the slightest compassion when the poor Malayans, who were acquainted with no other method of fishing except with spear, complained that the Chinese destroyed the fishing for them by using nets. In 1871, Singapore counted 97,111 inhabitants, and of these 54,570 were Chinese. While the Malayans are being exterminated as a race, the Chinese are supplanting them with a fine crossbreed, which there—as wherever the

---

[19] Later Formosa, now Taiwan.

108

Chinese are found—is exemplified by energy, strength, and animation. For economic reasons, the Chinese generally prefer not to take their women with them. For this reason they enjoy the benefit of much kindness from the women in foreign lands because of the humane attitude of the Chinese—an attitude they are not accustomed to from their own men.

In the Philippines,. for example, where the Tagals live, the Chinese have almost completely intermixed with the population and have bred a particularly sturdy, robust stock, the mestizos. But before being permitted to intermarry, the Spaniards force the Chinese to be converted to Christianity—an easy matter for one who looks upon religion with complete indifference. The country, which the Chinese honor with their visit, does not seem to gain anything else, for he never becomes permanently settled there. As soon as a Chinese has enriched himself, he returns to his homeland, leaving behind wife, children, and religion. It is true that he occasionally on his peregrinations to Singapore turns up as tiller of the soil, although in a way far from advantageous to the land. He ravaged the forests by burning them down in order to plant pepper. During the first years, the land produced rich harvests, but afterward it brought forth none; and then he abandoned the undertaking. His principal occupation is, however, trading. "Before the ship has dropped anchor, a Chinese is on board, making the acquaintance of the merchant. Not for a moment does he let the merchant out of his sight. He pays him money in advance, finds out his weaknesses, and ends up by being the owner of the cargo." By no means does he disdain taking up a trade. When he does, he can get along with a minimum of space and the simplest of tools, so that competing with him becomes impossible. It is so everywhere. In Calcutta, 400 (90%) of the shoemakers there are Chinese, in Manila, 633 out of 784, and in San Francisco the 214 cigar factories employ exclusively Chinese workers.

Nowadays those Chinese who have made their fortune in Singapore, retire to Malacca (Malay) or its environs, over whose landed estates and mining facilities they almost entirely rule. There they remain until their dying day. There they are free from the harassments of mandarins, and they are noted for their hospitality and gentleness and for their generous contributions to charitable causes.

Pulo Pinang, Prince of Wales' Isle, is presently in the hands of

Chinese. Like Singapore, it can not be considered actually a British possession. On the Sunda Isles, the Dutch have not had too agreeable relations with the Chinese. Between 1740 and 1742 they carried on a desperate warfare on Java and almost lost the island to the Chinese. Today there are still 274,097 Chinese in the Dutch India (Dutch East Indies).

But the emigration toward the south has not stopped here. In the goldmines of Australia one can find 40,000, and in Victoria alone there are no less than 17,000 Chinese. Through their ability to endure the climate, they are irresistible. The total Chinese population of Australia has, as mentioned, reached the high figure of 230,000. The coolie trade on the West Indies and South America has taken on such enormous proportions that, on the Guano Islands, for instance, 40,000 yellow men have died, victims of the unhealthful climate. In Cuba, the first coolies were imported in 1847. The greater part of these were Chinese. Since then the transportation of coolies to Cuba has continued until there at present time are 20,000. Besides California and Cuba, Peru is the destination for the coolie trade. In that country there are at present 140,000. In 1872, several thousand were occupied in building the transatlantic railroad. In Lima, they have their own theatre, and in Callao a benefit society.

As can be seen, the emigration has really reached stupendous proportions, and Europe is being assailed from both east and west—*assailed,* because it is as emigrants that the Chinese have at all times made their conquests. In spite of being the most *un*warlike nation in the world, it has—even though their country, or rather, their reigning dynasty, was conquered several times—nevertheless devoured their captors through their enormous population, and through immigration into the countries of their conquerors, subjugated and conquered the conquerors' lands. In that way they invaded and took over Mongolia by way of introducing its inhabitants to tea. The simpleminded shepherd folk adopted tea drinking as a habit, and in no time this article became a necessity. It was not long before the Mongols were caught in the clutches of the Chinese; and they were only too glad to give them long-term credit, and eventually took their land as security and settled on it as farmers and innkeepers. The shepherd and the hunter, who habitually shun the farmer, withdrew to the wildernesses, and the Chinese advanced as far as Kashgaria, near Turkestan. There he came upon the Osmanli, who at that time became the vanguard of the western world against the Hun. Battle ensued, and the Chinese, being inferior warriors, found themselves overpowered.

The Chinese can thus be said to loom as a power bent on conquest; and therefore the Americans and the Russians quite correctly drive him out. Like the wasp, he invades the hives of others, hunts on the soil of others, and intrudes upon and empties the nets of others. He does not till the soil himself but seeks out communities which have already been built. For there it is easier to gain profit, and the labor is not too heavy. His views of right and wrong differ from those of the westerner; his conscience is constituted differently. For that reason the westerner cannot reason with him, ought never to have anything to do with him. The contest will be uneven. The Chinese is slyer; and therefore the stronger. The day the coolies in the West Indies and the Chinese in California have been crowned as martyrs, their victory has been won. For there will always be a few sensitive souls who will want to improve upon the laws of nature, and they will call for emancipation for the Chinese. And when the Chinese is elected to the Congress, with a couple of centuries of inherited hatred stored up in him, the "the yellow peril" may with good reason be the cause of apprehension and fear for the future of western culture.

Should one try to determine the causes for this unceasing emigration, one must look for them behind the great Chinese wall. One hears talk about socialistic movements, overpopulation, general discontent with the government, corruption, oppression and tyranny, incompetent, weak rulers, and many other things. The intelligence one receives, varies greatly, depending upon the informant's particular position on the question. On one point there seems to be general agreement: that the Chinese empire, following the Tai-Ping revolution—one of the most phenomenal movements in the history of mankind—has been shaken to its very foundation; and that still more wide-spread movements can be expected, not only socialistic ones but also dynastic.

There are some, however, who prophesy that these upheavals and ferments are a portent of an approaching disintegration and breakdown. These declare quite frankly that the Chinese nation is bound to perish. They reason that the nation, having—according to them—remained static and unprogressive for many years, will gradually commence to disintegrate. Yet there are others who, by narrowly clinging to the emigration phenomenon, with misgivings elect to think that the Chinese will some day be the rulers of the universe. This opinion, which is a quite general one, has its roots in the usual prejudices against China; and these are based upon a lack of knowledge of the actual situation. It is my intention to attempt to throw some light on certain points in relation to the continued existence of that nation and to refute some of the more erroneous conceptions about the Chinese people's actual position and views in religious, political and social matters. This I shall do in an objective manner and without being in every respect an admirer of the Chinese, or suspected of being one.

*   *   *

China has always aroused curiosity, at times exaggerated admiration, sometimes repugnance and horror, and among the less educated almost generally levity and ridicule. One has been eager to discover the cause for this continually changing appraisal because of the fact that China has been so little known and so inaccessible that it—through its very segregation and detachment from the rest of the world—has acquired and retained an aura of mystery and interest. Even to this day one hears repeatedly, with pretensions to being the truth, that we in the main know nothing about this remarkable country. And yet China has been known from time immemorial. Marc Antony sent an envoy to "the land of silk" for the purpose of entering into trade relations with it. This mission, however, gave no results. The Nestorians brought Christianity to China as early as the year 635. In one city in the vicinity of Nanking there were in 1274 two Christian churches, the ruins of which still stand; and the Nestorian Mar-Sachis served as governor in that same city. The Arabs have chronicled travels in China between the years 850-77, when they in the city of Canton found a mosque which already then was described as ancient. When Genghis Khan founded the Mongolian-Tatarian dynasty, the Arab Ibn-Batuta visited China. In 1704, Pater Gazani called at a Hebrew colony in Li-paisse, a colony that had been there for centuries. The Hebrews had so lost the tradition about Jesus that they confounded him with Syrach. They had their synagogue and great sacred book and retained all the rituals and ceremonies. In the year 1246, Pope Innocentius IV dispatched the monk Giovanni Carpini to convert the Tatars and Chinese to Christianity. The striking similarity which exists between the Buddhistic and Catholic ecclesiastic customs pleased the monk highly, for he thought that Christianity had already been introduced among them. The same error was made by Rubricus, who had been sent there in 1253 by Louis the Saint. Under the Mongolian-Tatar Kublai Khan (1214-94), who conquered China in the year 1280, Marco Polo undertook his journey and became a favorite of the khan; and his descriptions of China remain to this day among the best and most authentic sources. In 1288, Nicolaus IV sent Giovanni of Corrino as his delegate to China, and he was the first one to succeed in gaining ground for the Roman Catholic religion, despite the protests of the Nestorians. Giovanni erected a church and had churchbells cast for the towers. Baptismals took place on a great scale, and Latin was studied in the parochial schools. In 1516, Portuguese merchant ships arrived at Canton, but the Portuguese behaved like robbers, and the Chinese grew to fear and hate Europeans.

Toward the end of the sixteenth century the Jesuit Fathers Ricci, Schall, and Verbiest came to China, and through their knowledge of mathematics they gained considerable standing, and the Emperor favored them with exalted offices. In the year 1692 the Christians were given religious freedom by Emperor K'ang-Hsi, and the Emperor himself wrote tracts in defence of Christianity. Then the Christians grew bold, and the Pope started to issue bulls against the Emperor; and this action had as a consequence that Christianity was forbidden through an edict of 1723. The lively relations that later existed between China and Europe through the East Indian companies have brought forth an immense literature, which principally, however, was based on such works as Mendoza's HISTORIA del gran REYNO de la CHINA, 1585, and Kircher's CHINA ILLUSTRATA, 1667, together with a few others. Since 1860, when China declared the open door policy, all its hidden mysteries have been laid bare and found to have already been exposed in the past, all the guesswork has been substantiated, and the many errors corrected. A Chinese bibliography, published in 1876 in Shanghai by P. G. and O. T. von Möllendorf, lists not less than 4,639 works in European languages which have been printed and

113

deal with China. But notwithstanding this, people persist in dogmatically voicing as their opinion that nothing is really known about this extra-ordinary country.

The true state of things is rather that the subject is practically exhausted and the material so abundantly rich that on the first attempt to penetrate into the mass of knowledge and information written about the 'Celestial Empire', one is faced with great perplexity since almost every author begins his book by tearing down the works of previous authors on the subject. For that reason the sinologists, in order to get to the bottom of the question and obtain a clear, concise and dependable idea of the subject, have turned to the original source, the literature of China, the foremost works of which can in our day be obtained in most European languages. But even this means has been enlarged upon, and after departments for the teaching of the Chinese language were endowed in the universities of Paris (1815), London, Munich and Berlin, sinology became a science which was not limited merely to the works of translation but as well extended to a more sensitive analysis of the syntax of the language. It has furthermore, ethnographically and archeologically, conducted investigations concerning China's ancient history and its original inhabitants; and this has led to most astonishing results— much too astonishing for me to dare present here and lay myself open to ridicule, before they have been confirmed through further, and more thorough, more exhaustive exploration.

Among the wrong opinions of China, gained in the main through missionaries and peregrinating seamen, these are the more generally propagated and most deeply rooted: that China, after a certain period of flourishing prosperity ages ago, stopped in its development, and from then on stood still until the present time. At the same time, China is denied having a history, and the assumption is made that— because of its segregation from the rest of the world—it has exerted no influence upon the great human progress in the world. It is further maintained that ever since time immemorial, China has been ruled by complete despotism and that this has been one of the reasons why its development has ceased. And the other reason, they say, has been the complete lack of religion, or unmitigated atheism and indifference to spiritual values. Added to this, it is asserted that China possesses no art, and that its only literature is prosaically sober, being today no different from what it was 2,000 years ago. And, as for

114

its people, they are a dirty, avaricious, slavish lot, deserving to be destroyed.

The history of China will disprove a great part of these allegations.

Like everything in history, the true facts get lost in the dim past of myths and fables. These old tales tell of three emperors who at the time of about 2600 B.C. are said to have given China its first civilization. The first one, Fu-Hsi, is credited with having introduced certain crafts; the other one, Shen-Nung, was the originator of agriculture; and the third one, Huang-Ti, is said to have divided the country into nine sections, of which one was cultivated for the needs of the state. In addition, the invention of the 60-year cycle, upon which the Chinese chronology is based, has been attributed to him, and as well the characters of the Chinese alphabet. When this latter great marvel happened, "then," relates a historian, "heaven, earth and all the gods were stirred. The inhabitants of the lower regions wept in the night, and heaven rained ripened harvests out of joy. After the completion of the invention, the human heart forged intrigues, which were set in motion; false tales were circulated and grew in number with every day, strife and conflict sprang up, and even deceitful speech became common, causing much evilness in the world, so that the shades of the departed dead wept in the night. But the invention of the written alphabet was also instrumental in bringing about polite customs, courtesy in social relations, and music. Common sense and justice and integrity came into being; social life became ordered and clarified; laws were enacted. Governors were given regulations to follow, students looked up to scholars [and authorities] and revered them—and that is why ripened harvests rained from heaven."

After this came "the five monarchs," leaving behind them as peaceful and unwarlike a history as the three emperors had done. During the reign of the last one of these emperors, Shun, a tremendous deluge is said to have taken place. Some chroniclers have paralleled it with the deluge of the mosaic tradition. With Yu, who—because of his meritorious efforts in checking the inundation—was elected regent, the first dynasty, Hsia, was founded. This house was succeeded by the Shang dynasty, said to have lasted until 1100 B.C., after which—following a palace revolution—Ch'en came on the throne. It was during his reign that Lao-Tzu, K'ung-Fu-Tzu and Buddha came upon the scene. From this period China's history dates,

115

chronicled by K'ung-Fu-Tzu in the fifth of the Canonical Annals (Ching), which has been given the name Ch'un-Ch'iu (Autumn and Spring). After the death of K'ung-Fu-Tzu in the year 477 B.C., conflict arose between the Emperor and the vassals. This strife continued until 231 B.C., when Shih-Huang-Ti of the Ch'in dynasty established the Chinese Empire. Under this regent—one of the greatest personalities in the history of China—the Huns began their migratory movements and incursions into the north. To protect his country from any threatening attacks, the Emperor ordered the Wall of China to be built. He also decreed that all books in praise of his predecessors be burned so that the memory of their attainments and heroic deeds be obliterated; and he dispatched the first colonists to Japan or to America.[1]

Since this time until 1644, when the Manchurians conquered China, that country has had fifteen different dynasties on its throne (while France, for example, has during the same time had only two). Besides, it was at one period during this time occupied by the Mongols (1280-1334), who under Kublai Khan (1261-1294) had invaded it. It had also been shaken by domestic and social upheavals. In the twelfth century a reformer, Wang-An-Shih, came forward as the leader of a socialistic party, bringing about a revolution. This in turn was the cause of an emigration to other lands; and this emigration may have given the impulse to the later migratory movements. In addition, there were the movements of the Mongols toward the west, and Genghis Khan's appearance on Chinese soil. In short, the history of China shows a series of vast reforms, which have made the country progress. And even though China, according to some, lay dormant

---

[1] On one of his journeys the Emperor came to the shore by the sea. He lingered there, filled with wonderment and awe. Then a priest of the Worshipers of Common Sense stepped forward and said: "In the islands on the other side of the ocean there grows a herb which bestows on one the gift of immortality. Shih-Huang-Ti, who was forever zealous to learn about anything that was new and strange, at once commanded that a like number of young girls and youths set out to search for the plant. They embarked in ships but a devastating storm bore down upon them, and only one ship came back." Compare Gützlaff's GESCHICHTE DES CHINESISCHEN REICHES (Publ. by K. F. Neumann. Quedlinb., Leipzig 1836. See also: D'Hervey de Saint Denys: MÉMOIRE sur le PAYS connu des Anciens Chinois sous le Nom de FOU-SANG. Paris, 1876.

for two hundred years, the important happenings between 1851 and 1865, when the Tai-Ping rebellion occurred, indicate that the nation has not been asleep. For this revolution had a political side to it. It was a war of independence, of liberation from foreign invaders, and would not have resulted in victory for the latter, had these not been aided by the intervention and support of European governments. Furthermore, the invasion had long been contemplated and prepared in secret by revolutionary organizations and factions, working together. China never has been seen as conqueror by war; its only martial engagements have been wars in defence of its civilization, and against the barbarians. Thus it has always pursued the same objectives as Europe has. How much Europe is indebted to China for its culture cannot yet be determined. But that the Mongols in the 12th Century emerged against Europe with cannon, and that printed books existed already in the 10th century, is indisputable. Relations with the Western hemisphere were at that time quite brisk. One author claims that long before the art of printing was invented in Europe, Chinese books were seen there. As far as the Chinese stagnation and unprogressiveness is concerned, it was actually not so very serious. China's real history begins in 722 B.C., consequently 54 years after the first Olympiad, and 31 years after the founding of the city of Rome. One asks how the development of Greece and Italy has progressed during the past centuries. In comparison with China, these countries could, perhaps, with even greater reason, be called "dead," and their languages as well. Having had a glorious past, both have now ceased— after a languishing existence—to exert an influence upon the historical-universal development. Their influence came to an end as far back as the beginning of the Christian era. China, on the other hand, has to this day survived within its own boundaries. Its language and culture remain the same without any borrowing from foregin sources —and this under the rule of a foreign dynasty. This is proof that, in that country at least, the history of the rulers is not synonomous with that of the people.

Concerning the despotic rule of the government—which is said to have been the cause of the refusal of an armistice—there is no great danger in that respect either. It is true that the Emperor is absolute ruler and on the whole enjoys the same sort of deference as the Russian czar, yet no more. At his side he has two councilors of State. The government is divided into three branches, namely the

Supreme Council of State, in Peking and the State Councils of the Provinces, and of the Colonies. The administrational departments are six in number. The centralization is complete. Thus it might appear as if the monarchy were governed by a single, personal will, since no sign of any other representation appears to exist, not even by name. But there are other checks and balances, which have nothing to correspond to it in Europe.

Above the entire government machinery there hovers namely the censorship administration. It has supervision over the *mores* of the people, over the deportment and conduct of the members of the Imperial family, the cabinet ministers and public servants. No one— not even the Emperor—is immune from the censors' admonishments; and these can be sharp enough, since the censor who delivers the reprimand or rebuke is free from any liability or prosecution. There is furthermore a Palace of Petitions, a sort of supreme court of appeal, which renders an account and opinion of petitions and representations received from the provinces, as well as of complaints over judgments rendered. There is no hereditary nobility, and the Emperor is required to choose his civil officials solely from among those who before The Society of the Learned have passed the prescribed tests and examinations for knowledge. The only accepted aristocracy is that of culture. Riches gain a Chinese neither rank nor esteem, and the civil officials possess higher rank than the military. In addition, the Chinese have a highly developed communal government. The village communities themselves elect through general voting a village overseer who is responsible for the collection of taxes, acts as police and justice of the peace, and also functions as intermediary between the villagers and the mandarins. This manner of governing has something humane and patriarchal about it. The Emperor regards himself as both "father and mother" to his subjects. That capriciousness and arbitrariness prevail among the appointed officials and that these, who are poorly recompensed, stoop to extortion, is a sad fact. It serves, however, to prove that China is not the Promised Land of higher public servants, as has been claimed. Neither is it overrun by public servants, for in 1840 their number did not surpass 14,000. By comparison, Sweden counted 19,000 civil and ecclesiastical public servants in 1850, before its [government owned] railway system had been opened [when the number increased]. The people do not complain over political oppression and possess an unbelievable freedom to express their grievances in print. For the moment that the government institutes any measure which displeases them, they start raining brochures, satirical pamphlets and, especially, they resort to plastering the house walls with posters.

In general, the laws are lenient. That corporeal punishment—which is not looked upon as a disgrace—is meted out more frequently than imprisonment, is of benefit to the naîion. And the people seem to be satisfied with their bamboo drubbing. One opinion, which appeared in the Edinburgh Review in 1810 upon the publication of G. T. Staunton's translation of China's penal laws, may have more truth in it since it is pronounced by an Englishman, the English being neither friends nor admirers of the Chinese.

"When we from Zend Avesta or Puranas look at the true quality of practicality and common sense, contained in this collection of laws, it is as coming from the dark into the light, from superstition and insanity into clarity of understanding. And however longwinded and trivial in certain instances these laws may be, we nonetheless can think of no European book of statutes that is so rich in content, so consequential, or so free from intrigue, bigotry and distortion of fact as this tome."[20] Characteristic of the, so to speak, genial, goodhumored manner in which the Emperor accepts his official duties, is the answer the excellent Emperor K'ang-Hsi (1661–1722) gave the censors when they complained about the provincial courts.

"If human beings were inclined to allow themselves to be led astray when it comes to personal advantages," he says, "there would be no end to strife and quarrels, and the one half of the nation would scarcely be sufficient in number to decide the questions at issue. It is therefore my wish that all who turn to the courts for redress shall be treated without mercy so that each and everyone may get a distaste for legal proceedings and tremble at the thought of appearing before a magistrate. In this way, evildoing will be pulled up by the roots. For respectable subjects, who happen to have a disagreement, will settle their disputes like brothers, by leaving their feuds to be arbitrated by the village overseer and old men of experience. On the other hand, the man who is full of fight, who is obstinate and incorrigible, is given justice when he is trampled by the court."

---

[20] *Ta Ch'ing lü-li*: The Penal Code of China, translated by Sir George Th. Staunton. 1810. [The title, as published in 1810, is: *Ta-tsing-leu-lee,* here corrected.]

Huc, the most benevolent among Christian missionaries, who has related this, adds that the Chinese are rather inclined to start lawsuits, despite their peacefulness, and that the Emperor's reply had a salutary effect.

The patriarchal relations between the absolute ruler and the people are evidenced by the law, proclaimed throughout the empire, calling for excerpts from K'ang-Hsi's *Sacred Edict*[21] to be read on the first and fifteenth day of every month in every city and community.

This edict consists of sixteen maxims of moral and economic content, with commentaries by his successor, Yung-Cheng, and interpreted and expounded upon by a superintendent of a saltmine, Wang-Yu-P'u. The verities are quite commonplace, and the style is anything but official. It is instead distinguished by a quite high degree of goodnatured simplicity. "People and warriors," it says among other things, "even though you by nature are stupid and illiterate, lacking in good sense and possessing no understanding of reason and justice, you ought to—out of consideration for your family and for your own sake—grasp that once the law catches you in its net, a thousand disagreeable things are in store for you. Is it then not better that you cleanse your hearts and repent your errors in the silence of the night than to wait for the moment when you fall prey to the rod and have to give out horrible screams? Instead of ruining yourselves and having to give up all your possessions for the sake of getting off unscathed from those punishments which are unavoidable, would it not be preferable to rid yourselves of your vices, return to a virtuous life, refrain from overstepping the laws, and thus safeguarding yourselves and your families?"

The rights and liberties of the Chinese are quite extensive. Many a constitutional monarchy in the West offers no more freedom. Freedom of religion, of thought, speech and press, communal voting right, right of petition, freedom from oppression by a hereditary nobility, and freedom from an internal military party are some of the enviable privileges. Besides, these rights and freedoms serve to safeguard against an absolute government and centralization of administration. In reality, China can boast of greater freedom than France under the Second Empire with its legislature, Senate and popular vote.

* * * *

[21] The Sacred Edict. William Milne, London 1817.

To present a clear picture of the religious situation in China is not so easy a matter. The reports and information furnished by the Catholic and Protestant missionaries are vastly contradictory. And the missionaries themselves have frequently been so antagonistic toward one another that they have inflicted injury to their mission. One must, however, in this respect, wholeheartedly approve of the Catholics' mode of action, for they sought their converts among the more cultivated, at the Imperial Court; and when K'ang-Hsi occupied the throne they succeeded in gaining his personal friendship. The Protestants, on the other hand, were generally uneducated, and they concentrated their efforts on the conversion of the masses, which are more open to persuasion. But let us momentarily leave the theological conflict and turn to the question as to whether or not the Chinese people are irreligious and if they actually are the atheists that they have been accused of being. Let us go to the source, the ancient annals, for an answer to this question.

In China there are three religions, but there is no state religion. This has been used as proof of the nation's religious indifference. The government and the cultivated classes adhere to K'ung-Fu-Tzu's noble teachings, which are found in *Shu-Shu, The Four Classical Books*. These are partly based on *Wu-Ching*, or *The Five Canonical Books,* collected by K'ung-Fu-Tzu. These books can even to this day be read with benefit by people the world over, without harm or injury to either religious or moral feelings. They contain nothing but worshipful praise of the Creator and of human virtues, in addition to golden rules to live by. The Christians have found it difficult to come upon anything in the sacred books which might be said to be heathenish. Long and sharp encounters were carried on before the missionaries thought that they had discovered a clue. *T'ien*—a frequently recurring word—means "heaven," but in the Books it is used in the sense of "The Creator." In *Meng-Tzu,* for instance, The Fourth of the *Classical Books,* Part V, Vol. II, Chapter 1, it says: "The plan of Heaven when it created mankind, was that. . . . etc.," and in the same Part V, Vol. 1, Chapter 6, we read: "Whatever takes place without the doings and dealings of human beings, is the work of Heaven. Whatever happens without being willed by the human being is done by the power of Heaven. . . etc." However, the word *T'ien* was used in the calendar, and the word for astronomy is *T'ien-wen* (the Science of Heaven). Therefore the missionaries took it for granted that the Chinese worshiped the visible heaven, and consequently were heathens who ought to be saved. Enlightened Jesuits did not share the same stupid opinion, and they submitted the matter to the Emperor. The Emperor issued an edict, still preserved in the archives, and in this he says: "We do not make sacrifices to the visible, earthly heaven but solely to the Lord and Master of Heaven and Earth, and the things he has created (as the Emperor Chao-Ting was likewise called, after the palace given that name— where the Emperor showed himself in his greatest glory). This is the reason that all tablets, before which offerings are made, carry the inscription *Shang-Ti the Elder,* Supreme Lord. Out of reverence one dares not speak his name aloud; one customarily invokes Him by His celestial name." The mandarins and the learned similarly expressed their astonishment over the fact that Europeans should believe that they worshiped a being without life, such as a visible heaven. "How could we believe," they asked, "that every family has a head, every city its governor, every province a vice-roy, our entire realm an absolute lord and master, and yet doubt for even a moment that there exists a prime intelligence, a supreme spirit, an absolute ruler of the universe who governs with wisdom and justice? Do our ancient writings teach otherwise?"[22] This question was voiced in 1700, yet as late as 1845 Gützlaff insists in his Chinese history that the Chinese by the word *t'ien* mean the material heaven, and laughs at the idea of a supreme spirit! This is what westerners call *mala fides.*

The state does not remunerate the priests and tries through edicts to counteract and put a stop to superstition and image worship. In both the *Penal Code and The Sacred Edict* it can be seen as protector of the pure teaching of a Supreme Spirit against Buddha's and Lao-Tzu's image worship and false inventions, showing a rather keen, although humane, zeal. The teaching of Buddha, to which we shall shortly return, is well known to us. Less known, perhaps, is that of Lao-Tzu, or Lao-Chün. This philosopher lived approximately a hundred years before *K'ung-Fu-Tzu* and is said to have travelled far to the west in his peregrinations. In conformity with the Pythagoreans and the followers of Plato he holds common sense to be the basic foundation in philosophy. "Before Kaos, who preceded the

---

[22] J. G. Kröger: Abriss einer vergleichenden Darstellung der Indisch-Persisch und Chinesischen Religionssystemen. Eisleben 1842.

Creator of Heaven and Earth, there existed only one being, boundless and silent, motionless and yet constantly at work: that is the original source of the universe. Its name is not known to me, but I apply the name of sense or reason to it. Mankind has as its prototype the earth; the earth has its prototype in sense and reason; and sense and reason theirs in themselves." Lao-Tzu's views are contained in *Tao-Te-Ching, The Road to Virtue*. Eduard von Hartmann opens his introduction to the German translation (1870) in the following emphatic manner:

"An ancient sanctuary from the furthest Orient opens its portals and cries out to the astonished westerner: Enter! Even *we* have our gods! Not an angry, miserly, bloodthirsty God's temple of worship desecrated and profaned by priestly thirst for power, greedily bent on increasing its hierarchical hold on the people at their expense—no, a temple of the Eternal, nameless God, whom all have met and yet no one can mention by name, a peaceful community's inviolable haven of refuge, a temple of the purest and most beautiful humanity, mistied by contemplative religious mysticism only sufficiently to find there the tranquil retreat to which an impotent humanity can flee after a day's trivial and petty interests and stormy passions. We know the quieting influence Goethe experienced on reading Spinozas *Ethics;* and here we have a work of an ethical nature—yet, much like Spinoza's first volume, dealing with metaphysics. But even here, despite a severe pantheism and similarities as to the all-comprehensive, absolute (*Tao*), what a difference! While Spinoza is a stony, rigidly sculptured Medusa head, gazing at us with a petrified look, Lao-Tzu seems like an old fresco painting with half faded contours. But it is a picture of enchanting beauty and mellowness, upon whose sympathy-compelling loveableness and gentleness one cannot gaze long enough."

Von Hartmann's testimonial may be valid, but the fact is that the cultivated Chinese, having once become accustomed to *K'ung-Fu-Tzu* and his disciples, have refused to be inspired by Lao-Tzu. The latter has instead been accepted by people who, without understanding his teachings, have out of it developed a school of soothsayers, alchemists, charlatans and astrologers, who have found followers among that segment of the populace who are not adherents of Buddha.

K'ang-Hsi's 17th maxim reads as follows: "Suppress all alien teachings so that the true faith may be promoted and advanced;" and the commentaries and the paraphrasings elucidate further the government's position toward the two sects and toward Christianity. After having proved the theoretical truth of the two sects, Lao's and Fu's, he adds: "Later there sprang up a class of roving persons who appropriated the names of these sects and distorted their tenets. Their intent is to augur misfortune or good fortune, all for the sake of gaining personal profit through their ghastly stories and their spurious panaceas. First they dupe the people of their money in order to fatten themselves, then they gather together a congregation of both men and women to burn incense. And in the paraphrase: "You say that to serve Fu is salutary and beneficent; that if you burn paper money, offer sacrifices, and fast before the countenance of the god Fu, he will avert danger, wipe out your sins, increase your happiness and lengthen your life! Ponder it! From early time, it has been said: "The gods are the essence of common sense and justice." If Fu were such a god, how could he possibly be enamoured of your golden paper money and your sacrifices and be expected to protect you because of these? Do you think that if you do not burn golden paper money and bring sacrifices to his altar, the god Fu will be displeased with you and visit his punishing judgment upon you? If this be so, then the god Fu is a despicable god! Let us, for example, take the mandarin in your district! Even if you should never cringe and fawn upon and flatter him, he would nonetheless—if you were honest men and women and carried out your duties—pay attention to you. But if you overstep the laws, commit violence or outrage, or are unjust to others, he would show displeasure, even if you tried to flatter him in a thousand ways. And he would surely rid the community of such a pest!"

From this can plainly be seen that the government seeks to put a stop to anything smacking of charlatanry in religion, and few governments have expressed themselves so frankly and unmistakably about false prophets.

Concerning the feeble success that Christianity has attained in China, the reasons for this goes deeper than mere apathy to religion, which has been assumed to be general. When the Catholic missionaries came to China, they discovered a similarity between their own religious rituals and those of the Buddhists so striking that they thought the country was Christian. And when they asked who Buddha was, they received the answer: "He is the Saviour of mankind." It is common knowledge that in many respects Christian and

Buddhistic traditions resemble each other. Buddha is said to have been born by a virgin about the year 960 B.C. He was baptized and given the name of Siddhartha. His teacher soon became embarrassed and perplexed by his disciple's questions; and since his teacher knew no other language than the Indian (Hindustani), his disciple instructed him in fifteen other tongues. Eventually he left his community and took refuge in the wilderness. There he was exposed to temptations. Later, when he in Benares appeared as prophet, he took the name of Sakya-Muni. In Benares he defeated the high priest in a disputation and shortly thereafter enunciated his basic moral teachings and the ten commandments:

1. Not to kill.
2. Not to steal.
3. To be chaste.
4. Not to bear false witness.
5. Not to lie.
6. Not to swear.
7. To avoid profanity.
8. To be unselfish.
9. Not to be revengeful.
10. Not to be superstitious.

He died at the age of eighty, after having taken leave of his disciples and prophesied that another Buddha would come into the world 5,000 years later. Buddhism is permeated with a spirit of meekness, equality and brotherliness. "My law is the law of grace and mercy for all," Buddha says.

When therefore the Catholics put into circulation their teachings and expounded the gospel of the coming of the Saviour of the world, this came as no news to the Chinese. Consequently it brought about many difficulties. These were heightened by the fact that the Buddhists used not only masses (liturgy), fastings, bells, palms, consecrated water, rosaries, incense, but as well images with burning candles [before them]—exactly as the Christians [Catholics] did. But the westerners were mistrusted. The Chinese could not understand why they should have travelled from so far away merely to preach about a new Buddha; and they suspected they must have come for some political or other motive. In the beginning no such motive was found. But in the eighteenth century, Jesuits and Dominicans became embroiled with each other in quarrels. This resulted in the Pope's being drawn into the struggle, and the Pope ended it by threatening to pronounce the ban of the Church upon the Emperor, at the same time declaring China to be a feudatory state. The animosity and rage of the Chinese grew, and the Christian missionaries were expelled. It is for this reason that it is said of the Christians in the above mentioned maxims: "The sect of the western ocean which worships the Lord of heaven belongs as well to that group of people that is harmful and detrimental. But because these men know mathematics, the government uses them. This you must carefully bear in mind."

The Chinese have never been religious fanatics. They willingly discuss Christianity, acknowledge its fine teachings, have never persecuted Christians because of their religion. But they have harrassed them on occasions because of their bold and often tasteless demeanor, such as when French missionaries journeyed through their land, attired in the colors of the Imperial family, despite the fact that they knew that this was not only against the law but as well against custom. The banishment of the Christians made them enraged; and the fanatic behavior of the Protestant missionaries hurt Christianity no less, especially since less intelligent and sensible heads were in charge of their missions. Appendix XVIII of the Penal Code includes two Imperial edicts of 1805 pertaining to Christianity. They contain some curious chapters which throw light on and show what serious misunderstandings arose through excessive zeal on the part of the faithful.

In the second edict the Emperor says that he has had his Councilors investigate the writings of the Christians and that he in them has found offensive and untrue statements. He mentions among other things the following, from *Essential Introduction to the Faith*: "Tien-Chu, i.e. the Lord of Heaven, is the Supreme King of all nations—but in the *Calendar of Saints* it says that "Jesus, the son, is the Supreme King of the Earth and of all creatures." Is this true or sound reasoning?. . " In *Instruction Concerning Marriage* it says that they who do not have any religion are nothing less than slaves of the devil."

Elsewhere it says that "once upon a time there was a *pei-tse* (i.e. a Tataric prince) who habitually committed evil deeds and paid no attention to his wife's entreaties when she tried to persuade him to lead a different life. One day a legion of devils pounced upon the

126

prince and carried him off to hell. And when T'ien-Chu(God) saw that *Fo-Chin* was a good and virtuous woman, he told her clandestinely that her husband was suffering eternal torments and tortures in a sea of fire." Added to this was the admonition that they who do not pay heed to the pious forewarnings and rebukes, shall be brought to suffer eternally by T'ien-Chu. We repeat: This is unreasonable and to the highest degree exaggerated. . . .It is evident that this story of a pei-tse being carried off by the devils to hell is fabricated without an iota of truth, and is unworthy of being believed."

The Christians were expelled, but were saved from being maltreated, despite the fact that worship of the devil is in the Penal Code punished by a couple of hundred lashes. The misguided were treated with respect, and the people were attached to them, for they were charitable toward the poor and the sick and never accepted any money in return—something that particularly impressed the Chinese, who were quite strictly kept in check by their bonzes. But besides the missionary activities, trade was carried on by the westerners all through the eighteenth century. The Chinese refused at first to embark upon such undertakings, for their country was in no need of importing anything, but the Europeans needed tea. A balance had to be affected, and the British taught the Chinese to smoke opium toward the latter part of the 18th century. From then on the relationship began to be muddied, and before long the British with their unscrupulous trade policy were to militate against and obstruct their own and the other western powers' efforts for the advance of Christianity.

Previous to 1767 the entire import of opium from India had risen to no more than two hundred chests. Gradually the Chinese government became aware of the unwholesome, injurious influence opium was having upon the population, and prohibited its sale. The first consequence of this was the increase in its price; and secondly, the British established opium plantations in India and inaugurated a shameless smuggling trade, protected by their government, and this continued until 1839. Then the government in Peking dispatched one of its emissaries to Kuang-Tung, requesting that there be put a stop to the lawless activity. Then Emperor Lin, a noble, vigorous and energetic character, steadfastly determined to save his fatherland from ruination, issued this edict:

"It is a known fact," Lin says to the British, "that the ships

127

arriving at Canton for the purpose of carrying on barter trade, yield a great profit there . . . . We hand over to you all our goods and commodities, unadulterated and genuine, to be carried by you over the seas. . . . Do you show yourselves grateful for this? Have you respected and lived up to our laws? Have you shown any consideration for the wellbeing of others while you have come to gain advantages? Why do you bring in opium here when its use is forbidden in your own country and possessions?"

The opium cargoes were in the beginning refused admittance, but eventually 20,000 chests fell into Chinese hands; and this occurence came to play the same historical rôle as the chests of tea in the Boston harbor. That was the beginning of the three opium wars, ugly pages in history, which Europe should much like to see torn out. Not until 1860 do the Chinese completely break down, and the Europeans leave behind a hated and despised name after the heinousness and outrages which were then perpetrated and which they do not like to recall.

Christianity's cause was from now on irretrievably lost. "It cannot be," says a Chinese who had read books on Christian teachings and found these to be consonant with K'ung-Fu-Tzu's, "it cannot be that the British are Christians. If they were, they would not transgress the ten commandments, they would not rape our country and our cities, nor would they kill our poor people. If they were Christians, they would not breach the sixth commandment, nor sell opium and spread death and destruction throughout our land. If they are truly Christian, then let these hypocrites who overrun us with their missionaries, bibles, and [religious] tracts, be taught [Christianity]; let them be taught the Christianity that they profess, the Christianity of virtue and righteousness. Neither do the Russians, you might retort, have the right—according to the teachings of *their* religion— to take from us one piece of land after another. And that Englishman Bowring—he is the most shameless of all. He had the temerity to assert in a conversation with His Excellency *Chien* that opium was no more harmful than our tea." When the conversation turned upon the British, the Chinese opened our catechism, pointed to the ten commandments, and said in a solemn tone of voice: "No, they are no Christians!"[23]

---

[23] K. Fr. Neumann: Ostasiatische Geschichte. Leipzig 1861 .

A particularly remarkable rôle was reserved for Christianity during the great religious war of liberation, which is known under the name of the Tai-Ping Rebellion. It deserves being mentioned briefly.[24]

Hsiu-Ch'üan was the name of a poor man's son in southern Kuang-Tung. Eager to educate himself, he tried in vain several times to obtain the lowest degree given for academic studies. When his [financial] resources were at an end, he gave up the thought of getting a degree and withdrew to the country, where he taught in a small elementary school. But the strain of what he had had to endure caused him to have a break-down in health. During his illness he saw visions, and these appeared to him as absolute, subjective reality. They continued to pursue him after he had passed through his illness, and people spoke of him as having lost his mind. In time he began to harbor thoughts of having been chosen for a divine mission. Through an unfortunate chance, a book by a Chinese convert, Liang-A-fa, a compilation entitled *Ch'üan-Shih-Liang-Yen,* fell into his hands. In its English translation it is called *Good Words Exhorting the Age.* This book, which in manuscript form has been shown to Dr. Morrison and been approved by him, contains isolated passages from *The Holy Writ* in addition to some spiritual tracts.

That the first chapter in The Book of Isaiah and of Genesis should make a vivid impression upon the visionary was to be expected; and he and some of his friends studied the magical book together. Of its origin and meaning he had not the slightest knowledge or understanding. His friends, however, observed that the words *I, we, you, he* frequently appeared at the beginning of the chapters, but they could not comprehend exactly to whom these pronouns referred. Hsiu-Ch'üan intimated that he knew very well to whom they referred. He had often seen the word *ch'üan* (whole; all); and before long he became convinced that it was his name [that appeared there]. Thus he rendered the fourth verse of David's 19th Psalm in this way: "Their words have gone out to the end of Ch'üan's land" [to the end of the world]; and the ninth and tenth verses he read as follows: "Ch'üan is righteous and more to be desired than gold" instead of "The judgments of the Lord are true and righteous altogether; more to be desired are they than gold." When they read

---

[24] See the account "Swedish Missionaries in China."

the description of the deluge, they were utterly consternated. They were not aware that a deluge had taken place in the past. And it was not long before Siu-Tsuen appeared as a fullfledged prophet, taking the name of Jesus' younger brother. He hurled forth the punishing judgments of the Old Testament, already fulfilled, upon China, and the people flocked to him in multitudes. Convinced of his divine mission, Hsiu-Ch'üan's desire was to free his country from image worshipers, to introduce the teachings of serenity and peace and, having accomplished that, to overthrow the Manchu dynasty. In 1853 Hsiu-Ch'üan was proclaimed emperor in Nanking; and the dynasty was given the name of Tai-Ping, The Realm of Peace, while the state itself was named The Celestial Empire.

This civil war of liberation lasted into the year 1865, when France and England again appear on the scene in a false position and put an end to the legitimate Tai-Ping dynasty (which, unlike the Manchu conquerors, was legitimately entitled to the throne), thus extinguishing the faint flame of Christianity which the young dreamer and zealot had lighted.

* * * *

One of the significant reasons for the vague European judgments of China is the lack of acquaintance with the Chinese language. And it is precisely through his language that one gets to know the Chinese best. The prejudice against—or rather the antipathy to—the Chinese language is unjustified. A language as ancient as the dead Sanskrit language yet as alive today as in the past, giving access to a literature, richer and more solidly genuine than that of India, ought not to be as neglected as it is. And this, despite the practical interest [in knowing it], which will grow with every new point of contact that is made between the East and the West. But even in this respect, traditional false ideas have flagrantly interfered. It has been notoriously and unmistakably declared that Chinese is a language that cannot be learned; that it counts no less than 80,000 characters, one for each word, and that not even the native Chinese themselves can ever learn the full alphabet. But the true fact is the following: K'ang-Hsi's dictionary, the largest compiled hitherto,[25] contains 44,441 words, of which only 24,235 are used generally. If one compares this with [Samuel] Johnson's English lexicon, which contains

[25] 1879.

approximately 50,000 words, of which Shakespeare—who was not sparing of words—employed only about 20,000; and when one considers that the average Italian opera text, nothwithstandig that it is called upon to give expression to quite varied moods, can get along with a mere 600 words; and moreover, when one learns that China's five canonical books, containing over 200,000 words, employ no more than 4,601 *different* characters, and that the Penal Code (in its French translation, approximately 1000 octavo pages) uses but 2,000 different characters, it need not be surprising to be told that the knowledge of four or five thousand words should be sufficient for all ordinary purposes. The great number of characters has its origin, namely, in the many existing synonyms. Callery, for example, mentions 42 different ways of writing the word *pao* (costly; expensive), 41 for *tsun* (honorable), etc.

Is the Chinese language difficult to learn, then? Not any more difficult, it must be said, than the European tongues are for a European. Rather, it is easier than most of them, as regards the grammatical accidence, which is non-existent. And as for the syntax, it is no harder to manage than the Latin syntax is for a German. Professor Stanislas Julien of the Collège de France taught himself the language in six months, and well enough to be able to translate Meng-Tse and have the work published by the Société Asiatique. The missionaries, who are not known for their acumen or sagacity—at least not the Protestant ones—do not consider the language an insurmountable hindrance. And the Office for the Propagation of the Faith in Rome has in its printing establishment a Chinese section, which is managed by Europeans.

For anyone who devotes himself to the study of the Chinese language almost all obstacles have been removed, for there are today many excellent grammars and dictionaries available. Among these, there are the Dominican P. Varo's grammar, the first *Arte de la Lengua mandarina,* Canton, 1703; Bayer: *Museum Sinicum,* Petropol, 1730; Fourmont: *Meditationes Sinicae,* Paris, 1737; the same author's *Linguae Sinarum mandarinicae et hieroglyphicae grammatica duplex,* Paris, 1742; Hager: *Elements of the Chinese language,* London, 1806; Marshman: *Clavis Sinica,* Serampore, 1814; Morrison: *A grammar of the Chinese language,* Serampore, 1814; Rémusat: *Éléments de la Grammaire chinoise,* Paris, 1822; Gonçalves: *Arte China,* Macao, 1829; Prémare: *Notitia linguae Sinicae,*

131

Malacca, 1831; Hyacinthe Bitchourin: *Kitiskaya grammatica,* St. Petersburg, 1838; (Gützlaff): *Notices on Chinese grammar,* Batavia, 1842; Endlicher: *Anfangsgründe der Chinesischen Grammatik,* Wien, 1845; *Premiers rudiments de la langue Chinoise,* Paris, 1844 (anonymous); Edkins: *A Grammar.* Shanghai, 1853 (second edition, Shanghai, 1857); Bazin: *Grammaire Mandarine.* Paris, 1856; Schott: *Chinesische Sprachlehre.* Berlin, 1857; the same author's *Zur Chines. Sprachlehre.* Berlin, 1869; Summers: *Handbook of the Chinese language.* Oxford, 1863; Lobsched: Grammar of the Chinese language. Hongkong, 1864; Isaiha: *Wwedenie w. Russko-kitaiskii slovar.* Peking, 1869; Castaneda: *Grammatica elemental de la lengua China, dialecto Cantoné.* Hongkong, 1869; Julien: *Syntaxe nouvelle de la langue Chinoise* 1,2. Paris, 1869; Rudy: *The Chinese Mandarin language after Ollendorf's new method.* Genève, 1872; de Rosny: *A Grammar of the Chinese language.* London, 1874. In addition to these publications there are 48 dictionaries, from Colladi's (Rome, 1632) to Morrison's (Shanghai, 1876), and in manuscript form there can be found a great many, compiled by Jesuits, in European libraries.

The Chinese language is not monosyllabic. The written characters are not symbolic, depicting images or figures, nor is it phonetic, expressing a sound. No more so than the English language, even if Pope once wrote verses such as these:

> "Ah, if she lend not arms as well as rules,
> What can she more than tell us we are fools?"

Neither are the Roman numerals symbolic because I, II, III are. The truth is that it is something in between, and that is *chung-yung* [the *juste-milieu*], which one learns by associating with the Chinese.

To the beginner it is a delightful and fascinating illusion to think that all the words are symbols, ingenious combinations of reproductions, hieroglyphics. He scans a text and finds a conglomeration of pictures. He sees images, birds, trees, flowers, demons, heaven, earth, sky, goldfish and dragons, houses and furnishings—all jumbled together! It is like an opium dream! But then the dictionary is consulted, and then the flower turns out to be an adverb, the beautiful lake a conjunction, and the sun and moon are found to mean "in the morning" [or tomorrow], and so forth; and one finds oneself face to face with the sharpest prose. In order not to lapse into overdoing it in another respect, it must be recognized that after gaining some familiarity with the actual symbols, which in word combinations do not function as sounds, one can, indeed—on perusing no matter which text—glean what it is about.

The Chinese characters can be divided into six categories or classes. *The first one* embraces simple likenesses, which, in the course of time, owing to transitions in graphic art, have undergone expedient changes. In this category can be counted 608 characters, some of which may be mentioned here.

> *Shan*=mountain.
> *Mu*=tree.
> *Jih*=sun.
> *Yueh*=moon.
> *Yü*=fish.
> *Ch'üan*=dog.

Even though these characters have been radically changed, they serve a definite purpose—once one has learned what they signify.

The second category comprises simple symbols with their signification transposed. These number 107. Among them are words such as *shou,* meaning *take;* a sun over the horizon=*morning;* a half moon=*evening;* something in the mouth=*sweet,* etc.

In *the third class* are found 740 characters, which readily could be ranged within class 2. These are the combined symbols, such as for example:

> Sun and moon=effulgence, brightness . . . *ming.*
> Eye and water=tears . . . *lei.*
> Man and mountain=hermit . . . *hsien.*
> Ear in a door=hear . . . *wen.*
> Woman, hand and broom=wife . . . *fu.*
> Mouth and bird=singing . . . *ming.*

Class 4 embraces such characters as have a reverse significance. These number 372 and include, among others, a hand pointing to the left, or, vice versa, to the right.

Class 5 numbers 21,810 characters, and it is in this category one encounters most of the words of which one part denotes the sound, the other the meaning. The word *cypress,* for instance, is called *pai.* But *pai* is also the character for *white;* and all species of trees are combined with the word for tree, *mu.* When the character for *white, pai,* is placed beside the character for *tree,* a compound image is formed, and *mu* loses its sound, *pai* its significance.

Here the question is not to solve a pictorial riddle, or guessing riddles; the only help is to be found through the dictionary.

Class 6 contains 598 characters, which are compounded symbols and differ from those in Class 2 merely through the fact that their origin is not too evident; and to this day they are the object of conjectures and investigations by the learned. Thus, for instance, someone broached the supposition—by no means unimportant to archeology—that because of the sign denoting a dwelling-house (a pig underneath a roof) pigs may have been the original domestic animals of the Chinese.

These six categories have no practical significance when studying the language. They are a modern invention. Indispensible for the student, however, is the knowledge of the 214 "keys", under which *all* the words in the language are classified, and under which they can be found in the dictionary. These keys are, one and all, more or less distinct symbols and signify parts of the body, zoological, botanic, mineralogical, meteorological elements, species, members and organs, etc., as well as household articles, [physical and mental] attributes and actions. These 214 signs, which are always found at the beginning of a dictionary, can serve both ideographically and phonetically—when, and in which way, is explained in the dictionary.

Once having found a word, one would be apprised of its meaning, if the language were monosyllabic. But this is not so. Without knowing the preceding and succeeding words, and after searching among the various compounds of the three words, one cannot learn the meaning of any word. That this is a necessary procedure in the study of Chinese becomes evident when one knows that the spoken tongue numbers only in the vicinity of 500 monosyllabic words. And these must give life to 50,000 dead characters, even though each word can be spoken with four different intonations. A person principally studying the written language need not occupy himself with the pronunciation. One can very well translate without having learned to read beforehand, for the written language is for the eye and need not reach the ear. For this reason a Chinese finds it difficult to grasp the content of a book when he hears it read aloud—a defect which authors seek to remedy by using synonyms. Therefore one usually comes across two verbs or two substantives of practically the same meaning, following each other.

The entire Chinese grammar is syntax, since the words cannot be inflected [or conjugated]. "The whole of Chinese grammar depends on position." The words are placed in rows from right to left, from above to below, and one must be well acquainted with the syntax in order not to make it read like balderdash. One must know that the genitive always precedes the governed word; and where one in German, for instance, usually finds the verb, one must learn to look for the relative, and so forth. The following stanza from Shi-Ching may serve as a simplified example of the compressed classical style, which quite prominently differs from the more profuse modern style.

Hsi=guide; lead.	Hui=dear; fond.	Yü=rain.	Pe=north.
Shou=hand.	Erh=and.	Hsüeh=snow.	Fêng=wind.
T'ung=together.	Hao=love.	Hsi.	Hsi.
Hang=go.	Wo=I.	P'ang.	Liang=cold.
		(iterative)	

If you examine the text you will discover in the character *fêng* the sign *blast* (gale; gust) = an insect under a bench; in the sign *liang,* an icicle (uppermost to the left); in *yü,* a rain; in *hsüeh* and *p'ang,* snowflakes; in *hui,* a heart (at the very bottom); in *hao,* a woman and a child (indicating intimacy); in *hsi,* a hand (to the left); in *shou,* a hand. This may not be very elucidating, but it gives at any rate the fundamentals of the content. That *pe* means *north,* that *hsi* indicates the pronouns *is, iste, ille* (here used as an expletive [superfluous or redundant] article, not to be translated), that *êrh* is the word for *and,* *wo* is *I,* that *t'ung* stands for *together,* and that *hang* is the character for *go* can only be gleaned by consulting the dictionary. In free translation the above reads:

The north-wind chills our neighborhood;
the snow falls in heaps;
you, who hold me dear,
place your hand in mine that we may wander from here together.

That which makes the Chinese language so intriguing to the student, in comparison with other languages, is the absence of accidence, the lack of conjugations, declinations and gender rules, the mechanical learning of which by heart can so easily diminish the interest and be deadly dull. Instead the mind sets to work from the very beginning by itself, leaving free scope for the imagination to work out the various combinations.

That China, far from having lived a cloistered life behind the Great Wall, has on the contrary always had contact with the West, can be seen by the foregoing. As far as Chinese relationship from ancient, primitive time with other inhabitants of the earth is concerned, the most astonishing opinions have been voiced and been refuted.

Thus, for instance, De Guignes writes and seeks to prove that China is an Egyptian settlement, ascribing it to the fact that there is a similarity between the Chinese characters and the hieroglyphics of Egypt. In *Mémoires Concernant les Chinois, XX,* a comparison is drawn between the hieroglyphics of both languages. While his opinion has been repulsed, the fact remains that the hieratic Egyptian and Chinese languages are built on the very same foundations: conceptual signs (genus) and phonetic signs (species). Joseph Hager issued in 1806 a publication containing 159 quarto pages called *Panthéon Chinois ou parallèle entre le Culte religieux des Grecs et celui des Chinois.* Hager's opinion has also been disproved, yet the construction of the Chinese temple which he has reproduced, surprises by its resemblance to that of the Greek temple; and the intricacy of the Chinese ornamentation still remains a marvel. In our time, an author[8] has called attention to hundreds of similarities between primitive customs and *mores* of the ancient people of China and those of Europe. The New Year (Christmas) is celebrated in China with great lantern feasts and fireworks. "Le boeuf gras" (Apis) is to this day part of a Chinese feast to the glorification of agriculture, and China's native inhabitants dance around a Maypole [as in Sweden]. When a person in China dies, a hole is made in the roof, through which to release the soul. (In northern Scotland, doors and windows are opened). Like the Scottish musical scale, the Chinese one is lacking in halftones; and when Fleming one day out in the countryside heard Chinese shepherd's tunes, such as one born in the Highlands or in a mountain region is familiar with, he was gripped by a violent longing for his homeland. To be henpecked (in Sweden, to be subjugated under the slipper) might even in China be a proverb, in reverse meaning, for there the wife hands to her husband on their day of marriage a pair of slippers, as a sign of subjection. The author, however, makes a reservation against any premature or untimely disposition of these facts as premise for immature inferences or conclusions.

---

[8] N. B. Dennys: The Folk-Lore of China and its affinities with that of the Aryan and Semitic Races. Hon(g)kong, 1876.

136

THE DANCE OF DEATH, PART I
THE DANCE OF DEATH, PART II
·

SWANWHITE
·

STORMCLOUDS
·

THE BLACK GLOVE

137

To the memory of John Gassner

THE DANCE OF DEATH

THE DANCE OF DEATH
(1900)
A drama in two parts

PART I.

PERSONS IN PART I:
Edgar, a captain in the fortress artillery.
Alice, his wife, formerly an actress.
Kurt, a quarantine master.
Jenny, a maid.
An Old Woman.
A Sentry. (Non-speaking rôle).

* * * *

The Setting:

The interior of a round fortress tower of granite.

At the rear, a gateway with French windows, through which can be seen a seashore with battery emplacements, and the sea.

On either side of the entrance, a window with flower-boxes and birds in cages.

To the left of the entrance, an upright piano; further downstage a sewing table and two reclining chairs.

On the right, half-way downstage, a writing table on which is placed a telegraph apparatus, and closer downstage stands a what-not with framed portraits. Nearby is a *chaise-longue* or a sofa, sufficiently ample to be used for sleeping. A buffet (or a cabinet) stands against the wall. A hanging lamp is suspended from the ceiling.

On the wall, against which the piano is placed, hang two large laurel wreaths, with ribbons attached; they flank the framed portrait of a woman in a stage costume.

A hat- and coat-tree with army equipment, sabres, etc., stands near the rear doors, and close by is a bureau-desk.

To the right of the doorway hangs a mercury barometer.

On each side of the room there is a door, the one on the left leading to the kitchen and the one on the right leading to other rooms, as well as outside.

ACT I: SCENE 1

A mild autumn evening. At the back of the tower room, the French windows stand open, and in the background outside—down by the coastal battery emplacement—can be seen an artilleryman with his plumed helmet, on sentry duty. From time to time his sabre reflects the crimson rays of the setting sun. The sea lies dark and calm.

The Captain is seated in the armchair on the right of the sewing table, fingering an unlit cigar. He is in fatigue uniform, somewhat worn, and is wearing riding boots with spurs. He looks tired and bored.

Alice sits in the armchair on the left of the sewing table. Unoccupied with anything, she also looks tired, yet seems expectant.

THE CAPTAIN: Won't you play for me a little something?

ALICE: *(In an indifferent tone, without being snappish.)* What do you want me to play?

THE CAPTAIN: Whatever you feel like.

ALICE: But you don't like anything I do play.

THE CAPTAIN: And you don't like to play what I like.

ALICE: *(Evasively.)* Do you want the doors to be left open?

THE CAPTAIN: If you so wish.

ALICE: Let's leave them open, then. *(Silence.)* Why aren't you smoking?

THE CAPTAIN: Strong tobacco doesn't agree with me any more.

ALICE: *(Almost in a kindly tone.)* Smoke something milder, then—since you say smoking is your only joy.

THE CAPTAIN: Joy! What is joy—tell me that?

ALICE: Don't ask me. I know as little about it as you do. —Don't you want to have your whiskey now?

THE CAPTAIN: Not just yet.—What are we having for dinner?

ALICE: How should I know? Ask Kristin.

140

THE CAPTAIN: Isn't it time for mackerel soon? It's fall, isn't it?

ALICE: Yes— it's fall. . . .

THE CAPTAIN: Both outside and inside! But no matter! Apart from the cold that comes with autumn—inside and out—a grilled mackerel with a slice of lemon, and a glass of white burgundy, is not to be disdained.

ALICE: The thought of that promptly made you eloquent, didn't it?

THE CAPTAIN: Have we any burgundy left in the wine cellar?

ALICE: I didn't know that we have had a wine cellar for the past five years.

THE CAPTAIN: You don't seem to know anything. However, we *must* stock up for our silver wedding.

ALICE: Are you really serious about celebrating it?

THE CAPTAIN: Of course, I am.

ALICE: It would be more fitting for us to hide our misery—our twenty-five years of misery. . . .

THE CAPTAIN: We have had our miseries, Alice dear, but we have also had our moments of joy. . . . And we have to make use of the little time that is left—for after that comes the end.

ALICE: The end, you say? I only wish it were!

THE CAPTAIN: It *is* the end!—and all that is left of us could be put in a wheelbarrow and used to fertilize a garden plot.

ALICE: And all this ado for a garden plot. . . .

THE CAPTAIN: That is how it is, however. And it is not of my doing.

ALICE: All this fuss! *(Silence.)* Has the mail come?

THE CAPTAIN: Yes.

ALICE: Was the butcher's bill there?

THE CAPTAIN: Yes.

ALICE: How much was it?

THE CAPTAIN: *(Takes a sheet of paper from his pocket, puts on his spectacles, but takes them off immediately.)* You read what it says—I can't make it out.

ALICE: What's the matter with your eyes?

THE CAPTAIN: I don't know.

ALICE: Old age.

THE CAPTAIN: Nonsense! I?

ALICE: Yes, you—not I!

THE CAPTAIN: H'm.

ALICE: *(Taking at look at the bill.)* Will you be able to pay this?

THE CAPTAIN: Yes—but not immediately.

ALICE: Some time in the future, of course—after a year, when you have retired on a small pension and are unable to pay it. And later, when sickness sets in again. . . .

THE CAPTAIN: Sickness? I have never been sick—only a trifle indisposed—one single time, that's all. And I have twenty years yet to go.

ALICE: The doctor had a different opinion.

THE CAPTAIN: The doctor. . . .

ALICE: Yes, who else could give a trustworthy opinion?

THE CAPTAIN: I have no illness, and have never had any, nor shall I ever have any. When I die, I shall die all of a sudden—just drop dead—like an old soldier.

ALICE: Speaking of the doctor—you know that he is giving a party this evening.

THE CAPTAIN: (*Agitated.*) Well, what of it? We are not invited because we are not on intimate terms with him and his wife; and we are not intimate with them because we don't want to be—because I have contempt for both of them. They are riff-raff.

ALICE: You say that of everybody.

THE CAPTAIN: Because that's all everybody is—riff-raff.

ALICE: With one exception—you yourself.

THE CAPTAIN: Yes—for among all sorts of conditions of life I have invariably deported myself correctly and decently. That is why I do not belong in their category.

(*Silence.*)

ALICE: Would you like to play a game of cards?

THE CAPTAIN: We may as well.

ALICE: (*Takes a deck of cards from the drawer of the sewing table and shuffles the cards.*) Think of it, the doctor is allowed to have the garrison band—for his private party!

THE CAPTAIN: (*Angrily.*) That's because he fawns on the Colonel in the city. Fawns, do you hear!—If I could only do that. . . .

ALICE: (*Dealing the cards.*) The doctor's wife, Gerda, and I were friends once; but she turned out to be deceitful. . . .

THE CAPTAIN: They are all false—all of them!—What's trumps? What's that card over there?

142

ALICE: Put on your spectacles!

THE CAPTAIN: It's no use. . . . Well, well. . . .

ALICE: Spades are trumps.

THE CAPTAIN: *(Displeased.)* Spades?

ALICE: *(Starting the game, she plays a card.)* Be that as it may—but, in any case, as far as the wives of the newly arrived officers are concerned, we are marked for ostracism.

THE CAPTAIN: *(Plays a card and takes a trick.)* What does it matter? We never give parties anyhow, so nobody will notice anything. I can stand being left alone. I have always kept to myself in the past.

ALICE: So have I. But the children. . . . The children will grow up without any companionship.

THE CAPTAIN: Let them find companions for themselves—in the city.—That's my trick. Have you another trump?

ALICE: I have one left. This trick is mine.

THE CAPTAIN: Six and eight makes fifteen. . . .

ALICE: Fourteen—fourteen!

THE CAPTAIN: Six and eight gives me fourteen. . . . I think I have forgotten how to count, too.—And two makes sixteen. . . . *(He yawns.)* It's your turn to deal.

ALICE: You are tired.

THE CAPTAIN: *(Dealing.)* Not at all.

ALICE: *(Listening, her ear cocked toward the open door.)* You can hear the music all the way here. *(There is a pause.)* Do you think Kurt is invited?

THE CAPTAIN: He arrived this morning, so he should have had time to get settled and unpack his evening clothes—even if he hasn't found time to call on *us.*

ALICE: Quarantine master. . . . is there to be a quarantine station here?

THE CAPTAIN: Yes.

ALICE: He is, after all, my cousin—we had the same family name. . . .

THE CAPTAIN: That's nothing to brag about!

ALICE: *(Sharply.)* Now—you leave my family alone, if you wish me to leave yours alone!

THE CAPTAIN: Now, now—are we going to start that all over again?

143

ALICE: Does a quarantine master have to be a physician?

THE CAPTAIN: No, he is merely a sort of civilian administrator or record-keeper; and Kurt never really made the grade.

ALICE: Kurt was always a weakling. . . .

THE CAPTAIN: . . . And has cost me a good deal of money. And when he abandoned his wife and children, it was a disgrace.

ALICE: You should not be so severe, Edgar.

THE CAPTAIN: Yes, it was scandalous. And what has he been doing in America since then? Well, I can't say I am looking forward to seeing him with any great joy; although as a young man he was agreeable enough—and I used to like to argue with him. . . .

ALICE: Because he would always yield to you!

THE CAPTAIN: *(Haughtily.)* Whether he gave in or not, he was nevertheless someone you could converse with. Here on this island I can't find a single person who comprehends what I am talking about. . . . It's a collection of idiots.

ALICE: Isn't it strange, though, that Kurt should arrive here just at the time of our silver wedding—whether we now celebrate it, or not?

THE CAPTAIN: Why is that so strange?—Oh, I see—yes, of course, it was he who brought us together, or married you off, as it was said.

ALICE: Well, he did, didn't he?

THE CAPTAIN: Yes, of course, he did. It was one of those ideas of his. . . .

ALICE: A giddy idea!

THE CAPTAIN: For which *we* have had to suffer—not *he!*

ALICE: Yes. Just think, if I had remained in the theatre! All of my women friends are now stars.

THE CAPTAIN: *(Rising.)* Well, well, well. . . . Now I'll have my drink of whiskey! *(He goes to the cabinet and mixes himself a drink, which he sips standing.)* We ought to have a rail here so that one could imagine oneself in Copenhagen—at the American Bar.

ALICE: We'll have one made; if for no other reason, to remind us of Copenhagen. For, after all, there is where we had our best moments.

THE CAPTAIN: *(Gulping down his drink violently.)* Yes—do you remember Nimb's *navarin aux pommes,* do you? Superb!

(He smacks his lips.)

144

ALICE: No, but I remember the concerts at the Tivoli.

THE CAPTAIN: You are so fastidious in your tastes.

ALICE: That ought to please you, having a wife with good taste.

THE CAPTAIN: It does.

ALICE: Whenever you feel it necessary to boast about her!

THE CAPTAIN: *(Drinks.)* They must be dancing over at the doctor's—I can hear the three-quarter time of the brass tubas—boom—boom-boom. . . .

ALICE: I can hear the strains of the *Alcazar Waltz*—from beginning to end. . . . Alas, it wasn't yesterday I last danced. . . .

THE CAPTAIN: You think you are still able to dance a waltz, do you?

ALICE: Still, you say?

THE CAPTAIN: Yes. . . . Your dancing days are over—yours as well as mine.

ALICE: I am ten years younger than you, remember!

THE CAPTAIN: Then we are both the same age, for the feminine half should always be ten years younger.

ALICE: Stop your impudence! You are an old man, and I am still in my best years.

THE CAPTAIN: Yes, yes, I know that if you want to, you can be very charming—to others. . . .

ALICE: Should we light the lamps now?

THE CAPTAIN: You may as well.

ALICE: Will you ring, then. . . .

> *(The Captain walks sluggishly to the writing table and rings.—Jenny enters a moment later from the left.)*

THE CAPTAIN: Jenny, will you be good enough to light the lamp.

ALICE: *(In a sharp tone of voice.)* I want you to light the hanging lamp.

JENNY: Yes, madam.

> *(She lights the hanging lamp. The Captain watches her.)*

ALICE: *(Curtly; harshly.)* Have you wiped the chimney properly?

JENNY: It's clean enough.

ALICE: What kind of answer is that?

THE CAPTAIN: Now, now, Alice. . . .

ALICE: *(To Jenny.)* You may leave. I'll light the lamp myself. It's much better that I do it.

JENNY: I think so, too.

> *(She goes toward the door.)*

145

ALICE: *(Gets up.)* Leave!

JENNY: *(Lingering.)* I wonder what you'd say, madam, if I did leave?

> *(Alice is silent. Jenny goes out. The Captain steps over and lights the lamp.)*

ALICE: *(Worried.)* Do you think she means to leave?

THE CAPTAIN: It wouldn't surprise me. And then we'd be in a predicament.

ALICE: It's you who are to blame. You spoil them.

THE CAPTAIN: I do nothing of the sort. Don't you see how respectful they always are to me?

ALICE: Yes, because you fuss over them. Besides, you toady to all your subordinates; and that's because you are by nature a slave, and therefore a despot.

THE CAPTAIN: You don't say!

ALICE: Yes—you cringe before your men and your non-commissioned officers, but you can't get on with your equals and your superiors.

THE CAPTAIN: Ugh!

ALICE: You are like all tyrants. . . . Do you think she will leave?

THE CAPTAIN: She will—if you don't go out and say a friendly word to her.

ALICE: I?

THE CAPTAIN: If I went out, you'd say I was flirting with the maids.

ALICE: But think—if she should. . . . Then I would have to do all the work in the house, just like the last time, and my hands would be spoiled.

THE CAPTAIN: That wouldn't be the worst! But if Jenny goes, Kristin goes, too; and after that we would never be able to get another servant to come out to this island again. The mate on the steamboat scares away any newcomer on her way to seek employment with us. And if he does not do it, then my gunners will attend to it.

ALICE: Yes, your gunners—whom I have to feed in my kitchen just because you haven't the guts to show them the door.

THE CAPTAIN: No—for then they, too, would leave us in the lurch when their enlistment period was up; and then we would have to close up shop.

ALICE: That would be our ruin!

THE CAPTAIN: And that's why the Officers Corps is planning to petition the Crown for a special subsistence appropriation.

ALICE: Subsistence for whom?

THE CAPTAIN: For the gunners.

ALICE: *(Laughs.)* You are nothing short of crackbrained!

THE CAPTAIN: That's right, laugh a little for me! It does me good to hear!

ALICE: I have almost forgotten how to laugh. . . .

THE CAPTAIN: *(Lighting his cigar.)* You must never forget how to laugh. . . . Life is boring enough without it.

ALICE: It certainly is not much fun. . . . Do you want to continue the game?

THE CAPTAIN: No, I've had enough.

ALICE: You know, it frankly irritates me that the new quarantine master—who, after all, is my cousin—should visit enemies of ours the very first day he is here.

THE CAPTAIN: Well, forget about it!

ALICE: Yes, but did you see the notice in the newspaper about his arrival? They spoke of him as a man of means. He must have come into money.

THE CAPTAIN: A man of means? So-o? A rich relation! Certainly he is the first and only one in *this* family. . . .

ALICE: In your family, yes. We have had many rich men in *my* family.

THE CAPTAIN: If he has come into money, I suppose he is overbearing; but I'll hold him in check—and I won't give him a peek at my cards.

(The telegraph apparatus starts clicking.)

ALICE: Who can that be?

THE CAPTAIN: *(Remains still.)* Quiet, please.

ALICE: Go over there and listen!

THE CAPTAIN: I can hear—It's the children . . .

(He goes over to the apparatus and taps out an answer; the clicking continues for a while, after which the Captain again answers.)

ALICE: Well?

THE CAPTAIN: Wait a little. . . *(He taps out the concluding signal.)* It was the children—they are at headquarters in the city. Judith is ailing again and is staying home from school.

ALICE: Again?—What else did they say?

147

THE CAPTAIN: Money, as usual.

ALICE: Why must Judith be in such a hurry to graduate? It would be time enough if she took her examinations next year.

THE CAPTAIN: Tell her that, and you'll see how much good it does.

ALICE: *You* ought to tell her.

THE CAPTAIN: How many times haven't I done so! But you should know by this time that children do as they please.

ALICE: At any rate, in this house. (*The Captain yawns.*) Must you yawn?

THE CAPTAIN: What else is there for me to do? Hasn't it occurred to you that we keep repeating the very same things to each other, day after day? When you a moment ago delivered your old stand-by-reply: "At any rate, in *this* house," I should have answered with *my* old stand-by: "It is not my house alone." But as I have already delivered this speech well over a hundred times, I yawn instead. My yawning may then signify that I am either too bored to answer, or it may mean: "You are right, my angel," or: "Let's put an end to this."

ALICE: You are really quite amiable tonight.

THE CAPTAIN: Isn't it time for dinner soon?

ALICE: Did you know that the doctor and his wife have ordered supper tonight from Grand Hôtel in the city?

THE CAPTAIN: You don't say! Then they'll be having woodcock! Superb! Woodcock, you know, of all birds is the greatest delicacy . . . . but to roast it in pigs' fat is nothing short of barbaric, uncivilized.

ALICE: Ugh! Stop talking about food!

THE CAPTAIN: How about wine, then? I wonder what those barbarians are having with their woodcock?

ALICE: Would you like me to play for you?

THE CAPTAIN: (*Seating himself at the writing table.*) The last straw! Yes—if you will stop playing those funeral dirges and lamentations of yours. . . . It always sounds as if you picked your selections with a view to the effect they have on me. And as an obligato I have to hear your eternal cry: "Oh, I am so unhappy! Miaow, miaow! What a terrible husband I have! Grumble, grumble! Oh, if he would only die! . . . Rapturous rolling of drums, and fanfares!—and at the end the *Alcazar Waltz* and the *Champagne Galop!*" Speaking of champagne, I think we have two bottles left, haven't we? Shall we have them brought up and make believe we have company? Shall we?

ALICE: No, we shall not—for it's my champagne—it was a present to me.

THE CAPTAIN: You are always so frugal.

ALICE: And you are always so miserly—to your wife, at least!

THE CAPTAIN: Then I don't know what else to propose.—Perhaps you would like me to dance for you?

ALICE: No, thanks! Your dancing days are over. . .

THE CAPTAIN: You ought to ask some woman friend to come and stay with you.

ALICE: Thanks!—You should invite one of your men friends here.

THE CAPTAIN: Thanks—that's been tried, and to our mutual dissatisfaction. But interesting as the experiment may have been, the upshot of it was that the moment a guest arrived, we were happy—that is, at first. . . .

ALICE: And then. . . .

THE CAPTAIN: Oh, let's not talk about it!

(There is a knock at the door, right.)

ALICE: Who can that be—at this late hour?

THE CAPTAIN: Jenny is not in the habit of knocking.

ALICE: Go over and open, and don't shout "Come in!"—the way they do in shops. . . .

THE CAPTAIN: *(Going toward the door on the right.)* You don't like workshops, eh?

(Another knock is heard.)

ALICE: Open then, open!

THE CAPTAIN: *(Opens. A visiting card is handed to him.)* It's Kristin. . . . *(To Kristin, who remains unseen.)* Has Jenny left?

(The answer is not heard.)

(To Alice.)

Jenny has left!

ALICE: So now I am a domestic again!

THE CAPTAIN: And I the handy man.

ALICE: Couldn't we get one of your gunners to help in the kitchen?

THE CAPTAIN: Not these days.

ALICE: But the card? It couldn't have been Jenny's card that Kristin handed to you!

(The Captain puts on his eyeglasses and glances at the card, then hands it to Alice.)

THE CAPTAIN: You read it, I can't. . . .

149

ALICE: *(Reading the card.)* Kurt! Why, it's Kurt! Go out and ask him to come in!

THE CAPTAIN: *(Goes outside, right.)* Kurt! Well, what a pleasure!
(Alice, seemingly come to life, is seen arranging her hair.— The Captain enters from the right with Kurt.)
Here is our renegade! Welcome, old boy! Let's give him a hug!

ALICE: *(Coming up to Kurt.)* Welcome to my home, Kurt!

KURT: Thank you. . . . It's a long time since we have seen one another.

THE CAPTAIN: How many years is it? Fifteen years! Old age is setting in. . . .

ALICE: Oh, Kurt looks the same as ever, it seems to me.

THE CAPTAIN: Sit down, sit down. . . . And, first of all, have you any plans for the evening? Are you invited anywhere?

KURT: I have an invitation from the doctor, but I haven't promised to come.

ALICE: In that case, you must stay with your relatives.

KURT: That would seem to be the natural thing to do—but the doctor is my superior, in a way, and it might cause me embarrassment if I didn't go.

THE CAPTAIN: What kind of nonsense is that? *I* have never had any fear of my superiors. . . .

KURT: Afraid or not, embarrassments will always crop up. . .

THE CAPTAIN: Here on the island, I am the master. Take refuge behind my back, then no one will dare touch you.

ALICE: Now be' quiet, Edgar! *(She takes hold of Kurt's hand.)* Neither superiors nor others are going to keep you from staying with us. It is both fitting and correct that you should.

KURT: Very well, then.—Especially since I find myself so welcome here.

THE CAPTAIN: Why shouldn't you be welcome? There is no dissension between us, is there?
(Kurt shows he is a little embarrassed.)
Why should there be? You were a little careless once, when you were young—but all that has been forgotten. I never hold grudges.
(Alice shows irritation. All three sit down at the sewing table.)

ALICE: Well, you have been travelling far and wide, haven't you, Kurt?

150

KURT: *(To Alice.)* Yes, and now I find refuge with you. . .

THE CAPTAIN: . . . whom you married off twenty-five years ago.

KURT: That isn't the precise truth, but it doesn't matter. I am glad to see that you have stuck together this many years.

THE CAPTAIN: Yes, we have dragged along . . . sometimes only so-so, but nonetheless we have stuck it out. And Alice has no cause to complain. We have had plenty of everything, and no lack of money. Perhaps you don't know that I am now a celebrated author—an author of textbooks. . . .

KURT: Yes, I recall that when we last saw each other you had had a manual of rifle instruction published and told me it had a good sale. Is it still being used in the military schools?

THE CAPTAIN: It is still used and holds its own against a second-rate work which they have tried to substitute for it, and which is totally worthless—but nonetheless finds a market. . .

　　　(There is a painful silence.)

KURT: You have done some travelling abroad, I hear.

ALICE: Oh yes—we have been to Copenhagen five times! Think of it!

THE CAPTAIN: Yes, you see, when I took Alice from the theatre. . . .

ALICE: *(Bitingly.)* Oh, you *took* me, did you?

THE CAPTAIN: Yes, I took you—the way a wife should be taken. . . .

ALICE: How intrepid and gallant you have grown!

THE CAPTAIN: But as my wife soon after hurled the taunt at me that I had meddled with and ruined her brilliant stage career—h'm—I had to make restitution for it by promising to take her to Copenhagen. And this promise I have kept—kept dutifully. We have made five trips there. Five!

　　　(Holds up his hand, the fingers spread apart.)

Have you ever been in Copenhagen?

KURT: *(With a smile.)* No, I have spent most of my time in America.

THE CAPTAIN: America? That must be a horribly uncivilized country, isn't it?

KURT: *(Unpleasantly affected.)* It is not Copenhagen.

ALICE: Have you—have you heard anything of your—your children?

KURT: No.

ALICE: Forgive me, Kurt dear, but wasn't it a little rash of you to leave them the way you did?. . .

KURT: I did not abandon them—they were awarded to the mother by the Court. . .

151

THE CAPTAIN: Let us not bring up that subject now. . . . For my part, I think it was a good thing that you got out of that mess.

KURT: *(To Alice.)* How are *your* children?

ALICE: They are well, thank you. They go to school in the city and will soon be grown up.

THE CAPTAIN: Yes, they are both fine youngsters, and the boy has a brilliant head. Brilliant! He is bound for the General Staff. . .

ALICE: If they'll accept him.

THE CAPTAIN: Accept him? Why, he has the makings of a Minister of War in him!

KURT: From one thing to another—there is to be a quarantine station here—for the plague, cholera, and so forth—and the Doctor, as you know, will be my superior. What sort of man is this doctor?

THE CAPTAIN: Man, you say? He is not a man—he is an illiterate blackguard!

KURT: *(To Alice.)* That makes it very disagreeable for me. . .

ALICE: Oh, he is not as bad as Edgar says, but I can't deny that to me he is anything but sympathetic.

THE CAPTAIN: He is a scoundrel, a scoundrel! And that goes for the rest of them, too,—the customs officer, the postmaster, the female telephone operator, the apothecary, the pilot, the. . . . the—whatever they call it—the alderman—or councilman. . . . they are all scoundrels—everyone of them, and that's why I refuse to have anything to do with them.

KURT: Are you at loggerheads with all of them?

THE CAPTAIN: All of them! All!

ALICE: Yes, it's true—one can't associate with any of these people.

THE CAPTAIN: It is as if all the tyrants in the land had been sent to this island—it's a concentration camp!

ALICE: *(With irony.)* There you speak the truth!

THE CAPTAIN: *(Goodnaturedly.)* H'm. Are you alluding to me, eh? I am no tyrant—at any rate, not in my home. . .

ALICE: You had better not be!

THE CAPTAIN: *(To Kurt.)* Don't believe everything she says. I am a very wellbehaved and reasonable husband, and the old woman here is the best wife in the world.

ALICE: Would you like something to drink, Kurt?

KURT: No, thank you, not just now.

THE CAPTAIN: *(With a touch of sarcasm.)* You haven't turned. . . . Have you?

KURT: Simply a little moderate, that's all.

THE CAPTAIN: The American habit, eh?

KURT: Yes.

THE CAPTAIN: None of that for me! If I can't drink all I want, then I leave it alone. A man should be able to hold his liquor.

KURT: But, to return to our neighbors here on the island. . . . In my position I shall come in contact with them all—and it won't be easy to stay clear of the rocks. No matter how hard you try to avoid entanglements, you can't help being drawn into other people's intrigues.

ALICE: By all means, Kurt, mix freely with them; you will always come back to us, for in us you have your true friends.

KURT: Don't you find it dismal to sit here so aloof—marooned among enemies?

ALICE: It is not pleasant.

THE CAPTAIN: It is not dismal at all. I have had nothing but enemies all my life; and instead of being a hindrance, they have been a help to me. And when my time comes to die, I can truthfully say that I am indebted to no one, and that no one has ever given me anything. Everything I have gained, I have had to fight for.

ALICE: Yes, Edgar's career has been no path of roses. . .

THE CAPTAIN: No—of thorns, and rocks—rocks of flint. . . . By my own strength and stamina—if you know what I mean?

KURT: *(Simply.)* Indeed. I came to recognize my own deficiencies in that respect ten years ago.

THE CAPTAIN: Then you are a weakling.

ALICE: *(To the Captain.)* Edgar!

THE CAPTAIN: Yes, he is a weakling if he is lacking in guts and will-power. It's true, of course, that when the mechanism ceases to function, all that remains of us is a barrowful, to be dumped on some flowerbed in a garden. But while the mechanism functions, you have to kick and fight with hands and feet as long as there is life in you! That's my philosophy.

KURT: *(With a smile.)* Your discourse is entertaining.

THE CAPTAIN: But you don't believe it's really so?

KURT: No, I don't.

153

THE CAPTAIN: Nevertheless it is.

> *(It has commenced to be windy outside during the preceding scene, and suddenly one of the French windows slams shut. The Captain gets up.)*

It's beginning to be windy. I felt it coming.

> *(He goes over and closes the doors, then taps the barometer.)*

ALICE: *(To Kurt.)* You will stay for dinner, won't you?

KURT: Yes, thank you.

ALICE: It'll be very simple—our maid has just left us.

KURT: I am not finicky.

ALICE: You are so easy to please, Kurt dear.

THE CAPTAIN: *(By the barometer.)* If you could only see how the barometer is falling! Yes, I could feel it was coming.

ALICE: *(To Kurt, unobserved by the Captain.)* He is nervous.

THE CAPTAIN: It's about time we had dinner. . . .

ALICE: *(Getting up.)* I am just going out to see about it. You two sit and philosophize.

> *(In an aside to Kurt.)*

Don't contradict him—then he'll be offended and lose his temper. And whatever you do, don't ask him why he hasn't been promoted to major!

> *(Kurt nods understandingly. Alice goes out, left.)*

THE CAPTAIN: *(Seating himself at the sewingtable, near Kurt.)* And see to it that we get something good to eat, old girl.

ALICE: Let me have some money, then, and you'll get your wish.

THE CAPTAIN: *(Handing her some money.)* Forever money. . . .

> *(Alice goes out.)*

Money, money money! From morning till night I go about opening my purse. It has gotten to be such a habit that I have come to imagine myself being a purse. . . . Can you understand how a feeling like that can take hold of you?

KURT: Yes, I can—but with this difference that I fancied myself being a wallet.

THE CAPTAIN: Haha! So you, too, have had your experiences? Ah, these women! Haha! And you certainly picked the right kind, didn't you?

KURT: *(Without rancor.)* No use bringing that up now!

THE CAPTAIN: She was a regular jewel! . . . Well, no matter what you may say, I got myself a *good* woman—for, despite everything, she is honest and reliable.

KURT: *(With a goodnatured smile.)* Despite everything. . . .?

THE CAPTAIN: Don't laugh!

KURT: *(As before.)* Despite everything. . . .

THE CAPTAIN: Yes, she has been a faithful wife—excellent mother —really splendid, but *(Glancing toward the door, left)* she has a diabolical temper. Do you know—there have been times when I have cursed you for harnessing me to her.

KURT: *(Goodnaturedly.)* But I didn't!—Listen to me, Edgar. . . .

THE CAPTAIN: Cha-cha-cha! All you talk is twaddle and you conveniently forget things that are unpleasant to remember. You mustn't be offended—I am accustomed to giving orders and commands and to be blustering. . . . But you know me, and you won't take offense, will you?

KURT: Certainly not. But I did not harness you to your wife—quite the contrary.

THE CAPTAIN: *(Without letting Kurt interrupt him in his tirade.)* Don't you really think life is strange?

KURT: It is, indeed.

THE CAPTAIN: And that we should have to grow old! It is no fun, but it is interesting. . . . I am not really old, yet I am beginning to feel my years. One by one your acquaintances die off, and you are left desolate, companionless.

KURT: The man who can grow old with a woman by his side, is indeed fortunate.

THE CAPTAIN: Fortunate? Yes, it is fortunate—for your children leave you, too. You should never have left your children.

KURT: Yes, but I didn't. They were taken from me.

THE CAPTAIN: You must not be angry when I say this to you.

KURT: But such was not the case!

THE CAPTAIN: Well, whichever way it was, it is all forgotten. But you *are* alone.

KURT: We get used to anything and everything, my dear Edgar.

THE CAPTAIN: Do you think one can. . . . Can one get used also to be—to be completely alone?

KURT: Look at me!

THE CAPTAIN: What have you been doing these fifteen years?

KURT: What a question to ask! These fifteen years. . . .

155

THE CAPTAIN: I hear you have come into money and are rich.

KURT: I am not rich.

THE CAPTAIN: I have no intention of borrowing. . . .

KURT: If you had, I wouldn't refuse you.

THE CAPTAIN: That's very generous of you, but I always try to make both ends meet. You see. . . .

(With a glance toward the door on the left.)

. . . . here in this house there must be no lack of anything; and the day there was no more money—she would leave me!

KURT: Oh no!

THE CAPTAIN: No? Well, I know better!—Will you believe it— whenever I am out of money, that is the time she pounces on me, simply to give her the satisfaction of showing me that I am failing to support my family.

KURT: But I remember you told me you had an ample income.

THE CAPTAIN: So I have—I have a large income; still it is not enough.

KURT: Then it is not really large—generally speaking.

THE CAPTAIN: Life is strange; and so are we. . . .

(The telegraph apparatus starts clicking.)

KURT: What is that?

THE CAPTAIN: Just a routine time signal.

KURT: Have you no telephone?

THE CAPTAIN: Yes, in the kitchen. But *we* use the telegraph because the telephone girls blab everything we say.

KURT: You must lead a dreadful life out here in this community by the sea. . . .

THE CAPTAIN: Yes, it's nothing short of horrible. And life itself is horrible. But you, who believe in a life after this, do you really think you will find peace in the hereafter?

KURT: No doubt we shall have storm and struggle there also.

THE CAPTAIN: There also—if there is a hereafter! But rather than that, annihilation!

KURT: How do you know that annihilation will come without pain?

THE CAPTAIN: When I die, I am going to go like that! *(He snaps his fingers.)* Without any pain!

KURT: Are you so sure of that?

THE CAPTAIN: Yes, I am.

156

KURT: You don't seem to be satisfied with your life?

THE CAPTAIN: *(With a sigh.)* Satisfied? The day I die I shall be satisfied!

KURT: *(Rising.)* That is something you don't know.—But tell me— just what is going on in this house?—What takes place here? There is an odor as if the wallpaper were poisoned; you feel sick the moment you come inside. . . . Had I not promised Alice to stay, I would leave this place without hesitation. There is a corpse buried here—and I feel a hate here so venomous that I can hardly breathe.

> *(The Captain collapses in his chair and stares into space.)*

What is wrong, Edgar?

> *(The Captain remains motionless. Kurt pats him on the shoulder.)*

Edgar!

THF CAPTAIN: *(Recovering somewhat, he glances about.)* Eh? Did you say something? I thought I heard Alice. . . . Oh, it's you? Tell me. . . .

> *(He relapses into insensibility.)*

KURT: This is frightful.

> *(He goes over to the door on the left and opens it.)*

Alice!

ALICE: *(Comes in; she is wearing a kitchen apron.)* What is the matter, Kurt?

KURT: I don't know. . . . Look at him!

ALICE: *(Calmly.)* His mind goes blank like that once in a while.— I'll play something. That will wake him.

> *(She walks over to the piano.)*

KURT: No, no—leave him to me. . . . Can he hear us? Can he see?

ALICE: Just now he can neither hear nor see.

KURT: And you say that so calmly!—Alice, what is going on in this house?

ALICE: Ask him there!

KURT: Him there, you say! Why, he is your husband!

ALICE: To me he is a stranger—as much a stranger as he was twenty-five years ago. I know nothing whatsover about that man other than that. . . .

KURT: Sh! He may hear you. . . .

157

ALICE: He can't hear

> *(The sound of a bugle is heard from without. The Captain leaps to his feet and snatches his sabre and cap.)*

THE CAPTAIN: Excuse me! I have to inspect the guard!

> *(He rushes out through the French doors.)*

KURT: Does he suffer from some illness?

ALICE: I don't know.

KURT: Is he mentally disturbed?

ALICE: I don't know.

KURT: Does he drink?

ALICE: He boasts more about his drinking than actually doing it.

KURT: Sit down and tell me all—but calmly and truthfully.

ALICE: *(Sits down.)* What can I tell you?—that I have spent a lifetime in this tower, this prison, guarded by a man I have always hated, whom I still hate so boundlessly that I would laugh wildly the moment he gave up the ghost.

KURT: Why haven't you divorced him?

ALICE: That's a good question! We broke off our engagement twice—and ever since, we have been trying to get away from each other. But we are welded together and we can't break the link. We did separate once—living apart here in this house—for five years. Now only death can part us—and we know it—and that is why we keep waiting for death as our deliverer.

KURT: Why have you no one you can associate with?

ALICE: Because he keeps me isolated. First he rooted out my brothers and sisters from our home—he used that very word: root out—and after that he did the same to my women friends and others.

KURT: But what about *his* relations? Did *you* remove them?

ALICE: Yes—for after stripping me of my good name and honor, they very nearly robbed me of my life. Finally I was forced to rely upon that telegraph apparatus over there as my only contact with people and the world outside—for the telephone girls listened in and kept us from using that convenience. He is unaware that I have taught myself to tap out messages; and you must not mention it to him. He would kill me if he knew.

KURT: Horrible—horrible!—But why does he reproach me for having married you off to him? Let me tell you how it came about. . . . Edgar and I were childhood friends. The moment he saw you, he fell in love with you. And he came to me and asked me to intercede for him. I promptly refused—I was aware of your domineering and unfeeling nature, dear Alice. And I warned him. But when he nonetheless persisted, I told him to go to your brother and ask him to speak for him.

ALICE: I believe what you say; but since he has been deceiving himself for all these years, you will never get him to believe anything else.

KURT: Well, then let him put the blame on me—if that will ease the pain for him.

ALICE: But that is more than. . . .

KURT: I am used to it. . . . But what *does* wound my feelings is his unjust imputation that I have deserted my children.

ALICE: That is the way he is—he says whatever he feels like saying; and having said it, he believes it. Yet he seems to have an attachment for you, because you don't contradict him. . . . But please try not to get tired of us now! That you should have come at this very time was indeed fortunate for us, a stroke of fate, I believe. . . . Kurt, you must not get tired of us, for in all the world I don't think there are two beings more miserable than we.
    (She weeps.)

KURT: I have seen one marriage at close quarters—and that was appalling! But this is almost worse!

ALICE: Is that what you think?

KURT: Yes.

ALICE: Who is to blame?

KURT: Alice! If you will stop asking who is to blame, it will help to ease your mind. Try to look upon it as a fact, a trial, which must be borne.

ALICE: I can't do it! It is too much to bear! *(She gets up.)* There is no help for it!

KURT: I pity you both!—Do you know why you hate each other?

ALICE: No—it is the most senseless hate—there is no ground for it—completely uncalled for—and there will be no end to it. And do you know why he so vehemently hates to die? He is afraid I'll get married again!

KURT: Then he still loves you.

ALICE: I suppose so. But that doesn't deter him from hating me.

159

KURT: *(As if speaking to himself.)* They call it love-hate, and it stems from the bottom of hell.—Does he derive any pleasure from your playing for him?

ALICE: Yes, but he only likes horrid pieces—such as for instance that ghastly 'The Entry of the Boyars'. Whenever I play that, he starts behaving as though he were possessed and wants to dance.

KURT: He dances?

ALICE: Yes, he acts quite silly at times.

KURT: If you'll forgive me, there is one thing I would like to ask you—where are your children?

ALICE: You don't know, perhaps, that two of them are dead?

KURT: So you have had to suffer that, too?

ALICE: Is there anything I haven't been through?

KURT: But where are the other two children?

ALICE: In the city; I could not have them at home—he incited them against me.

KURT: And you did the same, didn't you?

ALICE: Why, certainly. And so there was partisanship and prejudice— bribes and vote buying; and in order not to corrupt the children we had to send them away. What was to have been a bond uniting us, became instead a sword between us; what was to have been the blessings of a home turned out to be a curse. . . . Yes, there are times when I think there is a curse upon our whole family!

KURT: Yes, ever since the Fall—yes.

ALICE: *(With a venomous glance and sharpness of voice.)* Which fall?

KURT: The parents of mankind.

ALICE: Oh—I thougnt you referred to some other fall! *(There is a moment of silent embarrassment. Alice wrings her hands.)* Kurt! You are my cousin, my childhood friend. . . . I have not always behaved toward you as I should have; but now that you see me receiving my punishment, you have been given your revenge.

KURT: No, no, not revenge! It's not in my nature—no, no!

ALICE: Do you recall one Sunday when you were engaged and I had invited you to dine with us?

KURT: Sh! Sh!

ALICE: No, no, I must speak! Do be lenient with me! . . . When you

160

arrived we were not at home, and you had to turn about and go home.

KURT: You had been invited out yourselves. . . . But why bring all this up now?

ALICE: Kurt! When I just now invited you to stay for dinner, I thought there was enough food in the house. . . . *(She covers her face with her hands.)* . . . but there isn't a thing—not as much as a crust of bread!

KURT: My poor, poor Alice!

ALICE: And now—when he comes home and wants his dinner and finds there isn't any, he'll fly into a rage. You have never seen him in a rage! Oh God, what a humiliating existence!

KURT: Why don't you let me go and straighten out this whole thing?

ALICE: There is nothing to be bought on this island.

KURT: Not for my sake, but for his—and your own sake—let me think up something—something. . . . We must treat the whole matter with levity—we must laugh over it when he comes back. . . . I'll propose that we all have a drink—and in the meantime, I'll get some sort of idea. . . . We'll put him in a good humor—play for him—any kind of trash. . . . You sit down at the piano now and be prepared.

ALICE: Look at my hands! How can I play with such hands? I have to polish the brass, do the dishes, tidy up the house, make the fires, and. . . .

KURT: But you have two servants, haven't you?

ALICE: We have to say we have two because he is an officer—but they are always leaving so that we are sometimes—most of the time—without any. . . . I don't know how to get out of this—this predicament with the dinner? Oh, I wish the house would go up in smoke!

KURT: Alice! Alice! Don't!

ALICE: Or that the sea would roll in and swallow us!

KURT: No, Alice! No, I won't listen to you!

ALICE: What will he say? What will he say? Don't leave me, Kurt, don't leave me!

KURT: My poor Alice! No—I shan't leave you!

ALICE: Yes—but after you have gone. . . .

KURT: Has he ever struck you?

161

ALICE: Struck me? Oh no! Then I would leave him—and he knows it! I hope I have *some* pride left!

> *(From outside can be heard the challenge of the sentry: "Halt! Who goes there?" and the answer: "Friend.")*

KURT: *(Rising.)* Is that he coming?

ALICE: *(Frightened.)* Yes, that's he!

> *(There is a silence.)*

KURT: What in the world shall we do?

ALICE: I don't know—I don't know!

THE CAPTAIN: *(Enters from the rear; he is in a jovial mood.)* Now that's done! Free again! Well, has she had time to weather her troubles, eh? Doesn't she lead a dreadful life, eh?

KURT: How is the weather outside, Edgar?

THE CAPTAIN: Stiff gale! *(Jestingly he opens one of the doors slightly.)* Sir Bluebeard and the maiden in the tower—and outside the sentry paces back and forth with drawn sword, keeping watch over the fair one. And then the brothers arrive. But the sentry is at his post, doing his duty! Look at him! Hip, hip! One, two; one, two! He is on the alert! Look at him! Melitam-tam-ta—melita-lee-ah-li! Let's have the sword dance—I want Kurt to see it!

KURT: No, let's have 'The Entry of the Boyars' instead.

THE CAPTAIN: You know that, do you?—Alice-in-the-kitchen-apron, come and play! Come on, I say! *(Alice goes reluctantly to the piano. The Captain pinches her arm.)* You have been talking about me behind my back, haven't you?

ALICE: I? *(Kurt turns away from him. Alice plays 'The Entry of the Boyars'. The Captain goes into some kind of Hungarian dance, in back of the writing table, to the obligato of jingling spurs. He suddenly collapses and falls in a heap, without being noticed by Kurt and Alice. Alice continues playing and finishes the dance music, after which she—without turning—asks:)* Shall I play it again? *(Silence. Alice turns around and sees the Captain lying unconscious behind the writing table, where he cannot be seen by the audience.)* God in heaven! *(She stands motionless, with arms crossed, and gives a sigh as of relief and gratitude. Kurt turns and sees what has happened, then hurries over to the Captain.)*

KURT: What's the matter? What's the matter?

162

ALICE: *(In an extreme state of tension.)* Is he dead?

KURT: I don't know. Help me!

ALICE: *(Standing still as before.)* I can't touch him. . . . Is he dead?

KURT: No, he is breathing.

> *(Alice gives a sigh. The Captain gets up, aided by Kurt, who places him in a chair.)*

THE CAPTAIN: What's wrong? What is it? *(Silence.)* What is it?

KURT: You fell.

THE CAPTAIN: Well, what of it?

KURT: You fell to the floor! How do you feel now?

THE CAPTAIN: How do I feel? There's nothing wrong with me! Why should there be? Why do you stand staring at me?

KURT: You are not well.

THE CAPTAIN: Stop talking nonsense! Keep on playing, Alice. . . . Oh, now it's coming back again. . . .

> *(His hands go to his head.)*

ALICE: You see—you are ill!

THE CAPTAIN: Stop screaming—it's nothing but a touch of dizziness. . . .

KURT: We must get the Doctor for you. I'll go out to the kitchen and telephone.

THE CAPTAIN: I will have no doctor!

KURT: You must, Edgar! For our own sake, we must call him, or we'll be held responsible.

THE CAPTAIN: I'll kick him out if he comes—I'll shoot him! Oh, it's coming back. . . .

> *(Again his hands go to his head.)*

KURT: *(Goes to the door on the left.)* I'm telephoning this minute. . . .

> *(He goes out. Alice removes her apron.)*

THE CAPTAIN: Will you get me a glass of water?

ALICE: I suppose I have to.

> *(She pours him a glass of water.)*

THE CAPTAIN: *(With irony.)* How tenderhearted you are!

ALICE: Are you sick?

THE CAPTAIN: Forgive me for being indisposed!

ALICE: Will you take care of yourself now?

THE CAPTAIN: I don't suppose you care to look after me.

ALICE: I certainly don't!

THE CAPTAIN: The moment you have been waiting for so long has come. . . .

ALICE: Yes—the moment you thought would never come.

THE CAPTAIN: You mustn't be angry with me.

(Kurt enters from the left.)

KURT: This is an outrage! . . .

ALICE: What did he say?

KURT: He hung up without even answering me!

ALICE: *(To the Captain.)* There you see the consequences of your monstrous arrogance.

THE CAPTAIN: I think I am getting sicker. . . . Try to get the doctor from the city. . . .

ALICE: *(Goes over to the telegraph apparatus.)* We'll have to use the telegraph, then.

THE CAPTAIN: *(Half way getting up out of the chair, in consternation.)* Do—you—do you know—how to use the telegraph?

ALICE: *(Tapping the keys.)* Yes, I do.

THE CAPTAIN: So-o?—Well, go on then. . . . What a false woman! *(To Kurt.)* Come here and sit by me. . . . *(Kurt goes to him.)* Take my hand. Here I am—sitting up—yet I have the sensation of falling—falling. . . . Can you imagine—falling—as from a precipice. . . . Such a strange feeling!

KURT: Have you had similar attacks before?

THE CAPTAIN: Never.

KURT: While we are waiting for an answer from the city, I am going over to see the doctor and have a talk with him.—Has he looked after you before?

THE CAPTAIN: Yes, he has.

KURT: Then he knows your condition?

(He goes toward the right.)

ALICE: *(To Kurt.)* They'll come back with an answer shortly.—You are being awfully nice, Kurt. . . . But don't be away long. . . .

KURT: I'll be back as soon as I can.

THE CAPTAIN: Kurt is nice, isn't he? And hasn't he changed?

ALICE: Yes, and for the better. But I feel sorry that he should be dragged into our misery, just as he has come back.

THE CAPTAIN: But a lucky thing for us!—I wonder how things really are with him. Did you notice how reluctant he was to talk about his own affairs?

164

ALICE: I noticed it, yes; but I don't think anyone asked him about that, anyhow.

THE CAPTAIN: Just think, what a life he has led! And think of ours! I wonder if everybody leads such an existence as we do?

ALICE: Perhaps. But they don't talk about it so much.

THE CAPTAIN: There are times when I think that misery attracts misery and that people who are happy keep away from anything of an unhappy nature. That is why *we* never meet anything but misery.

ALICE: Have you ever known anyone who was really happy?

THE CAPTAIN: I'm trying to think. . . . No. . . . Yes—the Ekmarks.

ALICE: You don't mean it? But the wife was operated on last year!

THE CAPTAIN: Oh yes, I forgot.—Well, then I can't think of anyone. . . . Yes, the von Kraffts!

ALICE: Yes, there is a family which for fifty years lived a truly bucolic life. They were all respected and well off financially, their children were wellbehaved and they married well. And then that cousin of theirs committed a crime and was sent to prison. And that had consequences for the rest of them; for after that, their peaceful existence was at an end. The family name was disgraced in all the newspapers. The Krafft murder case put an end to all their social relationships; this despite the fact that they were once held in the highest esteem. And the children were forced to leave school. . . . Oh God!

THE CAPTAIN: I wonder what my sickness can be?

ALICE: Haven't you any idea?

THE CAPTAIN: It could be the heart, or the head. I feel as if my soul was trying to fly out of my body and go up into a cloud of smoke.

ALICE: How's your appetite?

THE CAPTAIN: Yes—what about dinner?

ALICE: *(Suddenly begins to pace the floor uneasily.)* I'll ask Jenny.

THE CAPTAIN: But she has left.

ALICE: Yes, yes, of course.

THE CAPTAIN: Ring for Kristin—I'd like to have some fresh water.

ALICE: *(Rings.)* Could *she* have. . . . ?
      (She rings again.)

THE CAPTAIN: Go and see. . . . She couldn't have gone, too, could she?

ALICE: *(Goes to the door on the right and opens it.)* What's this?

Her trunk is in the hall—all packed.

THE CAPTAIN: Then she has gone.

ALICE: This is truly hell!

(She bursts into tears, falls to her knees and, with head resting on a chair, sobs.)

THE CAPTAIN: Everything comes at once! And just our luck that Kurt should come and find us in this muddle! If any more humiliations are in store for us, we may as well have them all come at the same time. . . .

ALICE: Do you know—something just strikes me! When Kurt went, he had no intention of coming back. . . .

THE CAPTAIN: That would not surprise me in the least!

ALICE: Yes, we are under a curse!

THE CAPTAIN: Stop talking nonsense!

ALICE: Don't you see how everybody shuns and turns away from us?

THE CAPTAIN: What do I care? *(The telegraph apparatus starts clicking.)* There is your answer now. Quiet, I want to hear. . . . No one can spare the time. . . . Evasions, excuses!—Such rabble!

ALICE: This is what you get for treating your doctors so contemptuously and always ignoring their bills.

THE CAPTAIN: That is not true!

ALICE: Even when you could well afford it, you refused to pay them, because you questioned their competence—just as you looked down upon what I and others did for you.—And now they refuse to come to you. And the telephone has been cut off because you considered it unnecessary. Nothing is worth anything to you except your guns and your rifles!

THE CAPTAIN: Don't stand there talking rubbish!

ALICE: Everything comes back to us. . . .

THE CAPTAIN: What sort of superstition is that? You sound like an old crone.

ALICE: You will see!—We owe Kristin six months' wages—you know that.

THE CAPTAIN: She has stolen that much.

ALICE: And I have had to borrow from her, besides.

THE CAPTAIN: It doesn't surprise me at all!

ALICE: What an ungrateful person you are! You know that I borrowed the money for the children so they could get to the city.

THE CAPTAIN: *(Sarcastically.)* Kurt certainly came back, didn't he?

166

He is another rogue. And he is weak, besides. Didn't have the courage to admit that he had had enough of us here, and that he would have more fun at the Doctor's dance. I suppose he was afraid he would get a poor meal here with us. The scoundrel has really not changed very much.

KURT: *(Enters speedily from the right.)* Now, my dear Edgar, this is how the matter stands. . . . The Doctor knows every nook and cranny of your heart. . . .

THE CAPTAIN: My heart?

KURT: Yes, you have long been suffering from calcification of the heart.

THE CAPTAIN: A stony heart?

KURT: And. . . .

THE CAPTAIN: Is that something serious?

KURT: Well—it is. . . .

THE CAPTAIN: It is serious.

KURT: Yes.

THE CAPTAIN: Fatal?

KURT: You must be careful—very careful! The first thing you have to do is to stop smoking. *(The Captain throws away his cigar.)* And the next thing: no more whiskey. And then, to bed.

THE CAPTAIN: *(Alarmed.)* No—that I won't do—I refuse to go to bed. That would be the end of me! Once put to bed, you never get up. . . . I am going to sleep on the sofa tonight.—What else did he say?

KURT: He acted very friendly, and if you should need him, he will answer your call without delay.

THE CAPTAIN: He was friendly, was he, the hypocrite? I have no wish to see him.—He will let me eat, at least?

KURT: Not tonight. And for the next few days, nothing but milk.

THE CAPTAIN: *(Makes a wry face.)* Milk! I can't stand the taste of it!

KURT: You had better get used to it.

THE CAPTAIN: No, I am too old to learn new tricks! *(His hands go to his head.)* Oh, there it is again. . . .
(He remains sitting in his chair staring into space.)

ALICE: *(To Kurt.)* What did the Doctor say?

KURT: That he may die—without warning.

ALICE: Thank God!

167

KURT: Watch yourself, Alice, watch yourself!—And now—go and get a blanket and pillow. I'm going to put him to bed here on the sofa. And I'll spend the night in that chair.

ALICE: What shall I do?

KURT: You go to bed. It seems to make him worse when you are about.

ALICE: You tell me what to do, and I'll obey, for I know you mean what is best for us both.

(She goes out, right.)

KURT: *(Calling after her as she is leaving.)* Remember—what is best for you both! I am taking no one's side in this. *(Kurt takes the water decanter and goes out, left. Outside the wind is blowing, and suddenly the French doors are blown wide open and an old woman, shabbily dressed and with ugly, horrid features, peeps into the room. The Captain is awakened, sits up, and looks about.)* So-o? They walked out on me, the miserable creatures! *(He catches sight of the old woman and is terrified.)* Who are you? What do you want?

THE OLD WOMAN: I only wanted to close the door, dear sir.

THE CAPTAIN: Why close it? Why close it?

THE OLD WOMAN: Because it blew open just as I was passing.

THE CAPTAIN: You were going to steal, weren't you?

THE OLD WOMAN: Not much to steal here, Kristin tells me.

THE CAPTAIN: Kristin!

THE OLD WOMAN: Good night, sir. Sleep well. . . .

(She goes out, closing the doors after her.—Alice enters from the right, carrying a blanket and pillows.)

THE CAPTAIN: Who was that at the door just now? Was anybody here?

ALICE: It was old Maja from the poorhouse—she was just passing by.

THE CAPTAIN: Are you sure that it was she?

ALICE: Are you afraid?

THE CAPTAIN: I—afraid? Of course not!

ALICE: Since you won't go to bed, lie down here, then.

THE CAPTAIN: *(Goes to the sofa and lies down.)* This is where I want to lie. *(He takes her hand, but she withdraws it. Kurt enters with the water decanter.)* Kurt! Don't leave me!

KURT: I am staying with you all night. Alice is going to bed.

THE CAPTAIN: Goodnight, then, Alice!

ALICE: *(To Kurt.)* Goodnight, Kurt!

(Kurt takes a chair and seats himself close by the Captain.)

KURT: Don't you want to take off your boots, Edgar?

THE CAPTAIN: No! A soldier should always be fully armed and equipped.

KURT: Are you getting ready for a battle, then?

THE CAPTAIN: Perhaps. . . . *(He sits up.)* Kurt! You are the only one I have ever taken into my confidence. I want you to listen to me now.—If I should die tonight—look after my children!

KURT: I promise you that.

THE CAPTAIN: Thank you! I know I can trust you.

KURT: Will you tell me just why you trust me?

THE CAPTAIN: We have not been friends—I put no faith in friendship—and our two families were born enemies and have always been at war. . . .

KURT: And nevertheless you trust me?

THE CAPTAIN: Yes—and I don't know why I do. *(There is a silence.)* Do you think I am going to die?

KURT: You—as all of us. You are not immune.

THE CAPTAIN: Do you feel embittered?

KURT: Yes.—Are you afraid of dying? Of the wheelbarrow and the garden plot?

THE CAPTAIN: But think—if that were not the end?

KURT: Many think not.

THE CAPTAIN: And what then?

KURT: Perhaps wonder without end. . . .

THE CAPTAIN: But we have no conclusive knowledge of that.

KURT: No. that's just it! And so we have to be prepared for anything.

THE CAPTAIN: You are not childish enough to believe in a hell?

KURT: Don't you—who are living in one?

THE CAPTAIN: That's only in a figurative sense.

KURT: Your description of your own hell was realistic enough to exclude any thought of being metaphorical, whether poetic or otherwise.

(Silence.)

THE CAPTAIN: If you only knew what agony I am going through?

KURT: Physical pain?

THE CAPTAIN: No—not physical.

169

KURT: Then I suppose your misery is mental or spiritual—there could be no other.

(Silence.)

THE CAPTAIN: (Sits up suddenly.) I don't want to die!

KURT: A moment ago you were asking to be blotted out of existence.

THE CAPTAIN: Yes—if there were no pain. . . .

KURT: But it doesn't seem to be painless, does it?

THE CAPTAIN: Is this the end then?

KURT: The beginning of the end. . . .

THE CAPTAIN: Goodnight!

KURT: Goodnight!

END OF SCENE 1

ACT I: SCENE 2

The setting is the same as in Scene 1.

The lamp is flickering out. Through the windows and the glass panes in the French windows, Center, can be seen the overcast sky, and the sea in motion. A sentry is doing guard duty at the battery emplacements, as in the preceding scene.

The Captain is lying on the sofa, asleep. Kurt is sitting in his chair near the sofa. He looks pale and weary from lack of sleep.

ALICE: (Enters from the right.) Is he sleeping?

KURT: Yes, from the time the sun was due to rise.

ALICE: What kind of night did he have?

KURT: He slept in fits and starts but kept talking continually.

ALICE: About what?

KURT: He kept arguing about religion like a schoolboy; and at the same time claimed to have solved the riddle of the universe. Finally, toward morning, he had discovered the immortality of the soul.

ALICE: For his own glory!

KURT: Precisely. He is actually the most overbearing and self-opiniated person I have ever met. "I exist, therefore God must exist."

ALICE: Now you see, don't you. . . . Look at his boots! With them he would have trampled the earth flat, if he had had his way; with them he has trampled other people's fields and flowerbeds; with them he has trampled on people's toes, and on my nerves, my spirit. . . . Voracious bear! At last you have been given your deathblow!

KURT: He would have been comic had he not been so tragic; yet even in his pettiness, there is a touch of grandeur. Isn't there a single kind word you can say about him, Alice?

ALICE: *(Sits down.)* Yes—if only he doesn't hear it; for if one has one word of praise for him, he at once becomes madly overweening. *(With a nervous glance at the Captain.)*

KURT: *(Reassuring.)* He can't hear a word we say; he has been given morphine.

ALICE: Edgar was reared in a poor home. He had many brothers and sisters. In his youth he had to support the family by tutoring because his father was a good-for-nothing, or even worse. It must be hard for a young man to have to give up all the pleasures of youth and have to slave for a lot of ungrateful children whom he has not brought into the world. I was a little girl when I first saw him—he was already a young man then—going about without overcoat in the cold of winter, with the thermometer at 25° Centigrade—while his small sisters were wearing duffel coats. That was generous of him, and I admired him for it, even though I was repelled by his ugly face. Don't you think he is exceptionally ugly?

KURT: Yes, there is something repulsive about his ugliness, as you say. I noticed it particularly every time there was a break in our friendship; and when we were separated from each other, his image grew, took on hideous and formidable proportions, and he actually haunted me.

ALICE: Then think of me!—But his first three years as an officer were unquestionably a painful, difficult trial for him, although he from time to time received help from some rich benefactors. However, he would never acknowledge this, and he accepted everything he could get hold of as if it were due him—and without ever offering a word of thanks in return.

KURT: We were to speak well of him, weren't we?

ALICE: After he is dead, yes. Well, I can't remember anything more now. . . .

171

KURT: Have you found him ill-natured, spiteful?

ALICE: Yes—and still he can be both kind and overemotionally tender.—As an enemy he is absolutely horrible.

KURT: Why has he never been promoted to major?

ALICE: You ought to understand that yourself. Nobody wants to have a man like him as a superior, a man who—already as a subaltern—was a tyrant. But never breathe a word about that to him. He himself says he has no desire to be a major.—Did he say anything about the children to you?

KURT: Yes, he wished he could see Judith.

ALICE: I can well understand that. Do you know what Judith is like? She is his image—and he has trained her to agitate and hound and pester me. Imagine it—my own daughter—my own daughter has raised her hand against me.

KURT: Oh no! That's a little too much!

ALICE: Sh! I see him moving. . . . Just think, if he has heard what we said. . . . He is crafty, you know. . . .

KURT: *(In a subdued voice.)* He does seem to be awake.

ALICE: Doesn't he look like a troll? He frightens me!
    (There is a silence.)

THE CAPTAIN: *(Stirring, he wakes and sits up, then looks around.)* It's morning—at last!

KURT: How do you feel now?

THE CAPTAIN: Badly.

KURT: Would you like to have the Doctor?

THE CAPTAIN: No—I want to see Judith—my child!

KURT: Wouldn't it be advisable to adjust your family affairs before you . . . in case something should happen?

THE CAPTAIN: What do you mean? What could happen?

KURT: That which happens to all of us. . . .

THE CAPTAIN: What nonsense! I shan't die as quickly as you think, so don't gloat prematurely, Alice.

KURT: Think of your children, Edgar! Make your will so that your wife will at least have the furniture.

THE CAPTAIN: Is she to inherit it while I am alive?

KURT: No—but if anything were to happen, she should not have to be thrown out of house and home. Anyone who for twenty-five years has dusted and polished the furniture and kept the house in order, should be entitled to keep it.—Will you let me call the judge advocate?

THE CAPTAIN: No!

KURT: You are a cruel husband, more cruel than I thought!

THE CAPTAIN: *(Collapses without warning and falls backward on the sofa.)* It's coming back again. . . .

> *(He loses consciousness.)*

ALICE: *(Walking toward the door, left.)* I hear someone in the kitchen—I have to go out there.

KURT: By all means—there is not much you can do here. *(She goes out.)*

THE CAPTAIN: *(Regaining consciousness.)* Well, Kurt, what are your plans for the quarantine station here?

KURT: Oh, everything will work out satisfactorily, I am sure.

THE CAPTAIN: Yes, but don't forget that I am in command on this island, and you will have to deal with me.

KURT: Have you ever seen a quarantine station?

THE CAPTAIN: Have I? Certainly, before you were born. And let me give you a piece of advice. Don't place the disinfecting-ovens too near the shore.

KURT: I was of the opinion that proximity to the sea would be the most favorable location.

THE CAPTAIN: That shows how much you know about it. Don't you know that water is the favorite element of bacilli—the element that gives them life?

KURT: But the salt water of the sea is essential for washing away impurities.

THE CAPTAIN: Idiot!—Well, now that you are set in your quarters, you must bring your children here.

KURT: Do you think they will yield to my entreaties?

THE CAPTAIN: Of course, if you have any kind of backbone. You would make a good impression on your associates here if they saw that you fulfilled your duties in that respect, too. . . .

KURT: I have always fulfilled my duties in that respect.

THE CAPTAIN: *(His voice growing loud.)* . . . in that respect—for it is there that you have been most neglectful.

KURT: But I have told you. . . .

THE CAPTAIN: *(Interrupting and persisting in his badgering.)* For a father does not desert his children that way. . . .

KURT: Keep right on!

THE CAPTAIN: As a relative of yours—who is also your elder—I feel I have a right and duty to speak out, even if the truth is painful to hear. And you should not be offended.

KURT: Are you hungry?

THE CAPTAIN: Yes, I am.

KURT: Would you like something light?

THE CAPTAIN: No, I want something substantial.

KURT: That would put an end to you.

THE CAPTAIN: Isn't it enough that I am sick; must I starve, too?

KURT: That's how it has to be.

THE CAPTAIN: Not even a drink—and can't smoke! Then life is not worth living. . . .

KURT: Death has to have his sacrifices, or he'll be ready with his scythe.

(Alice enters with several bouquets of flowers, a few telegrams and letters. She throws the flowers on the table.)

ALICE: These are for you.

THE CAPTAIN: *(Flattered.)* For me? Let me see!

ALICE: They are only from the non-commissioned officers, from the band, and the artillerymen.

THE CAPTAIN: You are envious.

ALICE: Anything but that! Had they sent you a laurel wreath—that would have been a different matter. But they would never give you one of those.

THE CAPTAIN: H'm. Here is a telegram from the Colonel. You read it, Kurt. . . . I must admit he is a gentleman, no matter what you say. . . . even if he is a bit of an idiot.—Here is one from. . . . what does it say? It's from Judith. . . . Telegraph her, please, and ask her to come out by the next boat.—And this—well, I see I am not entirely without friends, and it pleases me that they give me a thought when I am sick; after all, I think I deserve it, being a man without fear or favor, and far superior to his rank. . . .

ALICE: I don't quite understand—are they congratulating you because you are sick?

THE CAPTAIN: Hyena!

ALICE: *(To Kurt.)* You know, we had a medical officer here on the island who was so disliked that when he was leaving, he was given a banquet. But it was not a farewell affair in the usual sense; it was given in celebration of his departure!

174

THE CAPTAIN: Put the flowers in vases. . . . I don't think anyone can accuse me of being gullible—and people are all a lot of riff-raff—but, by God, these simple tributes can be nothing but heartfelt!

ALICE: Ass!

KURT: *(Reading one of the telegrams.)* Judith says she cannot come. The steamboat isn't running because of the storm.

THE CAPTAIN: Is that all?

KURT: Well, no—there is something else.

THE CAPTAIN: Out with it!

KURT: Well, she begs her father not to drink so much.

THE CAPTAIN: What impudence!—And that from my children—my own beloved daughter—my Judith, the apple of my eye!

ALICE: The image of you!

THE CAPTAIN: That is life for you! And the sweetest of its blessings! To hell with it!

ALICE: Now you are reaping the harvest of what you have sowed. You set her against her mother, and now she turns against her father. . . . Now tell me there isn't a God!

THE CAPTAIN: *(To Kurt.)* What does the Colonel have to say?

KURT: He grants you leave of absence—that's all he says.

THE CAPTAIN: Leave of absence? I have asked for no leave of absence. . . .

ALICE: But I have.

THE CAPTAIN: I refuse to accept it.

ALICE: The order has already been issued.

THE CAPTAIN: That's none of my concern!

ALICE: You see, Kurt, that for this man no laws exist—neither constitutional nor statutory, nor any prescribed authority. He is a law unto himself, above everything and everybody—the universe was created for his personal convenience and advantage —the sun and the moon exist merely that their rays may carry his praises to the stars. That is the kind of man my husband is! The insignificant captain who could not even rise to the rank of major; at whose pomposity everybody snickers, while *he* thinks that they hold him in awe—this petty creature who is afraid of the dark and whose faith is centered in the high and low of the barometer—all this, in addition to, and as a final curtain: a barrowful of manure—and not of the best brand either.

175

(All through this scene the Captain has been fanning himself with a bouquet of flowers with evident self-complacency and conceit, and without paying any attention to what Alice is saying.)

THE CAPTAIN: Have you invited Kurt to have some breakfast?

ALICE: No.

THE CAPTAIN: Then fix us at once two steaks—two succulent Chateaubriands.

ALICE: Two?

THE CAPTAIN: I am having one myself.

ALICE: But we are three here!

THE CAPTAIN: Are you having one, too? Very well, then—three.

ALICE: But where am I to get them? Last evening you invited Kurt to have supper with us, and we didn't have so much as a piece of bread in the house. Kurt has been up all night, watching over you, and hasn't had a bite to eat; he hasn't even had a cup of coffee, because none is left, and our credit is gone.

THE CAPTAIN: *(To Kurt.)* She is angry with me because I didn't die last night. . . .

ALICE: No, because you didn't die twenty-five years ago—because you did not die before I was born.

THE CAPTAIN: *(To Kurt.)* Listen to her! There you see what happens when you bring two persons together in marriage, my dear Kurt! One thing is certain: our marriage was not made in heaven. *(Alice and Kurt exchange meaningful glances. The Captain gets up and walks toward the doors, Center.)* However, you may say what you like, now I am going on duty. *(He puts on an old fashioned artillery helmet with a plume, girds on his sabre, and then puts on his cloak. Alice and Kurt try vainly to prevent him from going out.)* Out of my way!

(He goes outside.)

ALICE: Yes, go! You always do—always turn tail and beat a retreat when the battle goes against you; and then you let your wife lead you to safety, you drinking-hero, you braggart among braggarts, you archliar! Phew!

KURT: This is a bottomless hell!

ALICE: Oh, but you don't know it all yet. . . .

KURT: Is there still more?

ALICE: Oh, I feel ashamed!

176

KURT: Where is he going now? And how can he have the strength?

ALICE: You may well ask. Now, of course, he is going over to the non-commissioned officers to thank them for the flowers—and then he will eat and drink with them. And then he'll malign his fellow-officers. . . . If you only knew how many times he has been threatened with dismissal—only regard for his family has kept him from being dismissed. And yet he conceitedly thinks it is out of fear of his superiority. And those poor officers' wives who have taken our part he both hates and slanders.

KURT: I must confess that I applied for this post hoping to find some peace out here by the sea. I knew nothing about your circumstances or the strained relations between you.

ALICE: Poor Kurt! How will you now get something to eat?

KURT: Oh, I can go over to the Doctor's; but how about you? Do let me see about something for you. . . .

ALICE: Don't mention anything to him, however, for then he would kill me.

KURT: *(Looking out through the French windows.)* Look, there he stands on the rampart—the wind whirling about him.

ALICE: What a pity that he behaves the way he does.

KURT: You are both to be pitied. But what can you do about it?

ALICE: I have no idea. We received a stack of bills this morning— but he didn't see those.

KURT: Sometimes it is better not to see. . . .

ALICE: *(At the window.)* His cloak is wide open and the wind is beating on his chest. . . . He evidently wants to die.

KURT: I don't think he does. Only a moment ago, when he felt his life ebbing, he hooked on to me and started to meddle in my personal affairs as though he were about to crawl into me and live my life for me.

ALICE: That is his vampire nature manifesting itself—laying hold of other people's fates, sucking interest out of other people's lives, regulating and managing the affairs of others, because his own life is so completely lacking in interest. And remember, Kurt, never allow him to be part of your family life and let him never meet your friends, for he will steal them from you and monopolize them. He is nothing short of a wizard when it comes to that. And if he were to meet your children, it wouldn't be long before you found them on most intimate terms with him;

177

he would advise them and bring them up according to his ideas and, most important, contrary to yours.

KURT: Alice, tell me—was it he who took my children away from me at the time of the divorce?

ALICE: Now that it is all over—yes, it was he.

KURT: I have suspected it, but wasn't sure. So it *was* he, then!

ALICE: When you—with full confidence in my husband—sent him as peacemaker to your wife, he started a flirtation with her and showed her the trick whereby she obtained the custody of the children.

KURT: Oh God! God in heaven!

ALICE: There you have another side of him you didn't know.

(Silence.)

KURT: Can you imagine that last night, when he thought he was dying, he—he made me promise to look after his children?

ALICE: You are not going to take out your revenge on my children?

KURT: By keeping my promise? Yes! I shall look after your children.

ALICE: You couldn't take a more stinging revenge, for there is nothing he abhors more than nobility of mind, and magnanimity.

KURT: In that case, I may consider myself revenged—without taking it.

ALICE: I take a passionate delight in revenge as a means of justice, and I revel in seeing evil get its just punishment.

KURT: You are still harping on that!

ALICE: And always shall! If you should ever hear me say I forgave, or loved, an enemy, I would be a hypocrite.

KURT: Alice—there are times when it may be a duty not to tell everything, not to see everything. This is what we call tolerance, or forbearance. It is something we all need.

ALICE: Not I! My life is an open book, and I have always played the game fairly.

KURT: That's saying a good deal.

ALICE: Yet not enough. What I have suffered innocently because of this man—whom I have never loved. . . .

KURT: Why did you marry him?

ALICE: That is the question.—Because he took me—seduced me. . . . I don't know . . . and then I wanted to advance myself socially. . . .

KURT: And so you gave up your stage career.

ALICE: Which he looked down upon. . . . But, you see, he deceived

178

me. He held out to me the alluring prospect of a genial, cheerful life—a beautiful home—and he turned out to be over head and ears in debt. The only gold he possessed was the uniform buttons—and even they were mere imitation. He tricked me!

KURT: Wait a moment! When a young man falls in love, he looks to the future with great expectations. . . . That his hopes are not always realized, we must not hold against him. I myself have the same kind of deceit on my conscience—yet I do not consider myself perfidious or lacking in integrity. *(To Alice, who is looking out of the French windows.)* What do you see out there on the rampart?

ALICE: I am looking to see if he has fallen.

KURT: Has he fallen?

ALICE: No, unfortunately. He always fools me.

KURT: Well, I'm going over to the Doctor now, and to the judge advocate.

ALICE: *(Seating herself by the window.)* Yes, you do that, Kurt dear. I'll wait here. That's something I have learned—to wait. . . .

—END OF ACT I—

THE DANCE OF DEATH
Part I

ACT II, SCENE 1

The setting is the same as in Act I.

It is daylight—The sentry on guard duty at the battery paces back and forth.

Alice is seated in the armchair, left. She has now turned gray.

Kurt enters from the right, after having first knocked.

KURT: How-do-you-do, Alice?

ALICE: How-do-you-do, Kurt dear. Sit down.

KURT: *(Seating himself in the armchair, right.)* The steamboat is just arriving.

ALICE: Then I know what we can expect, if he is on board.

KURT: Yes, he's on board—I saw his helmet gleaming in the sun.— What has he been doing in the city?

ALICE: I have a good idea of that. Because he was dressed in parade uniform, he must have gone to see the Colonel; and since he wore a pair of fresh gloves, he must have paid some visits in town.

KURT: Did you notice how quiet he was all day yesterday? Ever since he gave up drinking, and eats with moderation, he is a different person: quiet, reserved, and considerate.

ALICE: I know the symptons! If that man had always stayed sober, he would have been a menace to humanity. Perhaps it is fortunate that he has made himself ridiculous, and so innocuous through his drinking.

KURT: The spirits in the bottle have punished him!—But have you noticed that since death has put its mark on him, he has acquired a semblance of sublime dignity. It is not impossible that he— with the recently awakened thought of immortality germinating in him—has come to have a different view of life.

ALICE: You are deceiving yourself! His intentions are evil. And do

180

not believe him, for he lies deliberately; and he knows the art of intrigue as no one.

KURT: *(Regarding Alice.)* Alice! What do I see? In these two nights your hair has turned gray.

ALICE: No, my friend, it's been gray for years. But now that my husband is practically dead for me, I have stopped tinting. Walled in for twenty-five years in a prison!—Do you know that this fort was used as a prison in olden days?

KURT: A prison. . . . I can tell from the look of the walls.

ALICE: And from my complexion! Even the children developed prison-pallor in this house.

KURT: I can't imagine little children prattling within these walls.

ALICE: You seldom heard any prattling. And the two who died, they faded away for lack of light.

KURT: What do you think will happen next?

ALICE: The decisive attack on us two. When you read that telegram from Judith, I saw a glimmer in his eye—an expression I know only too well. It was, of course, intended for her, but—as you know—she is sacred to him, and so he vented his ire on you instead.

KURT: What can he do to me, do you think?

ALICE: That's hard to say. But he has a phenomenal talent—in addition to luck—for snooping out other people's secrets. And you couldn't have helped noticing how he, all through the day, almost lived in your quarantine station—how he gobbled up interest in life from you—and how he devoured your children alive. . . . I know him too well, you see, this man-eater! His own life is almost at an end—practically gone. . . .

KURT: I have the same feeling—that he is already on the other side. . . . His face sort of phosphoresces—as if he were in a state of dissolution—and his eyes glimmer and flicker like will-o'-the-wisps over marsh and grave.—Here he comes. . . . Tell me—has it ever occurred to you that he might be jealous?

ALICE: Oh no, he is much too conceited for that! "Show me a man of whom I would have to be jealous!" Those are his own words.

KURT: So much the better; even his faults can be used to our advantage, then.—Shall I get up and greet him—what do you think?

ALICE: No, be discourteous to him, or he will think we are deceitful. And when he starts telling his lies, act as though you believed

181

him. I am an expert at translating them, and—with the aid of my dictionary—I always manage to get at the truth. . . . I sense something sinister is afoot—but, Kurt, don't lose your equanimity. In the long struggle between us, my one advantage has been the fact that I was always sober and therefore never lost my self-control. Whiskey was his downfall. Well, now we'll see. . . .

> *(The Captain enters from the right, dressed in parade uniform with helmet, cloak and white gloves. He is calm, but pale and holloweyed, and carries himself with dignity. As he walks, he stumbles, and seats himself at the extreme left, at a distance from Kurt and Alice. Throughout the ensuing scene he rests his sabre between his knees.)*

THE CAPTAIN: Howdoyoudo.—Pardon me for sitting down like this, but I am a little tired.

ALICE AND KURT: Howdoyoudo. And welcome back.

ALICE: How are you feeling?

THE CAPTAIN: Splendidly. But a little tired.

ALICE: What news from the city?

THE CAPTAIN: Oh, one thing and another. I saw the doctor, among others, and he said nothing was wrong with me and that I could live another twenty years if I took care of myself.

ALICE: *(To Kurt, in a low tone of voice.)* Now he is lying. *(To the Captain.)* That's good to hear, Edgar dear.

THE CAPTAIN: Yes, it was.

> *(There is a silence, during which the Captain keeps looking at Alice and Kurt as if he were imploring them to say something.)*

ALICE: *(To Kurt.)* Don't say anything—let him speak first; then he'll show his cards.

THE CAPTAIN: *(To Alice.)* Did you say something?

ALICE: No, I didn't say anything.

THE CAPTAIN: *(Deliberately.)* Listen, Kurt. . . .

ALICE: *(To Kurt.)* Here it comes. You'll see. . . .

THE CAPTAIN: I—I have been in the city, as you know. . . . *(Kurt nods an acknowledgment.)* And—h'm—I—I made some acquaintances . . . among others, with a young cadet officer . . . *(Lingering.)* . . . in the artillery. *(There is a pause, during which Kurt is beginning to show uneasiness.)* And since . . . since we

are particularly in need of cadet officers here, I am arranging
with the Colonel to have him assigned here. . . . That ought to
gratify you, especially when I inform you that the young man—
is—your own son.

ALICE: *(To Kurt.)* There you see—the vampire!

KURT: Under ordinary circumstances this would be pleasing news
to a father, but in my case it is only distressing.

THE CAPTAIN: I don't see why it should be.

KURT: You don't need to—it's enough that I oppose it.

THE CAPTAIN: So-o, that's how you feel about it, eh? Then I must
tell you that the young man has already been ordered to report
here and that from now on he is under my command.

KURT: In that case, I shall force him to apply for transfer to another
regiment.

THE CAPTAIN: You can't do that—you have no rights over your son.

KURT: Haven't I?

THE CAPTAIN: No, the Court awarded all rights to the mother.

KURT: Then I'll get in touch with her.

THE CAPTAIN: You don't need to.

KURT: Don't need to?

THE CAPTAIN: No, for I have already seen her. Cha!

    (Kurt gets up but sinks back into his chair.)

ALICE: *(To Kurt.)* This is his death-doom!

KURT: Yes, he is a man-eater! That's what he is!

THE CAPTAIN: Well, that was that! *(Facing Alice and Kurt.)* Did
you say anything, eh?

ALICE: No. Don't you hear well?

THE CAPTAIN: No—not too well—not always. . . . But if you will
come a little closer, I have something to tell you—in strictest
confidence. . . .

ALICE: No need for that! And it may be of advantage to both parties
to have a witness.

THE CAPTAIN: You are quite right—it's always a good thing to have
witnesses. . . . But, first of all, did you receive the will—is it
ready?

ALICE: *(Hands him a document.)* The Judge Advocate has drawn it
up himself.

THE CAPTAIN: In your favor. Good. *(He glances over the document,
tears it carefully into strips, which he throws on the floor.)*

183

That was that! Cha!

ALICE: *(To Kurt.)* Have you ever seen a human creature like him?

KURT: He is not human!

THE CAPTAIN: Oh yes—there was something I wanted to say to Alice. . . .

ALICE: *(Uneasily, yet somewhat ironically.)* By all means!

THE CAPTAIN: *(Cool and unruffled as before.)* On account of your frequently expressed desire to put an end to this miserable life, this unhappy marriage, and because of the heartlessness with which you have treated your husband and children, and the carelessness you have displayed in handling the household affairs, I have now—during my trip to the city—filed an application for divorce in the Municipal Court.

ALICE: So-o? And on what grounds?

THE CAPTAIN: *(Cooly as before.)* Besides the grounds I just mentioned, I have others of a purely personal nature. As I have now learned that I can expect to live another twenty years, I am thinking of exchanging this miserable marriage of ours for one that suits me better and is more becoming to my rank, and to join my destiny with that of some woman who can bring youth and, let us say, a semblance of beauty into the home, in addition to devotion.

ALICE: *(Takes off her wedding ring and throws it at the Captain.)* There you have my answer!

THE CAPTAIN: *(Picks up the ring and pockets it in his waistcoat.)* She threw away her wedding ring. The witness will please note this!

ALICE: *(Rises in agitation.)* So it is your intention to throw me out and put another woman in my place?

THE CAPTAIN: Cha!

ALICE: If that's the case, then let us not mince words! Cousin Kurt, this man is guilty of attempted murder on his wife!

KURT: Murder?

ALICE: Yes—he pushed me into the sea!

THE CAPTAIN: *Without* witnesses!

ALICE: Another lie! Judith saw it!

THE CAPTAIN: What if she did!

ALICE: She can testify!

THE CAPTAIN: Oh no, she can't. She saw nothing, she says.

184

ALICE: You have taught her to lie.

THE CAPTAIN: I didn't have to—you taught her that.

ALICE: Have you seen Judith?

THE CAPTAIN: Cha!

ALICE: Oh God! Oh God!

THE CAPTAIN: The fortress surrenders. The enemy will be granted ten minutes to withdraw and march off at liberty. *(He puts his watch on the table.)* Ten minutes! The time is ticking!

> *(He remains standing; his hand suddenly goes to his head.)*

ALICE: *(Goes to him and grasps him by the arm.)* What's the matter?

THE CAPTAIN: I don't know. . . .

ALICE: Is there anything I can bring you? Would you like something to drink?

THE CAPTAIN: Whiskey? No—I don't want to die!—So it's you! *(He pulls himself together and straightens up.)* Don't touch me! —Ten minutes—or the garrison will be struck down! *(With partly drawn sabre.)* Ten minutes!

> *(He goes out, rear.)*

KURT: What specimen of man is this?

ALICE: He's a demon—not a human being!

KURT: What does he want of my son?

ALICE: He wants him as a hostage so that he can dominate you; his plan is to isolate you from the authorities on the island.—Do you know that the natives here call this island "the little hell"?

KURT: I hadn't heard that. . . . Alice, you are the first woman to stir me to compassion. . . . All the others I felt deserved their fate.

ALICE: Don't desert me now! Don't leave me—he would strike me. . . . He has threatened to do that for twenty-five years—and in the presence of the children—he has pushed me into the sea. . . .

KURT: When I heard that, I had no more use for the man! I came here without harboring any rankling over his past humiliations. I even forgave him after you had told me that it was he who was responsible for my children being taken from me. I forgave him because he was ill and dying; but when he now wants to take my son from me—he must die! It is either he—or I!

ALICE: You are right! Don't give up the fortress. . . . Even if we have to blow it up, and him with it, with us two keeping him company. I'll handle the powder-keg!

KURT: When I came here, I had no rancor in me, yet I felt like

185

leaving, when I sensed that your hate was contaminating me.
But now I feel an irrepressible urge to hate this man as deeply
as I have always hated all evilness.—What can we do now?

ALICE: I have learned the tactics from him: drum up his enemies
and let us find allies.

KURT: To think that he could ferret out my wife! Why couldn't
these two have met a generation ago! There would have been
conflict enough to make the earth tremble!

ALICE: But now that their two souls have met . . . they must be torn
apart! I believe I know where he is most vulnerable—I have
long had my suspicions. . . .

KURT: Who is his most obdurate enemy on the island?

ALICE: The ordinance officer.

KURT: Is he an honorable man?

ALICE: Yes, he is. And he knows what I—what I know, too. He
knows what intrigues the sergeant major and the Captain have
been up to.

KURT: What have they been up to? You don't mean that. . . .

ALICE: Embezzlement!

KURT: That is disgraceful!—No, I refuse to have anything to do
with that!

ALICE: Ha, ha! You mean you refuse to strike down an enemy?

KURT: There was a time when I could. I can't any more.

ALICE: Why?

KURT: Because I have learned—that in the end justice prevails.

ALICE: But in the meantime your son will be taken from you! Look
at my gray hair—if you feel it, you will see it is still thick!—
He intends to marry another, and then I am free—to do the
same.—I'll be free again! And in ten minutes he shall be under
arrest—down below—in the dungeon. . . . *(She stamps on the
floor.)* . . . down in the dungeon . . . and I shall dance on his
head—I shall dance to the tune of 'The Entry of the Boyars'. . . .
(She takes a few steps, dancing with her hands on her hips.)
Hahahaha! I shall hammer on the piano so that he will hear!
(She bangs on the piano.) Oh! The fortress gates shall open
and the sentry with drawn sabre will no longer be guarding me,
but him . . . Meli-tam-tam-ta—meli-tah-lee- ah-li! He shall be
guarding him—him—him!

KURT: *(Looking at her, bewitched.)* Alice! Are you, too, a demon?

ALICE: *(Jumps up on a chair and pulls down the laurel wreaths.)* I am going to take these with me when I march off. . . . The laurels of triumph with their fluttering ribbons. . . . A trifle dusty, but eternally green—like my youth. . . . I am not so old, am I, Kurt?

KURT: *(his eyes gleaming.)* You are a demon!

ALICE: In 'little hell'!—And now I am going to get dressed. . . *(She takes down her hair.)* I'll be ready in two minutes—it will take me two minutes to get to the ordinance officer—and then . . . then up goes the fortress! Up in the air!

KURT: *(As before.)* You are a demon!

ALICE: You used to call me that when we were children also. Do you remember when we were children and said we were engaged? Do you? *(She laughs.)* You were bashful, as always.

KURT: *(In a serious tone.)* Alice!

ALICE: Yes, you were—and it was becoming to you. You know, there are rude women who like timid, bashful men—just as you may find shy men who are partial to rude, overpowering women.— I imagine you sort of liked me then? Didn't you?

KURT: I don't know—I am lost. . . .

ALICE: You are not lost—you are with me, an actress with uninhibited views, but who nonetheless is an exemplary woman. Yes, indeed! And now I am free—free—free! Now—if you will turn your back to me, I'll just change this shirtwaist. . . .

> *(She unbuttons her shirtwaist. Kurt rushes up to her and embraces her, then lifts her high in the air. Biting her neck, he causes her to cry out. Then he throws her down on the sofa and runs out, right.)*

—END OF SCENE 1—

ACT II, SCENE 2

The same setting. It is now evening.

The sentry at the battery emplacements can still be observed through the French window panes. The laurel wreaths are hung over the arms of a chair. The ceiling lamp is lighted. Faint music is heard from the outside. The Captain, pale and hollow-eyed, his hair

187

iron-gray, is seated at the writing table, playing solitaire. He is wearing spectacles, and is dressed in a worn fatigue uniform and riding boots.

The entr'acte music continues after the rise of the curtain until the next character appears on the stage.

The Captain lays out the cards; occasionally he gives a start, his face twitching, looks up and listens anxiously.

He seems to have difficulty making the cards come out, grows impatient, and puts away the deck, walks over to the window on the right, opens the door and flings the pack of cards outside. He leaves the door open; and one can hear it rattling on its hinges.

He goes over to the cabinet, but is frightened by the sound of the creaking, rattling door; he turns to see what causes the sound, and then takes out three square, dark-colored whiskey bottles, regards them hesitatingly and then throws them out of the door. Similarly he takes out several boxes of cigars, opens one and sniffs of it, then throws them all outside.

This done, he takes off his spectacles, wipes them and puts them on again to see whether they improve his sight; and then they are tossed out the same way as the other things. He stumbles against the furniture as if half-blind and lights the six candles in the candelabrum on the chest of drawers. When he notices the laurel wreaths on the armchair, he snatches them up and is about to throw them out of the window also, but changes his mind and walks to the piano. He takes off the piano cover, folds it carefully round the wreaths, fastening the corners together with pins which he picks up on the writing table; and then he places them on a chair. After that, he goes back to the piano, hammers on the keys with his fist, slams down the lid and locks it, whereupon he throws the key out of the French window. He then lights the candles on the piano, walks over to the whatnot, takes his wife's photograph from it, gazes at it and tears it into pieces, which he scatters on the floor. The door shakes and rattles, and again he is frightened.

Having regained his poise, he takes the portraits of his son and daughter, gives them a fleeting kiss and puts them in his breast pocket. The rest of the portraits he sweeps off with his elbow and, with his boot, kicks them into a pile on the floor.

Wearied, he then sits down at the writing table, his hand going to his heart. He lights the reading lamp, sighs, and stares into space as if he were having a horrible vision. He rises and goes over to the bureau-desk, opens the lid and takes out a bundle of letters, tied with a blue silk ribbon, and throws it into the stove, after which he closes the lid of the bureau-desk.

The telegraph apparatus clicks once, after which there is silence. The Captain shrinks in deadly terror and remains standing, clutching at his heart, and listening. As there is no further sound from the apparatus, he turns his ear in the direction of the door on the right and then goes over and opens it, takes a step across the threshhold and comes back, carrying on his arm a cat, which he strokes. Then he goes out, left, and the music ceases.

> *(Alice enters from the rear, dressed in a walking suit, with hat and gloves; her hair is now black. She looks about and is surprised to see all the lights lit.—Kurt enters from the right; he seems nervous.)*

ALICE: It looks like Christmas Eve in here.

KURT: Well?

ALICE: *(Offers him her hand to kiss.)* Thank me! *(Kurt kisses her hand reluctantly.)* Six witnesses, four of whom are completely dependable. The complaint has been entered and the answer will be coming here by telegraph—right here in the prison.

KURT: Yes, I see. . . .

ALICE: Instead of saying 'yes, I see!' say 'thank you'.

KURT: Why has he lighted all the candles?

ALICE: Because he is afraid of the dark.—Look at the telegraph apparatus—doesn't it look like the handle of a coffee grinder? I grind, I grind—and the beans crackle and crack—as when you pull teeth. . . .

KURT: What has he done to the room here?

ALICE: It looks as if he were about to move. *(With a gesture toward below.)* Down there—there is where you are moving. . . .

KURT: Don't, Alice, don't! I think it is sad. He was, after all, my boyhood friend, and many a time when I was in dire need, he helped me out. . . . I feel pity for him.

ALICE: What about me? I have done nothing to hurt him—and I gave up my career for this monster!

KURT: How about your career? Was it so very brilliant?

ALICE: *(Enraged.)* What was that you said? Do you realize who I am—what I was?

189

KURT: Now, now. . . .

ALICE: Are you, too, going to start—so soon?

KURT: So soon?

> *(Alice throws her arms round Kurt's neck and kisses him. He lifts her in his arms and bites her neck; she gives a shriek.)*

ALICE: You are biting me. . . .

KURT: *(Beside himself.)* Yes, I want to bite your flesh and suck your blood like a lynx! You have roused the beast in me—the beast which I have tried for years to conquer by privation and mortification. I came out here, and at first I believed myself to be better than you; but now I am more miserable than either of you. Since I came here and saw you—saw you in all your horrible nakedness, my vision warped by passion, I have learned to know the awesome power of evil. The ugly becomes beautiful; what is good turns ugly and despicable. . . . Come here, I want to suffocate you—with a kiss. . . .

> *(He embraces her.)*

ALICE: *(Holding out her left arm.)* Do you see the imprint of the shackles that you released me from? I was the thrall, the bond-woman—and now I am free. . . .

KURT: But I shall bind you. . . .

ALICE: You?

KURT: Yes, I!

ALICE: I thought for a moment you were. . . .

KURT: A pietist?

ALICE: Yes, you kept prating about the Fall. . . .

KURT: Did I?

ALICE: And I thought you had come here to preach. . . .

KURT: Did you?—In an hour we shall be in the city and then you will find out if I'm a preacher. . . .

ALICE: And we'll go to the theatre in the evening, just to show ourselves. You understand, if *I* leave *him,* the shame will be his. You understand, don't you?

KURT: I am beginning to. . . . Imprisonment alone is not enough. . . .

ALICE: No, it is not! He must be shamed, too!

KURT: A curious world! *You* commit the shameful act, and *he* has to bear the shame of it!

ALICE: As long as the world is so stupid!

KURT: It is as if these prison walls had absorbed all the wickedness and depravity of the criminals; merely by breathing the air here, one is contaminated. You, I suppose, were thinking about theatre and supper; I was thinking about my son.

ALICE: *(Strikes him across the mouth with her glove.)* Old fogey! *(Kurt raises his hand to box her ears. Alice shrinks back.)* Tout beau!

KURT: Forgive me!

ALICE: On your knees, then! *(Kurt kneels.)* And on your face! *(Kurt bends to the floor.)* Kiss my foot! *(Kurt does so.)* And never again! Now get up!

KURT: *(Rises.)* What have I come to? Where am I?

ALICE: You know very well.

KURT: *(Glancing about in horror.)* I would almost think that. . . .
(The Captain enters from the left; he is leaning on a walking stick and looks miserable.)

THE CAPTAIN: *(To Alice.)* Will you let me speak with Kurt? Alone.

ALICE: Is it about our departure and the safe conduct?

THE CAPTAIN: *(Seating himself at the sewing table.)* Kurt! Will you be good enough to sit down here with me for a moment? And will you, Alice, let us have one moment of—of peace?

ALICE: *(To the Captain.)* What are you up to now? New signals? *(To Kurt.)* Please be seated. *(Kurt sits down reluctantly.)* And listen to words of wisdom, and of age! *(Pointing to the telegraph apparatus.)* If a message should come—then let me know.
(She goes out, right.)

THE CAPTAIN: *(After a pause, with dignity.)* Can you understand a human destiny like mine, like ours? Can you?

KURT: No—not any more than I can understand my own.

THE CAPTAIN: What meaning is there to all this turmoil, chaos and confusion?

KURT: In my more sanguine moments I have felt its meaning to be that we were not to know, or question, the meaning of life, but simply be submissive.

THE CAPTAIN: Be submissive! With no fixed extraneous point, I can't be submissive.

KURT: Quite correct. But you, as a mathematician, ought to be able to find that unknown point, when you have several given ones.

191

THE CAPTAIN: I have searched for it, but—I haven't found it.

KURT: Then you have made some mistake in your calculations. Start all over again!

THE CAPTAIN: I'll do that.—Tell me, from where did you get your resignation, your humility?

KURT: I haven't any left. Don't overestimate me.

THE CAPTAIN: As you may have noticed, I have summed up the art of living this way: eradicate—rub out! And keep going! In other words: obliterate! Early in life I made myself a sack, into which I crammed all my humiliations; and when it was brimfull, I tossed it into the sea.—I don't believe any man has suffered so many humiliations as I have. But when I blotted them out, and kept on going, they ceased to exist.

KURT: I have noticed how you have shaped not only your own life but life about you, out of your poetic imagination.

THE CAPTAIN: How should I have been able to live otherwise? How could I have endured life?

(He clutches at his heart.)

KURT: How are you feeling?

THE CAPTAIN: Poorly. *(Silence.)* But then comes the moment when your imagination—when your poetic imagination, as you call it, runs out—when you can no longer create. And *then* you find yourself face to face with reality in all its nakedness.—That is what is so terrifying! *(He suddenly begins to speak like an old man, with tears in his voice and drooping chin.)* You see, my dear friend. . . . *(He controls himself and reverts to his usual manner of speech.)* I beg your pardon!. . . When I was in the city I consulted the doctor there, and he said. . . . *(Again with tears in his voice.)* . . . he said that my health was broken and . . . *(In his ordinary voice.)* and that I hadn't long to live.

KURT: He said that?

THE CAPTAIN: Yes, that's what he said.

KURT: So it wasn't true, then. . . ?

THE CAPTAIN: What?—Oh, I see. . . No—it wasn't true.

(Silence.)

KURT: Then the other thing you mentioned wasn't true either?

THE CAPTAIN: What other thing do you mean, Kurt?

KURT: What you said about about my son being ordered here as cadet officer.

THE CAPTAIN: I have never heard a word about that.

192

KURT: You know, your propensity for erasing your own misdeeds is unbounded.

THE CAPTAIN: I don't know what you are talking about, my dear Kurt.

KURT: In that case, you are at the end of the road.

THE C PTAIN: Yes—there isn't *much* left of me.

KURT: And I suppose you haven't filed a petition for divorce either— an action that would cast such a disgrace upon your wife?

THE CAPTAIN: Divorce, did you say?—No, I know nothing about that.

KURT: *(Getting up.)* Then—will you admit that you have been lying?

THE CAPTAIN: My dear Kurt, you use such strong words. We have to be tolerant, Kurt,—all of us.

KURT: You have come to realize that, have you?

THE CAPTAIN: *(Resolutely, in a clear voice.)* Yes, I have come to that conclusion. Will you therefore forgive me, Kurt? Forgive everything?

KURT: There you spoke like a man.—But I have nothing to forgive you. And I am not the man you always believed me to be—not any longer. And least of all am I worthy of receiving your confessions.

THE CAPTAIN: *(In a clear voice.)* Life for me has been so strange— so hostile, so vile—ever since my childhood . . . and people so mean, and as a consequence I grew to be mean also. *(Kurt paces about uneasily and keeps glancing at the telegraph apparatus.)* What are you looking at?

KURT: Can a telegraph set be turned off?

THE CAPTAIN: No, not very well.

KURT: *(With increasing uneasiness.)* Who is Östberg, the sergeant major.

THE CAPTAIN: He is a very honest fellow. A bit of a businessman, however.

KURT: And who is the ordinance officer?

THE CAPTAIN: Although he is my enemy, I have nothing bad to say about him.

KURT: *(Noticing the light from a lantern in motion, outside the French windows.)* What are they doing with that lantern out by the battery?

THE CAPTAIN: You see a lantern there?

193

KURT: Yes—and people moving about. . . .

THE CAPTAIN: I assume it's what we call a detail.

KURT: And what's that?

THE CAPTAIN: A corporal and a few men. Probably some poor fellow they are taking to jail.

KURT: Oh!

(There is a pause.)

THE CAPTAIN: Well, now that you know Alice—what do you think of her?

KURT: I can't answer that. . . . I don't understand people in the least. She is as much a riddle to me as you are, not to mention myself. You see, I am approaching the age when sensible people acknowledge that they know nothing, understand nothing. But whenever I see anything being done, I want to know the reason for it.—Just why did you push her into the water?

THE CAPTAIN: I don't know. She was standing there on the pier, and on the spur of the moment it seemed quite natural to me that she ought to be in the water.

KURT: Didn't you ever feel sorry about it?

THE CAPTAIN: Never!

KURT: That is extraordinary!

THE CAPTAIN: Yes, it really is. It is so weird that I can't believe I ever did such a nefarious deed.

KURT: Hasn't it occurred to you that she might seek revenge?

THE CAPTAIN: I think she has taken sufficient revenge on me—and I find that just as natural.

KURT: What has made you so cynically resigned suddenly?

THE CAPTAIN: Since I looked death in the eye, I have come to view life differently. Tell me, Kurt—if you were to judge between Alice and me—whom would you say was in the right?

KURT: Neither. But for both of you I have pity—endless pity— perhaps a little more for you.

THE CAPTAIN: Give me your hand, Kurt!

KURT: *(Putting one hand on the Captain's shoulder he extends the other to him.)* My old friend!

ALICE: *(Carrying a parasol, she enters from the right.)* Well, well, how intimate we've become! Oh well, such is friendship! Hasn't any message come yet?

KURT: *(Coldly.)* No.

ALICE: This waiting makes me impatient; and when I become impatient I expedite matters promptly.—Now, Kurt, see me fire the final shot at him—and that will be the end of him. . . . First, I load—I know the manual, his famous rifle manual that never sold even five thousand copies—and now I take aim. . . . *(She aims her parasol at him.)* How is your new wife? Your young wife—the beautiful one? You don't know! But I know how my lover is! *(She puts her arms round Kurt's neck and kisses him. He pushes her away.)* He is in excellent health, but he has not got over his bashfulness. *(To the Captain.)* You miserable creature, whom I have never loved! You never realized how I led you by the nose, because you were too conceited to be jealous!

> *(The Captain draws his sabre and rushes toward her threateningly. Slashing right and left he, however, only damages the furniture.)*

ALICE: *(Screaming.)* Help! Help!

> *(Kurt stands motionless. The Captain collapses and falls to the floor, still clutching the sabre.)*

THE CAPTAIN: Judith! Avenge me, Judith!

ALICE: Hurrah! He is dead!

> *(Kurt withdraws toward the rear door.)*

THE CAPTAIN: *(Struggling to his feet.)* Not yet!

> *(He puts his sabre back in the scabbard and goes to sit down in the armchair by the sewing-table.)*

ALICE: *(Going up to Kurt.)* Now I am ready—to come with you!

KURT: *(Pushes her away so that she falls to her knees.)* Go back to the depths from where you come!—Goodbye—for ever!

> *(He starts to leave.)*

THE CAPTAIN: Don't leave me, Kurt! She will kill me!

> *(Kurt leaves.)*

ALICE: Kurt! Do not leave me— don't desert me!

KURT: Goodbye!

ALICE: *(Suddenly changing her attitude.)* What a scoundrel! There is a friend for you!

THE CAPTAIN: *(Gently.)* Forgive me, Alice, and come over to me. Quickly!

ALICE: *(To the Captain.)* He is the worst scoundrel, the worst hypocrite I have ever met in all my life! No matter what you may say—*you* are a *man!*

195

THE CAPTAIN: Alice, listen to me. . . . I am not going to live much longer. . . .

ALICE: So-o?

THE CAPTAIN: The doctor told me.

ALICE: Then what you said before was untrue?

THE CAPTAIN: Yes.

ALICE: *(Beside herself.)* Oh! What have I done!

THE CAPTAIN: There is nothing that can't be helped.

ALICE: No, no—this is beyond all help!

THE CAPTAIN: Nothing is beyond help if you blot it out, rub it out—and then continue on. . . .

ALICE: But the telegraph message! . . .

THE CAPTAIN: Which message?

ALICE: *(Falls on her knees before the Captain.)* Are we rejected—doomed? Was this meant to happen? I have blown my life to pieces—destroyed us both! Why did you have to lie? And why did this man have to come and tempt me?—We are lost! Had you been noble and generous of heart, everything might have been forgiven.

THE CAPTAIN: What is there that cannot be forgiven? Have you ever done anything that I have not forgiven?

ALICE: Oh—but this is unforgivable!

THE CAPTAIN: I have no idea what it is, although I know how clever you are when it comes to inventing infamy and trickery.

ALICE: Oh, if I could only get out of this. If I could. . . . if I could—I would care for you, Edgar—I would love you. . . .

THE CAPTAIN: Now, listen to me. . . . What is it all about?

ALICE: Do you think anyone can help us—no! No one—no one in this world!

THE CAPTAIN: If not in this world—then who?

ALICE: *(Looking at him.)* I don't know.—Oh heavens! What will become of the children—with our name disgraced?

THE CAPTAIN: Have you brought dishonor to our name?

ALICE: Not I! Not I!—They will have to leave school! And when they go out into the world, they will be as lonely and alone as we are—and as mean!— *(Suddenly struck by a thought.)* I am just beginning to realize now you didn't see Judith, either!

THE CAPTAIN: No, but forget about that!

(The telegraph receiver starts to click. Alice leaps to her feet.)

196

ALICE: *(Screaming.)* Here comes the deathblow! *(To the Captain.)* Don't listen to it!

THE CAPTAIN: *(Calmly.)* I shan't listen, my dear child, you needn't get excited! *(Alice, over by the apparatus, is seen standing on tiptoe looking out of the window.)*

ALICE: Don't listen! Don't listen!

THE CAPTAIN: *(Covering his ears with his hands.)* I have my ears covered, Alice, my child.

ALICE: *(On her knees, with outstretched hands.)* Oh God! Help us!— The men on detail out there are coming. . . . *(She cries hysterically.)* God in heaven! *(Her lips move as if in silent prayer. The telegraph receiver is still heard, clicking faintly, and a long strip of paper has fallen from it. After another moment it stops clicking.—Alice rises, tears off the paper strip and reads it in silence. Then she casts her eyes heavenward and walks over to the Captain kissing him on the forehead.)* It is all over! It was nothing!

> *(She sits down in the other armchair and falls into violent weeping. She wipes the tears off her face with her handkerchief.)*

THE CAPTAIN: What are all these secrets you have. . . . ?

ALICE: Don't ask me! It is over now!

THE CAPTAIN: As you say, my child.

ALICE: You would never have spoken like this three days ago!—What has come over you?

THE CAPTAIN: You see, my dear—when I fell the first time, I was already on the other side of the grave—in the beyond. What I saw there I have forgotten—but the subconscious memory of it remains. . . .

ALICE: The memory of what?

THE CAPTAIN: Hope—the hope of a better life!

ALICE: A better life?

THE CAPTAIN: Yes—for I have never really thought of this life as the end of life. . . This life of ours is death itself, or something even worse. . . .

ALICE: And we. . . .

THE CAPTAIN: Our destiny is, no doubt, to torment one another— or so it seems. . . .

ALICE: Have we two tormented each other sufficiently, do you think?

197

THE CAPTAIN: I think we have! And wreaked chaos and destruction. *(He looks about.)* Shall we tidy up the mess we have made? And clean house?

ALICE: *(Rising.)* Yes—if we can. . . .

THE CAPTAIN: *(Looking around the room.)* It will take more than one day. No doubt of that.

ALICE: It might take more than that—many more. . . .

THE CAPTAIN: Let us hope. . . . *(There is a silence.)* *(The Captain seats himself again.)* And so you didn't get away from me this time! On the other hand, you didn't hook me, either! *(Alice seems taken aback.)* Yes, I knew you wanted to put me in prison —but I cross that off. It's erased—I imagine you have done worse things than that. . . . *(Alice is speechless.)* And I am not guilty of any embezzlement either!

ALICE: And now you want me to be your nurse?

THE CAPTAIN: If you so wish.

ALICE: What else is there for me to do?

THE CAPTAIN: I don't know.

ALICE: *(Sits down, listless, agonized.)* These are the torments of eternity! Is there no end to them, then?

THE CAPTAIN: Yes, if we have patience. Perhaps life only begins after death. . . .

ALICE: If it were so!

> *(Silence.)*

THE CAPTAIN: Do you think of Kurt as a hypocrite?

ALICE: I most certainly do.

THE CAPTAIN: I do not. But everyone who comes in contact with us, becomes tainted, turns evil, and leaves us. Kurt was weak—and evil is strong. *(Pause.)* Just think how banal life of today is! In olden days people fought; today people only shake a fist at you!—I am almost certain that three months from now we shall celebrate our silver wedding and that Kurt will give away the bride—and with the doctor and Gerda, his wife, present as guests. The ordinance officer will give the festal speech, and the sergeant major will be the cheerleader. If I know the Colonel aright, he will invite himself.—Yes, you may laugh—but do you remember Adolph's silver wedding—the fellow in the Riflemen's Corps, you know. . . . The silverbride had to wear her ring on her right hand because the bridegroom, in a moment of

198

tenderness, had cut off her ring finger with his saber. *(Alice suppresses a laugh by putting her hankerchief to her mouth.)* Are you crying?—No, I believe you are laughing!—Yes, my child, we cry one day, and the next we laugh. . . . And don't ask me which is the best for us. . . . I read in a newspaper the other day that a man had been divorced seven times. Finally—at the age of ninety-eight—he remarried his first wife. That's love for you! If life is a serious venture or merely a farce—that is a mystery I can't comprehend. When it plays pranks on us, it can prove to be most painful; and the serious aspect is really the more tranquil and peaceful. . . . But as soon as one finally grows to be serious—then someone suddenly appears to play pranks on you. Take Kurt, for example! . . . Do you want us to celebrate our silver wedding? *(Alice is silent.)* Say that you do!—People will be laughing at us, but what do we care! We'll laugh along with them; or we'll keep a straight face—whichever suits us best.

   (Alice is silent.)
ALICE: Well, let's celebrate then.
THE CAPTAIN: *(With a serious mien.)* Hence—the silver wedding! . . . *(He rises.)* Erase—and keep going! And so—let us go on!

END OF PART I

THE DANCE OF DEATH
(1900)

PART II

THE DANCE OF DEATH
PART II

PERSONS IN PART II:
Edgar
Alice
Kurt
Allan, son of Kurt
Judith, Edgar's daughter
The Lieutenant

THE SETTING.

An oval drawing-room in white and gold.

Set into the rear wall and occupying almost the whole breadth of it, a row of French windows, which stand open and reveal a terrace with a stone balustrade. On this are placed delicately blue majolica jardinères with petunias and scarlet geraniums.

The terrace serves as a public walk. Beyond the terrace can be seen the shore battery emplacements where an artilleryman is on sentry duty, and farther in the background is discerned the open sea.

In the drawing-room, on the left, stands a sofa, with gilt frame, a table and chairs; on the right is a grand piano, a writing table and a fireplace with mantel-piece. An American easy chair stands downstage. At the side of the writing table, a smaller table, beside which stands a floor-lamp of brass for reading.

On the walls are hung a number of old oil paintings.

ACT I: SCENE 1

ALLAN is seated at the writing table, struggling with a mathematical problem. JUDITH, with her hair hanging down in a braid, enters from the terrace. She is wearing a

202

short, summery dress and carries in one hand her hat, in the
other a tennis racket. She stops in the doorway.
ALLAN, serious of mien and courteous of manner, gets up
from his chair.

JUDITH: *(Similarly serious, and friendly in manner.)* Why don't
you come and play tennis?

ALLAN: *(Diffidently, struggling with his emotions.)* I have too much
to do.

JUDITH: Didn't you see that I placed my bicycle facing the oak, and
not the other way around?

ALLAN: Yes, I did.

JUDITH: Well, what does that mean?

ALLAN: It means—that you would like me to come and play tennis
with you. . . . But I have my work—I have some problems I
must solve, and your father is a pretty hard taskmaster. . . .

JUDITH: Do you like my father?

ALLAN: Yes, I do. He takes an interest in all his students.

JUDITH: He takes an interest in everybody and everything. Will you
come?

ALLAN: You must know that I would like to, but I must not.

JUDITH: I'll ask papa to excuse you.

ALLAN: No, don't! It'll only set people talking.

JUDITH: Don't you think I know how to handle him? He'll do what
I want.

ALLAN: I suppose that is because you are so insistent and unyielding.

JUDITH: That's what you should be, too!

ALLAN: I am not a wolf at heart.

JUDITH: No, you belong with the sheep.

ALLAN: I prefer that.

JUDITH: But tell me—why won't you come and play?

ALLAN: You know the reason.

JUDITH: But tell me the reason! . . . The lieutenant. . . .

ALLAN: You don't care the least about me—and you don't enjoy being with the lieutenant unless I am there, too, so that you can
see me suffer.

JUDITH: Am I really so cruel? I had no idea I was!

ALLAN: Now you know it!

JUDITH: Then I must make amends, for I don't wish to be cruel—I
don't wish to be bad—in your eyes.

ALLAN: You only say that so that you can dominate me. You already have me as your slave, but you are not satisfied with that. The slave has to be tortured and thrown to the wild beasts! You *have* the other one in your clutches—so what do you want with me? Let me go my way, and you go your way!

JUDITH: Are you telling me to go? *(Allan is silent.)* Very well, I'll go then!—Being cousins, we'll meet again, now and then, but I don't intend to bother you. . . . *(Allan seats himself at the writing table and continues wrestling with his problems. Judith does not leave, but instead moves toward him slowly, step by step, coming over to the table, where Allan sits.)* You don't have to worry—I am going immediately. . . . I just want to see what kind of quarters the quarantine master has. *(She looks about.)* White and gold!—A grand piano—a Bechstein—nothing less!—*We* are still living in the fortress tower after papa was pensioned off—the tower where mama spent twenty-five of her years—and we are living there on sufferance at that!—But you— you are rich. . . .

ALLAN: *(Quietly.)* We are not rich.

JUDITH: That's what you say, but you are always dressed in fine clothes. For that matter, whatever you wear is becoming to you. —Did you hear what I said?

ALLAN: *(Submissively.)* I heard.

JUDITH: How can you hear while you are sitting there making calculations, or whatever it is you are doing?

ALLAN: I don't listen with my eyes.

JUDITH: Your eyes, yes. Have you ever looked at them in the mirror?

ALLAN: Go away from me!

JUDITH: You despise me, don't you?

ALLAN: My dear Judith, I give no thought to you, one way or another!

JUDITH: *(Moving still closer to him.)* Archimedes sits occupied with his mathematics while the soldier comes and stabs him to death.
    (She rumples his papers with her tennis racket.)

ALLAN: Don't touch my papers!

JUDITH: That's exactly what Archimedes said. I suppose you go about imagining things, don't you? You imagine I can't live without you.

ALLAN: Why can't you leave me alone?

JUDITH: If you would be polite, I would help you with your examination.

ALLAN: You?

JUDITH: Yes, I know the examiners.

ALLAN: *(With severity.)* What if you do?

JUDITH: Haven't you learned to ingratiate yourself with your teachers?

ALLAN: Are you referring to your father and the lieutenant?

JUDITH: And the Colonel!

ALLAN: And so you mean to insinuate that with your help I could slip through without doing my lessons?

JUDITH: You are a bad translator. . . .

ALLAN: . . . of a bad original!

JUDITH: Aren't you ashamed of yourself?

ALLAN: I am—on your account as well as my own! I am ashamed of having even listened to you!—Why don't you run along?

JUDITH: Because I know you really like having me with you.—Oh yes,—for you always find occasion to pass under my window! You always manage to have an errand to do in the city and to take the same boat as I; and you never go sailing unless you have me to look after the fore-sheet.

ALLAN: *(Shyly.)* A young girl shouldn't talk like that!

JUDITH: Do you mean to say that I am a child?

ALLAN: Occasionally you act like a good child; and then again you act like a wicked woman. You seem to have chosen me to be your sheep.

JUDITH: You *are* a sheep, and that's why I want to protect you.

ALLAN: *(Getting up.)* Wolves make bad shepherds. . . . You want to devour me, that's the gist of it, no doubt. You want to palm off your beautiful eyes in exchange for my head.

JUDITH: Oh, you have been looking at my eyes, have you? I scarcely thought you had enough courage for that.

(Allan gathers his papers and is about to go out, left. Judith places herself before the door.)

ALLAN: Out of my way, or I'll. . . .

JUDITH: Or you will—what?

ALLAN: If you were a boy, I would. . . . Bah! But you are nothing but a girl!

JUDITH: And so. . . .

ALLAN: If you had the slightest trace of pride in you, you would have gone after my having practically shown you the door!

JUDITH: I'll repay you for that!

ALLAN: No doubt!

JUDITH: *(In a rage, going to the door.)* I—shall—pay you—back! *(She leaves.)*

KURT: *(Enters from the right.)* Where are you bound for, Allan?

ALLAN: Ah, it's you!

KURT: Who could that be who left in such a temper that even the shrubbery trembled?

ALLAN: It was Judith.

KURT: She is a little impetuous, a little vehement—but she is a nice girl.

ALLAN: Whenever a girl is mean and rude, she is called a nice girl. . . .

KURT: You must not be so severe, Allan.—Aren't you pleased with your new-found relations?

ALLAN: I like Uncle Edgar. . . .

KURT: Yes, he has many good sides. And how do you like your other instructors? The lieutenant, for example?

ALLAN: He is so petulant, so capricious. There are times when I think he harbors a secret grudge against me.

KURT: Oh no! You have a habit of imagining things about people, Allan. Stop fretting, and just do what you have to do—do the correct thing, and leave others to take care of their own affairs.

ALLAN: That's what I do, but I am never left alone. They draw you in—just like the squid down at the Jetty; they don't bite, but they stir up a whirlpool that sucks you in. . . .

KURT: *(Gently.)* I have a feeling that you are inclined to be morose and moody, Allan. Don't you feel happy being here with me? Is there anything you miss?

ALLAN: I have never enjoyed myself anywhere as much—but. . . . there is something here that suffocates me. . . .

KURT: Here—by the sea? Don't you like the sea?

ALLAN: Yes, the open sea! But along the shores here there are cuttle-fish, seaweed in which you get entangled, jellyfish, sea-nettle—or whatever it is called.

KURT: You ought not to stay indoors so much. Go out and play tennis.

ALLAN: I get no fun out of it.

206

KURT: I suppose you are angry with Judith.

ALLAN: Judith?

KURT: You are so choosy about those you associate with. That we can't be, for then we'll be left to ourselves.

ALLAN: I am not fussy, but—I feel as if I were at the bottom of a pile of wood—having to wait my turn to be cast on the fire. All the weight from above keeps pressing on me—pressing on me. . . .

KURT: Be patient—your turn will come—the pile will diminish. . . .

ALLAN: Yes, but it takes so long, so long. . . . Oh! And meantime I have to stay here and grow mouldy. . . .

KURT: To be young is no frolic. And yet you are envied.

ALLAN: Are we? Would you like to change place with me?

KURT: No, thanks.

ALLAN: Do you know what I find hardest to take? Having to keep silent when old people sit and talk twaddle and knowing that I know more about the subject they are discussing than they do. And still have to keep my mouth shut! You'll forgive me, but I don't include *you* among these old people, of course.

KURT: And why not?

ALLAN: Perhaps because we are only just now getting acquainted with each other?

KURT: And because. . . . because you have now come to have a different picture of me?

ALLAN: Yes:

KURT: I suppose that during the years we were separated, you didn't always have the friendliest feelings toward me?

ALLAN: No.

KURT: Did you ever see a portrait of me?

ALLAN: Only once—and that was anything but favorable.

KURT: Old-looking, eh?

ALLAN: Yes.

KURT: Ten years ago my hair turned gray, overnight; but—without my doing anything about it—it has come back to its natural color.—Let us talk about something else. . . . Look, there comes your aunt—my cousin. How do you like her?

ALLAN: I prefer not to say.

KURT: Then I shan't press you.

> *(Alice enters. She carries a parasol and is dressed in a very light-colored tailored summer suit.)*

207

ALICE: Good morning, Kurt.

> *(She indicates by a look that she would like to be alone with Kurt.)*

KURT: *(To Allan.)* We'd like to be alone, Allan.

> *(Allan goes out, left. Alice sits down on the sofa, right. Kurt seats himself on a chair beside her.)*

ALICE: *(Embarrassed.)* Edgar will be here any moment, so don't let it upset you.

KURT: Why should it?

ALICE: You—with your strict sense of honor and your correct behavior. . . .

KURT: As regards myself, yes.

ALICE: Exactly! I forgot myself one time when I thought you had come to deliver me—but you kept your self-control—and so there is no reason why we should not forget—what never was. . . .

KURT: Then, let us forget it.

ALICE: However, I don't think that *he* has forgotten.

KURT: Are you alluding to the heart attack he had that night when he collapsed—and when you gloated too prematurely, in the belief that he was dead?

ALICE: Yes. And now that he has recovered, after giving up drinking, he has learned to keep his mouth shut—and now he is abominable. He is up to something—something sinister; but what it is I cannot make out. . . .

KURT: Alice, your husband is a harmless buffoon—he is forever showing me kindnesses.

ALICE: I know his kindnesses. Be wary of them!

KURT: Now, now. . . .

ALICE: So he has blinded you, too? Don't you sense the danger? Don't you? Don't you notice the snares?

KURT: No.

ALICE: Then you are doomed to come to grief.

KURT: Heaven help us!

ALICE: Imagine my sitting here watching disaster creep upon you like a cat, and pointing it out to you—yet you cannot see it!

KURT: Allan, who is both clearheaded and unprejudiced, sees no danger either. But, then, he has only eyes for Judith; and that, in itself, is an assurance of a happy relationship among us.

ALICE: Do you know Judith—know her well, I mean?

KURT: A flirtatous little vixen with a braid down her back and with skirts that could be a little longer.

ALICE: Precisely. But I saw her the other day dressed up in a long skirt—and then she was a young lady; and when she put up her hair, she did not seem so very young any more.

KURT: I must admit she is rather precocious.

ALICE: And she is playing a game with Allan.

KURT: No harm in that, so long as it is only play.

ALICE: So-o? There is no harm in that, ha!—Edgar will be here any moment now, and he will seat himself in the easy chair there. . . . He is so passionately in love with it that he could steal it.

KURT: He can have it.

ALICE: Let him sit over there, and we'll stay here. And when he says anything—he always talks a lot in the morning—when he talks about trivial things, I'll translate for you. . . .

KURT: Oh, my dear Alice, you are far too clever, far too clever! What should I have to worry about, so long as I look after my quarantine station properly and otherwise conduct myself correctly?

ALICE: You believe in honor and justice, and that sort of thing. . . .

KURT: Yes. Experience has taught me that. There was a time when I believed the opposite; and I paid for it—paid for it dearly.

ALICE: *(With a look of warning.)* He is coming. . . .

KURT: I have never known you to be frightened before.

ALICE: My courage was merely ignorance of the danger.

KURT: Danger? You'll soon have me frightened, too.

ALICE: Oh, how I wish that I could.—Here he comes. . . . *(The Captain enters from the rear. He is in civilian dress, a black redingote, which he wears buttoned; on his head he has an officer's cap, and he carries a silver-topped walking-stick. He greets them with a nod and goes directly to the easy chair and sits down. Alice, to Kurt:)* Let *him* speak first.

THE CAPTAIN: This is a superb chair you have here, my dear Kurt, truly superb.

KURT: It is yours, if you will accept it as a gift.

THE CAPTAIN: It was not my intention to. . . .

KURT: But I meant what I said—sincerely. Think of all you have given me!

THE CAPTAIN: *(Volubly.)* What nonsense! . . . And when I sit here I have a bird's-eye-view of the whole island—of all the walks and thoroughfares—I can see all the people sitting on their verandas—all the ships out on the sea—ships coming and going. . . . You were indeed in luck when you got the best location on this island, which is certainly not an Isle of the Blessed. Or what do you say, Alice? Indeed, it is called 'Little Hell'; and here is where Kurt has built himself a Paradise—but without his Eve, of course. . . . for when *she* appeared, Paradise came to an end! I say, do you know that this was once a royal hunting-lodge?

KURT: So I have heard.

THE CAPTAIN: You live royally, Kurt, but I'm ashamed to admit that you have me to thank for that.

ALICE: *(To Kurt.)* Watch out, now he is about to fleece you!

KURT: *(To Edgar.)* I have much to thank you for.

THE CAPTAIN: Don't talk nonsense!—Tell me, did the cases of wine come yet?

KURT: Yes.

THE CAPTAIN: And are you satisfied?

KURT: Very. You can tell your wine dealer I am well pleased.

THE CAPTAIN: His wines are always top quality.

ALICE: *(To Kurt.)* At second rate prices, and you pay the difference.

THE CAPTAIN: What did you say, Alice?

ALICE: I? Nothing.

THE CAPTAIN: Yes—when this quarantine station was in the throes of being established, I seriously thought of applying for the post of quarantine master; and with that in mind I made a study of quarantine methods.

ALICE: *(To Kurt.)* He is lying!

THE CAPTAIN: *(Boastfully.)* I found I could not share the archaic ideas concerning disinfecting methods, which the department heads held. You see, I stood on the side of the Neptunists— that's the name we gave them because they were in favor of the water method. . . .

KURT: You'll forgive me, but I remember clearly that it was I who preached the water method, and you were for disinfecting by heat, that time.

210

THE CAPTAIN: I? Nothing of the sort!

ALICE: *(Aloud.)* Yes, I remember that, too.

THE CAPTAIN: You?

KURT: I recall it all the more clearly, since. . . .

THE CAPTAIN: *(Abruptly cutting him off.)* Be that as it may, it doesn't matter! *(His voice growing louder.)* However—we have now arrived at the point when a new set of circumstances. . . . *(To Kurt who is trying to break into his haranguing.)* . . . don't interrupt me. . . . when a new set of circumstances has presented itself, and the quarantine service is now in the process of taking a gigantic step forward.

KURT: That reminds me—do you know who it is who has been writing those stupid articles in that periodical?

THE CAPTAIN: *(Turning red in the face.)* I have no idea—but why do you call them stupid?

ALICE: *(To Kurt.)* Watch out! It is he who has written them!

KURT: *(To Alice.)* He? *(To the Captain.)* Well, at any rate, not too judicious, if you so like.

THE CAPTAIN: I don't think you are capable of being the judge of that.

ALICE: Are you going to start a quarrel now?

KURT: Oh no!

THE CAPTAIN: It is not so easy to keep things peaceful on this island, but we ought to set a good example. . . .

KURT I agree. But can you explain this to me? When I came out here, I at once became friendly with all those in official positions. With the Judge Advocate, in particular, I was on espcially intimate terms—as intimate as one can be at our age. Then, after a lapse of time—it was not long after you had recovered from your attack—one after another began showing coldness toward me; and yesterday the Judge Advocate refused to return my greeting when we met on the promenade. I can't tell you how it hurt my pride. *(The Captain is silent.)* Have you ever encountered any similar behavior toward you?

THE CAPTAIN: No, quite the contrary.

ALICE: *(To Kurt.)* Don't you understand? He has been stealing your friends!

KURT: *(To the Captain.)* I have been wondering whether it could have anything to do with the new stock issue which I refused to vote for.

THE CAPTAIN: Oh no!—But just why wouldn't you subscribe to it, tell me?

KURT: Because I had already placed my small savings in your soda water venture. And also because a new issue is an indication that the old stock is shaky.

THE CAPTAIN: *(His mind wandering.)* That's a superb lamp you have there. Where did you get that?

KURT: In the city, of course.

ALICE: *(To Kurt.)* Watch out for your lamp, Kurt!

KURT: *(To the Captain.)* You must not think that I am ungrateful, or that I mistrust you, Edgar. . . .

THE CAPTAIN: Yes, but it doesn't indicate much confidence if you withdraw from a business-undertaking that you have helped to start.

KURT: My dear Edgar, ordinary prudence demands that a person save himself and what is his in time.

THE CAPTAIN: Save, you say? Do you see any danger ahead? Is anybody trying to fleece you?

KURT: Why use such harsh words, Edgar?

THE CAPTAIN: Weren't you satisfied when I helped you to invest your capital at six percent, eh?

KURT: Yes, I even felt grateful.

THE CAPTAIN: You are not grateful—it is not in your nature to be grateful—but that is not your fault.

ALICE: *(To Kurt.)* Listen to him!

KURT: My nature has its shortcomings, no doubt, and my struggle against them has been far from successful; however, I recognize my obligations. . . .

THE CAPTAIN: Then show it! *(He stretches out his hand and picks up a newspaper on the table.)* Why, what's this? This death notice. . . . *(He reads.)* The senior medical officer of the Ministry of Health is dead!

ALICE: *(To Kurt.)* He is already speculating on how to profit from the corpse!

THE CAPTAIN: *(As if to himself.)* This will bring changes in its wake. . . .

KURT: In which respect?

THE CAPTAIN: *(Gets up.)* We'll see. . . .

212

ALICE: *(To the Captain.)* Where are you going?

THE CAPTAIN: I must go to the city, I think.

    (Suddenly he catches sight of an envelope on the writing-table and picks it up, as if absentmindedly, reads the sender's address and then lays it on the table.)

Excuse me for being a little absent-minded!

KURT: No harm done.

THE CAPTAIN: Here is Allan's case with his mathematical instruments.—Where is the boy?

KURT: He is out playing with the girls.

THE CAPTAIN: A big boy like him? I don't like that. And I don't want Judith to be running around in that fashion. You must keep an eye on your young gentleman; and I'll take care of my young lady! *(As he walks past the grand piano, he strikes a few notes on it.)* Superb tone this instrument has! A Steinbech? Eh?

KURT: Bechstein.

THE CAPTAIN: Yes, you have done very well, you have! Thanks to me who brought you here.

ALICE: *(To Kurt.)* He is lying—he tried to prevent your appointment.

THE CAPTAIN: Goodbye for a while. . . . I am taking the next boat.

    (As he goes out, he gazes covetously at the paintings on the wall.)

ALICE: *(To Kurt with a quizzical look.)* Well?

KURT: Well?

ALICE: I still can't figure out what he is up to. But tell me one thing—the envelope he picked up—from whom was it?

KURT: I am ashamed to admit it—it was my only secret.

ALICE: And he was on the scent of it! You see, as I told you before, he is a sorcerer.— Did the envelope have the sender's address on it?

KURT: It has the name of the Voters' League on it.

ALICE: Then he has guessed your secret. I understand you would like to get the nomination for Parliament. And now you'll see that he gets there instead.

KURT: Has he been thinking of running?

ALICE: No, but he will be from now on. I could read it in his expression while he was examining the envelope.

KURT: Was that the reason he decided to go to the city?

ALICE: No, he decided to do that when he read about the death of the Chief Medical Officer of the Ministry of Health.

KURT: What can he expect to gain from the Medical Officer's death?

ALICE: Well, tell me that! Perhaps he was an enemy of Edgar's, who stood in the way of him and his intrigues?

KURT: If he is really so dreadful as you tell me he is—then one has every reason to be afraid of him.

ALICE: Couldn't you see how greedily he wanted to capture you and tie your hands on the pretext of your owing him a debt of gratitude—a debt which does not exist. He was in no way, for example, instrumental in getting you your post here; on the contrary, he did everything he could to thwart it. He is a man-eater, an insect, a termite, who is bent upon devouring your innards until one day you are hollow as a dead pine.... Although he is bound to you by the memory of your childhood friendship, he nonetheless hates you. . . .

KURT: How sharp your wits become when you hate.

ALICE: And dulled when in love. Love both blinds and dulls.

KURT: Oh no, you mustn't say that!

ALICE: Do you know what people mean by a vampire? They say it is the soul of a dead human being in search of a body which it can take possession of as a parasite. Edgar is dead, ever since he collapsed and fell that time. He himself, you see, has no interests of his own, no personality, no initiative. But when he gets hold of someone, he hangs on to him with his tentacles, sends down his suckers, and starts to grow and thrive. Just now *you* are the victim.

KURT: If he comes too near to me, I'll shake him off.

ALICE: Try to shake off a burr, and see how it sticks.— By the way, do you know why he doesn't like to see Judith and Allan together so much?

KURT: I imagine he is afraid they might become emotionally entangled.

ALICE: Nothing of the sort. He wants to marry Judith off—to the Colonel!

KURT: *(Alarmed.)* That old widower!

ALICE: Yes!

KURT: Horrible!—And Judith. . . .?

ALICE: If she should get the General, who is eighty, she would take *h i m* merely to pique the Colonel, who is sixty. To spite and mortify people—that, you see, is what she lives for. To trample and to bully—that is the watchword of Edgar's family.

KURT: So Judith is like that? That proud, attractive, glorious young girl!

ALICE: Oh yes, I know all that!—May I sit down a moment and write a note?

(Kurt arranges the writing-table for her.)

KURT: Please sit here.

ALICE: *(Removing her gloves, she seats herself.)* Now I shall make an attempt at the art of warfare. My first attempt, when I tried to slay the dragon, was a failure. But since then I have learned how to master the craft.

KURT: You know that you have to load before you can fire, don't you?

ALICE: Oh yes—and this time—with live ammunition! *(Kurt goes out, left.—Alice sits cogitating, and then writes.)—(Allan rushes in, throws himself face down on the sofa, sobbing in a lace handkerchief. Alice—whom Allan did not notice when he entered—watches him for a moment. Then she gets up, walks over to the sofa, and speaks to him softly.)* Allan! *(Allan sits up, embarrassed, and hides the handkerchief behind his back.)* *(Alice says tenderly, with true womanly feeling:)* You should not be afraid of me, Allan,—I am not going to harm you. . . . Is anything wrong? Are you ill?

ALLAN: Yes.

ALICE: What is the matter?

ALLAN: I don't know.

ALICE: Have you a headache?

ALLAN: No-o.

ALICE: A pain in the chest? In the heart?

ALLAN: Ye-es.

ALICE: A pain—a pain as if your heart were about to melt away— and then it tugs—and tugs. . . .

ALLAN: How could you know?

ALICE: . . . and you want to die—you wish you were dead—and everything seems so utterly dark and dreary. . . . And you can think of only one—one only, and no one else—but if someone else should also be thinking of that same one—the sorrow falls heavily upon one of them. . . . *(Allan forgets himself and starts plucking at the handkerchief.)* This is a sickness for which there is no cure. You can't eat, can't drink, you do nothing but weep —and oh, how bitterly!—and preferably out in the woods, where no one sees you—for it is the kind of sorrowful affliction everybody laughs at, people being mostly cruel and mean. Ugh! What is it, then, you want of her? Nothing! You dare not kiss her mouth, for then, you think, you would die; and when your thoughts fly to her, you feel a sensation as if death were not far away. And a death it is, my child,—the kind of death that gives life. But at your age you would not understand that. . . . I feel the fragrance of violets—her fragrance. *(She approaches Allan and gently takes the handkerchief from him.)* It is she—her fragrance—she is everywhere—she is the one and only one. . . . Oh, my dear boy! *(Allan takes the only way out and hides his face at Alice's breast.)* You poor boy! You poor boy! How it must hurt you—how it must hurt! *(She wipes away his tears with the handkerchief.)* There, there, there! Cry—cry—then you will feel better! It eases the heart. . . . But now, Allan, you must be yourself again—be a *m a n*—else she will not give you a glance—that cruel girl, who does not mean to be cruel. . . . Has she tormented you? Made you jealous because of the Lieutenant? Listen to me, my boy! You must make a friend of the Lieutenant and then you two can talk about her and compare notes. That usually eases the pain.

ALLAN: I have no wish to see the Lieutenant!

ALICE: Now, now my boy! It won't be long before the Lieutenant will be coming to you and want to talk about the girl and compare notes, because. . . . *(Allan straightens up with a glint of hope.)* Shall I tell you why? *(Allan gives a nod of assent.)* Because he is just as unhappy as you are.

ALLAN: *(Beaming.)* You don't mean it?

ALICE: You can be quite certain he is, and whenever Judith wounds his feelings he needs to unburden himself to someone.—You already seem cheered up. . . .

ALLAN: Doesn't she want the Lieutenant?

ALICE: She wants neither him nor you, my dear Allan—she wants the Colonel! *(Allan's face shows disappointment and shock.)* So, it's raining again?—Well, you can't have the handkerchief because Judith is particular about her things and wants to keep

216

her dozen intact. *(Allan looks foolish.)* Yes, Allan—that is the way Judith is!—Sit over there now, while I finish another letter; then I'll let you do an errand for me.

> *(She goes to the writing-table and sits down, continuing her writing. The Lieutenant enters from the rear. He looks depressed, but without appearing comic. Unconscious of Alice's presence, he makes a straight line to Allan.)*

THE LIEUTENANT: Cadet Officer. . . . *(Allan rises and stands at attention.)* Sit down, please. *(Alice watches them. The Lieutenant goes up to Allan and seats himself beside him. He sighs, takes out a handkerchief, similar to the one Allan had, and wipes the perspiration off his forehead with it. Allan stares jealously at the handkerchief. The Lieutenant regards Allan with a sad face. Alice coughs. The Lieutenant leaps to his feet, stands rigidly erect, and bows.)*

ALICE: Please sit down.

THE LIEUTENANT: I beg your pardon, Madame. . .

ALICE: No need to apologize. Do sit down and keep Allan company. He feels a little forlorn out here on the island.

> *(She continues writing. The Lieutenant converses embarrassed with Allan in a subdued voice.)*

THE LIEUTENANT: It's frightfully hot.

ALLAN: Oh—yes. . . .

THE LIEUTENANT: Have you finished the Sixth Book yet?

ALLAN: I am in the midst of the last proposition.

THE LIEUTENANT: A little tricky, isn't it? *(Silence.)* Have you—have you been playing any tennis today?

ALLAN: N-no, the sun was too hot.

THE LIEUTENANT: *(In agony, yet without being comical.)* Yes, it is frightfully hot today.

ALLAN: *(In a whisper.)* Yes, it is very hot.

> *(Silence.)*

THE LIEUTENANT: Have you—have you been out sailing today?

ALLAN: No-o. I couldn't get anyone to take care of the fore-sail.

THE LIEUTENANT: Would you care to entrust me with it?

ALLAN: That would be asking too much of you, Lieutenant.

THE LIEUTENANT: Not at all, not at all!—Do you think that—that we will have a good breeze today—say, about midday? That's the only time I am free.

ALLAN: At noon the wind usually dies down, and—and Miss Judith has her lesson then.

THE LIEUTENANT: *(Downcast.)* Oh! Oh, well. . . . H'm.—Do you think that. . . .

ALICE: Would one of you gentlemen care to deliver a letter for me? *(The two young men look at each other suspiciously.)* It's for Miss Judith. *(Allan and the Lieutenant leap to their feet and rush over to Alice. They do this with a certain dignity, however, with an effort to conceal their excitement.)* I see we have two lettercarriers. So much the better—then the letter will certainly be in safe hands. *(She hands the letter to the Lieutenant.)* Oh, Lieutenant, may I have that handkerchief? It has to go into the wash. My daughter is rather particular about her finery, and besides is a little parsimonious. Give it to me, please.—I don't wish to laugh at you, but you must not make fools of yourselves —unnecessarily. And I don't think the Colonel wants to be an Othello! *(She takes the handkerchief from him.)* Be on your way now, young men, and try to hide your feelings as best you can. *(The Lieutenant bows and goes out, with Allan following him. Alice calls after him:)* Allan!

ALLAN: *(Reluctantly stopping in the doorway.)* Yes, Aunt ˙ˈice.

ALICE: Stay here, if you don't want to be more hurt than you can stand.

ALLAN: Yes, but *h e* is going to her!

ALICE: Then let him get burned. But you take care!

ALLAN: I don't want to!

ALICE: You'll end by shedding tears. And then I'll have the trouble of consoling you.

ALLAN: I want to go along with him!

ALICE: Then go! But come back here, you harebrained young scamp, so that I may have a good laugh at you!

> *(Allan races after the Lieutenant. Alice sits down at the writing-table again and continues her writing.)*

KURT: *(Enters.)* Alice, I have received an anonymous letter, which disturbs me.

ALICE: Have you noticed that Edgar has become a totally different person since he discarded his uniform? I never thought a uniform could make so much difference in a person.

KURT: You did not answer my question.

ALICE: That was not a question. It was a piece of intelligence. What are you worried about?

KURT: Everything.

ALICE: He went to the city. Whenever he goes to the city, it means that something sinister is afoot.

KURT: But how can I possibly do anything to thwart it when I haven't the faintest idea from where the attack is coming?

ALICE: *(Putting the letter in an envelope and sealing it.)* Now we'll see if I have guessed correctly. . . .

KURT: Are you willing to help me, then?

ALICE: Yes—but only so far as my own interests allow it. Mine—meaning my children's.

KURT: I quite understand.—Do you hear, Alice, how silent it is outside—on the sea—on the island—everywhere?

ALICE: But from beyond the stillness I hear voices—murmuring—outcries—shrieking—screaming. . . .

KURT: Hush! I hear it, too. . . . No, it was only the sea gulls. . . .

ALICE: I hear something else. . . . And now I am going to the post office—with this!

(She gestures with the letter.)

—END OF SCENE ONE—

ACT I. SCENE 2

The same setting.

Allan is sitting at the writing-table, studying.

Judith stands in the doorway. She is wearing a tennis hat and is carrying the handle-bar of a bicycle.

JUDITH: May I borrow your screw-wrench?

ALLAN: *(Without looking up.)* No, you may not.

JUDITH: You are rude to me because you think I am running after you.

ALLAN: *(Without being snappish.)* I am neither rude nor anything else, but I should like to be left alone.

JUDITH: *(Coming closer to him.)* Allan. . . .

ALLAN: Well, what do you want?

JUDITH: You must not be angry with me.

219

ALLAN: I am not angry.

JUDITH: Will you give me your hand on that?

ALLAN: *(Tractably.)* I don't want to shake hands with you—but I am not angry. What is it you want of me, anyhow?

JUDITH: You are so silly. . . .

ALLAN: You are welcome to think so.

JUDITH: You think I am mean and cruel and nothing else, don't you?

ALLAN: No, I don't—for I know that, when you want to be, you can be both friendly and nice.

JUDITH: Well, I can't help it if you—if you and the lieutenant go around shedding tears in the woods. Why do you weep? *(Allan, embarrassed, does not reply.)* Tell me. . . . You never see *me* cry. And why is it that you have become such good friends of late? What do you talk about when you saunter about, arm in arm. *(Allan is speechless.)* Allan—you will soon learn to appreciate what I am, and you will find out that if I care for anyone, I can be of help to him. And—even though I don't like to tattle, I can give you a piece of information. . . . You must be prepared for. . . .

ALLAN: Prepared for what?

JUDITH: Some unpleasantness.

ALLAN: From whom?

JUDITH: From where you least expect it.

ALLAN: I am quite accustomed to annoyances and have not had too much fun out of life. . . . What is it that's in store for me now?

JUDITH: *(Pensively.)* You poor boy!—Give me your hand! *(Allan gives her his hand.)* Look at me!—are you afraid to look at me?
(Allan rushes out, right, in order to conceal his emotion.)

THE LIEUTENANT: *(Enters from the rear.)* I beg your pardon—I thought the Cadet Officer was. . . .

JUDITH: Lieutenant! I'd like you to be my friend and let me confide something to you. . . .

THE LIEUTENANT: It makes me happy to think that you trust me!

JUDITH: I do.—Let me ask you in just a few words—not to desert Allan if anything unfortunate should happen!

THE LIEUTENANT: Unfortunate. . . .?

JUDITH: You will hear about it shortly—even today perhaps. . . . Do you like Allan?

THE LIEUTENANT: That young man is my best student, and I

220

respect him as well. He has stability of character. And that is
something we need all too often. . . . *(With emphasis.).* . . .
strength to bear up under adversities; in a word, to endure, to
suffer.

JUDITH: That was more than one word, I'd say. However, you do
like Allan, don't you?

THE LIEUTENANT: Yes, I do.

JUDITH: Then go and find him and keep him company.

THE LIEUTENANT: That was why I came here—for that purpose
only.

JUDITH: I had not supposed otherwise—as you seem to imply.—Allan
went out that way.

> *(She indicates the door on the right.)*

THE LIEUTENANT: *(Goes reluctantly toward the right.)* Yes—I'll
keep him company.

JUDITH: Do that, please.

> *(The Lieutenant goes out.)*

ALICE: *(Enters from the rear.)* What are you doing here?

JUDITH: I came to borrow a bicycle wrench.

ALICE: Will you listen to me for a moment?

JUDITH: Certainly, I will. *(Alice seats herself on the sofa; Judith
remains standing.)* But tell me quickly what you have to say. I
can't stand long lectures.

ALICE: Lectures?—Well, then, put your hair up and change into a
long dress.

JUDITH: Why?

ALICE: Because you are no longer a child. And you are too young
to go flirting about, acting younger than your age.

JUDITH: What are you leading up to?

ALICE: That you are old enough to marry. And that your way of
dressing is causing offense to people.

JUDITH: Then I'll conform to your wishes.

ALICE: You have understood, then?

JUDITH: Yes, indeed.

ALICE: On all points?

JUDITH: Even the most delicate!

ALICE: Will you at the same time discontinue playing a game—with
Allan?

JUDITH: You like me to be in earnest, then?

ALICE: Yes.

JUDITH: Then we may as well begin immediately.

> *(She puts away the handle-bar, lets down her bicycle skirt, and arranges her braid in a knot, which she fastens on top of her head with a hairpin, that she takes from her mother's hair.)*

ALICE: One does not do one's toilet at the home of strangers.

JUDITH: How do I look now?—I am quite prepared now! And so—come who may!

ALICE: Now you look respectable at least.—And from now on you leave Allan in peace.

JUDITH: I don't understand what is in your mind?

ALICE: Don't you see how unhappy he is?

JUDITH: Yes, I think I have noticed it, but I can't understand why.

ALICE: That is where your strength lies. But just wait—and some day you, too, will suffer! Oh, yes!—Now go home, and don't forget—that you are now dressed in a long skirt!

JUDITH: Am I to walk differently now?

ALICE: Go ahead—try!

JUDITH: *(Tries to walk like a lady.)* Oh, my feet are tied—I am tied—I can't run any more!

ALICE: Yes, my child, now the procession begins—the slow march toward the unkown, which one knows all about beforehand, yet must pretend not to know. Shorter steps—and slower, much slower, much slower. You must get rid of the shoes you've been wearing as a child and now wear young ladies' shoes, Judith.—You don't remember when you discarded your baby socks and stepped into shoes, do you, Judith?

JUDITH: This is more than I can stand!

ALICE: Still you must—you must!

> *(Judith goes over to Alice and kisses her casually on the check. Then she walks with dignity, like a lady, toward the door, rear, leaving the handle-bar behind.)*

JUDITH: Goodbye.

KURT: *(Enters from the left.)* You are here already?

ALICE: Yes.

KURT: Has Edgar come back yet?

ALICE: Yes.

KURT: How was he dressed?

ALICE: In gala uniform. Consequently he has been to see the Colonel. He wore two decorations.

KURT: Two? I knew he would be given the Order of the Sword on his retirement. What could the other one be?

ALICE: I am not familiar with these things, but it has a white cross on a red field.

KURT: Ah! Then it was a Portuguese order.—Let me think! The articles he wrote in that periodical—didn't they give an account of the quarantine stations in Portuguese harbors?

ALICE: Yes, I seem to remember they did.

KURT: And he has never been in Portugal, has he?

ALICE: Never.

KURT: But I have.

ALICE: Why should you always be so communicative? He is such a good listener, and he has such an excellent memory.

KURT: You don't think that Judith—is in any way responsible for his getting this decoration, do you?

ALICE: Oh now, Kurt! There is a limit. . . . *(She gets up.)* . . . and you are overstepping it. . . .

KURT: Are we going to start quarreling now?

ALICE: That is up to you. But do not meddle in my interests!

KURT: If they run counter to mine, I must deal with them, even if only lightly.—Here he comes now.

ALICE: This is the time for action.

KURT: What are you going to do?

ALICE: We shall see.

KURT: Let us proceed to the attack then, for this state of siege is tearing at my nerves. I haven't a friend left on the whole island.

ALICE: Let's see now!—He'll be taking the easy chair, no doubt, so you sit on this side, then I can prompt you.

> *(The Captain enters from the rear. He is in dress uniform and wears the Order of the Sword and the Portuguese Order of Christ.)*

THE CAPTAIN: Good morning. So this is where we meet!

ALICE: You are tired. Sit down. *(The Captain, contrary to expectation, seats himself on the sofa, to the right.)*
Make yourself comfortable.

THE CAPTAIN: I am comfortable here.—You are much too considerate.

ALICE: *(To Kurt.)* Be careful—he is suspicious of us.

THE CAPTAIN: *(Irritably.)* What was that you said?

ALICE: *(To Kurt.)* I think he has been drinking.

THE CAPTAIN: *(Boorishly and savagely.)* No, he has not. *(Silence.)* Well—what have you been doing to amuse yourselves?

ALICE: And you?

THE CAPTAIN: Are you looking at my decorations?

ALICE: No.

THE CAPTAIN: No, I can well imagine—you are jealous. Otherwise it is customary to congratulate a person when he has had a decoration conferred on him.

ALICE: *(Exaggeratedly; sarcastically.)* We congratulate you.

THE CAPTAIN: Instead of laurel wreaths given to actresses, *we* are given honors like these.

ALICE: *(To Kurt.)* Now he is dragging down the wreaths that hang on the wall in the tower. . ..

THE CAPTAIN: Which your brother gave you.

ALICE: Oh, keep quiet!

THE CAPTAIN: And which I have had to salaam to for twenty-five years. . . . and which it has taken me twenty-five years to expose.

ALICE: Have you been seeing my brother?

THE CAPTAIN: A good deal. *(Alice is crushed.)* How about you, Kurt? You are not saying anything.

KURT: I am waiting.

THE CAPTAIN: Oh, say! I suppose you have heard the great news?

KURT: No.

THE CAPTAIN: It's not precisely pleasant for me to be the one to bring. . .

KURT: Go ahead— don't hesitate.

THE CAPTAIN: The soda factory has crashed.

KURT: That is most unfortunate.—How will that affect you?

THE CAPTAIN: I'm in luck—I sold out in time.

KURT: That was sensible of you.

THE CAPTAIN: But how about you?

KURT: Wiped out!

THE CAPTAIN: You have only yourself to blame. You should have sold out in time, or taken the new stock.

KURT: If I had, I'd have lost that, too.

THE CAPTAIN: Nothing of the kind. For then the company would have survived.

KURT: Not the company, but the board members; and I considered the new stock issue exclusively a collection for them.

THE CAPTAIN: And can this way of looking at the matter save you now, do you think?

KURT: No—I'll be losing everything I have.

THE CAPTAIN: Everything?

KURT: Everything—down to the last stick of furniture!

THE CAPTAIN: This is dreadful!

KURT: I've been through worse.

> *(Silence.)*

THE CAPTAIN: That's what happens when amateurs try to speculate.

KURT: You astonish me, for you know that if I had not subscribed, I would have been boycotted. . . . "As a subsidiary means of livelihood of the coastal population, of the toilers of the sea. . . . unlimited capital, as inexhaustible as the sea itself. . . . philanthropy and national prosperity", and so forth." That is what you had printed and advertised—and now you speak of it as speculation!

THE CAPTAIN: *(Unaffected.)* What do you intend to do now?

KURT: Put my property up at auction, I expect.

THE CAPTAIN: You'll be doing the wise thing.

KURT: What do you mean by that?

THE CAPTAIN: Just what I said. There are, namely,— *(Slowly, with emphasis.)* certain changes to be made here. . . .

KURT: Here—on the island. . . . ?

THE CAPTAIN: Yes. Your official residence, for example, will be moved to more modest quarters.

KURT: H'm.

THE CAPTAIN: You see, the plan is to place the quarantine station on the outer shore of the island, by the open sea.

KURT: My original idea!

THE CAPTAIN: *(Drily.)* I don't know anything about that—I am not familiar with your ideas in the matter. However—this provides you with a suitable excuse to get rid of your furniture now, so that the scandal won't be too apparent. . . .

KURT: What did you say?

THE CAPTAIN: The scandal! *(Working himself up into a temper.)* For it is a scandal to come to a new post and immediately get involved in a financial mess which cannot bring anything but unpleasantness to, and reflect upon, the relatives—especially the relatives.

KURT: I should think I am the one who will suffer most!

THE CAPTAIN: I want to tell you one thing, Kurt: if you hadn't had me to intervene for you, you would have been discharged from your post.

KURT: That, too!

THE CAPTAIN: You have a tendency to be a little careless. Complaints have been made about your performance of your duties.

KURT: You don't mean justified complaints?

THE CAPTAIN: Cha!—for in spite of your otherwise respectable qualities, you *are* careless! Don't interrupt me—you are *exceedingly careless!*

KURT: This is really astonishing!

THE CAPTAIN: However—the change I just mentioned is planned to take place in the immediate future. For that reason I should advise you to have the auction without delay, or try to dispose of your property and household effects privately.

KURT: Privately? Where can I find a buyer here?

THE CAPTAIN: You couldn't expect me to make myself at home in your furniture, could you? That would be something to talk about. . . . *(By fits and starts.)*—h'm—especially—if one—if one considers—what happened—once in the past. . . .

KURT: What did happen? Or, do you mean—what did *not* happen?

THE CAPTAIN: *(Abruptly changing the subject.)* Alice is so quiet! What ails you, old girl? You are not sad, are you?

ALICE: I am thinking. . . .

THE CAPTAIN: Oh, heavens! Are you thinking? But you have to think fast, clearly, and correctly, if it is to do you any good!— So, go ahead and think! One—two—three!—Haha! You can't! Well, then, let me try!—Where is Judith?

ALICE: She is somewhere about.

THE CAPTAIN: Where is Allan? *(Alice does not answer.)* Where is the Lieutenant? *(Alice remains silent.)* Tell me, Kurt, what are your plans for Allan now?

KURT: Plans?

226

THE CAPTAIN: Yes, you can't afford to let him stay in the artillery any longer.

KURT: Perhaps not.

THE CAPTAIN: You have to try to get him into a cheap infantry regiment—up in Norrland, or somewhere far up in the north.

KURT: In Norrland?

THE CAPTAIN: Yes—or you may prefer to have him change to a more practical vocation, why not?—If I were you, I would have him take a position in an office. I don't see why not. . . . *(Kurt is silent.)* . . . in these enlightened times! Cha!—Alice is so exceptionally silent today. Yes, my children, such are the ups and downs on the see-saw of life. . . . One moment you are up in the air, looking down and around you with cockiness; the next you are all the way down—and then you are up again! And so on, and so forth. . . . That was that, yes. . . . *(To Alice.)* Did you say anything? *(Alice shakes her head.)* We can expect visitors here in a few days. . . .

ALICE: Are you speaking to me?

THE CAPTAIN: We can expect visitors in a few days. Important visitors.

ALICE: Who?

THE CAPTAIN: You see! You are interested!—Now you can sit there and guess who it is, and while you are guessing you might take another look at this letter and read it again!
(He hands her an opened letter.)

ALICE: My letter! Opened! Returned by the postmaster!

THE CAPTAIN: *(Getting up.)* Yes, in my capacity as head of the family and your guardian, I must exercise vigilance over the most sacred interests of the family; and any attempt to sever the family ties through correspondence of a criminal nature shall be cut off with an iron hand. Cha! *(Alice is overcome.)* I am not dead, remember that, but you must not get angry now when I am about to lift us all out of undeserved humiliation— undeserved *on my part,* at least!

ALICE: Judith! Judith!

THE CAPTAIN: And Holofernes—I suppose? Bah!
(He goes out, rear.)

KURT: Who is this man?

ALICE: I don't know.

227

KURT: We are beaten!

ALICE: Yes—we are beaten!

KURT: He has gnawed me out completely, and with such infernal cleverness that I can't accuse him of anything.

ALICE: *(Ironically.)* Accuse him? No, on the contrary, you owe him a debt of gratitude.

KURT: Is he conscious of what he is doing, I wonder?

ALICE: I can't believe he is. He does what his nature impels him to do and follows his instincts. For the moment he seems to be smiled upon by the powers that mete out fortune and misfortune, good and evil.

KURT: I imagine it is the Colonel who is coming here?

ALICE: Probably. And that is why Allan must be got rid of.

KURT: And you find that justified?

ALICE: Yes, I do.

KURT: Then we shall go our separate ways.

ALICE: *(Preparing to leave.)* But not too far apart. . . . We shall undoubtedly meet again.

KURT: No doubt.

ALICE: And do you know where?

KURT: Here.

ALICE: You have that feeling.

KURT: It is easy to guess: he takes my house and buys the household effects.

ALICE: I think you are right.—But do not desert me!

KURT: Not for so trifling a thing as that.

ALICE: Goodbye.

> *(She goes out.)*

KURT: Goodbye.

END OF ACT I, SCENE 2

ACT II.

The setting is the same.

It is a cloudy, rainy day.

Alice and Kurt enter from the rear, both in raincoats and carrying umbrellas.

ALICE: So you finally set foot here!—Kurt, I cannot be so cruel as to bid you welcome—in your own home.

KURT: Oh, why not? I have been through three compulsory sales, and even worse, so you couldn't offend me.

ALICE: Did *he* summon you here?

KURT: He sent me a formal summons—but what the reason for it is I am at a loss to know.

ALICE: But he is not your superior?

KURT: No, but he has made himself king of this island. And if anyone dares to oppose him, he immediately resorts to the use of the Colonel's name, and then they all submit.—Tell me, is it today the Colonel is due here?

ALICE: He is expected—but I can't be certain about it.—Please sit down.

KURT: *(Seating himself.)* Everything looks the same here.

ALICE: Don't let your mind dwell on it! Don't open up the wound and be in pain again!

KURT: Pain? I find this merely a little strange—as strange as the man himself.—Do you know that when I first made his acquaintance as a boy, I kept away from him. But he pursued me, flattered me, offered to be of help, and caught me in his net; and though I tried to escape, it was in vain. Now I am his slave!

ALICE: And why? It is *he,* who owes *you* a debt—and yet you are made to pay for it.

KURT: After having ruined me, he has offered to help Allan through his examination.

ALICE: And for that you will have to pay dearly.—Are you still a candidate for the Parliament?

KURT: Yes, as far as I can see nothing stands in the way of it.

(Silence.)

229

ALICE: Is Allan really leaving today?

KURT: Yes—unless I can prevent it.

ALICE: It was a short-lived happiness for you both.

KURT: That, like everything else except life itself, which is dreadfully long.

ALICE: It is, indeed.—Won't you come into the drawing-room and wait there instead? To me the atmosphere in this room is stifling —even if it does not trouble you.

KURT: Just as you wish.

ALICE: I feel ashamed—ashamed beyond words—but there is nothing I can do to change things.

KURT: Let us go in there, then, if you like.

ALICE: Yes, and besides—someone is coming.

(They go out, right.—The Captain and Allan enter from the rear. Both are in uniform, with cloaks.)

THE CAPTAIN: Sit down here, my boy. I want to have a talk with you. *(Seats himself in the easy chair. Allan sits down on the chair on the right.)* If it were not raining today, I could sit here and enjoy looking at the sea. *(Silence.)* Well, then—so you don't wish to leave?

ALLAN: I don't like to leave my father.

THE CAPTAIN: Your father, yes—he is a most unfortunate man. *(Silence.)* And parents rarely understand what is best for their children. There are, of course, exceptions, I'll admit. H'm. . . . Tell me, Allan, do you keep in touch with your mother?

ALLAN: Yes, I get a letter from her now and then.

THE CAPTAIN: You know that she is your guardian, don't you?

ALLAN: Ye-es.

THE CAPTAIN: And you know, Allan, that your mother has given me power-of-attorney to act on her behalf.

ALLAN: No, I didn't know that.

THE CAPTAIN: Now you know, however. Consequently, all discussion pertaining to your career is terminated, and you are going to Norrland.

ALLAN: But I have no means to. . . .

THE CAPTAIN: All that has been taken care of.

ALLAN: In that case, all I can do is to thank you, Uncle.

THE CAPTAIN: You, at least, are grateful—something I can't say

230

about everybody. H'm. *(Raising his voice.)* The Colonel. . . . Do you know the Colonel?

ALLAN: *(Nonplussed.)* No, I don't.

THE CAPTAIN: The Col-onel. . . . *(Holding on to the word.)* . . . is a particular friend of mine. . . . *(In a more casual manner.)* . . . as you undoubtedly know. H'm. The Colonel has condescended to take an interest in my family, including my wife's relations. Through his intercession, the Colonel has procured the necessary means for you to complete your training course.—So now you know to whom you are indebted—and to whom your father is indebted: the Colonel!— Have I made this sufficiently clear to you? *(Allan bows deferentially.)* Now go and pack your belongings! The money will be given to you at the gangway as you go ashore. And now—goodbye, my boy. *(He extends a finger to Allan as a goodbye gesture.)* Goodbye.

> *(He gets up and goes out, left.—Allan, now alone, stands dejected; he looks around the room. Judith enters from the rear. Dressed exquisitely, in a long skirt and with her hair done up, she carries an umbrella. Over her dress she wears a hooded raincoat or cape.)*

JUDITH: Is that you, Allan?

ALLAN: *(Turns about and scrutinizes carefully her appearance.)* Is this really you, Judith?

JUDITH: You don't recognize me? But where have you been all this time? . . . What are you looking at? . . . My long dress—and my hair. . . . You haven't seen me like this before?

ALLAN: No-o. . . .

JUDITH: Do I look like somebody's wife, eh? *(Allan turns away from her. Judith, in a more serious tone.)* What are you doing here?

ALLAN: I came to say goodbye.

JUDITH: What's that? Are you—are you going away?

ALLAN: I am being transferred to Norrland.

JUDITH: *(Struck dumb.)* To Norrland?—When are you leaving?

ALLAN: Today.

JUDITH: Whose idea is this?

ALLAN: Your father's.

JUDITH: I might have guessed it. *(She walks up and down, stamping her foot.)* I wish you could stay here today.

231

ALLAN: And meet the Colonel?

JUDITH: What do you know about the Colonel? Is it definite that you are leaving?

ALLAN: I have no choice in the matter. And besides—now I *want* to go.

> *(Silence.)*

JUDITH: Why do you want to?

ALLAN: I want to get away from here. Out into the world.

JUDITH: Yes, I know how you feel, Allan. It is too confined here, it is unbearable—with all their speculating—in soda water and in human beings. *(Silence. With true emotion and feeling.)* Allan—I am sure you have learned that it is not in my nature to feel so deeply that I suffer pain. . . . but now—now I am beginning to realize that I *can* suffer. . . .

ALLAN: You—Judith!

JUDITH: Yes—now I am beginning to feel it. . . ! *(She presses both hands to her breast.)* Oh—I suffer so terribly! Oh!

ALLAN: Where does it hurt?

JUDITH: I don't know. . . . I am suffocating. . . . I think I'm dying!

ALLAN: Judith!

JUDITH: *(Gives a loud cry.)* Oh!—Is this how you poor boys feel?

ALLAN: If I were as heardhearted as you, I would laugh!

JUDITH: I am not heardhearted! I just didn't know any better. I won't let you go! . . .

ALLAN: I must.

JUDITH: Then go—but give me something to remember you by.

ALLAN: What have I that I can give you?

JUDITH: *(From the depth of her bruised heart.)* Allan! Oh—this is more than I can bear. . . . *(With her hands pressed against her heart, she shrieks hysterically.)* Oh, the pain, the pain! What have you done to me? I don't want to live any longer after this! Allan—don't go—not alone! Let us go together—let us take the small sloop—the small white sloop—and let us sail away, but with sails flattened in—there is a good breeze blowing—and we shall sail until we go down to the depths of the sea—out to sea—away out into the beyond, where there is no eelgrass to snare us and no nettle-fish to sting. What do you say, Allan? Say something!—But we should have washed the sails yesterday—they should be snowy white—for at that final moment

232

I wish to see everything in pure white—and then you shall swim with me clinging to your arm, until you have no strength left—and then we shall sink—together. . . . *(With a sudden change.)* Wouldn't that be a beautiful way to end it all—much better than going about grieving and sending clandestine letters which Father will open, and then sneer and rail at. Allan! *(She takes hold of his arm and shakes him.)* Listen to me!

ALLAN: *(Regarding her with radiant eyes.)* Judith! Judith! Why haven't you spoken like this before?

JUDITH: Because I didn't know! How could I have told you what I had not felt?

ALLAN: And now I must leave you. . . . But perhaps it is for the best—the only thing I can do. . . . I can't compete with someone as. . . . someone who—who. . . .

JUDITH: Don't speak of the Colonel!

ALLAN: Isn't it true that. . . .

JUDITH: It is—and it isn't. . . .

ALLAN: Can't you make it *un*true—put an end to it?

JUDITH: Yes—now I shall—within an hour.

ALLAN: And you will keep your word? I can wait—I can be patient —I can work. . . . Oh, Judith!

JUDITH: Don't go yet.—How long must I wait?

ALLAN: One year!

JUDITH: *(Ecstatically.)* One year? I shall wait a thousand years, and if you should not come to me then, I shall turn the heavens about so that the sun will be rising in the West. . . . Hush—some-one is coming. . . . We must part now, Allan! Don't speak a word! Take me into your arms! *(They embrace.)* But you must not kiss me. . . . *(She turns her head away.)* Now go—go now!

> *(Allan goes to the rear and puts on his cloak. Then they spontaneously rush into each other's arms, and Judith is hidden inside Allan's cloak. They momentarily kiss. Allan runs out. Judith throws herself, face down, on the sofa and sobs. In the next moment Allan returns, rushes over to Judith and kneels beside her.)*

ALLAN: No, I cannot go! I cannot leave you!

JUDITH: *(Rising.)* If you only knew how beautiful you are this moment! If you could only see yourself!

ALLAN: Nonsense, no man is ever beautiful. But you, Judith—

you. . . . Oh, when you acted so tenderly just now—then I discovered in you another Judith—and *that* Judith is mine. . . . But if you should break faith with me now—then I shall die. . . .

JUDITH: I feel as if I could die! Oh, if I could only die now, this very moment, while I am happy!

ALLAN: Somebody is coming. . . .

JUDITH: Let them come! I have no fear of anything—not of anything in the whole wide world—any longer! Oh, I wish you would take me with you inside your cloak. . . . *(She playfully hides beneath his cloak.)* . . . and that I could fly with you to Norrland! What shall we do up there in Norrland? Become riflemen—one of those with plumes in their hats? They look so chic, and they would be so becoming to you. *(She fusses with his hair, and he kisses the tips of her fingers, one by one, after which he presses a kiss on her boot.)* What are you doing, silly boy! You'll get shoe blacking on your lips! *(Getting up abruptly, in mock anger.)* Now I can't kiss you any more!—Let us go! I am coming with you!

ALLAN: No—they would arrest me then!

JUDITH: Then I want to be arrested with you!

ALLAN: They wouldn't do that. . . . Now we *must* part!

JUDITH: Then I'll swim after the steamer . . . and you'll have to jump overboard and save me—and then it'll be printed in the newspapers—and then we'll be engaged! Shall we do that? Shall we?

ALLAN: You can still jest!

JUDITH: There will be time enough for tears!—Say goodbye to me now. . . .

> *(They fly into each other's arms, and then Allan, followed by Judith, walks slowly out through the door in the rear, which is left open. They can be seen embracing in the rain, outside.)*

ALLAN: You'll be getting wet, Judith.

JUDITH: I don't care!

> *(They tear away from each other. Allan leaves. Judith remains standing in the rain and wind, which tugs at her hair and clothes as she stands waving her handkerchief. Then Judith rushes inside, throws herself on the sofa, covering her face with her hands.)*

234

ALICE: *(Enters and sees Judith. She goes to her.)* What's this I see? Are you sick?—Stand up and let me look at you! *(Judith gets up. Alice regards her intently.)* You are not sick. . . . So I am not going to comfort you.

> *(She goes out, left.)*
> *(Judith returns to her position on the sofa. The Lieutenant enters from the rear. Judith gets up and puts on her raincoat and hood.)*

JUDITH: Will you do me a favor and come with me to the telegraph office, Lieutenant?

THE LIEUTENANT: Yes, if I can be of service to you, Miss Judith,—but I don't know whether it would be entirely proper. . . .

JUDITH: So much the better. That is exactly why I want you to come—so that you can compromise me—but without any illusions on your part. . . . You go ahead!

> *(They go out, rear. The Captain and Alice enter from the left. The Captain is dressed in fatigue uniform. He seats himself in the easy chair.)*

THE CAPTAIN: Have him come in.

> *(Alice goes to the right and opens the door. Then she seats herself on the sofa. Kurt enters from the right.)*

KURT: You wish to see me?

THE CAPTAIN: *(In a pleasant yet somewhat condescending tone.)* Yes, I have a number of things of importance to tell you.—Sit down!

KURT: *(Seating himself on the chair to the right.)* I am all ears.

THE CAPTAIN: Well, then. . . . *(Spouting.)* You are aware that our quarantine service has been sadly neglected for very nearly a century now . . . h'm. . . .

ALICE: *(To Kurt.)* The candidate for the Parliament speaking now. . . .

THE CAPTAIN: But in view of the unprecedented advances in every. . . .

ALICE: He is going to talk about communications, of course.

THE CAPTAIN: . . . in every possible direction, the government has been contemplating making provisions for expanding the scope of its service. In order to carry out this plan, the Ministry of Health has appointed inspectors—and. . . .

ALICE: *(To Kurt.)* He is talking like a phonograph record.

235

THE CAPTAIN: . . . and—I may as well tell you now as later—I have been appointed an inspector of Quarantine.

(There is a silence.)

KURT: My congratulations!—and at the same time I pay you my respects.

THE CAPTAIN: Because of the family ties that exist between us, there will be no change in our personal relationship. There is, however, a certain other matter, of which I would like to speak. Your son Allan has—at my request—been transferred to an infantry regiment in Norrland.

KURT: But I object to that.

THE CAPTAIN: Your wishes in this matter are subordinate to what his mother wants. And as his mother has authorized me to act on her behalf, I have made the decision I just mentioned.

KURT: *(Sarcastically.)* I admire you!

THE CAPTAIN: Is that how you are affected at a moment like this—when you are to be separated from your son? Haven't you any feelings—any human feelings?

KURT: You mean you would like to see me suffer?

THE CAPTAIN: Yes.

KURT: It would give you joy to see me suffer.

THE CAPTAIN: Can you really suffer, can you?—Once I was taken ill—you were present at the time—and all I can remember was an expression on your face—an expression of undisguised elation.

ALICE: That is a lie. Kurt sat beside your bed all that night and helped to calm you when your pangs of conscience became too much for you to bear. And when you recovered, you forgot to be grateful. . . .

THE CAPTAIN: *(Pretending not to have heard Alice.)* Consequently Allan must leave.

KURT: Who is going to pay for it?

THE CAPTAIN: I have taken care of that, that is, we—a—a group of us, who have taken an intereset in the young man and his future.

KURT: A group of. . . .

THE CAPTAIN: Yes.—And just so that you may see that everything has been done correctly, I'll let you take a look at these lists.

(He hands Kurt some sheets of paper.)

KURT: Lists? *(He reads.)* Why, these are nothing but pleas for charity!

THE CAPTAIN: Call it what you like.

KURT: Have you been begging for my son?

THE CAPTAIN: Are you ungrateful again? An ungrateful person is the heaviest burden upon this earth.

KURT: Now I am dead socially. And my candidacy is done for!

THE CAPTAIN: What candidacy?

KURT: For Parliament, of course!

THE CAPTAIN: You really did not dream you would get nominated, did you? Especially since I, as you might have known—I being the senior resident here—intend to run for that office. This indicates that you underrate me!

KURT: Well—so now that, too, is finished.

THE CAPTAIN: It doesn't seem to disturb you very much.

KURT: Now you have taken everything. Is there anything else you want?

THE CAPTAIN: *Have* you anything else? And have you anything to reproach me with? Think hard if there is anything you can reproach me for!

(Silence.)

KURT: Strictly speaking, there isn't anything. Everything has been done correctly and lawfully, as between honest, respectable citizens in everyday life!

THE CAPTAIN: You say this with a resignation which I should like to call cynical. But your whole nature has a predisposition to cynicism, my dear Kurt, and there are times when I am tempted to share Alice's opinion of you that you are a hypocrite—a hypocrite of the very first order!

KURT: *(Calmly.)* Is that what Alice thinks?

ALICE: *(To Kurt.)* I did think so at one time, but don't any more. To be able to bear what you have had to bear takes immeasurable courage, or—it might take something else!

THE CAPTAIN: I think we may now consider the discussion closed. Suppose you go and say goodbye to Allan, Kurt, since he is leaving by the next boat.

KURT: So soon?—Ah well, I've been through worse.

THE CAPTAIN: You say that so often that I am beginning to wonder what you could have done in America.

237

KURT: What I could have done? I'll tell you. I was beset by misfortune, that's all. And every human being has the undeniable right to be subjected to misfortune.

THE CAPTAIN: *(Cuttingly.)* There are misfortunes brought on by your own doings. . . . Were yours that kind?

KURT: Isn't that a question of conscience?

THE CAPTAIN: *(Rudely.)* Have you a conscience? You?

KURT: There are wolves, and there are sheep. To be a sheep is not considered any great human asset; but I would rather be a sheep than a wolf.

THE CAPTAIN: Haven't you heard the old saying that everyone forges his own destiny, eh?

KURT: And does that always hold true?

THE CAPTAIN: Haven't you learned that a man's own strength. . . .

KURT: Yes, I do know that—ever since the night when your own strength failed you and you lay prostrate on the floor.

THE CAPTAIN: *(Raising his voice.)* A man of my merits—yes, you may look at me—who has been pitted against the world for fifty years—and who has finally come out on top—through perseverance, by being loyal and true to duty—through energy and—*and* honesty!

ALICE: You should leave that to others to say.

THE CAPTAIN: That's something they don't do, for they are jealous. However—we have visitors coming. . . . My daughter, Judith, is to meet her intended here today. . . . Where is Judith?

ALICE: She is out.

THE CAPTAIN: In this rain?—Send for her.

KURT: Do you mind if I leave now?

THE CAPTAIN: No, stay—you stay!—Is Judith dressed? Dressed properly?

ALICE: Yes, sufficiently so.—Has the Colonel definitely said he would be here?

THE CAPTAIN: *(Gets up.)* Well—that is, he wants to come unexpectedly, as a surprise, as they say. . . . I'm waiting for word from him by telegraph any minute—any minute. . . . *(He goes out, left.)* I'll be back momentarily.

ALICE: There you have your man! Would you call him human?

KURT: The last time you asked me that question, I answered "no". But now I believe he is typical of the common-place creatures

238

who have taken possession of the earth. . . . Perhaps even we belong in that category of people who use others and take advantage of every opportunity from which they can benefit.

ALICE: He has eaten you and yours alive—and still you defend him?

KURT: I have suffered worse things.—But this man-eater has left my soul untouched; it was more than he could swallow.

ALICE: What have you encountered that could have been worse?

KURT: You ask me that?

ALICE: Do you mean to be rude?

KURT: No, I don't wish to be, and therefore—don't ask me again.

THE CAPTAIN: *(Enters from the left.)* The telegram was there waiting for me.—Will you read it to me, Alice, it's difficult for me to see. *(He seats himself haughtily in the easy chair.)* Read it!—Kurt can stay! . . .

> *(Alice reads the telegram hastily to herself, and shows consternation.)*

THE CAPTAIN: We-ell? Doesn't it please you, eh? *(Alice is silent and regards the Captain fixedly. The Captain, sarcastically.)* From whom is it?

ALICE: It's from the Colonel.

THE CAPTAIN: *(Self-satisfied.)* That's what I imagined. What does the Colonel say?

ALICE: This is what he says: "Because of Miss Judith's impertinent telephone message, I consider the relationship terminated for ever."

> *(She eyes the Captain fixedly.)*

THE CAPTAIN: Read it again—if you please.

ALICE: *(Reads speedily.)* "Because of Miss Judith's impertinent telephone message, I consider the relationship terminated—for ever."

THE CAPTAIN: *(Pales.)* This is just like Judith!

ALICE: And you—you are Holofernes.

THE CAPTAIN: What are you, then?

ALICE: You'll know soon enough!

THE CAPTAIN: *(In a rage.)* This is your handiwork!

ALICE: No. *(The Captain attempts to get up and unsheath his sabre, but collapses in his chair from a stroke of apoplexy.)* Now you have what you deserve!

THE CAPTAIN: *(Whimpering like a very old man.)* Don't be angry with me—I am so sick. . . .

239

ALICE: Are you? I am glad you are!

KURT: Let us take him out and put him to bed.

ALICE: No—I don't want to touch him.

> *(She rings.)*

THE CAPTAIN: *(As before.)* Don't be angry with me! *(To Kurt.)* Look after my children.

KURT: This is precious. He wants me to look after his children after having stolen mine from me.

ALICE: Self-deceiving, as ever.

THE CAPTAIN: Look after my children!

> *(He continues stammering and mumbling incoherent blah-blah-blahs.)*

ALICE: At last that tongue of his has been curbed.—Now he can no longer lie, or boast, or wound.—You, Kurt, who believe in a God, thank Him on my behalf—thank Him for setting me free from my imprisonment—from the wolf—from the vampire!

KURT: Don't, don't, Alice!

ALICE: *(Close to the Captain, in his face.)* Where is that strength of yours—your *own* strength—now? Where is it? And your energy? *(The Captain, speechless, spits in her face.)* So you can still spit venom, you viper, can you? Then I'll tear out your tongue! *(She slaps him in the face.)* His head is off, but still he blushes!—Oh, Judith! You marvelous, adorable girl whom I have borne, like my vengeance, under my heart. It is you who have set us all free!—If you have more than one head, you Hydra, we'll take them, too. *(She pulls his beard.)* Oh, to think that justice still exists on earth! There were times when I thought there might be—but I never quite believed it. Ask God to forgive me for doubting, Kurt. Yes, there *is* a justice! And now *I*, too, join the sheep. Tell Him that, Kurt! The merest taste of good fortune tends to make us better, but when we meet with nothing but adversity, we all turn into wolves. . . . *(The Lieutenant enters, rear.)* The Captain has suffered a stroke, Lieutenant. Will you help us, please, to roll the chair into the next room?

THE LIEUTENANT: Madam. . . .

ALICE: What is it?

THE LIEUTENANT: Why. . . . Miss Judith. . . .

ALICE: Help us with this first—then you can tell me about Miss

JUDITH. *(The Lieutenant and Kurt roll out the chair, left.)* Out with the cadaver! Out with it! And open the doors and windows wide—so that this room will be aired out! *(She throws open the French windows, rear. The weather has now cleared.)* Phew!

KURT: Are you going to desert him now?

ALICE: When a ship has foundered, the crew abandons it and saves itself. I don't see why I should lay out a decaying animal! Let the dissecting-room or the morgue take care of him! A flower-bed would be too good for such a wheelbarrowful of foulness! —Now I am going to bathe so that I may rid myself of all this filth and nastiness—if I can ever cleanse it away?

> *(Judith, hatless, is seen on the balustrade outside. She is waving a handkerchief to someone out at sea.)*

KURT: *(Calling in the direction of the French windows.)* Who is out there? Judith! *(Calls again.)* Judith!

JUDITH: *(Enters, cries aloud:)* He is gone!

KURT: Who?

JUDITH: Allan—he is gone!

KURT: Without saying goodbye?

JUDITH: He said goodbye to me, and sends his love to you, Uncle.

ALICE: Oh, so this is what. . . .

JUDITH: *(Throwing herself into Kurt's arms.)* He is gone!

KURT: He will be back, my dear child!

ALICE: Or we shall go where he is.

KURT: *(With a gesture toward the door on the left.)* And leave Edgar! What would people. . . .

ALICE: People! Bah!—Judith, come and embrace me! *(Judith goes to Alice, who kisses her on the forehead.)* Would you like to go to Allan?

JUDITH: How can you ask, Mother?

ALICE: But your father has been stricken. . . .

JUDITH: Why should I care—after what he has done?

ALICE: That's my Judith!—Oh, I love you, Judith!

JUDITH: Besides, Father is not small in anything he does—and he dislikes sickly sentimentality. You may say what you like, but Father certainly has a personality and style about him!

ALICE: Yes—of a certain kind.

JUDITH: But I imagine he has no great longing to see me after the telephone call I made to the Colonel!—Well, he should never

241

have tried to marry me off to that old fogy! No, Allan—Allan is for me! *(She throws herself into the arms of Kurt.)* I'm aching to go to Allan!

> *(She tears herself from Kurt and runs outside, waving her handkerchief. Kurt hastens after her and waves also.)*

ALICE: To think that a flower can sprout and grow out of filth and foulness! *(The Lieutenant enters from the left.)* Well?

THE LIEUTENANT: Oh, Miss Judith. . . .

ALICE: Do you find Judith's name so enchanting that you have to coo it, and forget the man who is dying?

THE LIEUTENANT: Yes, but she said. . . .

ALICE: She? Speak her name instead, then.—But tell me first—how is he now—in there?

THE LIEUTENANT: It is all over. . . .

ALICE: All over?—Oh God, I thank you—for myself, and for all others—thank you for having delivered us from this evil!— Let me take your arm, Lieutenant! I want to go out—out to breathe—to breathe! *(The Lieutenant offers her his arm. Alice stops abruptly.)* Did he say anything before the end came?

THE LIEUTENANT: Yes. He said a few words.

ALICE: What did he say?

THE LIEUTENANT: He said: "Father forgive them, for they know not what they do!"

ALICE: I do not understand. . . .

THE LIEUTENANT: Yes, Miss Judith's father was a good man, a noble man. . . .

ALICE: *(Calls.)* Kurt! *(Kurt comes in.)* It is all over!

KURT: Oh!

ALICE: Do you know what his last words were? No, you couldn't guess. . . . "Forgive them, for they know not what they do."

KURT: How would you interpret that?

ALICE: I assume he meant that *he* had always done what is righteous and died as a man who had been wronged by life.

KURT: He will be given a beautiful funeral oration, no doubt.

ALICE: And plenty of wreaths—from the non-commissioned officers.

KURT: Yes.

ALICE: About a year ago I heard him say: "It seems to me that life is a hoax."

KURT: Are you suggesting that, even in death, he is the buffoon, jeering at us?

ALICE: No. But now that he is dead, I suddenly feel a strange inclination to speak well of him.

KURT: Yes, let us do that.

THE LIEUTENANT: Miss Judith's father was a good and a noble man!

ALICE: *(To Kurt.)* There you hear!

KURT: "They know not what they do." How many times did I not ask whether he knew what he was doing? And you thought he didn't know. Let us therefore forgive him!

ALICE: Riddles! Riddles!—But now we have peace in the house— the awesome peace of death. . . awesome as that solemn and profound anxiety which prevails when a child is about to be born. I can hear the silence—can see on the floor the impression made by the easy-chair in which he was wheeled away. . . . And I have a feeling that my own life has now come to an end, that I am on the road to decay and dissolution! It is very strange, but do you know that these plain words uttered by the Lieutenant —and he is a simple-hearted, unsophisticated young man—they still ring in my ears. . . . But now they have become a weight on my soul. . . . My husband—the love of my youth. . . . Yes, you may laugh—but he *was,* in spite of everything, a good and noble man.

KURT: In spite of everything? Yes, and he did have courage—the way he fought for his existence, and his family's!

ALICE: Think of all the vexations and worries he had, the humiliations—all of which he erased, obliterated, so that he could continue and go on—and on!

KURT: He was a frustrated, defeated man—a man passed by! That is the sum total of it!—Alice—go to him—go inside!

ALICE: No—I can't. . . . While we were speaking, the image of him in his youth has come back to me. . . . I saw him—I see him now before me—see him as he was at the age of twenty. . . . I must have loved that man—once!

KURT: And—hated him!

ALICE: *And*—hated him!—May peace be with him!

> *(She walks toward the door on the left. There she stops, her hands clasped.)*

—END OF PART II—

To the memory of Mildred Morris

SWANWHITE
(1901)

A medieval fantasy in three acts

PERSONS IN THE PLAY:
(In the order of their appearance)

Signe ⎫
Elsa ⎬ The Three Maidens
Tova ⎭

The Duke

The Stepmother

Swanwhite

The Prince

Swanwhite's Mother

The Prince's Mother

Magdalena

The Major-domo

The Steward

The Warden of the Castle

The Master Cook

The Soldier in charge of the pillory

The Master of the Stables

The Riding Master

The Gardener

Four Maidens

Two Knights

The Fisherman (The Gardener)
    Men and Women.

THE SETTING

A stately bower in a medieval stone castle.

The ceiling is cross-vaulted and chalk white, as are the walls. In the center, rear, are three arched door-openings that lead to a stone terrace. These openings can be closed off by draperies. Beyond the terrace can be seen the tops of tall rose trees with white and pink blossoms, in a copse. Beyond the copse can be discerned a white, sandy beach and the blue sea.

To the left of the three archways is a small door; when open, it shows in linear perspective three connected rooms. The first one—which is the pewter chamber—contains vessels of pewter in rows on shelves; in the second one—which is the wardrobe chamber—are hung richly brocaded costumes; the third one—which is the fruit chamber—holds apples, pears, gourds and melons.

The floors throughout are uniformly patterned in red and black squares. In the center of the larger room of state is placed a gilt dining table covered with a brocaded cloth; there are also two gilt tabourets, a clock, and a vase filled with roses. A sprig of mistletoe hangs from the ceiling above the table. A rug of lion skin is on the floor, down stage. Above the archway, inside the larger room, can be seen two nests of swallows.

On the right, down stage, there is a white bed with a canopy, supported by two posts at the head; at the foot of the bed are no posts. The bed is made up in white, but the silken bedspread is of a most delicate shade of blue. A beautiful, white night gown, trimmed with lace, lies on the bed. Behind the bed is a cabinet for linen, bath accessories, etc. Close by the bed stands a small, gilt Roman table (round, on a columned leg) and on it is a Roman lamp of gold.

On the left is a beautifully sculptured fireplace. A white lily stands in a vase on the mantelpiece.

In the right archway a peacock is asleep on its perch, its back toward the audience.

In the left archway, a large golden bird cage with two doves at rest in it.

The setting remains the same throughout the play.

SWANWHITE

ACT I.

When the curtain rises, the three maidens are discovered, one in each one of three archways leading to the three chambers. The maidens are, however, only partly visible: they are slightly hidden by the door-post. The false maiden, Signe, stands in the doorway to the pewter chamber, Elsa in the wardrobe chamber, and Tova in the fruit chamber.

The Duke enters from the rear, followed soon after by The Stepmother, who is clutching a steel whip in her hand.

The stage is dimly lighted as they enter to the sound of a fanfare of horns.

The Stepmother: *(She looks around.)* Where is Swanwhite?

The Duke: You can see she is not here, can't you?

The Stepmother: I can see—but I don't see Swanwhite. Maidens! Signe—Elsa—Tova! *(The three maidens come forward, one after the other, and stand facing The Stepmother.)* Where is Princess Swanwhite?

Signe: *(With arms folded; she remains silent.)*

The Stepmother: You don't know? *(She makes a threatening gesture with the whip.)* You see what I am holding in my hand, don't you?—Answer me quickly!

Signe: *(Remains silent.)*

The Stepmother: Speak! *(She cuts the air with the whip.)* Do you hear the falcon whizzing through the air? He has talons of steel, and he has a beak! What would you say this is?

Signe: The steel whip!

The Stepmother: Yes, it's the steel whip! Now tell me, where is Princess Swanwhite?

Signe: I can't very well answer what I don't know, can I?

The Stepmother: Ignorance is not a virtue, but carelessness invites punishment! Is it not your duty to watch over the young princess?—Remove the kerchief from your neck!

    (Signe unties the kerchief in fear.)

246

THE STEPMOTHER: Get on your knees!

THE DUKE: *(Revolted, he turns his back on the spectacle.)*

THE STEPMOTHER: Let me see your neck so that I can adorn it with a necklace that will keep the young swains from pressing their kisses on it any more!—Let me have your neck! There—that's better!

SIGNE: Mercy! For the sake of Jesus!

THE STEPMOTHER: Letting you keep your life is mercy enough for you!

> *(The Duke removes his sword from the scabbard and tries the edge on his nails, then on his flowing beard. When he speaks, his words have a double meaning.)*

THE DUKE: Off with the head—put it in a sack—hang it to a tree. . . .

THE STEPMOTHER: That's just what should be done!

THE DUKE: For once we think alike!

THE STEPMOTHER: Unlike yesterday!

THE DUKE: And probably tomorrow!

THE STEPMOTHER: *(To Signe, who is trying to crawl away from her on her knees.)* Stop! Where are you going?

> *(She lifts the steel whip to strike her, but Signe evades the blow and the whip strikes the air.—Swanwhite comes forward from behind the bed and kneels before the Step-mother.)*

SWANWHITE: Here, I am, stepmother! The blame is mine! Signe is innocent!

THE STEPMOTHER: Say *mother!* You must call me mother first!

SWANWHITE: I can't! Of mortal born. . . . I have only one mother!

THE STEPMOTHER: Your father's wife is your mother!

SWANWHITE: My father's second wife is my stepmother!

THE STEPMOTHER: You are an unbending daughter, but steel is flexible and will help to make *you* so, too!

> *(She raises the whip as if to strike Swanwhite.)*

THE DUKE: *(Draws his sword and raises it.)* Watch your head!

THE STEPMOTHER: Who?

THE DUKE: You!

> *(The Stepmother pales, shows her temper and then sud-denly calms herself. She is silent. There is a long pause. When she realizes her defeat, she turns to another subject.)*

247

THE STEPMOTHER: Well—will Your Grace announce to his daughter what is now in store for her?

THE DUKE: *(Puts back his sword.)* Rise, my dearest child, and come into my arms! There you will find calm again!

SWANWHITE: *(Runs to her father, who embraces her.)* Father! . . . You are like a royal oak! My arms will not reach round you, but I am safe from all harm and all ills beneath your foliage. . . . *(She hides her head beneath his warrior's beard, which reaches to his waist.)* And on your branches I want to sway like a bird in the wind. . . . Lift me up, and I shall perch on your crown! *(The Duke stretches out his arm. Swanwhite climbs up and seats herself on his shoulder.)* Now I have the earth beneath me, and the air above. . . . Now I can look out over the rose garden, the white sandy shore, the blue sea—and over seven kingdoms!

THE DUKE: Then you must be able to see the young king also—your betrothed. . . .

SWANWHITE: No—I have never seen him. . . . Is he handsome?

THE DUKE: My dearest one. . . . that depends entirely upon your eyes—how you look at him!

SWANWHITE: *(Rubs her eyes.)* My eyes?. . . . My eyes see only what is beautiful!

THE DUKE: *(Kisses her foot.)* Your little foot—that is so black! Little blackamoor foot!

> *(The Stepmother has gestured to the maidens to resume their places in the doorways. She herself steals out like a panther through the rear archway.—Swanwhite jumps down from her father's shoulder. The Duke lifts her up on the table, then seats himself next to her on a chair. Swanwhite glances after the Stepmother meaningfully.)*

SWANWHITE: Did the sun just rise? Did the wind turn toward the south? Has spring come?

THE DUKE: *(Places his hand over her mouth.)* You little chatterbox! You joy of my old age, my evening star! Open your little rosy red ear and close your little purple red mouth. . . . Listen to me—obey me—and life will be good to you! . . .

SWANWHITE: *(Puts her fingers in her ears.)* I hear with my eyes— I see with my ears. . . . Now I see nothing—I only hear!

THE DUKE: My child!—While in your cradle, you were betrothed

248

to the young King of Rigalid. You have never seen him, for such is the custom among royalty. Now the day for the wedding is approaching. But in order to teach you court etiquette and prepare you for your regal duties, the King has dispatched a young prince here who will instruct you in the reading of books, how to play games, how to dance and to play the harp.

SWANWHITE: What is the prince's name?

THE DUKE: That, my child, is something you must not ask—neither him nor anyone else; for it has been foretold that whatever maiden speaks his name shall fall in love with him! . . .

SWANWHITE: Is he handsome?

THE DUKE: Yes—to your eyes he will be. . . .

SWANWHITE: But he *is* handsome, isn't he?

THE DUKE: He is—yes! And now guard your little heart, which belongs to the King, and never forget that you were cradled a queen. . . . Now, my beloved child, I have to leave you—for I am going away to war!—Be humble and obedient to your step-mother! She is a hard woman, but your father has loved her; and gentleness can change and soften hearts of stone. If her meanness—despite her vows and promises—should go beyond what you can endure, then blow this horn. . . . *(He takes from underneath his cloak a horn, carved in ivory.)* . . . and you will receive help.—But do not summon aid before aid is really needed, desperately needed!—Do you understand?

SWANWHITE: I do.

THE DUKE: And now—the prince is already here, waiting in the bower.—Would it please you to see the prince now?

SWANWHITE: How can you ask?

THE DUKE: Let me first bid you farewell!

SWANWHITE: You say the prince is here already?

THE DUKE: He is here, and I—I am already far, far away, where the heron of forgetfulness puts its head under its wing!

SWANWHITE: *(Throws herself into her father's lap and hides her head under his long beard.)* You must not say such things, father! Your little girl is ashamed!

THE DUKE: My little girl should be spanked for forgetting her old father so quickly for a young prince! For shame! *(The signal of a horn is heard from afar. The Duke rises hastily, picks up Swanwhite in his arms, heaves her in the air and then catches*

249

her again.) Fly, little bird, fly! And keep forever above the dust, and let the air be beneath your wings!—And now—down on the ground again!—Honor and battles call me!—while youth and love call you! *(He girds himself with his sword.)* And now—hide the miracle horn lest it fall into the hands of evil-doers!

SWANWHITE: Where—where shall I hide it?

THE DUKE: Hide it in your bed!

SWANWHITE: *(Hides the horn in her bed.)* Go to sleep now! Sleep well, little horn! When it is time for you to waken, I shall call you! And don't forget to say your prayers tonight!

THE DUKE: My child! Do not forget my final admonition: Be obedient to your stepmother!

SWANWHITE: In everything?

THE DUKE: Yes—in everything!

SWANWHITE: Not in anything impure or odious!. . . . My mother changed my linen twice a week—my stepmother makes me do with one! Mother gave me water and soap—my stepmother gives me neither! Just look at my poor little feet!

THE DUKE: My daughter, keep yourself clean inwardly, and you will be clean of body also. . . . Do you know that holy men who, for the sake of penitence, are forbidden the use of cleansing water, become white as white swans—while the unholy turn black as ravens!

SWANWHITE: I want to be white as a swan, father!

THE DUKE: Come into my embrace, my child!—And so—farewell!

SWANWHITE: *(Rushes into his embrace.)* Farewell, you mighty warrior, my great and glorious hero! May fortune follow you, my blessed, kind, victorious father!

THE DUKE: So be it—and may your gentle prayers protect me!
    (He pulls down the visor of his golden helmet.)

SWANWHITE: *(Springs up and kisses the closed visor.)* The golden gate is closed, but I can see your good and watchful eyes through the bars. *(She knocks on the visor.)* Open, open for your little Red Riding Hood!—Nobody at home. . . . "Come in, come in!" said the wolf, lying in the bed!

THE DUKE: *(Puts her down on the floor.)* You lovely little flower! Grow and spread your fragrance! If I come back—well, then so be it! If I fail to return, then I shall watch over you from the starry heavens above! And I shall never cease to see you!

Up there one becomes all-seeing like the Creator himself!. . . . *(He leaves her, warding her off with a gesture, and walks out determinedly.—Swanwhite drops to her knees and prays for her father.—The rose bushes outside sway in the wind. The peacock shakes his tailfeathers and his wings.— Swanwhite goes over to the peacock. She strokes his tail and his back.)*

SWANWHITE: Pavo. . . . dear little Pavo! What do you see? What do you hear? Do you hear someone coming? Could it be a little prince, could it? Is he handsome and is he kind? You should be able to see it with your many blue eyes. . . . *(She takes hold of one of the bird's rudder-feathers and scrutinizes its eyes keenly.)* Must you keep staring at us with your eyes, you naughty Argus? Are you trying to keep guard to see that two young people's tiny little hearts do not beat too fast?—You stupid little Pavo! I'll close the curtain so you will not be able to see! *(She closes the curtains which shield the peacock from view, although the landscape outside is still visible. Then she walks over to the doves.)* My white doves—white—white—white! You shall soon look upon the very whitest of all!. . . . Silence, wind! Silence, roses! Silence, doves! My prince is coming!. . . .

(She gazes outside. Then she withdraws into the doorway of the pewter chamber. There she places the door ajar in order to be able to regard the prince through the opening. She remains standing there, seen by the audience but unseen by the prince.—The Prince enters from the rear through the archway. He is dressed in black and wears armor. Having keenly observed the furnishings and decorations in the room, he seats himself at the table, removes the helmet and regards it. His back is turned toward the door behind which Swanwhite has hidden.)

THE PRINCE: If anyone is here, answer, please! *(Silence.)* Someone is here. . . . I can feel the warmth of a young body coming toward me like a wind from the south. . . . I hear a breath that has the fragrance of roses—however feeble it may be, it is strong enough to send a flutter through the feathers of my helmet. . . . *(He places the helmet to his ear.)* My helmet sings like a great sea shell. . . . it is the thoughts in my head that have collected like a swarm of bees in a log. Zum-zum, the thoughts say, exactly like the bees as they buzz round the queen—the queen of my thoughts, my dreams! *(He lays the helmet before him on the table and regards it.)* Dark and arched as the heaven of Night, but without any stars—for the black plume of mourning turns everything into blackness since my mother died. . . . *(He keeps turning the helmet, scrutinizing it.)* But there—in the darkness—way down—I glimpse a streak of light. . . . Has heaven been cleft?. . . . And through the cleft I see. . . . not a star—for a star is like a diamond—but a blue sapphire, the queen of precious stones, the blue of the summer sky, on a milky white heaven, shaped like the egg of a dove. . . . What is it? Can it be my ring? And a black, velvety, feathery cloud sweeps by—and the sapphire smiles—but the sapphire cannot smile—it shoots out lightning, a blue lightning—flashes of summer lightning—flashes of heat, without thunder. . . . What are you? Who are you? Where are you? *(He regards the inside of the helmet.)* Neither here nor there! Nowhere! *(He brings the helmet close to his face)* I come close to you, and you draw away from me!

SWANWHITE: *(Steals forward on tiptoe.)*

THE PRINCE: Now I see two—two eyes—two human eyes. . . . I kiss you! *(He presses a kiss against the helmet.)* *(Swanwhite advances to the table and seats herself slowly, face to face with the Prince.—The Prince rises, bows to her, his hand on his heart. Then he stands looking at her.)*

SWANWHITE: Are you the young prince?

THE PRINCE: I am the young king's faithful servant—and yours!

SWANWHITE: What message does the young king send to his bride?

THE PRINCE: He sends his greeting to Princess Swanwhite—a thousand dear greetings of love; and he says that the bliss and happiness in store for him shall ease the time of waiting of its pain and tediousness.

SWANWHITE: *(Who has regarded the Prince searchingly.)* Why does not my Prince sit down?

THE PRINCE: If I should be seated when you are, then I should have to kneel when you stand!

SWANWHITE: Tell me something about the King. What does he look like?

THE PRINCE: What does he look like? . . . *(He runs his hand over his eyes.)* How strange! I can't see him!

SWANWHITE: What do you mean?

THE PRINCE: He is gone from my sight. I just can't see him. . . .

SWANWHITE: Is he tall?

THE PRINCE: *(He fixes his eyes on Swanwhite.)* Wait! Now I see him! He is taller than I am!

SWANWHITE: Handsome?

THE PRINCE: He could not compare with you!

SWANWHITE: Speak about the King—not about me!

THE PRINCE: I am speaking about the King.

SWANWHITE: Is he fair or is he dark?

THE PRINCE: If he were dark, he would grow fair the moment he saw you. . . .

SWANWHITE: You speak more out of chivalry than with wisdom! Has he blue eyes?

THE PRINCE: *(With his eyes on the helmet.)* Will you let me look?

SWANWHITE: *(Holds up her hand to keep him at a distance.)* You. . . . you!

THE PRINCE: Y-o-u-you; y-o-u-t-h spells youth.

SWANWHITE: Are you teaching me the alphabet?

THE PRINCE: The young King is tall and fair. He has blue eyes, broad shoulders, and hair like a young forest. . . .

SWANWHITE: Why are you wearing a black plume?

THE PRINCE: His lips are red like cloudberries, his cheeks are white, and a young lion might be envious of his teeth!

SWANWHITE: Why is your hair so damp?

THE PRINCE: His heart is devoid of fear and has never shrunk from remorse over an evil deed!

SWANWHITE: Why is your hand trembling?

THE PRINCE: We were to speak of the young King and not of me!

SWANWHITE: Are you correcting me?

THE PRINCE: It is my mission to teach you to love the young King whose throne you are to share with him.

SWANWHITE: How did you arrive here across the sea?

THE PRINCE: By sail—in my sloop!

SWANWHITE: In this stormy weather?

THE PRINCE: One does not get far without wind!

SWANWHITE: How wise you are, young man!—Would you like to play a game with me?

THE PRINCE: Whatever I must do, I am glad to do!

SWANWHITE: I will let you see what I have in my treasure chest. *(She walks over to the chest and kneels beside it. Then she takes out several dolls, a baby rattle, and a hobby-horse.)* Here is the doll—she is my child of sorrow—she can never keep her face clean—I have carried her in my arms down to the wash-house and scrubbed her with the white sand. . . . But the dirt only clings to her still more. . . . I have given her a good spanking, but it does no good. . . . Now I have figured out what to do with her—the very worst that could happen to her!

THE PRINCE: What is that?

SWANWHITE: *(Looks around.)* She shall be given a stepmother!

THE PRINCE: But how will you do that? She must first of all have a mother, mustn't she?

SWANWHITE: I am the mother! And if I re-marry, then I will be her stepmother.

THE PRINCE: What's that you say! That isn't the way it is done!

SWANWHITE: And you will be her stepfather!

THE PRINCE: Oh, no!

SWANWHITE: But you must be good to her, even if she can't keep her face clean!—Pick her up, and let me see if you know how to hold a child! *(The Prince takes the doll unwillingly.)* You don't know how to hold her yet, but you will learn! Now take the rattle and rattle it for her. . . . *(The Prince takes the rattle.)* I can see that you don't know how to rattle either! *(She takes back the doll and the rattle and throws them into the chest. Then she picks up the hobby-horse.)* Here is my steed. He has a saddle of gold, and his hoofs are shod with silver. . . . He can travel more than forty miles in an hour! I have ridden him through the Wood of Sounds, across the Great Heath, over the Bridge of Kings, along the Great Highway, on the Road of Anxiety, as far as the Lake of Tears! There he lost his golden shoe. It fell into the Lake—and then a fish came along—and after that, a fisherman—and I got back the shoe! That was that! *(She throws the hobby-horse back into the chest, and takes out a chessboard with white and red squares and with chessmen made of gold and silver.)* If you would care to compete with me, then sit down on the lion skin there. *(She seats herself on the lion skin; then she sets up the chessmen.)* Sit down, won't you? The maidens can not see us here!

(The Prince seats himself timidly on the lion skin.)

SWANWHITE: *(Her hand runs over the lion's fur and mane.)* It's like sitting on the grass—not the green grass of the fields but of the desert—that has been scorched by the sun.—Now you must tell me something about myself! Do you like me a little?

THE PRINCE: *(Embarrassed.)* Shall we start playing?

SWANWHITE: Start playing? I don't care about playing. . . . *(She sighs.)* Oh!—You were going to teach me something. . . .

THE PRINCE: I am only a poor youth who can't do anything but saddle a horse and bear sword. And that wouldn't be of much help to you.

SWANWHITE: You seem sad. . . .

THE PRINCE: My mother is dead!

SWANWHITE: Poor little prince!. . . My mother is also up there with God in Heaven. She is now an angel! I sometimes see her at night. . . . Do you see your mother also?

THE PRINCE: No-o!

SWANWHITE: Have you a stepmother?

THE PRINCE: Not yet—my mother has only just died.

SWANWHITE: You must not feel sad. . . . You see, there is an end to everything. . . . Now I shall give you a banner to make you happy again. . . . But I just remember it's the one I made for the young King! Now I shall make one for you! . . . This is the King's—this one with the seven tongues of fire. I shall sew one for you with seven red roses! But you have to help me by holding the skein of yarn. . . . *(She takes out a skein of bright red yarn from the chest and hands it to the Prince.)* One-two-three! I am starting now—but your hand must not tremble!—Perhaps you would like to have some of my hair mixed in with the yarn? —Pull out a few hairs!

(She bends her head to him.)

THE PRINCE: No-no, I couldn't do that!

SWANWHITE: Then I shall do it myself! *(She pulls out a few hairs and winds them into the yarn.)* What is your name?

THE PRINCE: That is a question that you must not ask!

SWANWHITE: Why?

THE PRINCE: Didn't the duke, your father, tell you?

SWANWHITE: No! What would happen if you told me your name? Could it be the cause of something dreadful?

THE PRINCE: Didn't the Duke tell you?

SWANWHITE: I have never heard of such a thing! That a man can't speak his own name!

(The curtain, behind which the peacock is hidden, moves and an undefinable sound, as of castanets, is heard.)

THE PRINCE: *(Listening.)* What was that?

SWANWHITE: *(Disturbed.)* It is Pavo. . . . Do you suppose he can understand what we say?

THE PRINCE: Who can tell?

SWANWHITE: Well—what is your name?

(The peacock again makes a clucking sound with his beak.)

THE PRINCE: I am afraid! You must not ask me again!

SWANWHITE: He is just snapping his beak. . . . You must keep your hands steady!—Did you ever hear the story of the little princess who was never allowed to speak her prince's name lest something dreadful should happen? And do you know why?

(The drapery hiding the peacock is drawn aside, and the peacock is now turning his back on Swanwhite and the Prince. The bird's tail is spread into a fan, and all its "eyes" seem to be fixed on the two.)

THE PRINCE: Who drew aside the curtain? Who ordered the bird to look at us with all its many eyes? . . . Please do not ask me my name again!

SWANWHITE: Perhaps I had better not!—Lie down, Pavo! Lie down!

(The curtain closes again.)

THE PRINCE: Are there ghosts here?

SWANWHITE: If you mean that strange things happen here, yes. Many things take place here, but I am so used to them—and besides. . . . *(In an undertone.)* They say that my stepmother is a witch!—Ouch, I pricked my finger!

THE PRINCE: How did you do that?

SWANWHITE: There was a splinter in the wool! The sheep have been housed in the cattle-shed all winter—that's probably how the splinter got there.—Could you help me take it out?

THE PRINCE: Yes—but we have to sit at the table so that I can see. . . .

(They rise and go over to the table and sit down.)

SWANWHITE: *(Holds out her little finger to the Prince.)* Do you see anything?

THE PRINCE: *(Somewhat bolder than before.)* What do I see! I can see right through the rosy palm of your hand. . . . I see life and the world in glowing colors. . . .

SWANWHITE: Take out the splinter now—it gives me pain. . . .

THE PRINCE: But I shall have to hurt you!—Forgive me if I do!

SWANWHITE: Why, yes—only help me. . . .

THE PRINCE: *(Presses her little finger and pulls out the splinter with his nail.)* There it is, the nasty little thing that dared to give you such pain!

(He throws the splinter on the floor and makes believe he tramples on it.)

SWANWHITE: Now you must suck out the blood, or it will fester.

THE PRINCE: *(Sucks her finger.)* Now I have drunk of your blood! Now I am your foster-brother!

SWANWHITE: Brother and sister—well, but *that* we were the moment we saw each other. . . . Now I have a little brother—and it is you! . . . My little brother! Take hold of my hand!

THE PRINCE: *(Takes her hand.)* My little sister! . . . *(He notices her beating pulse under his thumb.)* What is it that is ticking: one—two—three—four. . . .

(He continues to count silently after having glanced at the clock.)

SWANWHITE: Yes—what is it that is ticking? One—two, one—two! Our hearts are not in our fingers—it's under one of the breasts. . . . Put your hand here and you will feel! *(The doves move close to each other and start cooing.)* What is it, my little white ones?

THE PRINCE: Sixty! Now I know what it is that is ticking. . . . It is time! Your little finger is the second hand. . . . It has ticked away sixty times in the minute that just passed. Do you think there is a heart inside the clock, too?

SWANWHITE: *(Fingering the clock.)* One can't get inside the clock! It's as hard as getting inside your heart. Feel my heart!

(Signe enters from the pewter chamber. She carries a steel whip which she lays on the table.)

SIGNE: The Duchess commands the children to seat themselves opposite each other, on each side of the table!

257

(The Prince seats himself opposite Swanwhite. They regard each other silently for a few moments.)

SWANWHITE: We have been placed far away from each other; yet we are closer.

THE PRINCE: Two beings are never so close to each other as when they are parted!

SWANWHITE: You have learned that!

THE PRINCE: I learned it this very moment. . . .

SWANWHITE: Now you are beginning to teach me something. . . .

THE PRINCE: And *I* am learning from *you*. . . .

SWANWHITE: *(Indicates the fruit bowl.)* Would you like to eat some fruit?

THE PRINCE: No—to eat is such an ugly habit!

SWANWHITE: Yes, it is!

THE PRINCE: There are three maidens standing here: one at the pewter chamber, one at the wardrobe chamber, and one by the fruit chamber. Why are they standing there?

SWANWHITE: They are there to guard us. . . . to see that we do nothing that is forbidden. . . .

THE PRINCE: Are we not permitted to go into the rose garden?

SWANWHITE: I am only allowed to go into the rose garden in the morning. In the afternoon my stepmother's bloodhounds are let out and are free to roam wherever they wish. I am never permitted to go to the beach—and that is why I never can bathe.

THE PRINCE: Have you never been to the seashore—never heard the sea wash the sands?

SWANWHITE: Never! All I can hear is the sound of the waves when a storm is raging. . . .

THE PRINCE: Have you never heard the whistling and whining of the wind when it sweeps over the waters?

SWANWHITE: It does not reach us here.

THE PRINCE: *(Moves his helmet over to Swanwhite.)* Listen within, and you shall hear. . . .

SWANWHITE: *(Holds the helmet to her ear.)* What is it that I hear?

THE PRINCE: The song of the sea, the whispering wind. . . .

SWANWHITE: No—I hear human voices. . . . Quiet now! . . . I hear my stepmother talking! . . . She is speaking to the overseer of the castle—she mentions my name—and the young King's! She uses harsh and evil words—she swears that I shall never be a

258

queen—and she vows that—that *you* shall marry her daughter—
the malicious Lena. . . .

THE PRINCE: Indeed! . . . Is that what you hear in the helmet?

SWANWHITE: Yes!

THE PRINCE: Why, I didn't know one could hear things in it! This
helmet was a baptismal gift to me from my godmother.

SWANWHITE: Will you give me a feather from your plume?

THE PRINCE: As surely as I live! . . .

SWANWHITE: But you must cut it into a quill so that I can write
with it.

THE PRINCE: You know how to write, do you?

SWANWHITE: Father has taught me. . . .

> *(The Prince pulls out a black feather from his plume, then
> produces a silver knife, richly inlaid, from his girdle and
> shapes the feather into a quill pen. Swanwhite brings out
> an inkwell and parchment from the table drawer.)*

THE PRINCE: Who is Princess Lena?

SWANWHITE: *(Writes.)* Who is she? Would you like to woo her?

THE PRINCE: There is evil afoot in this house. . . .

SWANWHITE: Do not fear! My father has given me a gift to help me
in the event of need!

THE PRINCE: What is the name of your gift?

SWANWHITE: It is the horn *Stand-by!*

THE PRINCE: Where have you hidden it?

SWANWHITE: *(In a suppressed tone of voice.)* You can read it in
my eyes—I dare not speak it aloud for fear that the maidens
might hear.

THE PRINCE: *(Looks into her eyes.)* I see it!

SWANWHITE: *(Pushes the inkwell, pen and parchment across the
table to the Prince.)* Write it!

THE PRINCE: *(Writes.)*

SWANWHITE: *(Takes the parchment and reads.)* Yes—there is
where it is!

> *(She writes.)*

THE PRINCE: What are you writing?

SWANWHITE: Names! All the beautiful names a prince might have.

THE PRINCE: All except mine!

SWANWHITE: Yours also!

THE PRINCE: Do not write it!

SWANWHITE: Now I have written all the names I can think of—twenty of them—and so yours must be one of them! *(She pushes the parchment across the table again.)* Read! *(The Prince reads. Swanwhite suddenly claps her hands.)* Oh! I read it in your eyes!

THE PRINCE: Don't speak it! In the name of the Merciful God—don't speak it!

SWANWHITE: Why not? What will happen? . . . Do you want Lena to speak it? Your bride—your beloved!

THE PRINCE: Oh, please don't say such things! Please don't!

(Swanwhite has risen and starts to dance on the floor.)

SWANWHITE: I know his name—the most beautiful in any land! *(The prince gets up and catches her. He puts his hand over her mouth.)* I'll bite your hand, I'll suck your blood, and we will be brother and sister twice over! Do you know what that means?

THE PRINCE: That means we are twin brother and sister!

SWANWHITE: *(Throwing her head back.)* Oho-ho-ho! Do you see—there is a hole in the ceiling and I can see heaven, a little bit of the heavenly sky—a window pane—and behind the pane I see a face! Is it an angel's? . . . Oh, but look, look! It is your face I see!

THE PRINCE: The angels are little girls—not boys!

SWANWHITE: But it is you!

THE PRINCE: *(Looks up at the ceiling.)* It is a mirror!

SWANWHITE: Woe to us! It is my stepmother's witchcraft mirror! She has seen everything! She has been watching us the whole time!

THE PRINCE: I can see the stove in the mirror—and in the stove I can see a pumpkin hanging!

(Swanwhite takes a motley colored pumpkin, strangely shaped, out of the stove.)

SWANWHITE: What is it? It looks like an ear. . . . And that witch has heard us, too, every word. . . . Heaven help us! *(She throws the pumpkin back into the stove. She runs limping across the floor toward the bed, stops suddenly and lifts up her foot, then sits down and rubs it. The Prince falls on his knees before Swanwhite, eager to help her.)* How horrible! She has put needles on the floor!—No—you must not touch my foot! You must not!

THE PRINCE: Dear heart, you must take off your stocking if I am to
help you!

SWANWHITE: *(Sobbing.)* You must not! You must not see my foot!

THE PRINCE: But why—why?

SWANWHITE: *(Hides her foot under her.)* I can't tell you why—I
can't tell you! Go away, go away from me!—I shall tell you
tomorrow! I can't tell you now! . . .

THE PRINCE: But your little foot is hurting you. . . . I have to take
out the needle!

SWANWHITE: Go, go, go!—No—no, I can't let you help me!—If
mother had been alive, this would never have happened! Mother
—mother—mother!

THE PRINCE: I can't understand you at all! Are you afraid of me?

SWANWHITE: Please don't ask me. . . . Only go away and leave me!
Oh!

THE PRINCE: *(Rises; sorrowfully.)* What have I done?

SWANWHITE: Don't leave me—I don't want to hurt you. . . . But I
can't tell you. . . . Oh, if I could only get to the shore and the
beautiful sand. . . .

THE PRINCE: What then?

SWANWHITE: I can't tell you! I just cannot! *(She hides her face in
her hands.) (The peacock is now heard clucking with its beak
and the doves are seen to move.—The three maidens enter in a
row.—A sudden gust of wind is heard and the trees in the rose
garden sway; the golden clouds over the sea disappear and the
blue sea changes into a dark surface.—Swanwhite has eagerly
been observing what is happening.)* Can heaven be sitting in
judgment on us? . . . Has misfortune come to our house? Oh,
if my grief could raise my mother from beneath the black earth!

THE PRINCE: *(Puts his hand on his sword.)* I would give my life
for you!

SWANWHITE: Not that! She has the power of blunting your sword,
too!—Oh, if only my grief could bring back my mother from her
grave! *(The swallows twitter in their nest.)* What was that?

THE PRINCE: *(Notices the nest of the swallows.)* A nest of swallows! I didn't notice before. . . .

SWANWHITE: Nor did I! When did they build it? How did they
happen to build it here?—No matter—it is a good omen; but

261

I am so worried—my brow is wet with perspiration—I feel choked up. . . . Look, even the rose there begins to wilt when that evil woman approaches—for, mind you, it is she who is coming. . . .

(The petals of the rose on the table start to close and the leaves begin to droop.)

THE PRINCE: But the swallows—from where did they come?

SWANWHITE: Certainly not from my wicked stepmother, for the swallows are birds of good will. . . . She is here now!

(The stepmother enters from the rear. She steals in like a panther.—The rose of the table withers completely.)

THE STEPMOTHER: Signe! . . . Go and get the horn from the bed!

(Signe goes over to the bed and takes the hidden horn.)

THE STEPMOTHER: My prince, where do you intend to go?

THE PRINCE: The day is growing toward its close, Duchess, the sun is about to set, and my sloop is anxious to return home. . . .

THE STEPMOTHER: It is far too late in the day—the gates are closed—and the dogs are let loose. . . . Do you know my bloodhounds?

THE PRINCE: Yes, I do indeed. But do you know my sword?

THE STEPMOTHER: Is there anything so remarkable about your sword?

THE PRINCE: It has known blood upon occasion!

THE STEPMOTHER: Oho!— You don't mean the blood of women, do you? Tell me, would Your Grace like to sleep in the blue chamber?

THE PRINCE: No, by God, I want to sleep in my own bed at home.

THE STEPMOTHER: Is there anyone else who would like to do the same?

THE PRINCE: Many more.

THE STEPMOTHER: How many? As many as this: one—two. . . .

(As the Duchess starts counting, a parade of the castle's servitors and retainers file by on the veranda, all with threatening mien. Some are armed. Looking rigidly ahead—without casting a glance into the room—are seen: The Majordomo, The Steward, The Warden of the Castle, The Master Cook, The Soldier in charge of the pillory, The Master of the Stables, The Riding Master, etc.)

THE PRINCE: I will sleep in the blue chamber.

THE STEPMOTHER: I thought you would. And now let me wish our infatuated knight-errant a thousand good nights. . . . and I feel certain that Swanwhite will wish you the same!

> *(A white swan flies by outside the rose garden; a poppy falls from the ceiling on the Stepmother, who swiftly falls into a slumber together with the maidens.—)*

SWANWHITE: *(Goes over to the Prince.)* Goodnight, my Prince!

THE PRINCE: *(Takes her hand, saying softly to her.)* Good night! . . . Oh, I am to sleep under the same roof as my princess—my dreams embracing your dreams; and tomorrow we shall rise to new adventures, to new. . . .

SWANWHITE: *(In a subdued voice.)* Now you are my one and only one on earth—you are my protector, now that she has separated me from my father's precious gift, from my mighty support. . . . Look, she is asleep!

THE PRINCE: Did you see the swan?

SWANWHITE: No—but I heard it! It was my mother!

THE PRINCE: Let us flee!

SWANWHITE: No—we must not flee—Patience! We shall meet in our dreams! Shall we not? . . . But for us to do that, you must. . . . you must love me more than anything on earth! Love me—oh, do, do!

THE PRINCE: My King, and my oath to him. . . .

SWANWHITE: I am your queen—I am your heart!

THE PRINCE: I am a knight!

SWANWHITE: I am not! And therefore—therefore I take you—as my prince. . . .

> *(She places her hands round her mouth and forms it as though she were speaking his name in a whisper.)*

THE PRINCE: Woe! Woe! What have you done?

SWANWHITE: I gave myself to you when I spoke your name—with me upon your wings, you are again yourself, you. . . .

> *(She whispers his name again.)*

THE PRINCE: *(As if he caught the name in the air with his hand.)* Was it a rose you threw to me? *(He kisses his fingertips and makes believe he throws her a kiss.)* Swanwhite!

SWANWHITE: You threw me a violet! That is what you are—that is what your soul is! Now I am drinking you in—I have you within me—in my heart! Now you are mine!

THE PRINCE: And you are mine! To whom do we then belong?

SWANWHITE: To us—to ourselves!

THE PRINCE: We—you and I!—I love you!

SWANWHITE: You love me!

THE PRINCE: You love me!

SWANWHITE: I love you! *(The stage grows light. The rose on the table comes back to life and rises and opens again.—The faces of the Stepmother and the maidens are lighted up and are given an expression of beauty, goodness and happiness. The Stepmother raises her sleepy head and, with eyes closed, she seems to regard the bliss of the Prince and Swanwhite with a sunny smile.)* Look, look! The cruel woman smiles as though dreaming of memories of youth. . . . and the false Signe is full of faith and hope. . . . the ugly Tova is beautiful, and the little Elsa has grown up. . . .

THE PRINCE: Our love has done it!

SWANWHITE: Has it really? May God bless love then! Bless it, mighty God of Creation!

> *(She falls on her knees and weeps.)*

THE PRINCE: You are crying?

SWANWHITE: Yes—but tears of happiness!

THE PRINCE: Come into my arms and you will smile again!

SWANWHITE: In your embrace I would die!

THE PRINCE: Then smile and die!

SWANWHITE: That's how I would wish to die!

THE PRINCE: *(Embraces her.)*

> *(The Stepmother wakes. When she sees the Prince and Swanwhite in an embrace, she strikes the table with the steel whip.)*

THE STEPMOTHER: I believe I have been sleeping! . . . Hoho! It's gone so far already! Did I say the blue chamber! I meant the Blue Tower! There is where the prince will sleep—with the iron maiden!—Maidens! *(She calls out and the maidens awaken.)* Show the Prince the shortest way to the Blue Tower! And should he make any misstep, then call the Warden, the Riding Master, the Stable Master, the Soldier in charge of the pillory!

THE PRINCE: There is no need for that! I can go through fire, through water, down into the earth, beyond the clouds. . . . and I shall meet my Swanwhite despite everything—for she is with me wherever I am! And now—I go to meet her—in the Blue Tower. . . . Can you do as much with your tricks of magic and your sorcery? I doubt it. . . . for you are lacking in love!

(He goes out, followed by the maidens.)

THE STEPMOTHER: *(To Swanwhite.)* You don't need many words to let me know what you wish for—so be brief!

SWANWHITE: First of all I desire clean water to bathe my feet in. . . .

THE STEPMOTHER: Hot or cold?

SWANWHITE: If I may be so bold—warm water.

THE STEPMOTHER: Anything else?

SWANWHITE: A comb to comb my hair with. . . .

THE STEPMOTHER: Of silver or gold?

SWANWHITE: Are you—are you being good to me?

THE STEPMOTHER: Silver or gold?

SWANWHITE: Wood or horn is good enough for me. . . .

THE STEPMOTHER: What else?

SWANWHITE: Clean linen. . . .

THE STEPMOTHER: Of silk or flax?

SWANWHITE: Flax.

THE STEPMOTHER: Very well!·I have heard what you desire. Now you shall hear what *I* desire! I want you to have no water, neither cold nor tepid; I want you to have no comb, neither of wood nor horn—much less of silver or gold! That is how good I am to you. And I want you to wear no undergarment of silk or flax, but I demand that you go at once to the wardrobe chamber and put on the black chemise of coarse homespun next to your body! Now I have told you what to do!—And if you try to leave these chambers—which you can not because I have placed traps outside—you will be dead. . . . or I shall mark your pretty little face with my steel whip so that no prince or king will ever want to look at you again!—And now you get to bed!

(She strikes the steel whip against the table top; then she goes out, slamming the golden gates of the archway shut, the gates closing with a creaking, squeaking sound.)

END OF ACT ONE

ACT II.

The setting is the same, except that the golden gates are closed. The peacock and the doves are sleeping. The golden clouds are now black as the sea and the land in the distance.

Swanwhite, in black homespun, is lying in the bed. The lace night-gown is no longer in sight.

The doors to the pewter chamber, the wardrobe chamber and the fruit chamber are open.

The three maidens stand immobile, their eyes closed, holding small, burning Roman lamps in their hands.

A swan flies over the rose garden outside. A chord, as of trumpet tones, is heard, as of swans on migration.

Soon after, Swanwhite's Mother, dressed in white, appears outside the gates. She carries the shade of a swan on one arm; on the other one, a small golden harp. She hangs the swan on the gate, which opens by itself and closes after her, when she has entered the room.

She places the harp on the table, looks around and observes Swanwhite. Then the harp begins to play; and the lamps which the maidens are carrying, go out, one after the other: the one furthest away first; the doors to the chambers close, one after the other, the one furthest away first. The clouds recapture their golden sheen.

The Mother lights a lamp on the golden lampadary and goes over to the bed. She kneels at its side. During the following scene the harp keeps playing.

The Mother rises, lifts Swanwhite from the bed and places her in a large chair with arm rests. Swanwhite is still sleeping. Then she kneels, removes Swanwhite's stockings and puts them under the bed. Weeping, she bends over Swanwhite's tiny feet as if bathing them with her tears. Then she wipes them with a white linen cloth and kisses them. She puts a pair of sandals on her feet, which now are pure white. She rises again, takes out a gold comb and combs Swanwhite's hair. Having done this, she carries her back to the bed and takes a white night-gown from her handbag and spreads it over the coverlet

266

beside Swanwhite. Having kissed her on the forehead, she prepares to leave. Just then a white swan again flies by outside, and the chord which was heard previously, is sounded.

At the next moment, the Prince's Mother, also dressed in white, is seen entering through the gate, on which she also hangs an image of a swan which she is carrying.

SWANWHITE'S MOTHER: Well met, sister! Will it be long before the cock crows?

THE PRINCE'S MOTHER: Not too long. . . . The dew is already lifting from the roses, the corncrake can be heard in the hay, and dawn is drifting in from the sea.

SWANWHITE'S MOTHER: Let us hasten to do what we have to do, sister. . . .

THE PRINCE'S MOTHER: You have summoned me to talk about our children. . . .

SWANWHITE'S MOTHER: I was wandering about in a greenclad field in the land where there are no sorrows. There I met you, whom I had not known before—yet had always known. . . . and you told me of your grief over your poor little lad who was so lonely down there in the valleys of sorrow. . . . You opened up my heart; and my thoughts—which still can not help being earthbound—went out to my poor abandoned little girl—now destined to become the wife of the young King, who is a cruel and evil man.

THE PRINCE'S MOTHER: Then I spoke, and you listened. . . . May he who is most worthy get the worthy maiden—may the power of love win and let these two distressed hearts be joined together that they may inspire and give comfort to each other!

SWANWHITE'S MOTHER: Their hearts have already exchanged kisses, their souls have embraced each other! May sorrow turn into joy for them, and the earth rejoice and exult at their newfound happiness!

THE PRINCE'S MOTHER: Oh, that heaven would let it come to pass!

SWANWHITE'S MOTHER: It will have to be through fires of suffering!

THE PRINCE'S MOTHER: (*Takes the Prince's helmet which he has left behind, in her hand.*) May sorrow turn into joy and happiness for them—on the morning of this day, a year after his mother was taken away from him!

(She exchanges the black plume in the Prince's helmet for one of red and white.)

SWANWHITE'S MOTHER: Give me your hand, sister, and may the hours of trial begin! . . .

THE PRINCE'S MOTHER: Here is my hand—and enclosed in it my son's!—Now we have bound them together. . . .

SWANWHITE'S MOTHER: In honor and chastity! . . .

THE PRINCE'S MOTHER: Now I shall go and open the Blue Tower! And then our two children may embrace each other. . . .

SWANWHITE'S MOTHER: In honor and chastity!

THE PRINCE'S MOTHER: *(Embraces Swanwhite's Mother.)* And we shall meet again on the fields of verdure, where no sorrows exist. . . .

SWANWHITE'S MOTHER: *(Indicating Swanwhite.)* Listen!—She is dreaming of him! . . . Oh, that vain, malicious woman who believes that she can tear apart those who love each other! . . . Now they are wandering hand in hand in the land of dreams beneath whispering pine trees, under happy linden trees. . . . and they are full of frolic and smiling. . . .

THE PRINCE'S MOTHER: Ssh! Morning is dawning—I can hear robin redbreast chirping—and the stars are withdrawing to their nests in the firmament. . . . Farewell, my sister!

(She leaves, taking along her swan.)

SWANWHITE'S MOTHER: Farewell! . . .

(She passes her hand over Swanwhite as though she were blessing her. Then she goes out, taking her swan with her. She closes the gate as she goes out.)

(The clock on the table strikes three times. The harp on the table is momentarily silenced, then commences to play a new, lovely melody.)

(Swanwhite awakens, looks around, listens to the music of the harp, gets out of bed, runs her hands through her hair, regards happily her tiny white feet, notices the white linen on the bed. Then she seats herself where she sat before at the table. She seems to be regarding someone sitting opposite her, where the Prince had been seated previously. She looks straight into his eyes, gives him a smile of recognition and extends her hand across the table. Her lips move as if speaking, but occasionally are motionless as if listening to an answer.

268

She points significantly to the white and red feathers of the helmet and leans forward as if she were whispering; she throws her head backward and inhales the air through her nostrils, as if drawing in a pleasant fragrance. She encircles the air with her hand as if to catch a kiss thrown to her, and then kisses her fingertips, returning the kiss sent to her. She writes with the quill pen after having first stroked it as one strokes a bird, then pushes the parchment to the opposite end of the table. She seems to be following "his" pen with her eyes as he is writing his reply to her; then she stretches forward to take back the parchment with his answer. She reads it and puts it away in her bosom. She feels of her black garment, indicating the sad change in her appearance. Then—with a gesture toward her bosom—she smiles at the surmised answer and breaks into happy, ringing laughter.

She shows by gestures that she has combed her hair, rises and advances to the center of the floor. With a shy expression she puts forward her white little foot, but stops suddenly, waiting for the answer, which she receives with puzzlement. She quickly hides her foot.

She then goes over to the chest, takes out the chessboard, which she places on the lion skin, makes a gesture as if bidding another player to be seated, lies down on the rug and sets up the chessmen. She then starts to move as though she were playing with someone present in the invisible.

The harp stops playing for a moment; then it resumes with a different melody.

The chess game ends and Swanwhite seems to be speaking with the invisible one. Suddenly she moves back as if the unseen one were coming too close to her. She wards him off with a gesture and springs up like lightning. She regards the unseen one with a long, reproachful look; then she picks up her linen and hastens to her bed, behind which she hides.)

THE PRINCE: *(Is seen outside the gates. He attempts to open them, but in vain. Despairing and sad, he glances above.)*

SWANWHITE: *(Steps forward.)* Who comes there at the dawning of the sun?

THE PRINCE: Your heart's beloved, your prince, your own!

269

SWANWHITE: From where does my heart's beloved come?

THE PRINCE: From the land of dreams, from the red, red dawn hiding behind rose tinted mountains, from whispering pines, from playful lindens. . . .

SWANWHITE: What did my heart's beloved do in the land of dreams behind the red, red dawn?

THE PRINCE: He played and smiled, he wrote her name, he played with golden chessmen on a rug of lion skin. . . .

SWANWHITE: With whom did he play—with whom did he play chess?

THE PRINCE: With Swanwhite!

SWANWHITE: It is he! . . . Welcome to my castle, to my table, and to my embrace!

THE PRINCE: Who will open the golden gates?

SWANWHITE: Give me your hand! . . . *(The Prince offers her his hand; she takes it.)* It is as cold as your heart is warm.

THE PRINCE: My body slept in the Blue Tower, while my soul wandered in the land of dreams! . . . It was cold and dreary in the Blue Tower—dreary and dark. . . .

SWANWHITE: At my bosom I shall warm your hand—with my glances I shall warm your hand—and I shall warm your hand with my kisses! . . .

THE PRINCE: Lighten my darkness with the light of your eyes!

SWANWHITE: Is it so dark for you?

THE PRINCE: In the Blue Tower you see neither sun nor moon!

SWANWHITE: Rise, sun! Bring warmth, wind! Keep rolling, billowing sea! . . . You golden gate—you think you can keep two hearts, two hands, two lips apart! But nothing can separate us. . . .

THE PRINCE: Nothing!

> *(Two portals are pushed from the sides—in front of the gates—and close off the view of the two lovers from each other.)*

SWANWHITE: Woe! What did we say—and who could have overheard us? Who is punishing us?

THE PRINCE: I shall not be kept from you, love of my heart! The sound of my voice will reach you—it will penetrate through stone and steel and metal—and will caress your dainty little ear—I embrace you in my thoughts—I kiss you in my dreams. . . . Never again shall anything on earth separate us! Nothing—ever!

SWANWHITE: Nothing—ever!

THE PRINCE: I see you even though my eye does not—I taste your fragrance—you are like the essence of roses. . . .

SWANWHITE: But I want you in my arms!

THE PRINCE: You have me!

SWANWHITE: No—I want to feel your heart close to mine. . . . I wish to sleep on your arm! Oh, let us, let us, kind God—let us have each other!

> *(The swallows twitter. A little white feather falls on the floor. Swanwhite picks it up and discovers it to be a key. She opens the portals and the gates with it.)*

THE PRINCE: *(Enters.)*

SWANWHITE: *(Throws herself in his arms. The Prince gives her a kiss on the mouth.)* You didn't kiss me!

THE PRINCE: Why, I just did!

SWANWHITE: I didn't feel your kiss!

THE PRINCE: Then you do not love me!

SWANWHITE: Embrace me!

THE PRINCE: *(Embracing her.)* I am taking your breath from you!

SWANWHITE: No! Now I can breathe!

THE PRINCE: Give me your soul!

SWANWHITE: Here you have it! . . . Give me yours!

THE PRINCE: Ah!—Now I have yours, and you have mine!

SWANWHITE: Give me back mine!

THE PRINCE: And I want mine!

SWANWHITE: Try to find it!

THE PRINCE: Woe, we are lost! You are I, and I am you!

SWANWHITE: We are one!

THE PRINCE: The dear God heard your prayer—we have found each other!

SWANWHITE: We have found each other—but now I have you no longer—I do not feel the clasp of your hand—or your lips when they touch mine—I cannot see your eyes—cannot hear your voice. . . . You are no longer near me. . . .

THE PRINCE: I am still here!

SWANWHITE: Down here, yes—but I wish to meet you up there—in the land of dreams. . . .

THE PRINCE: Let us fly there—on the wings of sleep. . . .

SWANWHITE: Resting on your arm!

THE PRINCE: In my embrace!

SWANWHITE: In your arms, yes!

THE PRINCE: This is Paradise!

SWANWHITE: Eternal bliss—without blemish—without end. . . .

THE PRINCE: Who can part us ever?

SWANWHITE: No one!

THE PRINCE: Are you not my bride?

SWANWHITE: Are you not my bridegroom?

THE PRINCE: Not here! But in the land of dreams!

SWANWHITE: Where are we?

THE PRINCE: Down here—on earth!

SWANWHITE: Where clouds drift by, where the sea roars, where the earth weeps on the grass at night before the sun goes up! Where the hawk destroys the dove, where the swallow kills the fly, where the leaves fall and turn to dust, where hair grows white and cheek becomes sunken, where the eye grows dim, and the hand withers. . . . Upon this earth—down here!

THE PRINCE: Let us flee!

SWANWHITE: Yes—let us flee!

> *(The Gardener, dressed in green, with cap, knee breeches, apron, shears and knife in his belt, suddenly appears behind the table. In his hand he carries a small wooden bowl from which he scatters seeds.)*

THE PRINCE: Who are you?

THE GARDENER: I sow seeds, I sow seeds. . . .

THE PRINCE: What are you sowing?

THE GARDENER: Seeds, seeds, seeds. . . .

THE PRINCE: What kind of seeds?

THE GARDENER: Seed buds and seed pods. One pulls this way, two pull that way; when the bridal gown is on, concord and harmony end! In discord, I shall sow; and in concord, you shall reap. One and one makes one, but one and one makes also three; one and one makes two, but two makes three! Do you understand?

THE PRINCE: Earthworm, digging in the dust—you, who walk with your brow toward the ground and turn your back on heaven—what is it you are trying to teach me?

THE GARDENER: That you are an earthworm digging in the dust! And because you turn your back on the earth, the earth shall turn its back on you!—Good morning!

272

(He drops out of sight behind the table.)

SWANWHITE: What was that? Who was that?

THE PRINCE: It was the green gardener.

SWANWHITE: Green? Wasn't he blue?

THE PRINCE: He was green, my dearest!

SWANWHITE: How can you say what is not so?

THE PRINCE: My dearest love, I only said what is true.

SWANWHITE: Oh woe, he does not speak the truth!

THE PRINCE: Whose voice is that I hear? It is not my Swanwhite's!

SWANWHITE: Who is this man I see before me?—Not my prince, whose very name once had the power to attract me like the Necken and his playing, like the song of the mermaids upon the green billows. . . . Who are you, you strange man with evil eyes and—and gray hair!

THE PRINCE: Not until now did you notice that my hair had turned gray during the night in the Tower—after hours of sorrow over losing my Swanwhite. . . . who now no longer exists!

SWANWHITE: Yes—Swanwhite is here!

THE PRINCE: No! I now see before me a maiden whose face is black. . . .

SWANWHITE: Did you not notice until now that I am black and that I am dressed in black?. . . . Then you cannot love me any more!

THE PRINCE: No! The maiden who stands here is mean and graceless!

SWANWHITE: Then you were false a moment ago!

THE PRINCE: No! For then I saw another maiden before me! Now —now you threw a stinking nettle in my face!

SWANWHITE: Now your violets reek of stinkweed! Faugh!

THE PRINCE: This is my punishment for being unfaithful to my young King!

SWANWHITE: I suffer at the thought of not having looked forward to seeing the young King!

THE PRINCE: Keep waiting! He will come!

SWANWHITE: I shall not wait! I shall go to meet him!

THE PRINCE: Then I shall remain!

SWANWHITE: *(Goes toward the rear.)* So this is what love is!

THE PRINCE: *(Beyond himself.)* Where is Swanwhite? Where— where—where? The dearest—the most beautiful—the most loving one!

SWANWHITE: Go seek—go search for her!

273

THE PRINCE: But not down here!

SWANWHITE: Then somewhere else!

> (*She leaves.—The Prince is alone. He seats himself at the table and weeps in his hands. Now a gust of wind sweeps through the room, causing the draperies and curtains to flutter; and the strings of the harp emit a soughing sound. The Prince rises, goes over to the bed and stops, regarding the pillow, on which can be seen the impression of Swanwhite's head. He picks up the pillow and presses his lips against it in a kiss. Then there is a noise heard outside. He seats himself at the table again. The doors to the chambers are thrown open. The three maidens appear, their faces now black. The Stepmother, also with black face, enters from the rear.*)

THE STEPMOTHER: (*In a gentle voice.*) I wish you good morning, my dear Prince! How did you sleep?

THE PRINCE: Where is Swanwhite?

THE STEPMOTHER: She has gone to her young King for their wedding. Isn't it time for you, my Prince, to be thinking of marriage, also?

THE PRINCE: I think of only one thing!. . . .

THE STEPMOTHER: Little Swanwhite?

THE PRINCE: Is she too young for me, do you think?

THE STEPMOTHER: Common sense usually goes with gray hair. . . . I have a daughter with good sense and understanding. . . .

THE PRINCE: Gray hair, did you say?

THE STEPMOTHER: He is not aware of it! He does not believe it! Maidens! Signe, Elsa, Tova! Isn't it to laugh—a young suitor with gray hair!

> (*The maidens burst into loud laughter, in which the Stepmother joins.*)

THE PRINCE: Where is Swanwhite?

THE STEPMOTHER: Trace her footsteps, why don't you! Here is a clue!

> (*She holds before him a parchment with writing on it.*)

THE PRINCE: (*Reads.*) She has written this?

THE STEPMOTHER: You know her handwriting, don't you? What has she written?

THE PRINCE: That she hates me, and that she loves another. . . .

that she has been playing with my feelings. . . that she spits out the kisses I have given her. . . and casts my heart to the swine. . . Oh, now I want to die! This is the end. . . .

THE STEPMOTHER: A knight does not wish for death merely because a maiden has made a plaything of his love! He proves himself a man by choosing another maiden!

THE PRINCE: Another's love? When there *is* only *one!*

THE STEPMOTHER: One? There are at least two! And my Magdalena possesses seven barrels of gold!

THE PRINCE: Seven barrels. . . .

THE STEPMOTHER: Yes, and even more!

(*There is a silence.*)

THE PRINCE: Where is Swanwhite?

THE STEPMOTHER: And Magdalena is skilled in many ways. . . .

THE PRINCE: Does she know witchcraft, too?

THE STEPMOTHER: I have no doubt she can bewitch a young prince. . . .

THE PRINCE: (*Regards the parchment.*) You say Swanwhite has written this?

THE STEPMOTHER: Magdalena would never write anything like that!

THE PRINCE: Is Magdalena good of heart?

THE STEPMOTHER: She is goodness itself! She does not play with sacred feelings—she does not seek revenge for any little wrong —she is faithful to the one she loves.

THE PRINCE: Then she is beautiful!

THE STEPMOTHER: No—that she is not!

THE PRINCE: Then she is not good! . . . Tell me some more about her!

THE STEPMOTHER: Take a look at her!

THE PRINCE: Where?

THE STEPMOTHER: She is here. . . .

THE PRINCE: And you say Swanwhite has written this?

THE STEPMOTHER: Magdalena would have written lovingly.

THE PRINCE: What would she have written?

THE STEPMOTHER: That. . . .

THE PRINCE: Speak the word! Speak the word *love* if you can!

THE STEPMOTHER: Lobb!

THE PRINCE: You can not say it!

THE STEPMOTHER: Lobb!

THE PRINCE: No! No!

THE STEPMOTHER: Magdalena can say it! May she come in?

THE PRINCE: She may come.

THE STEPMOTHER: *(Rises. She turns to the maidens.)* Bind a kerchief before the Prince's eyes—and then he shall discover in his arms a princess the like of which is not to be found in seven kingdoms!

SIGNE: *(Steps forward and covers the Prince's eyes with a kerchief.)*

THE STEPMOTHER: *(Claps her hand.)* Well?—Isn't she coming? *(The peacock clucks with his beak and the doves coo.)* Has my magic left me? Or what has happened?—Where is the bride?. . . .

> *(Four maidens enter from the rear, carrying baskets of white and pink roses. Music is heard from above. The maidens go over to the bed and sprinkle it with roses.*
>
> *Two knights, with dropped visors, enter. They take the Prince by the hand and escort him to the rear, where the false Magdalena meets them. She is accompanied by two matrons. The bride is heavily veiled.*
>
> *The Stepmother, with a gesture, bids all except the bridal couple to leave, after which she herself goes out, having first closed the curtains and the gates.)*

THE PRINCE: Is my bride here?

MAGDALENA: Who is your bride?

THE PRINCE: I do not remember her name. . . . Who is your bridegroom?

MAGDALENA: The one whose name must not be spoken!

THE PRINCE: Speak his name if you can!

MAGDALENA: I can—but I will not!

THE PRINCE: Say his name if you can!

MAGDALENA: Tell me *my* name first!

THE PRINCE: Seven barrels of gold—a crooked back—mean and malicious—and a hare-lip to boot! What is *my* name? Tell me if you can!

MAGDALENA: Prince Grayhair!

THE PRINCE: That is correct!

> *(The false Magdalena throws off her veil, revealing herself as Swanwhite. She stands before the Prince, dressed in white and with a wreath of roses round her brow.)*

276

SWANWHITE: Who am I?

THE PRINCE: You are a rose!

SWANWHITE: You are a violet!

THE PRINCE: *(Removes the kerchief from his eyes.)* You are Swanwhite!

SWANWHITE: And . . . you. . . . are. . . .

THE PRINCE: Do not say it!

SWANWHITE: You are mine!

THE PRINCE: But you went away—went away from my kisses. . . .

SWANWHITE: And came back—because I love you!

THE PRINCE: But you wrote wicked words to me. . . .

SWANWHITE: Which I have erased—because I love you!

THE PRINCE: And you said I was false!

SWANWHITE: What does it matter so long as I love you and you are faithful to me?

THE PRINCE: But you wished to go to the young king?

SWANWHITE: And I came to you—because I love you!

THE PRINCE: Now *you* must reproach *me,* too!

SWANWHITE: No! My love for you has made me forget all our discord. . . .

THE PRINCE: If you love me, will you be my bride?

SWANWHITE: I *am* your bride!

THE PRINCE: May heaven bless our union, then!

SWANWHITE: Our union—in the land of dreams!

THE PRINCE: In my arms! *(He leads Swanwhite to the bed, places his sword in the middle of it. Swanwhite and the Prince lie down on the bed, the sword separating them. The golden clouds turn a rosy red, there is a soughing in the rose garden, and the harp plays beautifully, ecstatically.)* Goodnight, my queen!

SWANWHITE: Good morning, dearest love of my soul! . . . I can hear your heart sighing like the billows of the sea, like the canter of a steed, like the eagle in flight. . . . Hold me by the hand!

THE PRINCE: There! Now we can lift our wings!

THE STEPMOTHER: *(Enters with the maidens, who bear torches. All four have gray hair.)* I must see my work completed before the Duke returns. Magdalena, my daughter, betrothed to the prince —while Swanwhite pines away in the Tower. . . . *(She advances toward the bed.)* They are sleeping in each other's arms. . . . Maidens! I call you as witnesses! *(The maidens approach the bed.)* What do I see! Your hair is gray!

SIGNE: And so is yours, Duchess!

THE STEPMOTHER: Mine? Let me look at myself! *(Elsa brings her a mirror which she holds up to her.)* This is the doings of evil powers!—And perhaps the Prince has been given back his black hair?—Let us have some light here! *(The maidens hold their torches over the sleeping couple.)* By God! It is indeed true! You see! Beautiful, isn't it? . . . . But the sword! Who has placed the sword between them?—That makes their union invalid!

> *(She attempts to remove the sword, but the Prince holds it firmly in place without waking.)*

SIGNE: Duchess—there is some devil's game here!

THE STEPMOTHER: How so?

SIGNE: This is not Princess Magdalena!

THE STEPMOTHER: Who is it? Tell me—my eyes fail me!

SIGNE: Why! It is Princess Swanwhite!

THE STEPMOTHER: Swanwhite!—Is this a deed of Satan, an illusion, or have I done what I least wanted to do? . . .

THE PRINCE: *(Turns in his sleep. His lips meet Swanwhite's.)*

THE STEPMOTHER: *(Is involuntarily moved by the beauteous sight.)* Never did I see a more beautiful sight! Two roses—meeting in the wind—two stars falling from the firmament, touching each other as they fall. . . . Oh, it is altogether too beautiful! Youth, beauty, innocence, love! . . . Memories—lovely memories—from the days when I lived in my father's home when *he,* the youth whom I never got was in love with me. . . . What did I say that he did?

SIGNE: Your Grace said that he loved you. . . .

THE STEPMOTHER: Then I did speak the great word correctly! *Beloved!* That is what *he* called me: *My beloved!*—before he went away to war. . . . *(She sinks into reverie.)* He never returned! . . . And so I had to take the other man, whom I couldn't suffer! . . . Now my life will soon have passed, and I have to be content with the happiness that might have been! I must learn to enjoy—the happiness of others. . . . for that, too, is love! . . . But my Magdalena? Will she enjoy happiness also? You, greatest of all Love, You—eternal God of Creation— how did You ever soften my hardened heart again? Where are my iron strength and will-power gone, where is my hate? Where is my revenge? *(She seats herself and gazes upon the sleeping lovers.)* I call to mind a song, a song of love, that he sang in my young days—the last evening that. . . . that. . . . *(She gets up as if awakened from a dream and flies into a violent rage. She shrieks out:)* Come hither, servitors,—all of you! Hasten, warden, steward, soldiers—all of you! *(She snatches the sword from the bed and flings it to the floor.)* Hither, people! *(There is a noise and racket. Servitors and people of the castle enter, as before.)* There you see the Prince, the vassal of the young King defiling his Lord and Master's bride! I call you to bear witness to this infamy, this outrage! Put this traitor to his King in chains and take him to his Royal Master and Benefactor! And place the concubine in the spiked barrel! *(The Prince and Swanwhite awaken.)* Soldier in charge of the stocks—Riding Master! Seize the Prince!

> *(The Soldier in charge of the stocks and the Riding Master seize the Prince.)*

THE PRINCE: Where is my sword? My sword, dedicated to slay all evil and to defend innocence and all that is good!

THE STEPMOTHER: *(With sarcasm.)* Whose innocence?

THE PRINCE: My bride's!

THE STEPMOTHER: His concubine's innocence! Prove it!

THE PRINCE: Oh, mother! My mother!

> *(The white swan is winging past outside.)*

THE STEPMOTHER: Bring me a pair of scissors, maidens, and I shall shear off the harlot's tresses!

SIGNE: *(Brings the Stepmother a pair of scissors. The Stepmother takes Swanwhite by the hair and is about to cut it off but the scissors, once opened, will not close.)*

THE STEPMOTHER: Now I shall remove your beauty—and your love! *(She is gripped by panic that communicates itself to the servitors, etc., and to the maidens.)* Has the enemy come upon us? Why do you show fear, maidens?

SIGNE: The dogs are barking, Duchess, and the horses are neighing! That forebodes visitors!

THE STEPMOTHER: Quick! Hasten to the drawbridge, men!—all of you! All! Mount the bulwark! Use fire—water—sword—broad-axe!

—END OF ACT TWO—

279

ACT III.

The three maidens are busying themselves in the chambers. Signe, the false maiden, is in the pewter chamber; Elsa, the youngest one, is in the wardrobe chamber; and Tova, the ugly and faithful one, in the fruit chamber.

THE GARDENER: *(Enters.)* Signe, my daughter, help me!

SIGNE: Tell me first who it was who came with such din and clatter? Was it the Duke, our sovereign master? Has he returned from the war?

THE GARDENER: No—it was not the Duke. It was an emissary from the young King, Princess Swanwhite's bridegroom, with a large, armed retinue! Misfortune is over us—we shall have war again . . . and the castle will be burned!

SIGNE: Your seeds have sprouted, your seeds of discord. . . . Now you will reap what you have sown. . . .

THE GARDENER: You false one, it was you who betrayed us when you provided the Duchess with the horn *Stand-by!*

SIGNE: A faithful servant must be false to her mistress's enemies. . . .

THE GARDENER: And now the castle will be destroyed unless the Duke returns in time! How can we bring back the Duke?

SIGNE: Wait until tomorrow and there will be a way out! First there will be the great festal banquet. I am scrubbing and cleaning the pewter, Elsa is brushing the raiments, and Tova is drying the fruit.—But the young King—did he not come, too?

THE GARDENER: Only the emissary and his retinue. . . .

SIGNE: Where is the young King?

THE GARDENER: Who knows? Perhaps he is among the retinue, masquerading as one of them. . . .

SIGNE: And the Prince?

THE GARDENER: In the Tower!—Why do you hate him?

SIGNE: I? I do not hate him—no, no, no!

THE GARDENER: Perhaps you—perhaps you. . . .

SIGNE: Do not say it! . . .

THE GARDENER: How can you hate someone you love?

SIGNE: If you can not have him. . . .

280

THE GARDENER: If you cannot have him? But Princess Swanwhite will not get her Prince; and she loves him even unto death—beyond death. . . .

SIGNE: Will the Prince be put to death?

THE GARDENER: You know that he is doomed!

SIGNE: No—by the God of Heaven—he must not die! Save him, save him!

THE GARDENER: How can I?

SIGNE: Through the secret tunnel—here is the trap-door—you can feel it—here in the floor. . . .

> *(She slides her foot along the floor.)*

THE GARDENER: The Duchess is having it flooded with water!

SIGNE: You can overcome that. . . . But save the Prince, save him! Waste no time! And then set out to sea—in the sailing vessel!

THE GARDENER: Very well, I shall go—and make restitution for the evil I have done. . . . And if I should not return, then—then I shall have atoned. . . .

SIGNE: May God protect you on your way. . . .

SWANWHITE: *(Enters from the rear.)* You evil man, what are you doing here?

THE GARDENER: *(Kneeling before her.)* I am here to do good in repentance for the evil I have done. . . .

SWANWHITE: How can you? You sowed seeds of enmity—what are you sowing now?

THE GARDENER: *(Scattering seeds.)* I am sowing seeds of concord and harmony, peace, and happiness of heart—for the good of all, to the detriment of no one!—Do not judge me, Princess,—for I am without blame in your feuding!

SWANWHITE: Feuding? About whether you were blue or green?

THE GARDENER: Yes, that is right!—Now gaze at me with both your beautiful eyes—with both of them?

SWANWHITE: I am looking at you!

THE GARDENER: *(He turns about.)* You see, then, that I am blue on one side and green on the other!

SWANWHITE: Thus you are both blue and green! You old codger—you have taught me wisdom. Thank you—But where are you going now?

THE GARDENER: To fetch the Prince!

SWANWHITE: You? Can evil turn into good?

281

THE GARDENER: Not always!—I am going to him now—through the secret passage. . . . If I do not come back with him—then I'll remain there—without him!

SWANWHITE: May God bless you and protect you!

THE GARDENER: *(Disappears through the trapdoor.)*

SWANWHITE: *(To Signe.)* Are you planning to betray your father?

SIGNE: No—not my father.

SWANWHITE: The Prince, then?

SIGNE: Not the Prince either!

SWANWHITE: Then me!

SIGNE: *(Remains silent.)*

SWANWHITE: Then me!

SIGNE: Princess! Disaster is hovering over us all—only one man can save us—the Duke, your father. . . .

SWANWHITE: Yes—the Duke—my glorious father! But he cannot hear us, now that you have betrayed me and given the horn into the hands of the Duchess.

SIGNE: Do you know where she is hiding it?

SWANWHITE: Let me think. . . .

> *(She reflects for a moment.)*

SIGNE: Where?

SWANWHITE: Hush! I see it—behind the mirror—in her. . . . in her silver chamber!

SIGNE: Then I shall go and fetch it. . . .

SWANWHITE: You? To help me?

SIGNE: Do not thank me! Disaster is upon us all. . . . No, no—do not thank me!

SWANWHITE: You are not betraying us, are you?

SIGNE: Us? Not all—nobody and somebody—one and one—I only wish I knew! Whomever one loves, one also hates—yet not always. . . . On the other hand, he whom one hates, one does not love—always! I am torn by my feelings. . . . We shall see, *Stand-by!* I shall help—but whether I shall stand by, I do not know. . . .

> *(She leaves.)*

SWANWHITE: Riddles and answers!—Elsa—Tova! Come here! *(Elsa and Tova enter.)* Come over here! *(She beckons.)* Here! We are being listened to!—Beautiful Elsa, good little Tova, stand close to me, help me! I have a premonition, a fear of

something—I do not know what! Someone is coming here—I
do not know who it can be! The ear of my heart tells me, and
I have a feeling in my heart that danger is lurking—a cold
breath is blowing on me—a breath cold as ice—a rude hand is
touching my tender young breasts, much as the hawk defiles the
feeble offspring of the dove. . . Woe, it is wild game—it is
cabbage and onions—all that is malodorous and stinking—it is
goat's beard and putrid nestle. . . . Now he is here. . . . the young
King! *(The King enters from the rear. He is in heat and
slightly inebriated from wine.)*
*(Swanwhite stands with Elsa and Tova in a cluster, Swan-
white in the back of them.)*

THE KING: *(He scrutinizes the three insolently.)* You three! Do you
know who I am?

ELSA: The knight-errant Wine-sack!

THE KING: You saucy little shrew, come here and give me a kiss!
I like you because you are tiny, lovely to look at and saucy! *(To
Tova.)* You look ugly and goodnatured! Tell me where Princess
Swanwhite is!

ELSA: Guess!

THE KING: Is it you? . . . Yes, so you are Swanwhite—but your
hands are red! You can't be a princess!—Do you know who
I am?

ELSA: Lord He-Goat!

THE KING: I like girls that are bold and impudent! Come here,
little one, and let me embrace you!

ELSA: You are in great haste, are you not?

THE KING: Just think if the Princess should hear us!

TOVA: She does not hear such things—she has only ear for the song
of the nightingale, the soughing of the linden trees, the whispering of the wind when it is ruffling the waves. . . .

THE KING: Don't be so long-winded, you ugly little maid! You take
too many words into your mouth at one time. . . . If you,
servant-girls, do not behave now and tell me where the Princess
is, I shall raise a fiery red trail on your backs with her stepmother's whip of steel, so help me Satan in Hell! Where is
Princess Swanwhite?

SWANWHITE: *(Steps forward.)* Here she is!

THE KING: *(Looks her up and down.)* You? *(There is a silence.)*

283

I can't believe it! I have seen the Princess's image, and on that she was a thing of beauty! But it had been painted by the treacherous Prince—no doubt for the purpose of deceiving me.— You have no nose, child,—you have weird looking eyes—and your lips are too heavy. . . . I am asking you now: Are you really Swanwhite?

SWANWHITE: I am Swanwhite.

THE KING: *(Seats himself.)* So this, then, is—all there is!—Can you dance? Can you play the harp? Can you play chess—or sing? *(Swanwhite is silent.)* None of it! . . . . And for such a nobody I am preparing to make an assault upon the castle—to burn, lay waste, to start a war! *(Swanwhite remains silent.)* You can, at least, speak, can't you? Can you while away a long dreary evening with talk?—Not even that!

SWANWHITE: *(In a dull voice.)* I can speak—but not with you!

THE KING: You sound like a chimney-sweep! Perhaps you are even deaf!

SWANWHITE: There are certain voices that fail to reach my ear.

THE KING: And perhaps blind and lame, too? *(Silence.)* Quite frankly, it is too much of an effort for so little gain! *(Again there is silence.)* Go in peace—or rather, let me go. . . Prince Faithless may pluck his goose with your parents if he so wishes! *(He gets up.)* And with me also! *(He goes out.)*

> *(Swanwhite, Elsa and Tova raise their hands in relief and remain in that position. The harp commences to play again.)*

THE PRINCE: *(Enters from the secret passageway.)*

SWANWHITE: *(Rushes into his arms.)*

> *(The harp plays. Elsa and Tova go out, rear.—*
> *The Prince tries to speak but cannot. Swanwhite has the same difficulty.*
> *The King appears in the wardrobe chamber, spying on them and listening to them.*
> *Swanwhite, recovering her composure, can at last speak.)*

SWANWHITE: Is this a farewell?

THE PRINCE: *(Now also recovering his voice.)* Speak not that word!

SWANWHITE: He has been here—he is here—the King, Your King!

THE PRINCE: Then it is farewell for ever!

SWANWHITE: No—he did not see me—he did not hear me—he did not like me!

284

THE PRINCE: But he is bent on taking my life!

SWANWHITE: All are bent on taking your life. . . . Where are you going?

THE PRINCE: To the seashore. . . .

SWANWHITE: And out to sea, in storm and current, you—my dearest of all, my heart and joy. . . .

THE PRINCE: I shall drink my wedding toast in the waves. . . .

SWANWHITE: Then I shall die!

THE PRINCE: Then we shall meet—never, never to be parted again!

SWANWHITE: Never again! But if I should not die, I shall grieve until you rise from your grave. . . .

THE PRINCE: My grave will be filled with blood for every tear from your radiant eye! But every time your heart is glad on this earth, my grave will fill with rose petals!

SWANWHITE: It is getting dark!

THE PRINCE: I am wandering in light—in your light—for I love you. . . .

SWANWHITE: Take my soul, take my life!

THE PRINCE: I have them both—take mine—take my soul, take my life! They are yours! My body leaves me—yet my soul remains!

SWANWHITE: My body remains here—but—my soul follows you!

THE PRINCE: *(Tries to speak but only his lips move.)*

SWANWHITE: *(Likewise goes through the same motion.)*

> *(The Prince descends into the secret passage.)*
>
> *(The King has followed the scene and has been so moved by varying feelings on discovering the Swanwhite he had not known, that he at first is ashamed, later is gripped by admiration and ecstacy. As soon as the Prince has left, he rushes forward and falls on his knees before her.)*

THE KING: Swanwhite, God's own beautiful creation, fear nothing! for now I have seen you, you perfect one,—now I have heard your voice of silver chords! But it was with *his* eyes I saw you, and with *his* ear I heard! I myself can never see or hear you, for your love does not belong to me. . . . I can tell by your stony glances that you do not even see me, and do not hear my words —that you exist for him alone! And if you were to be mine, I know I would hold a corpse in my arms! Forgive me for all evil I have done—forget that I have ever existed—and never think that I should even dare touch you with an unclean thought!

Only the memory of you shall follow me and punish me. . . . but before we part, let me hear your voice once more that I may keep the echo of it in my heart forever. . . . One mere word from you! No matter which! One mere word, one inspiring word from you!

(There is a silence.)

SWANWHITE: *(In a hard voice.)* Leave!

THE KING: *(Jumps to his feet.)* Raven! Now my answer is: blood! *(He draws his sword.)* And no one shall have you—no one but I! What I want is a raven! I love the strong—the hard—the rude—the coarse! The dove is no bird for me!

(Swanwhite has retreated behind the table.)

SWANWHITE: Help me, father. Stand by me—come to me, come!

THE KING: *(Falls back.)* There it came—the silver chord—the church bells on Angels' Day! . . . Now my power is gone! . . .

SWANWHITE: *(Almost singing the words.)* Come—come—come!

THE KING: How lovely a voice! My sword blushes out of shame and sheds tears! Go and hide yourself, sword! *(He puts back his sword in the scabbard.)* No—no sword! But the castle shall go up in flames and the traitor to his King shall suffer death!— Who is there?

TOVA: *(Enters with the horn.)* Here—here it is!

SWANWHITE: You, Tova! . . . And not Signe!

TOVA: I took it from Signe—she is forever faithless!

> *(Swanwhite blows the horn. In the distance is heard an answer from another horn.)*
>
> *(The King, stricken by panic, calls out to his men.)*

THE KING: To your horses! Loose the reins! Use your spurs! Do not spare your steeds!

> *(He flees, rear, and sets off to the right.)*
>
> *(Swanwhite blows the horn again. A horn answers outside.)*

TOVA: He is coming, our glorious hero! He is coming!

> *(There is a pause.—Again Swanwhite blows the horn.— The Duke enters. He and Swanwhite are alone on the stage, Tova having gone.)*

THE DUKE: My dearest child—what is wrong?

SWANWHITE: Father—your child is in danger. . . . You see that spiked barrel there!

THE DUKE: What has my little child done?

SWANWHITE: I learned the name of the prince by means that only love can provide. . . . I spoke his name. . . . and he fell in love with me. . . .

THE DUKE: That is not a matter of life and death! What else did you do?

SWANWHITE: I slept by his side, with the sword between. . . .

THE DUKE: Still not a matter of life and death—though not well advised! . . . What else?

SWANWHITE: That is all!

THE DUKE: *(To the Soldier in charge of the stocks.)* Roll out the spiked barrel! *(The Soldier leaves with the barrel.)*—Well, my child, and where is the Prince?

SWANWHITE: He is on his way back to his homeland in his sloop!

THE DUKE: In this frightful storm? . . . Alone?

SWANWHITE: Alone!— *(Anxiously.)* Could anything happen to him?

THE DUKE: That is for the Almighty to say, in whose hands he is!

SWANWHITE: Is there danger?

THE DUKE: The brave are often blessed with good fortune!

SWANWHITE: Then *he* deserves it!

THE DUKE: If he is without blemish or guilt, he will have it. . . .

SWANWHITE: He is! More so than I!

THE STEPMOTHER: *(Enters. She turns to the Duke.)* How did *you* come here?

THE DUKE: By the shortest way! I wish I had come sooner!

THE STEPMOTHER: Had you come earlier, your daughter would not have had this misfortune!

THE DUKE: What misfortune?

THE STEPMOTHER: The kind that cannot be helped!

THE DUKE: Have you proof?

THE STEPMOTHER: I have witnesses!

THE DUKE: Summon the Steward!

THE STEPMOTHER: He knows nothing!

THE DUKE: *(Rattling his sword.)* Summon the Steward!

THE STEPMOTHER: *(Shows fear. She claps her hands four times.)*
        (The Steward enters.)

THE DUKE: Prepare at once a dish of game, well seasoned with onion, parsley and cabbage!

THE STEWARD: *(Gazes at the Stepmother.)*

THE DUKE: Why these glances?—At once, I said! *(The Steward leaves.) (The Duke turns again to the Stepmother.)* Summon the gardener!

THE STEPMOTHER: He knows nothing!

THE DUKE: And he shall remain in ignorance! But I want him here! Summon him! *(The Stepmother claps her hands six times.) (The Gardener enters.)* Fetch me three lilies—one white, one red, one blue! *(The Gardener looks at the Stepmother.)* Watch your head, man! *(The Gardener leaves.)* Summon the witnesses!
(The Stepmother claps her hands once.)

SIGNE: *(Enters.)*

THE DUKE: Give your testimony! But in respectful words!—What did you see?

SIGNE: I saw Princess Swanwhite and the Prince in bed. . . .

THE DUKE: With a sword between them?

SIGNE: No—no sword!

SWANWHITE: Signe, Signe! You are giving false witness against me—against me, who saved your neck from the steel whip. . . . It hurts me—that you should do me this injustice! And you betrayed me that night, you know. . . . Why did you do this to me?

SIGNE: I did not know what I was doing—I did not want to do it— I carried out another's will—and now I do not care to live any longer. . . . For the sake of the Saviour forgive me! . . .

SWANWHITE: I forgive you. . . . but forgive yourself also—for you are without guilt—it was the evil will that held you captive. . . .

SIGNE: But you must punish me first!

SWANWHITE: Have you not been punished sufficiently, when you regret what you have done?

THE DUKE: I do not think so! . . . *(To the Stepmother.)* The rest of your witnesses!
(The two Knights enter.)

THE DUKE: Are you the knights who were in attendance?—Testify!

1ST KNIGHT: I escorted Princess Magdalena to her bed!

2ND KNIGHT: *(Parrots the 1st Knight.)* I escorted Princess Magdalena to her bed!

THE DUKE: What is this? A treachery that has backfired?—Other witnesses! *(Elsa enters.)* Your testimony!

ELSA: I saw Princess Swanwhite and the Prince—so help me God, the Great Judge, the Merciful One—fully dressed and with sword between them.

THE DUKE: One for and one against—two neither for nor against! —I shall leave it to God to judge!—Let us have the flower test!

TOVA: *(Steps forward.)* Gracious Lord and Master, noble Knight!

THE DUKE: Tell us what you know!

TOVA: My gracious Princess is innocent!

THE DUKE: Oh, my child, if you know Swanwhite to be innocent, then tell us!

TOVA: When I tell what is the truth, then. . . .

THE DUKE: . . . then nobody believes it! But when Signe speaks an untruth—then it is believed! . . . What has Swanwhite herself to say? Do not her steadfast eyes, her innocent mouth, her unblemished brow bespeak that she has been slandered? Does not my own fatherly eye see that this is not so? . . . And now—let us ask the Great Almighty to sit in judgment so that human beings may come to believe! *(The Gardener enters with the three lilies in a vase. The Duke places the flowers in a semicircle on the table. The Steward enters with a steamy dish on a platter.*

The Duke places the platter within the crescent of flowers.) For whom does the white lily stand?

ALL: *(Except Swanwhite and the Stepmother.)* For Swanwhite!

THE DUKE: Whose is the red lily?

ALL: *(Except Swanwhite and the Stepmother.)* The Prince's.

THE DUKE: Whose is the blue lily?

ALL: *(Except Swanwhite and the Stepmother.)* The young King's!

THE DUKE: Very well!—Tova, my child, you who believe in innocence because you are innocent yourself, will you now interpret the heavenly judgment and tell us the benign secrets of the flowers!—What do you see?

TOVA: I cannot speak of evil deeds!

THE DUKE: Then I shall! And then I shall let you speak of good deeds!—Look into the steaming blood of the wild game of the forest, look at the steaming herbs that awaken sensual pleasures. . . . What do you see?

TOVA: *(Regards the three lilies, which act as her words indicate.)* The white lily closes its petals in protection against impure influences. That is Swanwhite's.

ALL: Swanwhite is innocent!

TOVA: And the crimson one—that is the Prince's. . . . It, too, closes itself. . . . But the blue one—that is the King's—opens the jaws wide to breathe in pleasure. . . .

THE DUKE: You have interpreted with good sense! What else do you see?

TOVA: I see the red lily bend its head in respectful love to the white blossom—while the blue lily turns and twists in anger and envy. . . .

THE DUKE: Your interpretation is correct.—To whom, then shall Swanwhite belong?

TOVA: To the Prince—for his feelings are pure—and therefore stronger!

ALL: *(Except Swanwhite and the Stepmother.)* The Prince shall have his Swanwhite!

SWANWHITE: *(Runs to her father and throws herself in his arms.)* Oh, father!

THE DUKE: Summon back the Prince! Blow your horn and clarions! Put all the ships out to sea! But first—who shall be put in the spiked barrel? *(All are silent.)* Then I shall tell you!—The Duchess—this monstrous, lying woman!—Now you see, you evil woman, that your magic and your tricks, for all their power, were of no avail when confronted by love! . . . Leave—and speedily!

> *(The Stepmother makes a gesture with her hand that seems to silence the Duke.*
>
> *The Duke draws his sword, pointing it at the Stepmother, while carrying Swanwhite on his right shoulder.)*

Ugh, you wicked woman, my sharp sword will prick your evil schemes!

> *(The Stepmother drags herself out, weakening at the knees, facing the Duke like a panther.)*

And now—to the Prince!

> *(The Stepmother stops petrified on the terrace outside. Her mouth opens as if she were spewing venom. The peacock and doves fall down dead. The Stepmother begins to swell, her garments become inflated until the upper part of her body and her head are invisible. Her clothes are patterned in a design of snakes and branches.—*

The sun is now rising. Suddenly the ceiling descends slowly toward the floor, fire and smoke pour from the stove.

The Duke holds the sword handle, shaped like a cross, before the Stepmother.)

Pray to Jesus, pray to the Saviour!

ALL: Christ, have mercy!

> *(The ceiling rises and fire and smoke cease to pour from the stove.*
>
> *The sounds of voices and a disturbance outside are heard.)*

THE DUKE: What can be the matter now?

SWANWHITE: *(As if in a trance.)* I know it! . . . I see it! I hear the water dripping from his hair —I hear his heart silenced—he has stopped breathing. . . . I see it—he is dead. . . .

THE DUKE: Where—how—do you see this? Who is it you see?

SWANWHITE: Where, did you say? . . . I see it!

THE DUKE: I see nothing!

SWANWHITE: Oh—that they would come quickly. . . . for they must come!

> *(Four young maidens carrying baskets filled with white lilies and twigs of spruce enter, scattering them on the floor. Four young pages follow, ringing bells of silver, each one tuned in a different key; then the priest with the crucifix; the golden stretcher, on which the Prince is lying, covered with a white sheet, spun of flax. White and red roses are spread over the linen cloth.—The Prince's hair is now dark again, his cheeks rosy, and his face young. He is radiantly handsome, with a smile on his lips.*
>
> *The harp is playing; and the sun is rising. The stepmother's witch pack deflates, and she now appears as seen at first.*
>
> *The stretcher is set down and is illuminated by the rising sun. Swanwhite throws herself on her knees beside the stretcher, kissing the Prince's face.—All are weeping.)*
>
> *(Fishermen, who have carried the stretcher, are in the group.)*

THE DUKE: Fisherman, tell us briefly your tale. . . .

THE FISHERMAN: Noble Lord and Master, is it not plain to see? . . . The young Prince had already sailed across the sound—then, gripped by a violent longing, prompted by love,—he determined to swim back, despite the dangerous spring current, despite

291

weather and wind, after finding that his sloop would not respond to steering. . . . I saw his young head above the waves, I heard him cry out her name—and then—then we gently laid his dead body to rest on the white sand. His hair was grey from the night in the Tower, his cheek had withered from suffering and sorrow—a smile no longer dwelt on his dead lips. . . . And then—as he lay dead—he suddenly looked young and handsome again. . . . his dark hair crowned his brow—and the dead countenance smiled. . . . Look, he's smiling now! And the people that gathered down on the shore, carried away by the beautiful sight, turned to one another and said: Look! This is what love can do! . . .

SWANWHITE: *(Lies down beside the Prince's dead body.)* He is dead, his heart sings no more, his eyes no longer light my life, no longer do I feel the dew of his breath! He smiles—but not upon me—his smile is for heaven. . . . and I want to go with him on his pilgrimage!

　　　(She kisses his lips.)

THE DUKE: Do not kiss the lips of the dead! It is poison!

SWANWHITE: A sweet poison if it give me death—the death that to me means life.

THE DUKE: There is a saying, my child, that the dead do not meet according to their own desire. . . . and that that which we have loved in this life, has no value beyond the grave.

SWANWHITE: And our love—will not our love expand and endure to the beyond?

THE DUKE: Wise men hold a different view. . . .

SWANWHITE: Then he must come back here again, come down to me! Oh merciful God, release him from your heaven and send him back to me!

THE DUKE: Your prayer is in vain!

SWANWHITE: I cannot pray! Alas, the evil eye is still in power here!

THE DUKE: You mean the troll that burst in the sun! Let her be burned alive at the stake! Let there be no delay!

SWANWHITE: Burned—alive! No, no—not that! Let her merely go away from here!

THE DUKE: She shall be burned alive! Erect the stake on the shore that her ashes may be scattered by the wind!

SWANWHITE: *(Falls on her knees before the Duke.)* Oh no—I

plead for her—plead for my executioner! Have mercy on her! Have mercy!

(The Stepmother enters. She is now a changed woman, freed of bewitchery and enchantment.)

THE STEPMOTHER: Mercy!—Who spoke that sacred word? Who said a prayer from the depth of her heart for me?

SWANWHITE: It was I—I, your daughter,—mother!

THE STEPMOTHER: Oh God in heaven—she called me *mother!* What made you do that—who told you to?

SWANWHITE: It was love!

THE STEPMOTHER: Blessed be the love that can cause such wonders! —Believe me, my child,—your love can bring back the dead from the dark realms of the beyond! I myself have not the power, for love was denied to me—but *you* have!

SWANWHITE: What can I, poor little Swanwhite do?

THE STEPMOTHER: You can love—you can forgive. . . . yes, then you can do anything, you all-powerful little child! . . . Learn from me who no longer have any power! Go to your dearest one, speak his name, and place your hand on his heart! And with the aid of the Almighty—and alone with His help—your beloved shall hear you—if you have faith and believe!

SWANWHITE: *(With profound conviction.)* I do have faith—I believe—I pray!

(She goes over to the Prince's bier, places one hand on his heart; the other hand she raises heavenward. Then she bends down over the Prince and whispers in his ear, repeating this action two times. When she utters the words the third time, the Prince awakens. Swanwhite throws herself over him and he pulls her close to him. All those present kneel in prayer, giving thanks and praise to God.—Music.—)

CURTAIN

To the memory of George Freedley.

STORMCLOUDS
(1907)

A play in three scenes

PERSONS IN THE PLAY:

BRINK, a retired public official.
THE CONSUL, his brother.
STARCK, a pastry shopkeeper.
AGNES, his daughter.
LOUISE, Brink's housekeeper; a relative of his.
GERDA, Brink's divorced wife.
THE ICEMAN.
THE POSTMAN.
THE DELIVERY BOY.
THE DELIVERY GIRL.
THE LAMPLIGHTER.
MR. FISCHER, Gerda's present husband (mute character).
The voice of Mrs. Starck.

SCENE I.—The façade of an apartment house.
SCENE II.—The interior of Brink's apartment.
SCENE III.—The same setting as in Scene I.

The façade of a modern apartment-house, with a basement of granite. The upper floors are of brick, with a finishing coat of yellow plaster. The window casings and cornices are of sandstone.
In the center of the basement there is a low entrance door leading to the backyard and to a pastry shop.

The façade terminates left in a corner, where there is a square, planted with roses and other flowers.

There is a postbox at the corner. Above the basement is the first floor, with large windows that stand ajar; four of these open into the dining room, which is elegantly furnished.

On the floor above (second floor) the four center windows have their red shades pulled down, but the light penetrates from within.

In front of the house is the pavement, lined with trees. In the foreground, a green bench and a street lamp lighted by gas. It is unlit.

STARCK: *(Comes out, carrying a chair, on which he seats himself.)*

BRINK: *(Can be seen at table in the dining room. Behind him there is a stove of majolica, green in color and having a ledge on which a large, framed photograph is placed between two candelabra and two vases with flowers. A young woman, wearing a light-colored dress, is just serving the final course.)*

THE CONSUL: *(Enters from the avenue, right. He knocks on the window-pane with his walking-stick.)* Have you finished soon?

BRINK: I am coming directly.

THE CONSUL: *(Greets Starck.)* Good evening, Mr. Starck. The hot weather is still keeping up, isn't it?

(He seats himself on the bench.)

STARCK: Good evening, Mr. Consul. We are having real dog days, aren't we?—We've been busy making preserves all day. . . .

THE CONSUL: So-o? It's a good year for fruit, then?

STARCK: Fair.—We had a cold spring, but the summer has been insufferably warm. . . . We, who have to stay in the city, have certainly felt it.

THE CONSUL: I just came back from the country yesterday. . . . When the evenings begin to get dark, one longs for the city again.

STARCK: Neither I nor my wife have been outside the city limits this summer. Even though business is practically at a standstill, we have to stay in the city nonetheless and prepare for the winter. First there are the strawberries and the wild strawberries; then come the cherries—and then we have the raspberries, the gooseberries, melons, and the whole autumn crop. . . .

THE CONSUL: Tell me something, Mr. Starck, is this house for sale, do you know?

STARCK: I haven't heard so—no!

THE CONSUL: There are a great many people living here, aren't there?

STARCK: I think there are ten families here—if you count the people in the back. But we don't know one another. I must say there is unusually little gossip here in this house. It's almost as if the people here tried to conceal themselves. I have lived here now for ten years. The first two years I had as neighbors in the back a strange couple. They never made a sound all through the day— but at night people arrived in carriages, collected something, and drove away. Only at the end of two years did I find out that they kept some sort of nursing home. What they took away —was corpses!

THE CONSUL: How awful!

STARCK: And they call this house "the silent house". . . .

THE CONSUL: Well, I suppose the tenants here are quiet enough. . . .

STARCK: But there have been tragedies in this house, I can tell you. . . .

THE CONSUL: Tell me, Mr. Starck, who lives up there? . . . . *(He points to the second floor with his stick.)* On the second floor—above my brother?

STARCK: Well, up there—where the red shades are lighted up— there's where the previous tenant died this summr. Then the apartment stood vacant for a month. . . . and eight days ago a couple I haven't seen yet, moved in—I don't even know their name—and I never see them go out! . . . Why do you ask, Consul Brink?

THE CONSUL: Cha-a. . . . I don't know! The red shades make me think of a theatre curtain, behind which blood-curdling dramas are being rehearsed—at least that's what my imagination conjures up. . . . In the window stands a Phoenix palm looking like a birch rod, casting its silhouette on the window shade! If you, at least, could see somebody move about inside!

STARCK: I have seen quite a number of persons there, but not during the day—late at night. . . .

THE CONSUL: Women or men?

STARCK: Both, I think. . . . But now I must go down to my pots and pans. . . .

(He disappears through the basement entrance.)

296

BRINK: *(Has risen from the table and now lights a cigar. He speaks to the Consul from the window.)* I'll be ready in a minute—as soon as Louise has finished sewing a button on my glove.

THE CONSUL: Are you going downtown, then?

BRINK: We might take a stroll there, yes. . . . With whom was it you were talking?

THE CONSUL: It was only Mr. Starck, the pastry cook. . . .

BRINK: Oh, I see . . . yes, he is a nice man—and he has been my only company here this summer. . . .

THE CONSUL: You have stayed at home every single night—never gone out?

BRINK: Not once. These bright summer evenings make me shy. . . . There is no question but that it is beautiful out in the country. But in the city, summer seems contrary to the order of Nature. It gives you an almost ghastly feeling. . . . However, once the street lamps are lit again, I immediately feel at ease; and then I can start in taking my usual evening walk. It tires me, and so I sleep more soundly afterward. *(Louise comes with the glove and hands it to Mr. Brink.)* Thank you, my child. . . . Let the windows remain open, for there are no mosquitoes here. . . . Now I'll be with you right away. . . .

> *(He disappears in the direction of the postbox, in which he deposits a letter. He returns immediately and comes over to the Consul, and sits down on the bench beside him.)*

THE CONSUL: But tell me—why do you stay in the city when you *can* go to the country?

BRINK: I don't know. I have grown to be stationary, fixed. . . . I have become tied to this apartment through its memories; only in there do I find peace and protection. Yes—in there! It is interesting to look at one's home from the outside. . . . I make believe that some one else lives in there. Just think, I have lived there now for ten years!

THE CONSUL: Is it really ten years?

BRINK: Yes, time flies fast—once it has passed! But while it is passing, it is slow and tedious. The house was just being finished when I moved in. I saw them lay the parquet floor in the dining-room, saw them paint paneling and doors. *She* chose the wallpaper, that still covers the walls. . . . Well, that was that! Mr. Starck and I are the oldest tenants here; and he, too, has had his share of misfortune to contend with. . . . He is one of those who never seem to have too much luck. He is always in some difficulty. I have, as it were, lived his life and borne his troubles, while at the same time having my own burden to bear.

THE CONSUL: Is he a drinking man?

BRINK: Oh no! He doesn't neglect his business or his family. He just lacks enterprise and drive. And he and I know the history of this house. . . . Here they have drawn up in wedding carriages, and moved out in hearses—and the postbox over there has received a multitude of confidences.

THE CONSUL: You had a death here in the middle of the summer, didn't you?

BRINK: Yes, he died of typhoid—he was a bank auditor. And after his death the apartment stood vacant for a month. . . . First, however, the coffin came out, then the widow and the children—and last, the furniture. . . .

THE CONSUL: That was one flight up. . . .

BRINK: *(Pointing with his stick.)* Up there, yes, where you see the light. There are new tenants now, but I haven't met them yet. . . .

THE CONSUL: You haven't seen them either?

BRINK: I never inquire about the tenants. If they give me some confidence of their own volition, I accept it—but I never put it to wrong use or meddle in their affairs. I like to have some peace in my old age.

THE CONSUL: Old age, yes! To me old age is something to glory in. Then the rest of the journey won't seem so long!

BRINK: Why, certainly, it's nice to be old. . . . I am now balancing my accounts with life and human beings and have already started packing for the last journey. Being alone has its pros and cons, but as long as nobody has a stranglehold on you, you have at least your freedom. Freedom to come and go, to think and act, to eat and to sleep, just as you choose.

(A window shade is now pulled up in the apartment on the second floor, but only slightly. One sees a woman's gown for a moment; then the shade is quickly pulled down again.)

THE CONSUL: They are moving about up there. . . . Did you see?

BRINK: Yes, there is such a secretiveness up there—but it's worst at night. Now and then you hear music—bad music! And again I

298

think they must be playing cards—and late in the night, away after midnight, carriages draw up and call for. . . . I never complain about the tenants—for then they become vindictive, and retaliate. And they don't improve ever. . . . The best thing is to know nothing and say nothing!

> *(A man in black tie and dinner jacket comes from the square and deposits a large batch of letters in the postbox. Then he disappears.)*

THE CONSUL: That fellow had plenty of letters to post, didn't he?

BRINK: They seemed to be circulars. . . .

THE CONSUL: Who is he? Do you know?

BRINK: I don't suppose it could have been anyone but the new tenant who has moved in above me.

THE CONSUL: You think it could be he?—What do you think he looks like?

BRINK: I don't know. . . . Musician, some sort of theatreman, a touch of the operatic bordering on variety, professional card-player, Adonis—a little of everything!

THE CONSUL: He ought to have had black hair to go with his pale face; but it was brown, and therefore dyed, or perhaps a wig. Dinner jacket at home is an indication of an impoverished wardrobe; and the movements of his hands when he put the letters in the box made me think of someone mixing a deck of cards, cutting and dealing them! *(The faint sounds of a waltz being played on the piano can be heard from above.)* Always a waltz— perhaps they teach dancing. And nearly always the same one! What's the name of this waltz?

BRINK: I believe it is—yes, it's *Pluie d'Or*. . . . I know it by heart.

THE CONSUL: Did you yourself ever play it?

BRINK: Yes, both that one and the *Alcazar*.

> *(Louise can be seen inside the dining-room attending to various little chores on the buffet. She is arranging the glassware, among other things.)*

THE CONSUL: You still find Louise satisfactory?

BRINK: Very.

THE CONSUL: She is not planning to get married, is she?

BRINK: Not as far as I know.

THE CONSUL: You haven't seen anyone around, trying to court her?

BRINK: Why do you ask these questions?

THE CONSUL: Perhaps you yourself are smitten?

BRINK: I? Oh no, thank you! The last time I married, I was not too old. Didn't we have a child soon after? But now I am. And I want to spend my old age in peace.—Do you think I would want to take orders in my own home and be deprived of life, of everything I own, and of my honor?

THE CONSUL: At least, you saved your life, and your possessions that time. . . .

BRINK: What about my honor? Didn't I retain that, too?

THE CONSUL: You don't know? . . .

BRINK: What is it you are trying to say?

THE CONSUL: When she left you, she took your honor away from you. . . .

BRINK: Then I have been a living corpse for five years without knowing it.

THE CONSUL: You mean you were not aware of it?

BRINK: No—but now I shall tell you in just a few words exactly what happened. . . . When I, at fifty, remarried, I was wedded to a relatively young girl whose affection I had won. She gave me her hand in marriage without either fear or coercion. I promised her that if ever my age should prove burdensome to her youth, I would leave and give her back her freedom. . . . In due time, the child came, and neither of us wished to have any more. The child had shown signs of having outgrown her love for me; and I had begun to feel superfluous. So I left. That is, I took a boat—for we lived on an island. That was the end of that fairy tale. . . . I had redeemed my vow, and saved my self-respect.—What more could I do?

THE CONSUL: Yes, but she considered that a blemish on her honor. She felt that *she* should have left you. That is why she crucified you with surreptitious accusations—which never reached your ear.

BRINK: Did she accuse herself also?

THE CONSUL: No, she had no reason to do that.

BRINK: Well, then all is well, isn't it?

THE CONSUL: Do you know anything about her and the child since then?

BRINK: I don't wish to know anything about them. After I had suffered through all the horrors of losing her, I looked upon the experience as buried forever. And as this apartment held only beautiful memories for me, I stayed on. I am, however, grateful to you for having given me this precious information.

THE CONSUL: Which information?

BRINK: That she felt she had nothing to accuse herself of—for that would have been the same as an accusation against me.

THE CONSUL: I believe you are laboring under a great delusion. . . .

BRINK: Then let me continue to do so. A clean conscience—relatively clean—has always served me as a sort of diving suit, in which I could descend to the depths without fear of suffocating. . . . *(He rises.)* To think that I survived this with my life! I am glad it's over with.—Shall we go for a walk down the avenue?

THE CONSUL: Yes, let us. Then we can see the first street lamp being lighted.

BRINK: But I believe we are going to have moonlight tonight—August moonlight. . . .

THE CONSUL: Yes, and I believe full moon at that. . . .

BRINK: *(By the window. He speaks to Louise inside.)* Louise, will you please give me my walking-stick—the light summer one—just to have something in my hand.

LOUISE: *(Hands him the stick.)* Here you are, sir.

BRINK: Thank you, my child. And turn off the lights in the dining-room—unless you are busy with something. . . . We'll be gone for a while, I imagine—I can't say for how long. . . .

(Brink and his brother, the Consul, walk off to the right. Louise, in the window, watches them go off.)

STARCK: *(Comes from his pastry shop, through the basement door.)* Good evening, Miss. It's an infernal heat, isn't it? Have your two gentlemen gone out?

LOUISE: Yes, they have gone for a short walk on the avenue. It's the first time Mr. Brink has been out this summer in the evening.

STARCK: We old people love the twilight—it hides so many flaws and imperfections—both in ourselves and others. . . . Did you know, Miss, that my wife is going blind? But she refuses to have an operation. "What is there to look at?" she says; and sometimes she wishes that she was deaf also.

LOUISE: There are times when she could be right.

STARCK: You lead a nice, quiet life in there. . . . You have everything

301

you want, and nothing to worry about. I never hear anyone raise a voice or slam a door. Isn't it a little too quiet for a young girl like you?

LOUISE: No, indeed. I like the quiet. I like people who have some dignity, who are reserved and gracious, and whom one can converse with without stressing things; people with imagination. And who overlook the disagreeable things in our every-day life. . . .

STARCK: You never have any company either, do you?

LOUISE: No, the only one who calls, is the Consul. And never have I seen two brothers so devoted to each other.

STARCK: Who is the older of the two, anyhow?

LOUISE: I really don't know. There may be a difference of a year or two between them, or they may be twins. I don't know. But they both treat each other with mutual respect, as if the other one were the elder brother.

> *(Agnes comes out from the basement. She tries to steal past Mr. Starck, her father.)*

STARCK: Where are you going, Agnes my dear?

AGNES: I'm just going for a little walk. . . .

STARCK: That's right, but don't stay out too long. *(Agnes leaves. Starck again turns to Louise.)* Do you think that Mr. Brink still grieves over his dear ones?

LOUISE: He doesn't grieve—no! Nor does he miss them. . . . He has lost the desire to see them. But he lives with them in his memories. He dwells only on his moments of happiness.

STARCK: But he does worry about his daughter now and then, doesn't he?

LOUISE: Well, he can't help worrying, of course, that the mother might remarry; and then he would want to know what sort of stepfather the child would have. . . .

STARCK: I've been told that the wife at first gave up all claims to support, but five years later, through an attorney, sent a long statement with a demand for several thousand in payment.

LOUISE: *(In a tone of dismissal.)* That's something I don't know anything about.

STARCK: Be that as it may—I can't help thinking that the memory of his wife is dearest to him.

302

A Delivery Boy: *(Enters with a case of wine bottles.)* Excuse me, does Mr. Fischer live here?

Louise: Mr. Fischer? I don't know any Mr. Fischer here.

Starck: Perhaps it's he who lives upstairs, one flight up? Ring the bell one flight up around the corner!

The Delivery Boy: *(Goes toward the square.)*

Louise: Now we'll have another sleepless night since they have ordered wine.

Starck: What kind of people are they, anyhow? And why doesn't one ever see them?

Louise: I think they must go out the backway. I have never seen them—but I *hear* them.

Starck: *I* hear them, too,—banging doors and popping corks—and other noises besides. . . .

Louise: They never open the windows, not even in this frightful heat. They must be from some warm country. . . . Look, did you see the lightning—but there is no thunder. . . .

A Voice: *(From the basement.)* Starck dear, come down and help with the sugar syrup!

Starck: I'm coming, my darling!—You see, we are busy making preserves. . . . I'm coming, I'm coming. . . .

(He hurries down below.)

(Louise remains standing by the window.)

The Consul: *(Enters slowly from the left.)* Hasn't my brother come back yet?

Louise: No, Consul Brink.

The Consul: He stopped to telephone. . . . and I was to walk ahead. Well, I suppose he'll be here soon.—What's this lying here? *(He stoops and picks up a postal card from the pavement.)* What does it say on it? "Boston Club after midnight. . . . Fischer's"—Who is Fischer? Do you know, Louise?

Louise: There was a delivery boy here with some wine—he was looking for somebody by the name of Fischer on the second floor.

The Consul: The second floor—Fischer's! Red window shades that gleam like a cigar lantern in the night! I'm afraid you are getting bad company in this house!

Louise: What is a Boston Club?

The Consul: It may be something quite innocent—but somehow

303

. . . I don't know. . . . But how did the postal card. . . .? He must have dropped it a moment ago. I'll put it in the postbox. . . . Fischer? I've heard that name somewhere before—in connection with something—I can't remember just what. . . . Louise, may I ask you one question? Does my brother ever speak of— of the past?

LOUISE: Never to me.

THE CONSUL: Louise. . . . let me ask you. . . .

LOUISE: Excuse me, the girl is here with the milk. I have to take it in and put it away. . . .

> *(She leaves. The Delivery Girl can be seen, left, entering from the square.)*

STARCK: *(Comes out again. He removes his white cap, panting loudly.)* In and out, out and in, just like a badger from his hole. . . . It is downright insufferable standing over the stoves all day—and not even a semblance of breeze this evening!

THE CONSUL: We are going to have rain; it always follows lightning. . . . I won't say it is especially pleasant downtown, but out here you have it quiet. No noisy trucks or wagons, and no street cars! It's like being in the country.

STARCK: It's quiet enough, but too quiet for business. I know my trade but I am a poor salesman—always have been, can never learn to be one, or else something is wrong with me. Perhaps I haven't the right way about me? If a customer treats me as if I were a cheat and a fraud, I can't find words to answer him; and then I get as angry as I *can* get—I just haven't the strength to lose my temper completely any more. I'm worn out. Everything wears out. . . .

THE CONSUL: Why don't you go to work for someone instead?

STARCK: Who would want to hire me?

THE CONSUL: Have you tried?

STARCK: What good would it do?

THE CONSUL: Well—now. . . .

> *(At this moment a long drawn out exclamation of anguish is heard from the apartment on the second floor.)*

STARCK: What in heaven's name can they be doing up there? It sounds as if they were killing each other!

THE CONSUL: I don't like this new, strange atmosphere that has come over the house lately. It hovers over one like a red thunder

304

cloud. What sort of people are they anyhow? What are they doing *here*?

STARCK: It's a dangerous thing to poke about in other people's business. You get drawn into it. . . .

THE CONSUL: Do you know anything about these people?

STARCK: No, I don't know anything. . . .

> *(There is another sound from above.)*

THE CONSUL: Now there was another shriek—it came from the stairway this time. . . .

STARCK: *(Withdraws quietly to his shop.)* This is something I don't want to be mixed up in. . . .

> *(Gerda, Brink's divorced wife, is seen entering the square. She is bareheaded, her hair hangs loose in disarray, and she is agitated. The Consul walks over toward her. They recognize each other. She takes a step backward.)*

THE CONSUL: It is you! My former sister-in-law!

GERDA: Yes—it is I!

THE CONSUL: How did you happen to come to this house? Why couldn't you let my brother enjoy his peace here?

GERDA: *(Is taken aback.)* I thought he had moved. I was told another tenant had moved into the apartment. It is not my fault that. . . .

THE CONSUL: You have nothing to fear from me. You must not be afraid of me, Gerda. . . . Can I be of help to you? What is going on up there?

GERDA: He struck me!

THE CONSUL: Is your little girl living with you?

GERDA: Yes.

THE CONSUL: She has a stepfather, then?

GERDA: Yes.

THE CONSUL: Fix your hair and calm yourself. Then I'll try to straighten this out—but keep this from my brother. . . .

GERDA: He must hate me. . . .

THE CONSUL: No. Can't you see how tenderly he cares for your plants and your flower-beds here? You remember how he carried the soil here himself, in a basket? Do you recognize your blue gentians and mignonettes, your roses—*Malmaison* and *Mervielle de Lyon*—which he grafted himself. Do you understand now how he has cherished your memory—and your daughter's?

305

GERDA: Where is he now?

THE CONSUL: He is taking a stroll on the avenue. He'll be back by the time the evening newspaper is delivered. When he comes from the right, he usually goes in the backway. Then he seats himself in the dining room and starts to read. If you stand still, he won't notice you. . . . And then you are going up again—to your home, aren't you?

GERDA: I can't—I can't return to that man. . . .

THE CONSUL: Who—and what—is he?

GERDA: He has been a singer. . . .

THE CONSUL: Has been—and is now—an adventurer!

GERDA: Yes.

THE CONSUL: Keeps a gambling house—doesn't he?

GERDA: Yes.

THE CONSUL: And the child? Used as bait!

GERDA: Please. . . . don't say that!

THE CONSUL: *(With a shudder.)* Horrible!

GERDA: You judge too harshly.

THE CONSUL: *(With a touch of sarcasm.)* Filth should be touched gently, oh, so gently! But what is decent and respectable must be soiled and dragged down! And why did you delude me into becoming your accomplice? I was childish enough to believe what you said, and I defended your unjust cause against him.

GERDA: You forget that he was too old for me.

THE CONSUL: He was not so old then. You had a child by him, didn't you? And when he proposed to you, he asked you frankly whether you would like to have a child by him. . . . Furthermore, he offered to give you back your freedom as soon as he had fulfilled that promise and the years began to weigh him down.

GERDA: He abandoned me! That was an insult—an unforgivable insult!

THE CONSUL: Not in this case! Your youth shielded you from any stigma!

GERDA: He should have allowed *me* to leave *him!*

THE CONSUL: Why? Why should you have wanted to bring dishonor to him?

GERDA: It had to be one or the other, didn't it?

THE CONSUL: How strangely your mind works!—In any case, now

306

you have finished him. . . . And you tricked me into aiding you! But now—how can we right the wrong we two have done?

GERDA: If he were given restitution, it would be at my expense!

THE CONSUL: I can't follow you in your reasoning. It seems to be founded on nothing but hate. But let us forget about restitution for him and think of what we can do for his daughter. . . . What is there we can do for her?

GERDA: The child is mine. The Court has awarded her to me. And my husband is now legally her father. . . .

THE CONSUL: You are too hardfisted. And you have grown reckless and erratic. . . . Quiet—here he comes now. . . .

> *(Brink enters from the right. He carries a newspaper in his hand and walks pensively in through the back entrance. The Consul and Gerda stand motionless, out of sight, hidden around the corner of the house. The Consul and Gerda step forward. Immediately thereafter Brink can be seen seating himself in the dining room, perusing his newspaper.)*

GERDA: It was he!

THE CONSUL: Step over there and take a look at your home. . . . See how he has kept everything just the way it was arranged according to your taste?—Don't be afraid—he can't see us here in the dark; the light blinds him, you understand. . . .

GERDA: Oh, how he has lied to me!

THE CONSUL: What do you mean?

GERDA: He hasn't aged! He simply grew tired of me, that's all! Look at the collar he wears—and the scarf! The very latest in fashion! I'm sure he must have a mistress!

THE CONSUL: You can see her picture there on the majolica stove—between the candelabra.

GERDA: It's I—and the child! Does he still love me?

THE CONSUL: The *memory* of you!

GERDA: Strange! *(Brink stops reading and stares outside.)* He is looking at us!

THE CONSUL: Don't move!

GERDA: He is staring straight at me!

THE CONSUL: Stand still! He can't see you!

GERDA: He resembles a dead man. . . .

THE CONSUL: Remember, he was deprived of his life!

GERDA: Must you say these things?

    (The Consul and Gerda are suddenly illuminated by a sharp flash of lightning.)

    (Brink, inside, rises. He seems frightened. Gerda runs to the square and hides around the corner of the house.)

BRINK: *(At the window.)* Karl Fredrik!—Are you alone?—I thought that. . . . Have you somebody with you?

THE CONSUL: Can't you see I am alone?

BRINK: It is so sultry—and the flowers give me a headache. . . . Now I'll just finish my newspaper. . . .

    (He resumes his seat.)

THE CONSUL: *(At Gerda's side.)* Now—let us come back to your problem. Would you like me to take you upstairs to him?

GERDA: I don't know. . . . I'm afraid there will be a scene!

THE CONSUL: The child must be spared at all costs!—And I am a lawyer.

GERDA: Well—for the child's sake!—Come with me!

BRINK: *(From inside.)* Karl Fredrik! Come in and play a game of chess with me!—Karl Fredrik!

—END OF SCENE I—

SCENE II.

The dining room. In the rear, a majolica stove; on its right, an open door leading to the butler's pantry; on its left, a door leading to the hall.

On the right, a buffet, on which stands a telephone.

On the left, a piano and an ornamented wall clock.

In each wall, right and left, there is a door.

LOUISE: *(Enters.)*

BRINK: Where did my brother go?

LOUISE: *(Ill at ease.)* He was outside just a minute ago. He can't have gone far.

BRINK: What a terrible disturbance they are making upstairs. I feel as if they were treading on my head. . . . Now they are pulling out bureau drawers. . . . one would think they were getting ready to take a trip—or even to move out, abscond. . . . Oh, if you only knew how to play chess, Louise!

LOUISE: I play a little.

BRINK: Oh well, if you know how to move the chessmen, you'll soon learn. . . . Sit down, my child! *(He sets up the figures on the chess board.)* They make such a racket up there that the chandelier is shaking. And down below, the pastry cook is firing away with his stoves. I think I'll have to move soon.

LOUISE: I've been thinking for a long time you ought to do so anyway.

BRINK: Anyway, you say?

LOUISE: It is not a good thing to linger too long among old memories.

BRINK: Why so? With age all memories take on beauty.

LOUISE: You may still live another twenty years; and that's too long to live with memories of the past. They might fade. They might even take on different color. . . .

BRINK: That's as much as you know about it, my dear child.—Come now, you start. Take a pawn. But not the queen's—for then I'll chessmate you in two moves.

LOUISE: I'll start with the knight, then. . . .

BRINK: That's just as dangerous, my dear.

LOUISE: Just the same, I think I'll start with the knight.

BRINK: Very well. In that case, I'll use my bishop's pawn and. . . .
   (Starck appears in the hall with a tray of pastry.)
LOUISE: It's Mr. Starck with the pastry for the tea. He makes no more sound than a mouse.
   (She gets up and goes out into the hall. She takes the tray and disappears into the butler's pantry with it.)
BRINK: Well, Mr. Starck, how is your wife now?
STARCK: Oh, thank you, it's her eyes that bother her as usual. . . .
BRINK: You didn't see my brother, did you?
STARCK: I think he is strolling about outside.
BRINK: Is anybody with him?
STARCK: No, I don't think so.
BRINK: It wasn't yesterday you first saw this apartment, Mr. Starck, was it?
STARCK: Oh no, it's an even ten years!
BRINK: Since you brought the wedding cake. . . . Can you notice any difference?
STARCK: Not in the slightest.—The palms, of course, have grown. . . . No, it looks exactly as it did ten years ago.
BRINK: And will stay so until you bring the funeral cake. Once we have passed a certain age, nothing changes, everything remains the same—while we are skidding downhill like a sledge.
STARCK: Yes, that's the way it goes. . . .
BRINK: And living like this makes for quiet. . . . No love, no friendships—only a visitor or two to break the loneliness. And it is then that we begin to act like true human beings—are really true to ourselves. We don't try to possess others, to dominate or snare their feelings and sympathies. In that way we go out like an old tooth that comes loose and falls out by itself. We feel no pain—we don't miss it. Take Louise, for instance; she is a young, beautiful girl at whose very sight I feel exhilaration—as when seeing a work of art. One enjoys it—yet one has no desire to possess it. Nothing disturbs our good relations! My brother and I see each other regularly—two old men who never impose upon each other or try to pry into each other's secrets. By being neutral in our relations with people, one gains a certain distance; and at a distance we always appear better. In brief, I am content with old age and its quiet peace. . . . *(He calls.)* Louise!

310

LOUISE: *(In the doorway, right.)* The laundry has just come and I have to go over it. . . .

BRINK: Perhaps you, Mr. Starck, would care to sit down and chat with me? Perhaps you play chess—do you play chess?

STARCK: I don't dare to take too much time away from my pots and pans. . . . And at eleven I have to start the fire in the bake oven. But it's good of you to invite me. . . .

BRINK: If you see my brother, please ask him to come in and keep me company. . . .

STARCK: I certainly will. I'll be glad to. *(He leaves.)* *(Brink is alone. He keeps moving the chessmen on the board for a few seconds. Then he rises and starts to pace up and down the floor.)* The peace of old age, yes! *(He sits down at the piano and strikes a few chords. Then he gets up and starts pacing again.)* Louise! Can't you let the laundry wait?

LOUISE: *(Enters through the door, right.)* No, I can't do that. . . . The laundress is in a hurry, and her husband and children are waiting for her.

BRINK: Oh well. . . . *(He seats himself at the table and starts drumming it with his fingers. Then he tries to read the newspaper again, but tires of that. He strikes a few matches and blows out the flame; he looks at his watch, and at the clock on the wall. There is a shuffling sound in the hall.)* Is that you, Karl Fredrik?

THE POSTMAN: *(Appears.)* It's I—the postman. . . . Excuse me for coming in, but the door was open. . . .

BRINK: You have a letter for me?

THE POSTMAN: Only a postal card.

(He hands it to Brink and disappears.)

BRINK: *(Reads the card.)* Mr. Fischer again! The Boston Club! It's the man right above me! That fellow with the pale hands and the dinner jacket! And to me! This is an impertinence! I simply have to get out of this house!—Fischer! . . . . *(He tears the card into pieces. A noisy sound is heard from the hall.)* Is that you, Karl Fredrik?

THE ICEMAN: It's the iceman. . . .

BRINK: Thank heavens we get some ice—in this heat! But be careful of the bottles in the ice box! And put the cake of ice on its edge—so that I can hear the water dripping as it melts: it's my water timepiece. It measures out the time—the slow hours. . . .

311

Tell me, where do you get your ice—where do you take it from?
—Did he leave? They all go to their homes so that they can hear
themselves talk and have some company. . . . *(There is a silence.)*
Is that you, Karl Fredrik? *(From the floor above can now be
heard Chopin's Fantaisie Impromptu, Opus 66, played on the
piano. Only the first part is played.—Brink listens. He seems
to be coming to life. He looks up at the ceiling.)* Who is that
playing my Impromptu? *(He places his hands over his eyes,
listening.—The Consul enters from the hall.)* Is that you, Karl
Fredrik?

> *(The music stops.)*

THE CONSUL: Yes—it's I.

BRINK: Where have you been all this time?

THE CONSUL: I had to straighten out a certain matter. . . . Have
you been alone?

BRINK: Yes, of course. Come and sit down and play a game of chess
with me. . . .

THE CONSUL: I'd rather sit and talk. And I guess you need to hear
your own voice, too, don't you?

BRINK: Yes, you are right. . . . The only trouble is that it's so easy
to get back into the past. . . .

THE CONSUL: Then, at least, you forget the present!

BRINK: There is no present. What occurs in the present is nothing
but empty nothingness. In the future, and the past—and preferably in the future—there lies our hope!

THE CONSUL: *(At the dining-table.)* Hope for what?

BRINK: A change!

THE CONSUL: Oh, what you want to say is that you have had
enough of the peace that comes with old age?

BRINK: May be so?

THE CONSUL: That's the same as an affirmation. And if you now
were to choose between loneliness and the past. . . .

BRINK: Now don't bring back any ghosts!

THE CONSUL: How about the memories?

BRINK: They are not ghosts. They are my poems, created out of concrete reality. But if the dead should come back—they would be
ghosts!

THE CONSUL: In any case, which one of the two, the woman or the
child, brings back the loveliest mirage among your memories?

BRINK: Both! I can't separate them. . . . That is why I never tried to keep the child. . . .

THE CONSUL: But do you think you acted rightly? Did the possibility of a stepfather never occur to you?

BRINK: I didn't think of that eventuality then; but I did later. I have indeed—reflected—over it.

THE CONSUL: A stepfather—who mistreated—perhaps even defiled and injured your daughter?

BRINK: *(With suppressed emotion.)* Stop it! Stop! *(In a whisper.)* Quiet!

THE CONSUL: Do you hear anything?

BRINK: I thought I heard somebody walk softly—those short, tripping footsteps I used to hear in the corridor when she came to visit me.—I almost think it was the child who was dearest to me then—that brave, confident little soul who was afraid of nothing—who was innocently unaware of the treachery of life, who had nothing to hide! I remember her first experience with the evil of this world. She was in the park one day, and she happened to see a lovely looking child there. With open arms she toddled toward the little stranger to embrace and kiss her. The handsome child responded to her friendly impulse by biting her cheek, and then she stuck out her tongue at her. You should have seen my little Anne-Charlotte! She stood as though petrified—not from the pain, but from the horror of finding this limitless abyss which we call the human heart suddenly opening itself. I myself once experienced the very same thing when from a pair of the most beautiful eyes I suddenly saw two strange eyes protrude—the eyes of a vicious beast. . . . I became literally frightened—so frightened that I looked to see if someone stood behind her, manipulating a mask; for that was what her face resembled. But why do we sit here discussing these things? Can it be that the heat, or the lightning. . . . or what? . . . .

THE CONSUL: Loneliness breeds thoughts. . . . You should have people around you. Being in the city this whole summer seems to have affected you.

BRINK: It is only these last few weeks. . . . the sickness and the death upstairs affected me to such a degree that I suffered through the ordeal myself. Mr. Starck's griefs and worries have become mine. I can't help feeling uneasy over his economy, his wife's eye troubles, his future. And lately I have been dreaming night after night about my little Anne-Charlotte. . . . I see her in all sorts of danger—dangers of the kind I never even could have imagined before, never realized existed! And before falling asleep—when one's hearing is sharpened unbelievably—I hear her delicate little footsteps—and once I heard her voice. . . .

THE CONSUL: Where is she now?

BRINK: Well. . . .

THE CONSUL: If you were to meet her on the street. . . .

BRINK: Then I imagine I would either lose my mind or drop dead! . . . . When my youngest sister was growing up, I spent some years abroad. When I returned, I found a young girl waiting for me on the pier. She embraced me. I met with horror two eyes that penetrated into mine with an expression of the deepest disappointment and alarm because she was not recognized. "It's I," she repeated again and again before I realized that I had my sister before me.—In about the same manner, I imagine, a reunion with my daughter would turn out. At her age, five years of separation could make her difficult to recognize. But just think: a father not knowing his own child! His own child! A child who is a stranger to him! I should never be able to survive that! No—then I prefer to keep the memory of her as she was at four. . . . *(He points to the photograph on the ledge of the stove.)* I have no desire for any other image of her. . . . *(There is a silence.)* Is that you, Louise, pottering about in the linen closet? There is such a clean smell coming from it—it reminds me of. . . . Yes, a housewife and her linen closet—she is the good fairy who watches over and renews everything—the housewife with the pressing iron—who smoothes away and removes all wrinkles. . . . Yes, the wrinkles. . . . Now I shall go in—and write a letter. Will you stay here? I won't be long. . . .

> *(He goes out to the right.)*
> *(The Consul coughs audibly.)*
> *(Gerda is seen in the doorway to the hall. The clock in the dining room strikes.)*

GERDA: Are—you. . . . Oh God! This sound—which I have carried in my ears for ten long years! This clock that never kept good time, but measured out the hours, day and night, during five long years. . . . *(She looks around.)* My piano. . . . my palms!

314

The dining-table—he has kept it unblemished—it's shinning like a mirror! My buffet! With the knight-errant and with Eve— Eve with her basket of apples. . . . There used to lie a thermometer in the drawer on the right—away back in the drawer. . . . *(There is a pause.)* I wonder whether it is still there? . . . . *(She goes over to the buffet and pulls out the drawer on the right.)* Yes, it's still there!

THE CONSUL: Has the thermometer any special meaning for you, then?

GERDA: Yes—it turned out to be a symbol toward the end. . . . A symbol of the inconstant, the variable!—When we set up housekeeping, the thermometer was to have been placed outside the window. I had promised to put it there; and I forgot it. Then *he* was going to place it there—and *he* forgot. And the thermometer just kept lying there. Then we started nagging each other; and finally, in order to get away from it all, I hid it here in the drawer. . . . I began to hate it, and so did he. Do you realize now what it came to signify? . . . . Neither of us had any faith in the durability of our marriage! We had begun our life together by throwing off our masks and by showing our antipathies! We spent our first days together as if on the run— ready to flee without notice.—That was the thermometer—and it is still lying there!—Up and down, forever changeable—just like the weather. . . . *(She puts away the thermometer and then goes over to the chessboard.)* My chess set! He bought it to while away the long days before the baby came. . . . With whom does he play now?

THE CONSUL: With me.

GERDA: Where is he now?

THE CONSUL: He is in his room, writing a letter.

GERDA: Where?

THE CONSUL: *(Points to the right.)* In there.

GERDA: *(Shrinks.)* And here he has lived for five years?

THE CONSUL: Ten years. Five alone.

GERDA: He enjoys his loneliness, doesn't he?

THE CONSUL: I think he has had enough of it now.

GERDA: Do you think he will ask me to leave?

THE CONSUL: You have to wait and see. You are not taking much of a risk. He is always the gentleman.

315

GERDA: That table runner there—I didn't make that!

THE CONSUL: *(Preoccupied, he does not hear her remark.)* Of course, you have to expect that he will ask about the child.

GERDA: That's precisely why I have come. . . . He will have to help me to get her back. . . .

THE CONSUL: Where do you think Fischer has gone to? And what do you think he intends to do—disappearing like that?

GERDA: His first idea is no doubt to get away from a neighborhood that did not fit in with his plans. And then, I imagine, he thought I would pursue him. He took the child along as hostage. He wanted to train her to become a ballet dancer. As a matter of fact, she had shown both talent and desire for it.

THE CONSUL: Ballet dancer? Don't tell that to her father! He dislikes anything that has to do with exhibition on the stage.

GERDA: *(Sitting down by the chess table and aimlessly setting up the chessmen for a game.)* The stage? But *I* have been on the stage, you know.

THE CONSUL: You!

GERDA: I used to play accompaniments.

THE CONSUL: Poor Gerda!

GERDA: Why do you say that? I loved it! When I was imprisoned here, it was not the keeper whom I blamed for my unhappiness, for my not feeling at home,—it was the prison!

THE CONSUL: And now you feel you have had enough?

GERDA: Now I love to have quiet and to be alone. . . . But above all, I love my child!

THE CONSUL: Hush! He is coming. . . .

GERDA: *(Rises, as if about to flee, but falls back into the chair again.)* Oh!

THE CONSUL: Now I shall leave you!—Don't think about what to say. . . . The words will come by themselves.—just like the next move when you play chess.

GERDA: What I fear most is his first glance. . . . I shall read at once in his eyes whether I have changed to my advantage or disadvantage—whether I have become old, and ugly. . . .

THE CONSUL: *(Withdrawing to the left.)* Should he find that you have aged, it will give him courage to approach you. But if he finds you as young as ever, then there is no hope for him. . . .

And he is more modest and reasonable than you think!—So—
now. . . .

> (*Brink is seen slowly coming from the room, right, walking
> past the open door leading to the butler's pantry, right. He
> carries a letter in his hand. He goes into the pantry, but
> soon after appears in the hall and is seen going outside.*)

THE CONSUL: (*In the doorway, left.*) He went out to post a letter.

GERDA: I shall never be able to go through with this! How can I
ask him to help me through the ordeal of this divorce? I must
go—I can't stay!—It is too much to ask of him! Too brazen
of me!

THE CONSUL: You must stay! You know how good he is—there is
no limit to his kindness! He will help you, for the child's sake.

GERDA: No, no. . . .

THE CONSUL: And he is the only one who can help you!

> (*Brink enters briskly from the hall. He gives a nod to
> Gerda, whom he—in his nearsightedness—assumes to be
> Louise. He walks over to the telephone on the buffet and
> rings a number; in passing, he addresses a word to Gerda.*)

BRINK: Already done, eh? Set up the chessmen, then, Louise, and
let's start a new game. (*Gerda is petrified. She fails to grasp
what he means. Brink, his back turned to Gerda, speaks into
the receiver.*) Hello!—Good evening! Is that you, Mother?—
Oh yes, thank you—I feel well. Louise is waiting to play a
game of chess with me.—She is a little tired, having had much
to contend with today. . . . Yes, it's over now, and everything
is fine.—Oh, just some trifling thing!—*If* it is warm? It has
been roaring and thundering over our heads—yes, directly over
us—but it didn't strike. . . . just a false alarm.—What's that
you say? The Fischers! Well, but I think they are about to go
off on a trip. . . . Why? What makes you think so?—I don't
know anything about that; I have heard no particulars.—Is
that so? Is that so?—Well, yes—it leaves at 6.15—takes the
outer route through the skerries, and arrives—let me see—it
arrives at 8.25.—Well, did you enjoy yourselves, then? (*He
gives a chuckle.*) Yes, he really can be quite amusing when he
wants to be. . . . What did Marie think about it?—What kind
of summer I have had? Oh, so-so, not too bad. . . . Louise and

317

I have kept each other company—she has such a nice and even temper. Oh, she is so kind and thoughtful—so extremely nice!—No, thank you—not that! *(Gerda has begun to realize the situation. She rises, panicstricken. Brink continues his telephone conversation.)* My eyes? Yes—my sight is getting worse. But I say as Mrs. Starck does: "There is nothing to see! Would like to be a little deaf, too! Deaf and blind!" The neighbors up above make such a racket at night they must be conducting some sort of gambling club. . . . There—now somebody is breaking in on the line to listen in, I suppose. . . . *(He puts down the receiver and rings again. Louise appears in the doorway leading to the hall. Brink does not observe her. Gerda regards Louise with mingled envy and admiration. Louise withdraws through the door on the left.)*

BRINK: *(Still at the telephone.)* Is that you, Mother? The idea—to interrupt a conversation just to listen in! Well, then—tomorrow—at six fifteen!—Thank you ever so much! The same to you!—Of course I will. . . . Goodnight, Mother! *(He rings off.—Louise is no longer visible.—Gerda is standing in the center of the room.—Brink turns around. He faces Gerda. Gradually he recognizes her. His hand fumbles toward the heart.)* Oh, God in heaven, it's you? It wasn't Louise, then,—a moment ago? . . .

GERDA: *(Is silent.)*

BRINK: *(In a faint voice.)* How—did you—happen—to come—here?

GERDA: Forgive me, I—I came here on a trip—was passing through—and had a sudden longing to see my former—my old home—again. . . . The windows were open, and. . . .

(There is a silence.)

BRINK: Has it changed, do you think?

GERDA: It looks the same as it did in the past—yet it is different—something has crept in here. . . .

BRINK: *(Ill at ease.)* Are you satisfied—with your new life?

GERDA: Oh yes. It's—as I wanted it. . . .

BRINK: And the child?

GERDA: Oh, she is growing—and is happy—she is well taken care of.

BRINK: Then I shall not ask any more questions. *(Silence.)* Is there anything you wish—can I be of service to you in any way?

GERDA: Thanks, but—there is nothing I need—but I am glad to see

318

that you, too, are getting along well. . . . *(There is a pause.)* Perhaps you would like to see Anne-Charlotte?

(There is another silence.)

BRINK: I think not—now that I hear she is being well taken care of. —It is so trying to go back into the past. . . . like recapitulating old lessons that one actually knows, even if the teacher thinks differently. . . . I have grown so out of all these happenings of the past; my thoughts are so far away from them—I've left them for other things—and I can't renew the past. . . . I find it hard to be discourteous, but I cannot ask you to sit down. . . . You are now another man's wife—and you are no longer the woman I separated from.

GERDA: Am I—so—changed?

BRINK: So—strange! Your voice, your gaze, your manner. . . .

GERDA: Have I grown old?

BRINK: I don't know!—They say that after three years we haven't the same atoms left in our bodies—and after five years, everything has been renewed. . . . That's why you, standing there, are a different person from the one who lived and suffered here. It's hard for me even to call you by your first name any longer— that is how much of a stranger you are to me now! And I am afraid it would be the same if I should meet my daughter again. . . .

GERDA: Please don't speak such words—I would rather see you angry!

BRINK: Why should I be angry?

GERDA: Because of everything mean I have done to you.

BRINK: Have you? I don't feel that you have! I am not aware of it!

GERDA: Didn't you read the document when I brought action against you?

BRINK: No, I didn't—I merely sent it to my attorney.

(He seats himself.)

GERDA: And the judgment?

BRINK: I never read that either. As I had no intention of remarrying, I had no need of any such papers.

(There is a silence.)

(Gerda sits down.)

BRINK: What was in these documents? That I was too old? *(Gerda affirms his supposition by her silence.)* Well, it was nothing but the truth, wasn't it? So don't let that embarrass you. I said exactly the same thing in my counter suit, and asked the court to give you back your freedom.

GERDA: You wrote—that. . . ?

BRINK: I said that I *was not too old,* but *would be,* eventually, *for you.*

GERDA: *(Hurt.)* For me?

BRINK: Yes.—I could not, of course, say that I was too old when we were married. Then the child's parentage could have been open to all kinds of unpleasant interpretations. And the child was *ours,* wasn't it?

GERDA: You know that perfectly well!—But. . . .

BRINK: Do you want me to feel ashamed of my age? Of course, if I suddenly took it into my head to start dancing a Boston and to spend the nights playing cards—then I would soon be eligible for a wheelchair or the operating table! And that would be a shame, wouldn't it?

GERDA: You don't look as if you would. . . .

BRINK: Did you think I would pine away after the divorce? *(Gerda remains ambiguously silent.)* There are some who think that you dealt me a death blow.—Do you think I look like the victim of a murderer? Do you?

GERDA: Why did you marry me?

BRINK: You know very well why a man marries. And you know also that I didn't have to plead for your love. And you will remember how we both used to laugh at all the wise and witty advisers who warned you against marrying me. . . . But *why* you captivated me is something I just can't explain. . . . After the wedding ceremony you acted as if you didn't even see me. You behaved as if you were present at someone else's wedding. It occurred to me then that you might have made a wager to destroy me. Being the head of my department in the government service, I was naturally hated by my subordinates. No sooner had I made an enemy than he became your friend. This caused me to say to you: It is true that you shall not hate your enemies; but neither must you love *my* enemies! However, when I saw where I had you, I started packing. Yet I wanted first to have a living witness to prove that you had been telling lies about me behind my back.

That's why I waited until the baby arrived.

GERDA: To think that you could be so false!

BRINK: I was secretive—but I never told an untruth!—Gradually you transformed my friends into detectives. You even tricked my brother into losing faith in me. But worst of all, you created doubts as to our child's parentage by your thoughtless, inconsiderate, senseless prattle!

GERDA: I have retracted everything I said!

BRINK: Once over the lips, a word cannot be caught by the wings again. And the very worst is that your false gossip has reached the child, who now thinks of her mother as a. . . .

GERDA: Oh, no! . . .

BRINK: Yes—that's what you have done!—You built a tall tower on a foundation of lies! And now the tower is crumbling—crushing you—burying you!

GERDA: It is not true!

BRINK: Yes, it is! I have just seen Anne-Charlotte. . . .

GERDA: You have seen her. . . ?

BRINK: We met on the stairway—she said I was her uncle. . . . Do you know what that means? An older friend of the family—a friend of the mother! I have also heard that I have been called the same in her school!—This is horrible, insufferable—for the child. . . .

GERDA: You mean you have met. . . ?

BRINK: I have! But there was no need for me to mention it to anyone. Haven't I the right to keep silent if I so wish? Besides, the encounter affected me to such a degree that I erased it from my mind as though I had not seen her.

GERDA: Is there nothing I can do to repair the hurt?

BRINK: If there is anything you can do? No—you cannot restore my honor! How could you?—No—that is something I alone can do! *(They stare at each other challengingly and at length.)* As a matter of fact, I have already been given restitution.

(There is a silence.)

GERDA: Can't I make amends? Won't you forgive me—and forget? . . .

BRINK: Just what do you mean?

GERDA: Can't I make up for—undo. . . .

321

BRINK: You mean—that we should renew our union—start all over again—reinstate you as my lord and master? No, thank you! No—never again!

GERDA: I had to live to hear this!

BRINK: Now you know how it feels. . . .

(There is a long pause.)

GERDA: That's a very nice table runner you have there. . . .

BRINK: Yes—it is.

GERDA: Where did you get that?

(Pause.)

(Louise appears in the doorway to the butler's pantry. In her hand she has a household bill.)

BRINK: *(Turns around.)* Is it a bill? *(Gerda rises. She pulls on her gloves with such vehemence that the buttons fly off.)* *(Brink counts out the money for the bill.)* Eighteen and seventy-two—the exact amount.

LOUISE: *(In a subdued, confidential tone of voice.)* May I have a word with you, Mr. Brink?

(Brink gets up and steps over to the pantry entrance. Louise whispers something to him.)

BRINK: Oh, for heaven's sake! *(Louise leaves.)* Poor Gerda!

GERDA: What do you mean? That I am jealous of your servant girl?

BRINK: No, I didn't mean that!

GERDA: Yes, you did! And you meant that you were too old for me, but not for her. I understand the affront. . . . She is pretty—I don't deny it—for a servant girl!

BRINK: Poor Gerda!

GERDA: Why do you keep saying that?

BRINK: Because I feel sorry for you. Jealous of my housekeeper! That is sufficient vindication!

GERDA: I—jealous?

BRINK: Why, then, do you keep raging against my nice, quiet little kinswoman?

GERDA: Kinswoman! And what else?

BRINK: No, my child, I have become resigned—long ago—I am content in my loneliness. . . . *(The telephone rings. Brink takes the receiver.)* Mr. Fischer? There is no Mr. Fischer here. . . . Oh, I see—yes, it's I. . . . yes.—He has run away?—He has?—But with whom—with whom has he disappeared?—Mr. Starck's

daughter—the pastry cook's daughter! Oh, God in heaven! . . .
How old is she?—Eighteen! Why, she is nothing but a child!

GERDA: That he had run away—that I knew. . . . But with a
woman. . . ? Now you are satisfied, aren't you?

BRINK: I am not glad—if that is what you mean. But I can't help
feeling a certain satisfaction, seeing that justice is not dead.
Life passes swiftly . . . and now our positions are reversed!

GERDA: She is eighteen, and I am twenty-nine! I am old—too old
for him!

BRINK: Everything is relative—even age!—But now let me ask
you something else. . . . Where is your child?

GERDA: My child! I had forgotten her! My child! God in heaven!
Help me! He has taken the child with him—he loved Anne-
Charlotte as his own daughter. . . . Come with me to the police!
Please come with me!

BRINK: I? Now you are asking a little too much!

GERDA: Help me!

BRINK: *(Goes to the door, left.)* Karl Fredrik! Come here—and
call a cab. . . . then take Gerda down to the police station. . . .
Will you do that?

THE CONSUL: *(Enters.)* Of course I will. We are human, aren't
we, after all!

BRINK: Hurry! But don't mention a word to Mr. Starck! There
is still time to put things right! Poor Mr. Starck!—And poor
Gerda!—Only hurry!

GERDA: *(Glances out through the window.)* It's starting to rain.
Could you lend me an umbrella? . . . Eighteen years old—only
eighteen years—let's hurry!

(She leaves with the Consul.)

BRINK: *(Alone.)* The peace of old age!—And my child! My child
in the clutches of an adventurer!—Louise! *(Louise comes in.)*
Come and sit down and play a game of chess with me!

LOUISE: Has the Consul left?

BRINK: He went out to do an errand.—Is it still raining?

LOUISE: No, it has stopped.

BRINK: Then I think I shall go out and get some fresh air. *(There
is a pause.)* You are a nice girl, Louise, and you are sensible. . . .
You know Mr. Starck's daughter, don't you?

LOUISE: Oh, just slightly.

BRINK: Is she attractive?

LOUISE: Oh—yes. . . .

BRINK: Do you know the family above us?

LOUISE: I have never seen them.

BRINK: Are you eluding my question?

LOUISE: I have learned to hold my tongue in this house.

BRINK: I can't help thinking that feigned deafness can be stretched too far and become a threat to life.—Have some tea ready when I come back. . . . I am going out to get a breath of fresh air.— One more thing, my child. You know what's going on here; but don't ask me about it. . . .

LOUISE: I——No, Mr. Brink, I am not at all inquisitive.

BRINK: Thank you for that, Louise.

(He starts to leave.)

END OF SCENE II

SCENE III.

The setting is the same as in Scene I.

A light is burning in the pastry shop. The apartment one flight up is also lighted, and the windows are open. The shades are raised.

(Mr. Starck stands outside the basement entrance. Brink is sitting on the green bench.)

BRINK: We had a nice little shower, didn't we?

STARCK: Yes, and it was a real blessing. Now we can expect the raspberries to come up again. . . .

BRINK: Then you must put aside some jars of preserves for me—we are getting tired of making our own. They start fermenting so quickly and get mouldy. . . .

STARCK: How well I know. . . . You have to keep watch over the jars every minute—just like naughty children. . . . Some people use salicylic acid—but that's nothing but a newfangled trick, and I won't have anything to do with it.

BRINK: Salicylic acid—well, it's an antiseptic, I understand; and it might not be a bad idea.

STARCK: Well, but you can taste it—and it's artificial.

BRINK: Tell me—have you a telephone, Mr. Starck?

STARCK: No, I have no telephone.

BRINK: Haven't you?

STARCK: Why do you ask, Mr. Brink?

BRINK: Well, I just thought—a telephone is almost a necessity for taking orders, important messages, and. . . .

STARCK: That may be—but sometimes it's a good thing to be without one, too, and fail to get—messages. . . .

BRINK: I agree—I agree with you there!—Ye-es! Whenever it rings, my heart starts pounding a little. . . . One can never tell *what* one may hear.—And I like peace—peace above all!

STARCK: So do I.

BRINK: *(Looks at his watch.)* I expect they'll soon be lighting the street lamp?

STARCK: The lamplighter must have forgotten us. The lamps on the avenue are already lit.

325

BRINK: Oh, he'll be here momentarily, then. It'll be a real joy to see one's street lamp lighted again. . . . *(The telephone rings in the dining room. Louise can be observed inside. Mr. Brink feels his heart. He tries to listen; the conversation, however, is inaudible to the audience.—Louise comes from the square.—Brink looks troubled.)* Anything new?

LOUISE: No change.

BRINK: Was it my brother?

LOUISE: No, it was the lady—Mrs. Fischer.

BRINK: What did she want?

LOUISE: She wanted to speak with you.

BRINK: No! No! Am I to console my executioner? I have done it in the past—now I am tired of it!—You see—look upstairs! They have left the lights burning. . . . Empty rooms flooded in light are if anything more awesome than if they were in darkness. . . . one can *see* the ghosts. . . . *(In a subdued tone of voice.)* And Mr. Starck's daughter, Agnes?—Do you think he knows? . . .

LOUISE: It's hard to say. He never speaks of his disappointments or sorrows—nor about anyone living in this house—this house of silence.

BRINK: Do you think we ought to tell him?

LOUISE: For heaven's sake—no!

BRINK: I have an idea it is not the first time she is causing her father grief?

LOUISE: He never speaks of her. . . .

BRINK: It's frightful, horrible! Will we ever see the end of this? *(The telephone rings in the dining room.)* There is the telephone again. Don't answer it! I don't want to know anything more!—My child! Among people like these! An adventurer, and a streetwalker!—It's frightful! Poor Gerda!

LOUISE: But isn't it better to know, to have certainty? I am going in to answer.—Mr. Brink—you must do something. . . .

BRINK: I find it impossible even to make a move! I can receive the blows—but to strike back, no!

LOUISE: But if you run away from danger, it will only come crowding upon you! And if you make no resistance, you'll be crushed!

BRINK: And if you don't let yourself become involved, you'll be beyond reach!

LOUISE: Beyond reach?

BRINK: It is much easier to unravel things, if one stops interfering and doesn't get entangled. How can I possibly take a hand while so many passions are erupting? I can't subdue their feelings, or change their course?

LOUISE: But the child?

BRINK: I have, as you know, given up my rights—and besides, speaking frankly, I am not anxious, not at all anxious; especially after her coming here and destroying all my remembrances, my memories. . . . She erased everything I had treasured—all that was beautiful! Now there is nothing left!

LOUISE: Then you are free, free at last!

BRINK: See how empty it looks in there now! As if no one lived there. . . . And up above—as if there had been a conflagration!

LOUISE: Who is that coming there? *(Agnes enters. She is agitated, frightened, but controls her feelings. She walks toward the entrance, where Starck is seated. Louise turns to Brink.)* It's Agnes! What do you suppose has happened?

BRINK: Agnes!—Well, now the tangle is beginning to unravel.

STARCK: *(Entirely self-possessed.)* Good evening, my child. Where have you been?

AGNES: I've been out for a walk.

STARCK: Mother has asked for you several times.

AGNES: Has she? Well, I'll go in to her.

STARCK: Go down and help her start the fire in the small stove, will you?

AGNES: Is she angry with me? Is she?

STARCK: Why should she be angry with you?

AGNES: Oh yes—but she never says anything.

STARCK: Well, isn't that a good thing, my dear child,—that you don't get scolded?

    (Agnes goes inside.)

BRINK: *(To Louise.)* I wonder if he knows? Or doesn't he know?

LOUISE: I hope he never will.

BRINK: But what do you suppose could have happened? A break between them? *(To Starck.)* Oh, Mr. Starck. . . .

STARCK: Did you say something?

BRINK: I just thought. . . . Did you see someone leave here a while ago?

STARCK: I saw the iceman—and the postman, I think. . . .

BRINK: Oh, I see! *(To Louise.)* Perhaps it was a mistake—perhaps they didn't hear rightly. I don't know how to explain this. . . . Perhaps he didn't tell the truth? What did the lady say when she telephoned?

LOUISE: She wanted to speak to you, Mr. Brink. . . .

BRINK: How did she sound? Was she excited?

LOUISE: Yes.

BRINK: I find it rather immodest that she should appeal to me in a matter such as this. . . .

LOUISE: What about the child?

BRINK: Imagine, I met the daughter in the stairway; and when I asked her whether she recognized me, she called me "uncle". . . . And she told me that her father was upstairs. He is, of course, her stepfather and has now all legal rights. . . . They have done nothing up there but extirpate and slander me. . . .

LOUISE: A cab is stopping at the corner. . . . *(Starck withdraws to his shop.)*

BRINK: I only hope they are not coming back here so that I'll have them on my neck. . . Imagine, having to hear my child singing the praises of her father—the other one, I mean—and then to have the old story start all over again: "Why did you marry me?"—"You know perfectly well. But why did you want to marry *me*?"—"You know perfectly well"—and so forth and so on, until the end of the world!

LOUISE: It's the Consul coming.

BRINK: Can you tell how he looks?

LOUISE: He doesn't look to be in a hurry.

BRINK: I suppose he is mulling over in his mind what to say. . . . Does he look happy?

LOUISE: Rather pensive. . . .

BRINK: So-o. . . . It was always like that. No sooner did he come close to her than he turned traitor to me. . . . She knew how to charm all—all except me. To me she was uncouth, ordinary, ugly—while to the rest she was a refined, delightful, beautiful and intelligent woman. All the hatred that my independent nature created around me turned into a mass of sympathy for her, who had wronged me. Through her they sought to influence and conquer me, wound me, and finally—to murder me!

LOUISE: Now I'll go inside so that I can answer the telephone if it rings again. This weather won't last forever, I hope.

328

BRINK: People will not tolerate anyone who shows independence. All they want is to lord it over you. Everyone of my subordinates, all the way down to the porters and janitors, wanted me to take orders from them; and when I refused, I was called a despot, of course. The maids in our home expected me to let them rule, and to accept warmed up meals. And when I declined, they set my wife against me. Finally my wife wanted me to take my cues from the child. . . . Then I rebelled and left. And promptly there was a conspiracy against the tyrant—who was no one but myself!—Hurry now, Louise, so that we can throw the bomb-shell here! *(The Consul enters from the right.)* What was the outcome?—Without details!

THE CONSUL: Let me sit down—I am a little tired.

BRINK: I am afraid the bench is wet from the rain.

THE CONSUL: If *you* have been sitting on it, I don't think it can be so very hazardous for *me!*

BRINK: Just as you say!—Where is my child?

THE CONSUL: Could I start at the beginning?

BRINK: Go ahead!

THE CONSUL: *(Slowly.)* I went down to the railroad station with Gerda. . . . We saw him and Agnes over at the ticket office. . . .

BRINK: Agnes was with him, then?

THE CONSUL: Yes—and your daughter.—Gerda remained outside— and I stepped over to him just as he handed the tickets to Agnes. But as soon as she glanced at them and found that they were for third class, she threw them in his face. Then she walked away and went outside and hailed a cab.

BRINK: Faugh!

THE CONSUL: The moment I pressed the girl's stepfather for an explanation, Gerda rushed forward and grabbed her daughter. . . . Then they disappeared in the teeming crowd.

BRINK: What did the bounder have to say?

THE CONSUL: Well—you know that when you have a chance to hear the other side—well, you. . . .

BRINK: I want to know. . . . Naturally he was not as bad as we thought he was. He had his good sides, of course!

THE CONSUL: Exactly!

BRINK: Of course he did! And now, I suppose, you expect me to sit here and hear you sing his praises—*his*—my enemy?

329

THE CONSUL: No, not his praises—but there were extenuating circumstances. . . .

BRINK: Were you ever eager to listen to me, when I informed you of the true facts, were you? Yes—you listened and answered with the silence of disapproval—as if I were fabricating lies. You were ever on the side of injustice—you believed only falsehood and rumors—and why? Because you were enamored of Gerda! But you had still another motive!

THE CONSUL: Don't say anything more now, Brother!—You always look at things from your own viewpoint.

BRINK: From what viewpoint do you want me to look? You don't expect me to raise a hand against myself, do you?

THE CONSUL: I am not your enemy. . . .

BRINK: You are, so long as you are friendly with someone who has wronged me! Where is my child?

THE CONSUL: I don't know.

BRINK: What was the upshot of the incident at the station?

THE CONSUL: The fellow took the train alone—he went south.

BRINK: And the others?

THE CONSUL: They disappeared.

BRINK: Then I can expect to have them over me again. *(There is silence.)* Did you observe whether the others followed him?

THE CONSUL: No, he went alone.

BRINK: Then, at least, we are free of him! Now to the second question—the mother and the child. . . .

THE CONSUL: Why are all the lights lit upstairs?

BRINK: Because they forgot to turn them off.

THE CONSUL: I'll go up there. . . .

BRINK: No—don't!—I only hope they don't come back! Recapitulate, recapitulate! Having to go over one's lessons—over and over—the same thing—again and again. . . .

THE CONSUL: But so far everything has come out the way it should. . . .

BRINK: But the worst remains. . . . Do you think they will return?

THE CONSUL: Not she! She would have to give you satisfaction in Louise's presence!

BRINK: I had forgot about that. She really honored me when she showed she was jealous. There is, after all, still some justice in this world!

THE CONSUL: And don't forget she saw that Louise is a good deal younger. . . .

BRINK: Poor Gerda! But in cases like this, one must not tell people that justice exists—an impeding justice. . . . For it is not true that people are in love with justice. And we have to go easy when we touch the filth and mess *they* make. And Nemesis— well, that's only for the others. . . . —Now the telephone is ringing. . . . It sounds like a rattle snake—that telephone! . . .
(Louise is seen answering the telephone.—There is a pause.)

BRINK: *(To Louise.)* Did the snake strike?

LOUISE: *(In the window.)* May I speak with you, Mr. Brink?

BRINK: *(Walks over to the window.)* Speak out!

LOUISE: The Lady has gone to her mother in Dalecarlia. She is going to remain there with the child.

BRINK: *(To Consul Brink.)* The mother and the child have gone to the country—to a good home! Now things are straightening out! Oh!

LOUISE: And she asked me to go upstairs and turn off the lights.

BRINK: Do that at once, Louise, and pull down the shades—then we won't have to look at this tragedy any longer!
(Louise goes out.)
(Starck comes out again.)

STARCK: *(Looking up at the sky.)* I believe the storm has passed.

BRINK: Indeed, it seems to have cleared—now the moon will come out.

STARCK: It was a blessing to have had that rain!

THE CONSUL: A heavenly rain it was!

BRINK: Here comes the lamplighter—at last! *(The Lamplighter enters. He lights the street lamp.)* The first lamp! Now autumn is here. . . . The season for us who are old. . . . Dusk is setting in—and that's when common sense sets in, too, lighting the way with its dark lantern. . . . so that we don't take the wrong path. . . . *(Louise is seen through the windows, up above. A few moments later, the night is dark.) (Brink speaks to Louise.)* Close the windows and pull down the shades. . . . then all the memories can go to sleep and rest in peace. . . . The peace of old age. . . . And this fall I shall move from the silent house. . . .

CURTAIN

331

To Tore Tallroth.

THE BLACK GLOVE
(1909)
(CHRISTMAS)
A lyrical fantasy in 5 scenes

PERSONS IN THE PLAY:
MRS. HARD
THE OLD MAN (The Taxidermist)
ELLEN
KRISTIN
THE JANITOR
THE GNOME
THE ANGEL OF CHRISTMAS
THE OLD LADY

SCENE 1:—The entrance hall of a large apartment house.
SCENE 2:—The entrance hall of the Hards's apartment.
SCENE 3:—The Janitor's quarters in the basement.
SCENE 4:—The Old Man's room in the attic.
SCENE 5:—The nursery room of the Hards'.

SCENE I.

THE ENTRANCE HALL.

In the background is seen the entrance door, on which are a letter box and name plate. To the left is an ice box; to the right, a bench.

332

Above the door is a translucent transom-window with a heart painted on it.

A black glove lies on the vestibule floor.

An elderly gentleman enters from the right. He is out of breath and seats himself on the bench to rest. On seeing the glove, he pulls it toward him with his stick and picks it up.

THE OLD MAN: What is this?—A glove? Black, a ladies' glove, size six—it is the young lady's in there. . . . I can tell by the indentation left by her rings: right hand, two plain rings, and a rose cut diamond on the ring finger. . . . A nice hand—but her grip is a little hard—silken finery with sharp nails. . . . I'll lay it on the ice box, where they can see it. . . .

THE JANITOR: *(Enters from the right.)*

THE OLD MAN: Good morning—and a merry Christmas to you!

THE JANITOR: Merry Christmas, Mr. Taxidermist. You are a taxidermist, aren't you?

THE OLD MAN: That's what I am, yes. I stuff birds and fishes and insects, but I can't preserve myself.—Even if I should use arsenic soap, my skin would wrinkle and my hair would fall off as on an old seal-skin trunk, my teeth would fall out. . . .

THE JANITOR: It's like the electric wiring here—it has to be repaired and replaced continually. . . .

THE OLD MAN: It's unfortunate that we shall have to be in darkness for Christmas. Can't you get the light to work?

THE JANITOR: I think there is a short-circuit somewhere, but it'll soon be remedied.—I'll try this one. . . . *(He presses a button. The colored window and heart light up.)* There, now they have light in the hall at least.

THE OLD MAN: You go about spreading light in the house. . . .

THE JANITOR: But live in darkness down in the cellar! All *we* have is a kerosene lamp. . . .

THE OLD MAN: It's nice to do things for others. . . . Heavens, how beautiful that heart is!

(He points to the painted window above the door.)

THE JANITOR: It is beautiful—even if a little too bright, not to say sharp.

THE OLD MAN: Like the young lady in here. If her heart were as good as she is beautiful. . . .

333

THE JANITOR: What's this? A glove!

THE OLD MAN: I found it here in the hall. Will you take care of it?

THE JANITOR: I'll take it with me and hang it on the board down below—the rightful owner will no doubt see it there. . . . I am on my way upstairs now. . . .

THE OLD MAN: And I'll sit here a while longer and rest my eighty years. . . . A happy Christmas to you!

THE JANITOR: *(Turns off the light in the transom-window and goes out, left.)* A happy Christmas!

ELLEN: *(Enters from the left. She opens the ice box and takes out a rack of milk bottles.)*

THE OLD MAN: Good morning, Ellen, and a merry Christmas.

ELLEN: A merry Christmas, Mr. Taxidermist!

THE OLD MAN: How is the little baby and your young mistress?

ELLEN: Oh, they both chirp in unison like canary birds. You can hear them all the way out here. . . . But that's only when they sing duets. . . . Believe me, the young lady is not so loving to the rest of us. She gives neither the janitor nor us any Christmas presents. She says we are beasts. . . .

THE OLD MAN: But you mustn't tell me these things. I am an outsider—and that is a family matter. They may say I am a gossipmonger.

ELLEN: Speaking of canaries—have you stuffed my lady's yet?

THE OLD MAN: Yes, that I have—but. . . . *(He masticates.)* She refuses to pay for it!—There, now I am gossiping. . . .

ELLEN: No, she never wants to pay for work done—and when her husband wanted to give us girls a little something extra when they moved back from the country, she went wild.—When he paid us anyhow, she turned off the water and the electric light all through the night.—And just because she couldn't have her way, she became sick—she almost died—and her husband had to send for the doctor. When he came, he said there was nothing the matter with her—that it was nothing but an act—and then she tried to take poison and threatened to turn on the gas and blow the house into atoms.

THE OLD MAN: Oh, may the Lord save us! Is that the kind of goings-on you have in your house?

334

ELLEN: But now and then she can be like an angel. And you ought to see her when she is playing with her child, or when she sits and sews Christmas gifts—as she is doing just now!—When she is at her worst, one would almost think she was possessed by evil spirits!—Poor little woman! I don't think she knows what she is doing!

THE OLD MAN: It is kind of you to say that, Ellen, and I think I would call her sick. I have seen similar cases before.—The root of the trouble is that they have it too good. The husband does nothing, because he is rich!

ELLEN: But he is out the whole day long, busy spending his money. This year he has bought three new sets of furniture for the drawing-room—one of black pear-wood, with silver trimmings. . . . And all of them landed in the attic.—As I said before: they have it too good, that's all!

KRISTIN: *(Enters from the left. She speaks in a mild tone of voice.)* What are you standing here for, Ellen? Mrs. Hard is completely beside herself because her ring has disappeared.

ELLEN: Which ring?

KRISTIN: Her most valuable one—the one with the blue stone—she paid two thousand for it. . . . And when she didn't see you around, she thought that. . . .

ELLEN: What did she think?

KRISTIN: That you had run away and taken the ring with you.

ELLEN: Well, I never heard the like of it! Never! What do *you* think, Kristin?

KRISTIN: I know, of course, that you are innocent, Ellen. When you know anyone by heart, as I know you, you can tell at once: this one is innocent; that one is guilty. . . .

THE OLD MAN: Are you so sure about that?

KRISTIN: You don't have to take an oath on it, but you can be sure anyhow.

ELLEN: And now I am suspected?

KRISTIN: When Mrs. Hard gets a fixed idea. . . .

ELLEN: But she can see that I haven't run away, can't she?

KRISTIN: That makes no difference.

ELLEN: And if the ring is found, then she'll be angry with me because I was innocent. . . . And because she had been wrong!

335

You know, I think I'll just pack up and leave. . . .

KRISTIN: Don't do that! Then she'll be convinced that she is right and she'll send for the police.

ELLEN: I see we are going to have a nice Christmas in this house!

THE OLD MAN: *(Rises.)* You will have a nice Christmas, girls, but *after* you have been through your trials. . . . After rain there always comes sunshine—and it will be the same here. Ellen is an honest girl—but she has to learn to have a little patience.

ELLEN: You say I have no patience?

THE OLD MAN: Yes—but you still have something to learn.—Now let me say once more, from the bottom of my heart and with utmost confidence: A merry Christmas, my children!
> *(He leaves, left.)*

ELLEN: If only a good conscience would help!

KRISTIN: It goes a long way! Come inside now—but remember to be calm and patient when the storm breaks!

ELLEN: How can you expect me to be calm?

KRISTIN: Look at Mr. Hard! He is the head of the house, isn't he? And he, too, is being suspected of having something to do with the ring. . . .

ELLEN: He, too?

KRISTIN: Yes, he too! But he doesn't rage—he doesn't get angry. It only distresses him.—Come along now. . . .

ELLEN: He, too! Well, then I don't have to feel so bad. . . . and if that's the case, I can stand it. . . .

KRISTIN: Come along now. . . .
> *(They go out, left.)*

THE GNOME: *(Enters, carrying a broom.)* Now I shall do the sweeping for Ellen and Kristin, for they are kind and good. But the neighbor's maid Ebba will get the sweepings, for she is mean. And then I'll dust off the bench in the hallway, clean the ice box, and polish the brass—but not for Ebba. . . . There now! But let's see what they are doing inside. . . .
> *(He lights a pocket lantern. The backdrop is lighted from behind and the hall within becomes visible. One sees a white ice chest, over which hangs a white mirror; beside it a small white chair, underneath which is placed a pair*

336

of baby galoshes. Mrs. Hard stands before the mirror, arranging her hair.)

THE GNOME: You beautiful little young mother, you may well admire the gifts nature has given you, but you must not idolize yourself! Now I'll give you a Christmas card! *(He searches among a batch of Christmas cards.)* Alpine rose—no. . . . violet —no. . . . snow berries—no. . . . mistletoe—no. . . . thistle— yes, that's the flower for you! It is a beautiful flower, but it pricks! *(He places a Christmas card in the letter box.)* Now let us hear what they are talking about in the kitchen! *(He extinguishes his lamp and stands listening toward the right.)* Ellen is being accused of having stolen a ring!—She has done nothing of the sort! Ellen wouldn't steal! Ebba might have done such a thing—yes! I know them all in this house—the tenants as well as the servants—everyone of them. . . . Ellen is weeping! Now I shall have to get busy finding that ring—I'll look for it from the basement to the attic, in the lift, in the bath rooms, in the vacuum cleaner—I know every nook and cranny here. . . . But first I must take a peek in the ice box and see if they keep it clean. . . . *(He opens the ice box and takes a glance, scrutinizing it and feeling with his hand inside.)* Yes, everything is as it should be. . . .

* * * *

CHRISTMAS: *(A woman in white, with stars of snow in her hair, appears.)*

What are you up to, little man?

You stand and listen—that's not nice!

THE GNOME:

A gnome does only what is right and good!

My mission is to keep the house in order.

I chasten and I love, bring comfort, tidy up.

CHRISTMAS:

You have a big house to look after. . . .

THE GNOME:

A tower of Babel with many kinds of people

And tongues of speech; six flights of stairs, and basement down below,

And three apartments on each floor;

337

A dozen cradles, seven pianos. . . .
A host of human fates are here in the making.
There's strain and there is tension
In minds and hearts and between temperaments—just as in
    stones and beams;
Yet—despite the strain—there is cohesion;
and neighbors, *un*known to each other,
must have consideration, also practice patience,
and overlook their neighbors' small caprices.
One plays piano after ten;
another one gets up too early and to bed too late—
and all that one can do is to adapt oneself, or try to.
You hear all the little sounds within the spiral stair case:
the squeaky lift, the trickling from the water pipe;
the radiators, sizzling like a water kettle,
the showers' running water, the sound of suction from a cleaner;
the slam of doors, a baby crying. . . .
Here lives a man just married—there one divorced. . . , and
    there a widower. . . .
There is confusion everywhere. The while, pianos
reverberate with rhythms of a waltz, a fugue, and a sonata.
The basement speaks of poverty, so does the attic;
wealth, vanity and luxury, and empty show are flaunted in the
    flats;
some manage to survive by cunning, some aggressively,
while others pinch and spare;
one day a death, the next a marriage or divorce;
one chronic fuss-box rows, complains, and keeps repairing;
but when he finds that discord does not pay,
he takes at last the one way out—and moves!
CHRISTMAS:
    Who lives in there?
THE GNOME:
    Here lives the little lady, whom they talk about so much.
CHRISTMAS:
    Oh, does she? Yes, I know her then!—
    Just listen! What a tempest in the kitchen. . . .
    Oh, dear me, I would not call this Yule tide peaceful! . . . .

THE GNOME:

Today we're on the eve of Christmas; the kitchen's therefore
in a mess.—
However, something else has happened here:
Poor Ellen has unjustly been accused. . . .

CHRISTMAS:

I know, and that's the final straw! . . .
The cup of grace has overflown,
and wine of wrath shall now be pressed from sour grapes. . . .
To mete out punishment is not my task, however;
to help, console and put things right is *my* chore.
But *y o u* can chastise, can handle them with firmness. . . .
Now listen! This young woman, endowed with beauty,
in honor of The Giver for the joy of mankind,
shall now receive a lesson—hard, but passing:
She's built her happiness on haughtiness;
from haughtiness derives her hard and cruel spirit—
therefore: remove her little child
that she may grieve the baby's loss. . . .
Don't fret! It will be given back to her tomorrow,
as Christmas Eve gift. . . . Yet mark this well: *but* as a gift!
What they will think? What does it matter?
It has been lost, has strayed—that's all!
But you must not resort to *un*truth. . . .
A lie will go to seed like any harmful weed. . . .

THE GNOME:

It's much too cruel. . . . she will not survive it!

CHRISTMAS:

She must and will! I shall protect her!
And way down deep her heart is not so bad—
it's merely sick. . . . and grief will cure her sickness. . . .
When blissful, radiant sun begins to burn,
then grass and flowers wither;
a passing cloud gives shadow, cools—
and clouds bring rain, and rain makes things grow green. . . .
The sky is darkened now. . . . Pray do not be too hard on her!

THE GNOME: *(Sadly.)*

Need you entreat me to be kind?—
She is so beautiful!

339

CHRISTMAS:
>She is—and soon she will be kind as well!
>Then will come happiness—the kind that lasts!

THE GNOME:
>Wait just a moment. . . . There is a poor old soul up in the attic,
>Who hungers for a gift from me for Christmas. . . .

CHRISTMAS:
>Who is this ward of yours, if I may ask?

THE GNOME:
>An old philosopher, who only yearns to meet with Death. . . .

CHRISTMAS:
>We cannot counsel; nor do we rule o'er life and death. . . .
>But if he is deserving, he shall have his gift.

THE GNOME:
>He broods forever o'er the riddle of this life. . . .

CHRISTMAS:
>Is that, then, something to be brooding over?

THE GNOME:
>He is a queer old zany, but he's kind. . . .

CHRISTMAS:
>What does he do then, up there in the attic?

THE GNOME:
>He stuffs dried fishes, birds, sticks pins in worms,
>and has a cabinet that's filled with yellow paper;
>and there he searches, searches day and night. . . .
>He searches for life's riddle in that cabinet!

CHRISTMAS:
>I know his kind—and he shall have his Christmas gift. . . .
>And now: a Merry Christmas. . . . and—to work!

—THE CURTAIN FALLS BRIEFLY—

SCENE II.

THE ENTRANCE HALL

The entrance hall of the Hards' apartment on the third floor of the building. A white ice box to the left. A white mirror hangs above it. The mirror has shelves above and below; on the lower one, a silver brush; on the upper one, a vase with tulips. Below the mirror a woven basket, intended for gloves. On top of the ice box lies The Gnome's Christmas card with the thistle. To the right, a white chair beneath the clothes rack; and under the chair a pair of tiny galoshes. A child's white fur coat and a white bonnet hang on the clothes rack. No other wearing apparel is seen.

The door leading to the drawing-room, rear, is ajar, and behind the draperies of yellow brocade can be seen the sewing table, on which stand an attractive lamp and a vase with beautiful flowers. Behind the table sits MRS. HARD. She is dressed in white. Her gown has a square cut neckline. Her black hair is arranged in Japanese fashion, showing the nape of the neck. She is busy sewing on a length of yellow silk that might conceivably be intended for a child's garment.

THE GNOME: *(In the hall. He picks up the Christmas card from the ice box.)*

Look, there's my Christmas card, adorned with thistle!—
You must expect some weeds among the wheat.
It pricks and hurts like you, but is a pretty blossom—
like you!
You pretty little mother!—Watch her hand moving, as though
    picking flowers. . . .
Her head is bowed—as in a prayer, or contemplation. . . .
And now she smiles: she hears the little child approaching,
the patter of her feet on slippery wooden tiles,
which yesterday were waxed and shined with oil from pine tree—
emitting fragrance of the woods in May, the spawning time
    of bream,
when Summer opens up the green and joyful world outdoors.
You lovely home, where lovely people live
in purity and beauty, protected from the dross of life. . . .

341

Regard the flowers on the mirror:
the turbaned tulips, green and yellow,
that hide their chubby cheeks, their budding lips,
that meet in kisses chaste—
the kind the water-lily gives its mate upon the lake's cool
   mirror. . . .
The mirror, yes! *There* can be seen the marks
of little fingers seeking her own image behind the glass,
thinking it is another little girl's. . . .
And here is Rosa on her little mother's chair,
watching her coat and tiny boots. . . .
Yes, all the charm that life and home can lend
can here be found behind closed doors—
yet is not valued, until it is lost. . . .
Now I'll put out the lights! May darkness hide the sorrow—
and what I am about to do, as it can't stand the light. . . .
   *(He snaps off the electric light switch on the wall. It is
   dark.)*
And when again there's light, you will have Christmas in this
   house. . . .
   (He hides behind the draperies, left.)
MRS. HARD: *(She rings a small service bell.)*
ELLEN: *(Enters with a lighted candle.)*
MRS. HARD: *(Is seen scolding her.)*
ELLEN: *(Weeps in her apron, then leaves.)*
MRS. HARD: *(Enters the hall with the candle, which she places on
   the ice box. She sees the Christmas card with the thistle.
   She reads it and tears it up. Then she takes a glance at herself in the mirror and arranges her hair.—
   Suddenly Beethoven's Sonata 31 opus 110: L'istesso tempo
   di arioso is heard being played on the piano in one of the
   neighboring apartments. MRS. HARD listens. Then she
   takes the silver clothes brush and starts to brush the little
   girl's garments. Picking the nap, and brushing, she discovers
   a loose button on the coat, picks up the doll from the chair
   and lays it on the ice box. She seats herself on the chair,
   takes a threaded needle from her bosom and sews on the
   button. MRS. HARD rises and removes a black glove
   from the woven basket. She hunts for the mate but without*

342

finding it. She searches for it inside the little girl's galoshes under the chair. Unable to find it, she puts the glove in her bosom with a forlorn expression.—

The music changes into Beethoven's funeral march. MRS. HARD listens intently and is gripped by fear and anxiety. There is a sound from the ice box, as of falling pieces of ice.—

A child's scream is heard. MRS. HARD shrinks in fright. She wants to leave, but stands paralysed.

There is a pounding in the walls, the lift squeaks and whines, the water pipes make a roaring sound, voices come humming and murmuring through the walls.)

KRISTIN: *(Rushes in with arms uplifted and her hands clasped, her face white. She speaks to MRS. HARD in an undertone and goes out quickly.)*

MRS. HARD: *(Wants to run after her, but her strength seems to fail her. She falls to her knees by the chair, hiding her face in the little child's cloak, which she strokes and fondles.)*

—THE CURTAIN FALLS FOR A FEW BRIEF MOMENTS—

SCENE III.

THE JANITOR'S QUARTERS

A room in the basement. In the rear a colored window, illuminated from the outside. Now and then it is darkened, while the lift moves up and down.

A table arranged for the Christmas celebration with white table cloth and a small Christmas tree, set in a cradle of wax. At one end of the table is a small keg of mead, wound with twigs of spruce; buns, butter dish, the head of a suckling pig, a shoulder of mutton, salmon, smoked goose, etc.

A candelabrum at the other end of the table; juniper twigs on the floor.

On the wall a colored print of The Nativity of Christ; underneath this, a rack with a number of keys.

A kerosene lamp illuminates the room.

THE JANITOR: *(Sits by the table, resting.)*
THE OLD MAN: *(Enters, carrying a Christmas sheaf of grain, under his arm.)*
>   Again my greetings, friend! You sit here all alone. . . .
THE JANITOR:
>   The aged tree would not grow old unless it stands aloof,
>   alone, uncrowded by the saplings in the forest—
>   and time has freely thinned the ranks about me. . . .
>   *(There is a silence. Then, with a gesture THE JANITOR bids THE OLD MAN to be seated.)*
>   One time I had a home so full we could not move. . . .
>   I'm not complaining—I had my happy days with wife and children;
>   and, after all, I'm not unhappy here—maybe better off. . . .
>   Time plays its part, and everything is relative. . . .
>   Now I am sitting in the shadow of my tree,
>   my Christmas tree, with grateful memories of the past—
>   for I have many! Yet there are those who *have* none,

344

who now sit fretting, sadly grieving over
not having owned what's now too late to gain. . . .
THE OLD MAN:
Yes, I too have had. . . . yet, I prefer not to remember. . . .
THE JANITOR:
Sit down! But I—born in the mining country,
raised inside a mine, beneath the earth—
I feel so free! . . . . That's why I am at home down here,
down in the shadowy crannies of this Babel's tower,
gazing at the light through colored windows—
the light that is my sun, occasionally eclipsed
by the shadow of the lift, resembling fleecy clouds.
THE OLD MAN:
Indeed, much like a mountain king you sit here
as ruler of the elements.
Of heat and fire you are master,
and you distribute water, hot and cold;
from darkened regions you spread light.
You vacuum terrestrial dust, collected
by human feet on their peregrinations,
with air, condensed and rarified;
by laws of gravity you regulate the lift
that tenants may be raised or lowered, as they wish.
THE JANITOR:
Indeed, my friend, you know how to make much of little. . . .
THE OLD MAN:
Oh no, for you are much, much more, as well!
I see you keep the keys to all the tenants' doors here;
and they possess the key to both your character and disposition;
you know the fates that here are being woven,
you hear all, can see through floors and walls,
and all come with their confidences, griefs and worries to you. . . .
THE JANITOR:
You honor me too much, my dear doctor,
but I can stand it, will be neither spoiled nor frightened;
and you have made my humble task here more agreeable:
you've given me new courage when depressed,
and changed my simple quarters to a palace.

345

THE OLD MAN:
>They're talking in the hall, I hear voices raised. . . .
>I hear shrieks, and weeping—soon they'll come to you,
>and you will have to sit in judgment,
>advise, unravel, quiet down, and end the spectacle of discord!

THE JANITOR: *(Listens.)*
>I think I know. . . . It is the pretty Ellen
>on the third floor, the little lady's maid.

THE OLD MAN:
>I'll take my sheaf and go to greet the little birds
>that sing in competition with the weather-vanes. . . .
>And now once more: a Merry Christmas!

THE JANITOR:
>The same to you, doctor!

THE OLD MAN:
>One thing! Whatever happened to the glove I found?

THE JANITOR:
>Oh yes, the glove—I lost it here on the stairs. . . .
>Well, well, a glove is not so much to lose.

THE OLD MAN:
>Oh, don't say that—for mate seeks ever mate, you know!
>*(He leaves.)*

* * * *

ELLEN: *(Enters, dressed to go out.)* Will you let me sit here a while with you?

THE JANITOR: Sit down, dear child!

ELLEN: I can't endure this any longer. . . . When the lights went out, I was scolded for it—and then I was accused again of taking the ring. Now she has reported it to the police.

THE JANITOR: What kind of Christmas is this? Your family is the worst I have in this house! But first of all let me give you some light. . . . *(He brings out some tools.)* My hammer—my pincers. . . . *(He removes several keys from the key rack.)* My keys—now I can go through locked doors. . . .

ELLEN: I think the heat is turned off, too. . . .

THE JANITOR: The heat, too! What in the world is happening up there? It's only in your apartment such things happen.

ELLEN: It is as if things were bewitched! I am frightened! I heard a child scream, and all kinds of strange, eery sounds from the

346

walls. . . . . I think Kristin may be leaving, too. We simply can't stand it!

THE JANITOR: But where is her husband? Isn't he at home?

ELLEN: I think he is away on a hunting trip. We haven't seen him the last two days. He couldn't stand it any longer, either. The taxidermist is quite right when he says that they have it too good. . . . They have nothing to do, have no appetite, no sleep. The only thing they have to worry about, is how to spend their money.

THE JANITOR: Without paying for work done! That's something they don't like to do.

ELLEN: You didn't get anything for Christmas?

THE JANITOR: Oh no! She became angry with me because I asked her not to stand too close to me in the lift. Of course, I may have said it a little sharply, for I had much to do and was in a hurry.

ELLEN: Sh! I hear Kristin on the stairs. . . . She has a lot more patience than I have, but even she can tire of all this.

THE JANITOR: To think that riches bring so few blessings to some. . . . There is a certain consolation in that, however, for us who are poor—small as it may be. . . . How did they acquire their money anyhow?

ELLEN: I suppose they inherited it.—Sh! Here she is now. I shouldn't be surprised if something else has happened up there in that spooky apartment. . . .

THE JANITOR: Why not say the spooky house! There are so many strange things happening here. It's almost as if all these contrivances and machines had something to do with it. . . . I heard Ebba upstairs say that she once saw the gnome sprawled on top of the lift and pulling against the rope. . . .

* * * *

THE GNOME: *(He is seen interchanging the keys on the rack.)*

* * * *

ELLEN: Yes, one could almost suspect that the gnome had something to do with it, for there are times when one can't find things where they have been placed. And again and again, the lock on a door catches—and sometimes hot water comes out of the cold water faucet. . . .

347

THE JANITOR: *(Intently listening.)* Is someone here? I thought I heard a rattling at the key rack. . . .

THE GNOME: *(Hides quickly.)*

THE JANITOR: *(Goes to the key rack and inspects the keys.)* I believe the Fiend himself has been here mixing up my keys. . . . Here is number 25 on 13, and 17 on 81; and Mr. Andersson's mail is mixed in with Judge Svensson's. . . . And I hear forever talking on the stairs, loud quarrelling and weeping! But when I go out to investigate, no one is there!

ELLEN: And now I can hear Kristin—that's a sure omen she is coming!

THE JANITOR: *(Makes believe he opens a door on the right.)* There is no living creature here. . . .

ELLEN: Now I am really frightened!—And sometimes I hear voices of children—sometimes the pigeons on the roof. . . . At times I can't help thinking it's the old taxidermist sitting up there on the top floor, who is the cause of all this mischief. . . . Who is he anyhow, the old codger?

THE JANITOR: He is a curious old fellow—but there is nothing malicious about him.

ELLEN: Tell me—you didn't find a glove on the stairs, did you?

THE JANITOR: Yes, I did—that is. . . . the taxidermist found it, and he gave it to me to take care of—and then I lost it!

ELLEN: You lost it! And if you knew what a to-do we had upstairs because of that glove—as much as about the ring!

(The telephone rings.)

THE JANITOR: *(Answers the telephone.)* Yes, she is sitting here. . . . Why no, that's impossible! I don't believe it! She wouldn't steal a pin! We know Ellen— she would never do such a thing—it's a false accusation. . . . But I'll let her know—yes, yes.

(He hangs up the receiver.)

ELLEN: I know what that was—it was from the police, wasn't it?

THE JANITOR: Yes, my child—it was a call to report. . . .

ELLEN: Then I'll jump in the lake!

THE JANITOR: No—you must go to the police station, Ellen. . . .

ELLEN: Never! Once I am there, they may never let me go.

THE JANITOR: Look at me!—Ellen!—Don't let yourself be worried by bad thoughts. . . . Go in peace now!

ELLEN: *(Gazes at him and conquers her fears.)* I'm going!—I looked

into your eyes—I heard your voice. . . . now I can go in peace—
I have no fear. . . .

THE JANITOR: *(Takes her by the hand and escorts her to the door.)*

ELLEN: And your hand gives me strength—it leads me—it supports
me. . . . I'm going!

(She leaves.)

* * * *

(There is a brief pause.)

AN OLD LADY: *(Enters with the black glove and a little child's
brown boot.)* See what I found in the lift. . . . Perhaps you can
find out whose it is.—You received your Christmas present from
me, didn't you?

THE JANITOR: Yes, thank you! *(The Old Lady hands the glove
to The Janitor.)* That's the glove that was lost. . . .

(He places it on the table, together with the little boot.)

THE OLD LADY: You have a real Christmas table—and Christmas
tree—and such a lot of food—suckling pig's head—well, well,
well!

THE JANITOR: You, who are rich, should not begrudge me, who am
poor. . . .

THE OLD LADY: I am sure you are not as poor as you may seem
to be. And I am not as rich as you may think I am. . . . And now,
take good care of the glove so that it won't be lost again.—It's
as black as mourning—but it helps to conceal a pale hand—
and perhaps more than that!

(She goes out.)

THE JANITOR: *(Gaping at the boot.)* Just look at the little boot—
look at it! The heel is all worn down. What a careless little tot!

* * * *

THE GNOME: *(Comes forward quickly, picks up the glove and then
hides again.)*

* * * *

THE JANITOR: It belongs to a little child—whether a boy or a girl
you can't tell, for the child is too young yet to tell the difference
between right and left—or between good and bad—because
the little ones belong to heaven. . . . But as they grow older—
ugh! Well. . . . *(He goes to pick up the glove.)* But where is

349

the glove? I put it here on the table! *(He searches.)* It's disappeared!

    (He continues to search for it.)

*   *   *   *

KRISTIN: *(Is seen standing in the room; she is in evident agony.)* Oh, just think, just think. . . .

THE JANITOR: What's that? Who is it?—Kristin!

KRISTIN: Just think! God help us!—The little child is gone!

THE JANITOR: Gone! What's happened?

KRISTIN: She has disappeared. . . . someone has taken the child. . . .

THE JANITOR: That's impossible! I would have noticed it—I would have heard something! That's what I am here for—to watch over the tenants!

KRISTIN: Then you haven't seen the child? Well, I am going to the police, then! . . . . Treat the poor mother kindly, if you see her. . . . She is sitting in the apartment—there is no heat, and no light. . . . Oh, it's too cruel—even for her!

    (She goes out.)

*   *   *   *

THE JANITOR: What in the world is the meaning of all this? It can't be the doing of human beings! That's why there is still hope. . . . *(He lays the boot on the table.)* Who is that coming here? It's she—the poor little mother herself. . . .

    (He withdraws to the left.)

MRS. HARD: *(Comes from the right, dressed as in the previous scene. She is seemingly out of her mind.)*

Where have I come?

Where am I?

Where did I come from?

Who am I?

Here lives someone who's poor—but why the many keys?

It's a hotel, then, is it?—

No—an underground detention house. . . .

There gleams the moon—but shaped into a heart—

and past it glide the jet-black clouds. . . .

There is a wood, replete with gifts and candles—

yet, it's a prison!—This is a different world. . . .

Is anybody here?

350

THE JANITOR: *(Is seen at the left, but only by the audience. Softly, to himself:)*
　　She is beside herself, her wits are gone. . . .
　　What mercy! Oh what mercy for one, who's thus afflicted!
MRS. HARD:
　　But wait! I now recall. . . . yet I remember but the past,
　　and I came here in-search of something—oh, but what?
　　What did I seek? . . . .
　　I'd lost a glove! Its color—it was black. . . .
　　Now my mind is blank again—
　　but in my darkness I see something blue—
　　much like the sky in spring, amid white clouds,
　　a mountain tarn set between towering shores:
　　that blue was my blue sapphire that I lost—
　　that has been stolen. . . .
　　I've lost so much—so much—these past few dreary days. . . .
　　I sat in darkness, freezing. . . .
　　Here it is warm, although oppressive;
　　I feel the weight of this tall tower,
　　the onerous layers of human fates
　　bear down on me, as if to press me to the earth,
　　squeezing my heart in its enfeebled cradle. . . .
　　I hunger for the words to speak, but cannot find them—
　　I feel like weeping, as though I were in mourning! . . . .
　　　　(She sees the little boot.)
　　But what is this?—A tiny baby boot!
　　A little stocking—such a little foot!—
　　What's that I heard?—And here's a candle
　　with sprouting branches growing from the roots
　　of the candlestick—soon to bear flowers,
　　three bluish flowers with a tinge of red. . . .
　　To think that candles can both grow and sprout!
　　I wonder to what parts of our world I've come?—
　　Here floats an anchor-buoy in wood of spruce;
　　a boar sticks up its head out of the sea foam;
　　and fishes swim about on *terra firma!* . . . .
　　　　(She notices the colored print of The Nativity of Christ.)
　　And what is this? . . . . A cradle in a stable!
　　　　(Coming out of her delirium somewhat.)

351

And the shepherd's dusky cattle keep gazing wide-eyed
On the little child—that's—sleeping in its cradle. . . .
(She is suddenly wide awake and gives a shriek.)
O God, Lord Jesus, Saviour of the World, oh, help me! I'm
dying! I am dying!—A child is born this night—a child is dead!
—There stands the janitor, who is angry with me because I did
not give him anything for Christmas! Don't be angry with me!
Don't take revenge on me! I'll give you all my jewels. . . .

THE JANITOR: *(Steps forward.)* I am not angry, and I am not
revengeful. Your child will come back to you. A child can't
disappear in a city like ours. Come with me now and I'll see
that you, first of all, get some light and heat. . . .

MRS. HARD: Say once again what you just said! That a child can't
disappear in our city. . . . Of course, I don't believe a word you
say—but say it anyhow. Say it over and over again. . . .

THE JANITOR: Come with me. And while I fix what's wrong, you
go upstairs to an old friend of yours three flights up and keep
yourself warm. He will talk to you—I can't—and he will console
you. . . .

MRS. HARD: You mean the assessor. . . . But *he* is angry with me,
too, isn't he?

THE JANITOR: No one is angry with you, Mrs. Hard. Just come
along now. . . .

MRS. HARD: Oh, how kind you are—bearing no grudge against me. . .

THE JANITOR: Oh, for shame, for shame! Such wicked thoughts. . . .

MRS. HARD: But my child!—My child! My child!

THE JANITOR: Come!

END OF SCENE III

SCENE IV

THE ATTIC

A room in the attic. In the rear, two windows, covered by light green curtains. Between the windows, a cabinet with manuscripts and books, on which stands an attractive lamp. To the right, an oaken table, covered with manuscripts. To the left, a reclining chair.

THE GNOME: *(Enters.)* This is the morning of Christmas Eve! But
   here—at the old philosopher's I see no sign of Christmas joy.
      (He draws aside the curtains.)
   But wait! He's placed his Christmas tree out on the balcony—
   for the sparrows and the pigeons—
   and a sheaf with a thousand yellow nibs,
   a grain in each one, to feed the birds of heaven
   that still are sleeping on the roof,
   their heads buried under their wings. . . .
   Soon the morning breeze will shake the weather-vanes
   upon the smoke-boards over the fire-places,
   where gay and sparkling log-fires
   give heat beneath the coffee pots and pans;
   then I cavort upon the ridges,
   inhaling the enticing fragrance,
   while the sun reflects its rays
   upon the telephone cables in the early morning. . . .
   And then the cables and the weather-vanes
   start singing, and the doves coo on the cornices—
   and then the children leave their beds. . . .

   What has he here?
   On yellow sheets, in thousands upon thousands,
   he has collected all his knowledge! . . .
   Straw beneath the hot-bed's litter
   that's been threshed through?—No, merely chaff,
   in which the grain has to be sorted out;

353

the kernels also he's collected in his barn
of carven oak, which holds the harvest. . . .
    (He rummages among the manuscripts.)
This is the index—the key to all his learning,
to the enigma of creation that he imagines he has solved.—
You foolish oldster, re-arranger of the universe—
now I stir up the sweepings
you raked together on the slopes and hillsides,
and so create anew a chaos.
You now will have to start once more from the beginning!
    (He shuffles the manuscripts, leaving them in disorder.)
I here see the wise man's spectacles;
the years have made him short of sight. . . .
therefore I give you now a Christmas gift
to make you see afar, beyond. . . .
    (He exchanges The Old Man's spectacles for another pair,
      which he takes from his pocket.)
I give you now a pair of eyes
that you may see what other mortals
do *not* see in their work-a-day pursuits. . . .
Where formerly you saw but laws,
you now shall meet The Good Creator,
and afterwards The Great Judge.
Where once you saw but Nature
and blind, hap-hazard devil's play,
there you will now find spirits
alike in nature to yourself. . . .

I hear the oldster is awake. . . .
Perhaps he has been up all night—
for night is much like day to him,
who aims to banish darkness. . . .
He's coming now—and I shall stay
and get acquainted with him;
and he will learn to know me, too. . . .
    (The Gnome withdraws behind the drapery, left.)
THE OLD MAN: *(Enters from the right. He is dressed in black,*
      wears a white tie, black skull cap of silk. His hair is long
      and white, and so is his beard.)

354

Be welcome, life! Good morning, labor!—
Through sixty years I've arranged the universe—
and now the day has dawned, the sun is rising
for my solution of the riddle.
It's all in order, like the strata of the earth—
deposited from fire and from water through the ages. . . .
Of stones and animals and vegetation,
sources of origin, forces, measures, numbers,
I have produced the slabs and stones
for the celestial steps to Babel's Tower.
On them I tread now, rising from the vale of tears,
to gain the mosque with its blue cupola
that rests upon the four points of the compass.

For sixty years I have calculated and collected;
and half-way on the road I solved the riddle.
It was one night—I made a note of it in writing. . . .
but it was buried, and, alas, is lost now.
It must be somewhere, but while searching for it
the stack has grown and grown—
my offspring's turned into a giant. . . .
I'm lame-struck when I try to delve in it,
I rummage in it as if digging after treasures—
but soon the spade falls from my hand,
my head grows weary, and my body wilts;
and often I collapse and lie like dead
when trying to review my work and find its core. . . .

Yet now I feel the moment's come—
for in a dream last night I saw. . . .
I saw the sheet of paper I was searching
for; a sheet of blue-white Regal, English Oliphant. . . .
    (He removes his cuffs.)
This time or never! It is you or I,
you stack of papers! Give up your secret—
I am your master, all you spirits!
And I alone can here command!
    (He puts on his spectacles and stars to rummage frantically
    through his papers.)

What in the world is this?—What *is* this?
There is no order here any more!
Here alphabet and figures have changed places:
a, b, c, d, h, r—I think the Fiend himself. . . .
And number 1,4, 7, 26 and 10. . . .
Some one's been here!
Alpha, beta, pi. . . . and my system of symbols that I had
evolved. . . . Now it's lost from my memory—I can't remember
it. . . . *(He keeps rummaging.)* Here I have a cue—but right on
top of the principal numeral there is a blot of ink. . . . I'll try
erasing it! *(He takes out a knife.)* It went right through the
paper!—Well, well! I'll have to continue searching. . . . I'll go
through every single piece of paper until I find it. . . . *(He
scrutinizes sheet after sheet.)* Now my neighbor is starting to
play. . . . Go on and play, neighbor! . . . You won't disturb
me—I have the whole day before me—and the night too, for
that matter. . . . I eat practically nothing and need little sleep. . . .

> *(While The Old Man keeps going through his manuscripts,*
> *page by page, Beethoven's Sonata 29, opus 106, andante*
> *sostenuto, is being played for several minutes on the piano.)*

I seem to be tiring quickly today. . . . I think I'll rest for a
while. . . . *(He walks miserably toward the reclining chair and
falls into it. The music continues.)* I seem to see so strangely—
what is near seems now so far away, what is distant seems so
close to me—and there is an emptiness in my head. . . .

> *(He closes his eyes. The music continues.)*
> *(The Old Man awakens and again goes to work on the*
> *piles of manuscripts; but he tires immediately and returns*
> *to the chair.—He rises and digs into the pile again; again*
> *he succumbs to tiredness and seeks the chair in exhaustion.*
> *He falls asleep there. His face has the semblance of death.)*

THE GNOME: *(Moves a reclining chair from the left and seats him-*
self playfully opposite The Old Man. The music stops. The Old
Man wakes up.)*
THE OLD MAN:
Who's there? Are you a being?
THE GNOME:
To be is to be felt, perceived. . . .

356

You have perceived me!
Thus I *am* one.

THE OLD MAN: *(Rises.)*
But I would feel you, I would like to touch you. . . .
You don't exist for me until I've done so. . . .

THE GNOME:
You don't get up and touch the rainbow—yet it's there!
And the mirage of sea and desert, too, exists.
I am a spirit—don't come near to me,
for then you'll cease to see me—
and yet I shall continue being.

THE OLD MAN:
In truth, your logic is so very right. . . .

THE GNOME:
And therefore it is plain you must believe your eyes.

THE OLD MAN: *(Demurs.)*

THE GNOME:
You waver 'cause I'm not included in your system—
your system rules you, masters you—
you are its slave. . . .

THE OLD MAN:
I rule supremely o'er my system. . . .

THE GNOME:
Then you must tell me in a few brief words
what is the basic thought of all the multiplicity of facts
you've gathered—else you have collected merely leaves,
and rain drops, grains of sand—all similar;
and still they're not at all alike. . . .

THE OLD MAN:
My basic thought idea that binds together
the millions of phenomena that meet the eye. . . .

THE GNOME:
Let's hear it! I like to glean some knowledge!

THE OLD MAN:
You little pilferer, you purloined my idea from me. . . .
a moment past it was so clear to me. . . .

THE GNOME:
And now—your thought is clouded like the crystal-clear ice

357

that melts and turns to slush in heat;
like water, evaporating into mist,
is dissipated! I'll condense it promptly
and enunciate your system, which you have forgot!
>   *(There is a pause.)*
The riddle of the earth is this: the harmonious unity of cosmos....
THE OLD MAN:
>   You hit it right! You are a clever little sprite
>   to find so promptly what I searched for thirty years:
>   the unity of matter! That's the answer—that's the core of it!
THE GNOME:
>   This was the system—now to the reality!
>   Now ponder he duality of Nature;
>   let's see if that hypothesis has more to recommend. . . .
>   *(There is a silence.)*
>   The element of moisture, water,
>   is a unity—yet it cannot be disputed
>   it is comprised of two: of oxygen and hydrogen;
>   magnetic force is polarized in north and south,
>   and electricity is positive and negative;
>   the seed of vegetation is divided into male and female,
>   and foremost in the chain—in its most perfect link—
>   you find duality: because it was not good
>   for Man to be alone on earth. . . .
>   Thus man and woman were created—
>   and: the duality of Nature has been proved!
THE OLD MAN:
>   You little devil! You have torn to pieces. . . .
THE GNOME:
>   . . . your plaything, you mighty fool. . . . Your chain is broken,
>   and now the links lie like a scrap-heap;
>   the cable you had wound is torn to tatters,
>   turned to rubbish, fit only for the junkshop now. . . .
THE OLD MAN:
>   Ha! Sixty years to blow an empty bubble
>   that burst as from a breath of air!
>   No longer do I care to live!
THE GNOME:
>   E'en though the bubble burst, you can blow others;

you need but water and the foam from soap,
which you whip up to look like something big—
yet is so little—almost nothing. . . .

THE OLD MAN:

And sixty years. . . .
>   *(He rises wildly and flings his manuscripts in all directions.)*

Out! Out with you—you vain illusions of the devil!
A rotten fruit of twenty thousand daily labors. . . .
Out! Out!—you dried up leaves that sapped my tree,
you will-o'-the-wisps, you lantern carriers, who misled me,
decoyed me into marshes, where I sank in mire
up to the neck, enticed me into deserts,
where piercing spines and thorns unmercifully stabbed my
>   hands! . . .
>   *(He empties the cabinet of its papers, but leaves a small box untouched.)*

Out, out, you spurious pilots—you, who made me go aground,
you guiding beacons, who led me down to the abyss of hell!—
A failure, bankrupt, I give up the struggle
and sit now, emptyhanded, on the ground you scorched. . . .
>   *(He sinks down into the chair.)*

A snail, whose shell was rudely crushed,
a spider, with his web destroyed,
a bird that lost his way upon the sea,
too far from shore to turn around and reach it,
he flaps his wings o'er the abysmal waves
until he wearily falls down—and dies. . . .
>   *(There is a silence.)*

THE GNOME:

Tell me! Would you begin all over? Be young again?

THE OLD MAN:

Be young again? No, thanks! Be given strength to suffer—
strength to weave false dreams again? No—no!

THE GNOME:

Do you crave gold?

THE OLD MAN:

To buy me what?—
I wish for nothing—save eternal sleep!

THE GNOME:

Quite so! But only after you've been reconciled to life. . . .

THE OLD MAN:

Be reconciled!—Be bound anew and pilloried? . . .
No, no—and no again! Else I shall never leave. . . .
"One handclasp more!—Take one more glass to warm you!"
"Oh, stay a little longer!"—And so—one stays. . . .
No, take the driver's seat and whip the nag,
and tear yourself away!—then you'll have no regrets!

THE GNOME:

You tore yourself away once from the throbbing life,
from home and hearth, from wife and children,
in vain pursuit of honor and its empty shell.

THE OLD MAN:

But partly true. . . . I merely went
in order not to see the others leave—who'd packed already!
When life then failed me, and the ship was sinking,
I made myself a life-buoy and inflated it
with air. . . . Thus far it's true. . . .
It held me up, supported me for quite a time—
and then it burst—and I—I sank. . . . Was that my fault?

THE GNOME: *(Has removed the box from the cabinet.)*

You have some jetsam here the sea gave up. . . .

THE OLD MAN: *(His strength gone.)*

Let be my box! . . . Don't bring the dead to life again!

THE GNOME:

You faithless Sadducee, who disbelieved
the resurrection. . . . why do you fear the dead?

THE OLD MAN:

Let be my casket!—You'll give birth to ghosts. . . .

THE GNOME:

Indeed! Then you will be aware that life is spirit,
though fettered in the body, in a thing, or being!
Take care, I now exhort,
I conjure forth. . . .

THE OLD MAN:

Ah! What fragrance! Is the clover blossoming
in rosy May, when apple trees burst out in bloom,
when west wind sways the crowns of lilac trees?

360

And freshly furrowed garden patch that yesterday
lay snowy white, now spreads its murky covering
of earthen soil o'er seed—but buried to arise and to be born.
  (Sinding's the Rustling of Spring is heard being played.)
I see—a little cottage, white with green shutters;
a window now is opened, and the curtains flutter
their wine-red colors. . . . A mirror deep within,
in sculptured empire frame, is seen;
and in the oval glass I glance as in a dream
and see the loveliest gift that life can give:
a mother, young in years, tends her little child,
combing its soft locks, washing the sleep
from innocent blue eyes that open wide now
from love of life—and smile to mother and the sun. . . .
The little foot stamps friskily the rug,
impatient like a foal that's eager for a frolic. . . .
I hear music! What melodies from days of youth,
half unremembered, that rise up in me again. . . .
the little brook that glides beneath the alders,
midsummer wreaths, and berry baskets, and the row-boat,
and pike, highspiritedly at play, and jumping 'gainst the
     thwart. . . .

THE GNOME: *(Takes out a small bridal crown and a white veil
from the box.)*

THE OLD MAN:
What's this I see? What have you there?
A little crown, fit for a queen, entwined with myrtle. . . .
now crushed and sealed. And then, a veil of gauze—
a morning mist in elfen dance at sunrise. . . .
Now I can see no more, my vision is befogged. . . .
Oh, God in Heaven!—All this did once exist
but is no more, will never come again. . . .
     (He weeps and collapses.)

THE GNOME:
All this you've once possessed and thrown away—
the flowers that were fresh—for wilted leaves;
warmblooded life, for ice cold thoughts. . . .
You poor, poor man! . . . What have I here?
     (He holds up a woman's black glove.)

THE OLD MAN: *(He regards the glove.)*
  A little glove! Now let me see—I don't recall
  how it came here!—But wait, I now remember:
  I found it yesterday upon the stairs. . . .
THE GNOME:
  And now I give it to you as a Christmas gift. . . .
  It holds its many secrets, and the dainty fingers
  have touched so many fates, and caused much harm;
  it stretches out its hand to you in friendship. . . .
  If you now give it to her, as I hope you will,
  then you'll have spread both happiness and solved
  a riddle much more priceless than the Sphinx's—which defeated
    you!
    (He locks up the box in the cabinet.)
THE OLD MAN:
  If I could still bring joy to one lone mortal,
  if I could but receive one glance of gratitude,
  console or stimulate an aching heart—
  then I'd have done away with all my agony!
THE GNOME:
  You've burned your ancient, withered woods—
  that was the bravest and the wisest you could do;
  and now—out toward the clearing! Ashes make things grow,
  and you can still have time to harvest *something!*
  Yet if you can't enjoy it for yourself,
  then give, for giving is more joy than to receive. . . .
  Besides it is a sacrifice that pleases. . . .
  Now I'm returning to my gloomy shed—
  but wish you first a merry, *merry* Christmas!
    (He disappears.)
THE OLD MAN: *(Alone; he scrutinizes the glove.)*
  A little hand held out in all the darkness—
  a glove thrown down—in peace, and not in challenge. . . .
  a hand, much like a child's, caressive, soft . . . .
  What secrets are concealed within your grasp?
  Perhaps it's meant to be a foolish jest
  to give this single glove as Christmas present?
    (There is a knock at the door.)

362

Come in, my unknown friend! A Christmas gift awaits
the one, who enters first. . . . Come in!

ELLEN: *(Enters.)*

Forgive me, doctor, for my coming here—
but you are known to be a friend to all. . . .
My life is lost, I'm in despair, abandoned. . . .

THE OLD MAN: *(Rises.)*

May God console you, child! Sit down!
What's happened? Oh—is it the ring again?

ELLEN:

I've been to the police—and I am still suspected—
and have been searched. . . . I thought of drowning,
but lacked the courage. . . . Do let me stay, please,
and say something to me—say: "You are innocent!"

THE OLD MAN:

My dear, be at ease—and let me think. . . .
What was it I. . . . oh yes, I have a gift,
a Christmas present from a stranger!

ELLEN:

What is it—oh, a worn-out glove!

THE OLD MAN:

Yes, I fail to grasp it, but it has been lost
and found, and lost again, and found again. . . .

ELLEN:

Why, I believe it is my mistress's!
Let's look inside it for the size. . . .
    (She turns the glove inside out. The ring falls out.)
For heaven's sake! There is the ring!
    (She weeps.)
Then I am saved! And you had no idea it was in the glove? . . .

THE OLD MAN:

I had no idea. . . . Now wipe away your tears!

ELLEN:

You have a blesséd heart! I knew that you
were good to beasts and flowers. . . .

THE OLD MAN:

Hush! Hush! I have no share at all in this. . . .

ELLEN:

To save a human being—isn't that a deed of goodness?

THE OLD MAN:
   I'm not the giver—merely an instrument. . . .
ELLEN:
   Now reap your bliss! I wish that I were you,
   who's been so graced as to bring joy to me, poor girl. . . .
THE OLD MAN:
   Go now and set things right and vindicate yourself,
   and share the joy the whole house feels. . . .
ELLEN:
   How can I?—The little child has not been found;
   how can we then be happy in this house of sorrow?
THE OLD MAN:
   The little child, yes? I've heard that fairy tale—
   but here, forsooth, the game of hide and seek is being played.
   That's all I know—but with a different view of things,
   I think, and hope, believe that ere the day is over,
   each one of us has fought his way through these besetting tribu-
      lations!
      (He sinks down into the chair and falls asleep.)

END OF SCENE IV

SCENE V.

THE NURSERY

The nursery. In the background handsome draperies, hiding an alcove. In front of it is a small table, on which stand two silver candle sticks with lighted candles. Between the candle sticks, a portrait of a little girl. It has been decorated with flowers. Behind these things, a mirror, reflecting the lighted candles.—On the right side of the room, a child's small, white table and a tiny chair, on which Rosa, the child's doll, is seated. On the table is placed a miniature Christmas tree and a number of Christmas gifts.

A white rocking horse stands beside the bed.

MRS. HARD: *(Enters. She is dressed in a black gown. In her hand she carries a piece of crape, which she tears or cuts in strips to fit the various objects in the room, covering them: the Christmas tree, the doll, the rocking horse, etc.)*
We are in mourning! But we've been blessed with something
that fills the emptiness that grief creates:
the winter's here and cools us off,
the darkness hems us in and hides us
as does the blanket we creep under
on sleepless nights, to flee from visions conjured by our fears.
You, Rosa, you miss your little mother, don't you?
Your cheek's so pale, your hands are freezing. . . .
Would you not like the Christmas tree to play its song of lamentation?
(She winds up a music box and places it beneath the Christmas tree.)
And you, poor little horse, with band of mourning. . . .
I call to mind last year, when we departed
to visit with my parents in the country,
and you were left behind, alone, in these cold rooms!
But Mary—she kept worrying:
"My little horse is all alone, and freezing;

365

she may be frightened also by the darkness!"—
When she returned, you had, indeed, a cold:
you suffered in your throat, and she took care of you,
and wound her nicest stocking round it—
then kissed you on your sweet, white muzzle;
she combed your mane and bound a golden ribbon
around your forehead!—Yes, you had it good, then. . . .
But now—now we are all beset by sorrow!
You, little bed, stand empty—like a skiff at sea
after the ship has sunk, helplessly rocking. . . .
For whom shall I make up the bed now—
my little precious one, who now is dead?—
My mind goes back to that last evening,
when—after supper—you found crumbs in bed
and I had to make up your bed again. . . .
You thought it was the Sandman, who had sprinkled
sand in it, as I would sometimes tell you;
I used to mingle fairy tales with your goodnight-prayer,
and ballads, too, to lull you on your gay adventure
into the greenleafed woods, and lakes so blue in dreamland. . . .
Her eyelids closed, like daisy petals,
above her rosy cheeks, beneath her elfen hair. . . .
And now she's gone! A little dimple in the feather pillow
is all the image—an empty void—I now have of my darling,
where she once slept beneath her canopy of blue,
now darkened by the clouds of sorrow. . . .
Where is my child? Where are you? Answer!
Have you gone yonder to the stars,
to play with other children, yet unborn—
perhaps the dead, re-born up there?
Have you gone out in search of fairy tales,
to meet Tom Thumb, or little Blue Bird,
Red Riding Hood, or little Solyman,
irked by us and by our quarrelling?
Oh—I would like to follow you! I never felt at home here;
it held much promise, but my hopes were shattered,
forever unfulfilled: a mere shadow life;
a work of art, no doubt, and yet not flawless:
too much the physical, too little soul;

366

and it was agony one could not be,
was not allowed to be, what one most yearned to be!
(There is a pause.)
It is so dark. . . . I'm banished from the light. . . .
(She vainly snaps the electric button.)
And it's so cold here—even heat is taken from me!
(She wrings her hands before the grilled outlet.)
And I've no water! My flowers parch with thirst!
(She tinkles a small service bell.)
And no one comes! They all have left me!
Could I have been so mean, then? No one knows
what everybody knows—or think they know!
All were subservient to me, and no one had the courage
to tell me how I ought to act.
Yes—the mirror dared, but it turned out to be a hypocrite:
the slippery glass gave nothing in return but flattery.
(There is a pause.)
But what is this?—My glove—that I had lost!
And here—inside the finger—is my ring!
Then she was innocent—my poor, poor Ellen!
Now she'll revenge herself; *her* punishment shall now be mine,
and I shall suffer tortures worse than ever!
Perhaps be put in prison?—No, no I won't—I'll hide the
ring. . . .
(There is a pause.)
No!—Yes!—What's that I felt? A soft caressing on the cheek!
Is someone here? I heard a whisper. . . .
a child that breathéd in its sleep. . . .
And now. . . . It is the weather-vane upon the neighbor's roof!
Sh, listen, it sings up there above the chimney. . . .
What does it say: "My Mary—Mary, Mary!"
And now: "Poor Ellen, Ellen!" Oh, poor Ellen! . . .
I hear a siren! It is the police!
What can have happened? What? What have I done?
Yes, right must be right, and having trespassed
I now must take my punishment!
ELLEN: *(Enters.)*
MRS. HARD: *(Falls on her knees before her.)*
ELLEN: Rise up, rise up, in God's name—please! It makes me feel

terrible, poor dear Mrs. Hard, that you should be so unhappy! Rise up, I can't bear to see you like this. . . . The whole thing is a mistake—it's nothing to speak about—we all have to take things as they come—everything is in a mess anyhow. I've heard it said somewhere it's so hard to live—it's almost impossible. . . . Now, now!

MRS. HARD: Ellen! Forgive me!

ELLEN: Of course—I've already done so, poor dear Mrs. Hard. . . . Now get up—and then I'll have something to tell you. . . .

MRS. HARD: *(Rising.)* Is it about. . . ?

ELLEN: No, it has nothing to do with this. It has to do with something else—some one else—The old man up in the attic. . . . he passed away. . . . happy and reconciled to life as he had longed to be. . . . And when we went through his papers, . . . we found his right name. . . . and. . . .

MRS. HARD: Then I know!—He was my lost father. . . .

ELLEN: Yes!

MRS. HARD: And he died without seeing his child once more!—But we shall meet again! . . . This mysterious house, where human fates are stacked, floor upon floor, the one above the other, and next door to each other!—Where is my husband? Has any word come from him yet?

ELLEN: He'll be home for dinner—not before.

MRS. HARD: To our Christmas dinner! In cold and darkness—and no water! In a house of sorrow, and a house of death! My poor husband! Now I shall go to my father!—How did he die, Ellen?

ELLEN: He burned his papers and said it was nothing but rubbish.— And it was he who found the ring.—When I told him how overjoyed I was, he said: "Now I die happy—having been blessed by bringing happiness to a human being!"

MRS. HARD: He was right!—I felt no love for him, but I want to close his eyes and do him the last service—as one should do! Won't you come with me, Ellen?

    (They go out.)

    (There is a pause.)

KRISTIN and THE JANITOR: *(The Janitor carries his tools. They walk slowly across the stage.)*

THE JANITOR: It's clearing up! It's clearing up!

KRISTIN: *(Indicating the little bed.)* Hush! Hush!
    (They steal out.)
THE GNOME: *(Enters. He is visible at the far left.)*
CHRISTMAS: *(Is similarly seen at the right.)*
    Our task will soon be over now;
    I've heard the word that will atone for everything: "Forgive!"
    The word's been spoken, all is done—
    and now let grief depart, let only gladness reign!
THE GNOME: *(Steals about, removing the black mourning gauze,*
    which he gathers in one hand.)
    I blow the dust away, I sweep and tidy up,
    I clean the brass, grown tarnished from bad breaths,
    I spray the flowers now with water,
    lest they grow thirsty—and the maid forgets.
        (He waters the flowers by the mirror.)
    The curtains I shall fold that they may look their best,
    and straighten out the rugs. I can mess up things, too—
    but not in here, and not today. . . .
    You little mother, you beautiful young wife,
    now you have suffered! Don't forget this lesson!
    The tears of remorse and sorrow
    will make your eyes so lovely, so bright, so mild;
    but should you cry in anger, you'll turn ugly. . . .
    Now, Angel! May we wish you now: A Merry Christmas!
CHRISTMAS:
    She comes now for her task of love:
    she's closed the eyes of her dead father,
    who, only after death, was given back his child. . . .
THE GNOME: *(Goes to the bed and peeks into it. He rocks it gently,*
    lifting his finger as if to say: "She's sleeping. . . .")
CHRISTMAS:
    Now she'll receive what's hers—but still alive and breathing. . . .
    Be ready now: go to the faucets and electric buttons. . . .
THE GNOME:
    I'll go, and then make ready for the curtain fall!
        (They go out in opposite directions.)
        *(There is a pause; then music: Sinding's **The Rustling of**
        Spring.)*

MRS. HARD: *(Enters. She is wearing a cloak.)*
    Oh, blessed warmth! Have you returned again?
    Is south-wind here—has the sun of winter risen
    from the equator—is it summer?
        (The stage is lighted brightly.)
        (Drops her cloak on the floor.)
    O God!—One word!—And there was light!
    Have You once more unclosed Your heaven
    that I may see her precious features,
    her little smile, between white clouds—
    her tiny hands stretched out to me; her little mouth. . . .
    But listen!
        *(She stands listening as if hearing a sound from the little
        bed. Then she looks around.)*
    What's happened here?—Is the day of mourning over?
        *(She goes to the bed. She sees the child (not visible to the
        audience) asleep under the canopy.)*
    Yes! The Lord took away—and The Lord has given back!
    I'm still unworthy of such blessing. . . . *(She kneels by the bed.)*
    The joy a mother feels when she can close her child again in
    her embrace cannot be measured or expressed. . . . It makes me
    weep for joy!
THE GNOME: *(Is seen on the extreme left. He waves his head covering, throwing kisses to the mother and the child.)*

CURTAIN

PERFORMANCE NOTES

THE DANCE OF DEATH

THE DANCE OF DEATH had its first performance at the end of September, 1905, at the Residenztheater in Cologne, Germany, and following its original première there, Parts I and II were given in forty cities.

In the fall of 1905 both parts were also given in Berlin, and in the fall of 1906 by Josef Jarno in Vienna. During the next two years the play was acted in Mannheim, Hamburg, Bremen and Berlin. In Riga it was presented in 1909.

The Swedish première took place at The Intimate Theatre (The Strindberg Theatre) in Stockholm on September 8, 1909, when Part I was given; and on October 1 Part II was presented. Strindberg instructed August Falck, who played the Captain, as follows: "First and last, the Captain must look old! His ugliness, age, and whiskey imbibing must show!" The critical reception after Part I was mixed, but after Part II less stinging. The play was given *en tour* in 1911.

In 1912 Max Reinhardt produced both parts at the Deutsches Theater in Berlin. Gertrud Eysoldt acted Alice and Paul Wegener the Captain's rôle. In 1915 Reinhardt brought the play to Sweden, where it was given at the Royal Theatre with Wegener and Rosa Bertens in the two leading rôles; and during the war it was given in Germany with tremendous success (1916).

In 1919 The Swedish Theatre presented the play with Tore Svennberg as the Captain and Pauline Brunius as Alice, touring with it 1920-23. In the fall of 1921 Part II was given at Malmö Theatre with Harriet Bosse in Judith's rôle.

The Royal Theatre gave Part II in the autumn of 1921. 1923 and 1924 Tore Svennberg again triumphed as the Captain opposite Hilda Borgström as Alice. 1926 it was given at the People's Theatre in Gothenburg, and the same year August Falck and Manda Björling acted the play at the Civic Theatre in Helsingborg. 1934-37 Olof and Anna Hillberg played in it 423 times in the provinces.

In 1937 Poul Reumert of the Royal Danish Theatre gave guest

appearances at the Royal Theatre in Stockholm in the rôle of the Captain, playing opposite Tora Teje. In the spring of 1938 it was produced at the Gothenburg Civic Theatre, and in the fall of that year the travelling government theatre presented the play in the provinces. In 1944 the Vasa Theatre in Stockholm produced it, and in 1949, the government theatre took it to various parts of Sweden. The same year, it was seen at the Blanche Theatre in Stockholm; and in the spring of 1952 Keve Hjelm staged the play at the Civic Theatre in Helsingborg. The Chamber Theatre in Stockholm gave Part II in the spring of 1954.

In 1954 the Halmstad Theatre was inaugurated with a performance acted by the Gothenburg Civic Theatre Company, and in the same year the Norrköping-Linköping Civic Theatre had its opening with the play, which later was acted by the ensemble in the provinces, and also in Denmark. In the fall of 1957 Sammy Friedman acted the Captain again at the Chamber Theatre, and in 1959 the Royal Theatre gave the play with Lars Hanson as the Captain. *The Dance of Death* was acted by the Royal Theatre Company *en tour* that same year, when it also appeared in Finland.

In 1928 the distinguished Poul Reumert of the Danish Royal Theatre was invited to appear in the play at the Odéon in Paris, where he proved his virtuosity by giving a flawless performance in superb French—a performance greatly admired by Antoine and Lugné Poe, who were among the audience.

The play has been given in practically every European country as well as in America, Mexico and South America. In England Robert Loraine gave a most successful performance of the play, although somewhat melodramatic, in the 1920's. It was also filmed in Italy, with Erich von Stroheim as the Captain. It has received extensive productions on radio in Sweden, Norway, Denmark, Latvia, Germany, Finland, Russia, Austria, France and in the U.S.A.

SWANWHITE

This fairy play of Strindberg's had its first performance at the Swedish Theatre in Helsinki, Finland, on April 8, 1908. Its first presentation in Sweden took place at the Intimate Theatre in Stockholm on October 30, 1908. One critic called the play "one of the most enchanting things written by Strindberg. This beautiful fairy tale is not only a poetic tale to be read; its characters become alive even on the stage." It was a great public success for Strindberg's theatre and was presented 153 times. The theatre company later took it *en tour,* finishing up at the New Theatre in Gothenburg on December 11, 1909.

It was given in the open air theatre at Skansen, the famous ethnological and zoological park in Stockholm, where it received ten performances in the summer of 1910. In 1911 it was again presented by a touring company, and in 1914 it was given at the Swedish Theatre in Stockholm with Tora Teje as Swanwhite and Gösta Ekman as the Prince. Pauline Brunius—later to become director of the Royal Theatre—acted the role of the Stepmother. The incidental music was by Sibelius. The distinguished actor Tore Svennberg played the Duke. In the spring of 1915 Tora Teje and Ekman performed in the play at the Grand Theatre in Gothenburg.

In January, 1916, SWANWHITE was produced by the Vasa Theatre in Stockholm with Inga Tidblad as the young Princess. Uno Henning acted the Prince. Under the direction of Stig Torsslow it was performed at the Royal Theatre in the autumn of 1942. Carl-Hugo Calander was excellent as the Prince, and Ninni Löfberg played Swanwhite's rôle. In 1954 an attempt to adapt the play to "the demands of modern audiences" at the Marsyas Theatre in a Stockholm basement turned out to be a parody of the play.

In 1912 SWANWHITE scored a success when it was produced at the New Theatre in Budapest. It was also given at the Swedish Theatre in Helsinki that year; and the following year Max Reinhardt staged it at the Schauspielhaus in Berlin with Helen Thimig in Swanwhite's rôle. In the spring of 1919 SWANWHITE was seen at the Thalia Theatre in Hamburg, in which city the play was again acted in 1933 and 1953. In 1920 Strindberg's fairy play was given in Swedish at the Academy of Music in Brooklyn, and in the spring of 1925 it was seen at the Dagmar Theatre in Copenhagen. It was given fifteen performances at the Hall of Knights there in 1942.

It has been heard on radio, with the incidental music of Sibelius, in Sweden, England and the United States.

An opera, based on SWANWHITE, has been composed by Julius Weissmann. SCHWANENWEISS had its original performance in Duisburg, after which it was given in other German cities 1923-25.

STORMCLOUDS

This chamber play had its original première at the Intimate Theatre on December 30, 1907. It was revived at the New Intimate Theatre in 1915, staged by Mauritz Stiller and with Lars Hanson in the rôle of the Gentleman (Mr. Brink); and again at the Grand Theatre in Gothenburg in 1918.

On December 12, 1920, Max Reinhardt presented it at the Royal Opera in Stockholm, with the distinguished Albert Bassermann playing the leading male-rôle.

In the fall of 1933 Alf Sjöberg staged the play at the Royal Theatre, with Harriet Bosse in the rôle of Gerda. Early in 1951 Knut Ström gave a performance of the play at the intimate theatre of the Gothenburg Civic Theatre. He had previously staged it in Düsseldorf in 1917 and also at the Grand Theatre in Gothenburg, as well as having directed the play for radio in 1933. In 1955 the government travelling theatre gave the play with Victor Seaström in the rôle of Mr. Brink; and in the fall of 1956 the Malmö Civic Theatre presented it on its intimate stage.

1913-14 Reinhardt first staged the play at his Kammerspieletheater in Berlin, when Albert Basserman and Gertrud Eysoldt appeared in the leading rôles. It had previously been staged at the Königliches Schauspielhaus in Dresden—where it had its original German première—on May 18, 1912. Lothar Mehnert created the rôle of Brink (the Gentleman). In 1923 it was produced at the Theater an der Josefstadt in Vienna; and in 1916 the play (WETTERLEUCHTEN) was given at the Irving Place Theatre in New York, in German.

The Swedish Theatre in Helsinki produced the play in 1914, and in 1938 the Finnish National Theatre presented it. August Falck appeared in it at the Royal Theatre in Copenhagen in 1917; and 1920 Reinhardt's company was seen in it at the Casino Theatre. In 1960 Poul Reumert was heard in the play on radio. In Norway the National Theatre in Oslo presented the play with Halfdan Christensen and Ragna Wettergren in 1951; and in France it was presented under the title ORAGE at the Théâtre de Poche in the fall of 1943, Jean Vilar acting the leading rôle.

It has been given extensively in Scandinavia, Finland, France, Germany and England on radio.

THE BLACK GLOVE
(Christmas)

The original première took place at Christmas time 1909, when the play was first produced by a travelling company. Greta Strindberg, the author's daughter, acted the rôle of the young lady, Mrs. Hard. It was played through the spring of 1910, but for lack of proper staging and stage settings, the play was not considered a success. At Christmas time 1911 it was given at the New Intimate Theatre under the title CHRISTMAS, directed by Emil Grandinson. One critic thought it the most beautiful and poetic among Strindberg's chamber plays. In 1920 it was produced at the Lorensberg Theatre in Gothenburg, again at Christmas time, under the title MERRY CHRISTMAS, and this time it achieved much praise. But despite the fact that the critics gave praise to the play, it was felt that full justice had not been given it by the director. They pointed out that it required a particularly tender and deft treatment throughout in order to bring out the lyrical and imaginative values in the play and emphasized the importance of proper rhythm for the play.

During the Christmas holidays 1946, THE BLACK GLOVE was presented over the radio, directed by Olof Molander and with Inga Tidblad as the Young Lady. The performance was highly praised. In 1957 THE BLACK GLOVE had a performance in television, with Olof Widgren as the old Taxidermist. In 1910 Greta Strindberg acted in the play in Oslo and the Norwegian provinces. In the spring of 1918 it was performed at the Kammerspieletheater in Berlin with Johanna Terwin as the Lady and Gertrud Eysoldt as the Gnome.

To the memory of Fredrik Vetterlund

POEMS

SATURDAY EVE
(1883)

The wind is stilled, the cove lies like a mirror;
the windmill sleeps, the sailor takes down sail;
the oxen are let out into the green-grassed pasture,
and all is readied for the day of rest.

The woodcocks fly in flocks across the forest;
the farmhand at the barn plays his accordion;
the porch is being swept, the yard is raked;
the garden-beds are watered, and the lilacs plucked.

Upon the flowerbeds the children's dolls are resting
beneath the motley-colored bells of tulips;
a ball lies in a corner, camouflaged by grass;
inside a water barrel is a bugle, drowned.

Green-painted shutters have been closed already,
the doors are bolted, safely locked,
the mistress of the house puts out the final candle,
and soon the whole house is asleep in dreams.

The soothing June night slumbers tranquilly,
and weather-beaten farm yard now is quiet. . . .
but on the shore the sea is still in motion;
yet it is but the ground swell from the last days' storms.

THE ESPLANADE SYSTEM
(1883)

Where ancient hovels stood abreast
and shut out light from every nook,
a crowd of youngsters, full of zest,
came bearing axes, bars and hook.

> Soon chaff and dust
> flew in the air
> as crowbars thrust
> through floor and stair.

> And sand and lime
> from rottened beams,
> dried up by time,
> burst from the seams.

> With axe and pick
> and iron bar
> the walls of brick
> were split ajar.

> With rope that lashed,
> and iron hook,
> the roof soon crashed,
> the chimney shook.

> From door to door
> they thus went on
> through every floor
> till all was gone.

An oldster passes there one day
and sees, amazed, the dreary sight.
He stops, shows sadness and dismay
while stalking through the dismal blight.

"What do you plan to build here now?
A row of private homes? A mansion?"—
"We're building nothing! This is how
we clear for the street expansion!"

"Yes, tearing down! The habit of our day!
But building up? . . . It's horrifying!"—
"For light and air we're making way!
Is it not well that we are trying?"

POETRY EXCERPTS
FROM PLAYS

THE OUTLAW
·
THE KEYS OF HEAVEN
·
A DREAM PLAY
·
THE GREAT HIGHWAY

To the memory of Vilhjalmur Stefansson

THE OUTLAW
(1871; publ. 1880)

ORM: *(Takes the harp and speaks the following verses, plucking the strings with his fingers between each stanza.)*

When May wind blew
over billowing sea
and the shoots sprang up
from the tawny soil,
then the king pulled out
his ship from the shed
and sailed bravely off
upon white-edged waves.

Our ship we then steered
toward Leiregård,
where the king of the Danes
gave us mead to drink.
Then we sailed toward the east,
where with dark-eyed maidens
we drank of the wine
in Micklagård.

But when shield was hoisted
to masthead high
bucklers were shattered,
and coats of mail,
while the arrows were singing:
"It is spring! It is spring!"
And like sap from the birch
sprang blood from the wounds.

No woman did dare to
reject our embrace;
from the tiller of soil
we took what we wished.
And if he were stubborn
and-hid his gold,
we roasted his cattle
in the flames of his farm.

How glorious the life
we lived in those days!...
When the sea trolls pounded
'gainst ironclad prow—
then the viking's heart
felt joy in living
and, plucking the harp strings,
great songs were sung.

The praise of the vikings,
their manhood, their boldness,
was sung by troubadours
throughout the wide world . . .
But now the swords rust,
and extolled is weakness. . . .
and sea-kings are sleeping
by grimy hearth.

What now can the bard praise,
with brave deeds gone? . . .
Prattle and vanity
are not for harp strings. . . .
I shall put it away—
hang it on the wall—
having sung my farewell
to brawn and brave deeds.

* * * * * *

THORFINN: Alone ... Alone ... Alone!
  (There is a silence.)
  I call to mind—it was in autumn. . . .
  The equinoctial gale raged furiously
  over England's sea. My ship was wrecked;
  and I alone was cast upon a rock. . . .
  Then calm set in, dead calm.—What trying days!
  For all I saw was cloudless sky
  and endless, deep-blue sea about me!
  Not e'en a sound of living creatures;
  no sea gull waked me with its screeching;
  no breeze to cause the very lightest wave
  to plash against the rock. . . .
  It seemed to me as though I'd lost my life;
  I spoke aloud, I shouted, screamed—
  was frightened by my voice. . . .
  Then dryness tied my tongue—
  and all that made me know I lived
  was that my heart still beat. . . .
  However, after listening to its sound,
  I suddenly no longer heard it. . . .
  Then I sprang up in fear,
  again and still again, until I swooned.—
  When finally I wakened, I then heard
  quite close to me a sound as of a heartbeat;
  I heard a panting from a mouth that was not mine,—
  and courage grew again within my soul. . . .
  I looked around.
  It was a seal which lingered to find rest. . . .
  It gazed at me with tearful eyes
  as though it felt compassion for me. . . .
  Now I no longer was alone!
  With outstretched hand I tried to stroke
  its shaggy body; then it fled—
  and I was doubly lonesome. . . .
  Again I stand upon a rock. . . .
  What do I fear now? Aloneness!
  Then—what is loneliness?
  It is myself!

Who am I then that I should fear?
Am I not Thorfinn Jarl, the strong one,
who bends yet thousands to his mighty will—
who never asked for friendship or for love,
but kept unto himself his sorrows!
No! No! I am another—
and that's why I, Thorfinn the Strong,
now dread Thorfinn the Weak!—
Who took away my strength? Who weakened me?
Was it the sea? Did I not conquer it
a score and ten times; yet it defeated me
but once—and then to death. . . .
The sea is stronger thus. It is a god. . . .
But who subdued the sea and pacified it
when raging? Who did it? Who? Who? Who?—
It was the one still stronger!
Who are you, then, you who are the stronger?
Oh, answer, that I may believe in you! . . .
He does not answer! There is but silence! . . .
Now I can hear again my heartbeat!
Oh help—oh help! I am so cold. . . .
I'm freezing. . . .

To the memory of Gösta, Hans Georg, Ethel, Hampus and
Geraldine Mörner.

SCENE FROM ACT II OF
THE KEYS OF HEAVEN
(1892)

COURTESAN

If you're of noble birth, as seemingly you are,
you will not ask me what my name is!

THE SMITH

I do not ask; I merely inquire. . . .

THE COURTESAN

Pose any question that you like,
but do believe my honesty,
my virtue, and my unjust sufferings in the past.

THE SMITH

I've faith in you, both for your virtue and your beauty,
which I can plainly see with my own eyes—
such beauty as I've never seen before.

THE COURTESAN

I was convinced you were a noble man. . . .
Then hear . . . my father wants to force me into marriage!

THE SMITH

Ha! Now I understand! And you—
you love another!

THE COURTESAN

No!—But this is my own secret.
You must not ask again—just promise
that you will let me be your sister,
and that as such I'll have your kind protection.

THE SMITH

My sister! All too gladly, gentle maiden,

if you don't think your charm and noble ways
put me too deeply in the shadow
and make the kinship seem incongruous.

THE COURTESAN

Oh, speak not of beauty—least of all of mine!
Beauty is but a guise, a cloak. . . .

THE SMITH

A guise? It is a shining light that warms like sunbeams!

THE COURTESAN

Like the fire of the trolls on marshy heath.

THE SMITH

That is not true—no, no, it cannot be,
for only beauty is a sign of goodness,
as when it's speaking through your lovely eyes;
I can't conceive that any evil word
could pass such lips as yours! Nor that this fair brow
was ever wrinkled from vile anger;
and neither can this little hand be lifted
except to shake a hand, and to forgive. . . .
Will you not come with me—but not as sister?

THE COURTESAN

How many have not asked the same, yet changed their mind!
You do not know me, you have no idea
how poor I am, and how oppressed! . . .

THE SMITH

So much the better! They get on best who are alike.

THE COURTESAN

. . . . how sick I am. . . .

THE SMITH

I will forever care for you. . . .

THE COURTESAN

. . . how terrible my temper is. . . .

THE SMITH

Another virtue! It shows strength.

THE COURTESAN

Suppose I beat and scold you?

THE SMITH

't will help to soften up my wretched disposition.

THE COURTESAN

In truth, this indicates a deep and honest love!

390

Confess, man, can you love a woman,
no matter what?—No, do not touch me!
But tell me, could you—if I lost my beauty
through grief, old age, or sickness—
still love me just as dearly, just as deeply?

THE SMITH

Once having looked upon your countenance
I never could forget its beauty.
The memory of it would ever hide,
much like a mask, the ravages of age—
yes, even if the plague should place its imprint on it;
if fire scorched your pure white cheeks,
and if your eyes turned into boils,
I still would see you as before!
The image that I carry in my heart
is dear to me—I see it everywhere.

THE COURTESAN

Then look—look at a leper and abide the test!

(She removes a mask and shows a leper's ravaged face.)

THE SMITH

(Somewhat taken aback at first, but collecting himself.)

I sorrow, as in snowy winter
one grieves the summer's withered blossoms. . . .
But sorrow is the snow of love,
and underneath the snow the rose is forced. . . .
I love you as before—
yes, even more!
I love you as I love the memory
of one I loved! Beloved!
I give you as my pledge my pristine kiss. . . .

(He is about to embrace her.)

THE COURTESAN

Do not touch me! Upon my lips I bear
the sting of death!

THE SMITH

Alas, then let us die together—
and then we never will be parted. . . .
No strife, no passion, and no trivial worries,
no calumny, no envy. . . . and we can die
in bliss—as they do who are young!

THE COURTESAN

O God, I never dreamed there could be such a love!

THE SMITH

That's why you should not put your faith in dreams!

SAINT PETER: *(Who in the preceding scene has been visible intermittently in the background, comes forward.)*

Now I think we have found the heavenly kingdom, for
a love like this is the love of angels!

To the memory of Charity Grace; and to H. Stilwell Clapp.

A DREAM PLAY
(1901)

THE DAUGHTER OF INDRA: *(Accepting the Poet's petition to Indra,*
she speaks the words without glancing at the scroll.)

Then I shall give voice to your prayer. . . .
    "Why must you be born in anguish,
    child of mankind? Why must mothers
    suffer birth pains when you bring her
    the most precious of all gifts:
    motherhood, life's greatest blessing?
    Why must you to life awaken? . . .
    Why do you salute the sunlight
    with a cry of pain and mean ill-temper?
    Why do you not smile on dawning life,
    mortal child, since human happiness
    has been promised as your birthright?
    Why must we be born like beasts—
    we, descendants of both gods and mortals?—
    Better guise could have been given us than this
    wretched body, spun of blood and slime. . . .
    and why must this image of the gods shed teeth?"

Silent, rash one! Blame the image—not the Maker!
No man yet has solved life's riddle!

    "Started thus, the pilgrimage begins
    over stones and thorns and thistles. . . .
    Should it lead across a beaten path,
    you will find the road forbidden;

and if you should pluck a flower,
you'd be held for trespass—and for thieving also;
if a field should stop you from advancing
and you take a short cut through it,
you will trample down the farmer's crops;
others do the same to you,
equalizing thus the damage!—
Every moment that gives joy
brings to others only grief;
your own sorrow spreads, however,
not much gladness anywhere:
thus it's sorrow after sorrow! . . .
So the pilgrimage goes on—
even death brings gain to others!"

Is it this way, you—the son of Dust—
mean to come before the Great Almighty? . . .

* * * * * * *

THE FINAL SCENE OF THE DAUGHTER OF INDRA IN A DREAM PLAY

My life on earth is ending—it is time to leave. . . .
Farewell, you mortal child, you poet-dreamer,
who—better than the rest—have learned to live. . . .
Borne upon wings, you soar to heights beyond this earth,
yet sometimes fall into the mire,
but don't get caught in it—you merely graze it!

Now that I leave, the loss of what has been,
what I have loved, and the remorse for things left *un*done,
arises in me, as—when parting from one's friends—
one says Godspeed to them, and to the places one holds dear. . . .
Oh! In this moment I can feel the utter pain of *being*,
of *living*, and of being mortal. . . .
One misses even what was once disdained
and feels a guilt for wrongs that one did never do. . . .
One longs to leave—yet yearns to stay. . . .
Thus in a tug of war the heart is torn in twain
and feelings rent asunder by the beasts
of conflict, indecision, and disharmony. . . .

Farewell! And tell your earth-kin I shall never
forget them where I go—and I shall bring
their plaint to Indra—in your name. . . .
Farewell. . . .

*   *   *   *   *   *   *

Dedicated to the memory of
H. L. Mencken and George Jean Nathan.

THE FINAL SCENE FROM
THE GREAT HIGHWAY
(1909)

THE TEMPTER. *(Enters)* So there you are! Now we'll have
a little chat, but it's a shade too dark here, so let us have some
brightness . . . *(It grows light)* . . . so we can see each other. We
must, of course, be able to see each other in order to talk reason . . .
I come from the grand duke—he values you for your talents . . . He
offers you the post of court architect, with so and so much salary,
together with maintenance, firewood, etcetera . . . you understand . . .

THE HUNTER. I desire no post . . .

THE TEMPTER. Wait a moment . . . but I have to ask that you . . .
well—in a word—that you behave like a human being . . . like an
ordinary, normal human being . . .

THE HUNTER. Go on . . . it would interest me to know how a
normal human being behaves.

THE TEMPTER. Don't you know?—Why do you look so mystified?

THE HUNTER. I shall answer your last question as briefly as I
can. I seem mystified because I am confused. I have belonged to
that category of people namely that believes what a person says—
without any doubt of his word. Therefore I have been stuffed full of
lies. Everything I have believed in has proved to be a fraud. For
that reason my whole life has become a lie. I have been going
around with false notions and ideas of people and of life, have calculated with false figures, have unknowingly deceived with base
counterfeit: thus I am not the one I seem to be. . . . I can't be among
other human beings, can't rely on, or quote, or repeat what others

396

have said—can't trust in any one's word, for fear it may be a lie. In
several instances I have entered as an accomplice in the chain smithy
that is called society—but when I found myself becoming like the rest,
I broke away, took refuge in the woods, and turned huntsman.

THE TEMPTER. All this is just talk. Now let us get back to the
grand duke who requests your services.

THE HUNTER. He does not desire my work—he demands my
soul . . .

THE TEMPTER. He demands that you interest yourself in his
great project . . .

THE HUNTER. I can't do it . . . Now go away—I have not long
to live and wish to be alone to go over my accounts . . .

THE TEMPTER.
Haha! if now the day of reckoning's at hand,
Then I shall come with invoices,
With bills aplenty, summonses . . .

THE HUNTER.
Then come—come with the agony,
You tempter, who would bribe me to deny,
With cowardice, our good Creator. . . .

(The Tempter leaves)

I came down from the pure air of the alps
To mingle yet a while with human beings,
To share with them their trivial little sorrows;
But there was no wide, open roadway—
A narrow, thorny path was all—
And, caught in the brambles, I was rent,
Leaving a shred of myself here and there . . .
Good deeds were but a cloak for selfish purpose—
A gift bestowed: a trick to snare a debtor;
One rendered service but to dominate—
And liberated merely to enslave. . . .
My lone companion lost his way—
I met with untold snares repeatedly;
Was dragged into a mill wheel—
Came out of it the other side;
Met there a child whose starry eyes
Lit up the road that led me here—
Into this darkness.

Now you come forward with your bills. . . .
  (He turns and finds that The Tempter has left)
What! Has he, too, disappeared!

And so I am alone!
In night and blackness . . .
Where trees are sleeping, and the grass weeps tears
From cold, bereft of sun. . . .
The beasts—not all, though—are on the alert. . . .
The night owl spins its dark intrigues,
The snake is coiled 'neath poisonous toadstool,
Nocturnal badger moves about again
After its day of hibernation . . .
Alone! . . . Why? . . .
A traveller in foreign land
Is ever there a lonely stranger.
He goes to city, village, town,
Takes lodging, pays, and then continues on,
Until his journey's at an end—and he's at home again!
Yet that is not the end. . . .
I hear still: the snapping of a rotted branch—
An iron heel against the mountain rock . . .
It is the fierce, frightening smith . . .
I see the idol-worshipper, with knife of flint—
He's seeking me . . .
The miller and his mill wheel
That dragged me in,
And where I nearly perished . . .
The people of the thoroughfare . . .
A trap, easy to get into—
But hard to get out of. . . .
And the murderer Möller . . .
With bills galore and summonses—
And alibis and libel threats . . .
Abominable beast! . . .

What do I hear now? . . . Music! . . .
I recognize your tones, your gentle hand . . .
But do not yearn to meet you . . .

The fire warms at comfortable distance,
But not too close—for then it injures!—
And now: a child's voice in the darkness. . . .
You, little child, you last bright memory
That follows me into the gloomy forest
On the last journey to that far-off land—
The Land of the Fulfilled Desires—
That beckoned from the alpine heights,
But from the valleys seemed obscured
By dust from highway and the smoke from chimneys. . . .
Where are you gone, oh, beautiful sight,
Land of longing and of dreams?

If but a dream, I wish again to see you,
From snow-white heights, in crystal-clear air,
At the hermit's; there I shall remain,
To await the liberation! . . .
No doubt he'll offer me a resting place
Beneath the white and icy blanket—
And write, perhaps, in snow a casual inscription:
Here rests one Ishmael, son of Hagar—
Whom once they gave the name of Israel,
Because he'd battled with the Lord
And had not given in till he was felled,
Conquered by the bounty of God's almightiness. . . .

Eternal One! I won't let go Your hand,
Your strong, firm hand, till You have given me Your blessing!
Oh bless me, bless Your humankind
That suffers—suffers from Your gift of life!
Me first, who's suffered most . . .
Who's suffered most: from grief, from anguish
Not to be able to be as I wanted to be—
The one I longed to be! . . .

EXCERPTS FROM NOVELS

THE NATIVES OF HEMSÖ
·
THE SCAPEGOAT

Dedicated to the memory of Dudley Nichols.

THE NATIVES OF HEMSÖ
(1887)

(From Chapter I.)

It was now quiet in the kitchen, and the only sound heard was that of Rundquist snoring over by the kitchen stove. Carlsson lay awake. He was pondering the future. What the widow Flod had said to him about holding himself a bit above the rest of the folks and about putting the farm back on its feet again had stuck in his head like a spike. He felt an aching and swelling and festering around this spike. It was as though a growth had taken root in his brain. He lay thinking about the mahogany chiffonier and about the son's whitish hair and his suspicious glances. He saw himself going about with a big bunch of keys on a steel ring, jingling them in his pants pockets; and in his mind's eye he could see one of the hands coming to him for a loan or an advance of money—and then he would thumb the keys as though he were picking oakum—and when he had found the smallest one, the one that opened the lid to the money drawer in the chiffonier, he would fit it into the keyhole, the way he had poked his little finger into it earlier in the evening. But the keyhole—which before had looked like the pupil of an eye—now took on a different appearance: it grew rounder and larger, and black like the muzzle of a shotgun—and at the other end of the barrel he saw the son with his ruddfish eye stealthily taking deliberate aim at him, as though to defend his earthly possessions.

At that moment someone came into the kitchen and Carlsson was awakened from his daydreams. In the middle of the floor, where the moonbeams had now shifted their configurations, Carlsson saw two white bodies standing upright. A second later they dove into a bed, which received them with a loud, creaking sound much like

403

that of a boat sideswiping a shaky pier. After that there were a few lively signs of life beneath the sheets and some subdued tittering—and then at last there was quiet in the kitchen.

"Goodnight, my little doves," came from Rundquist, whose voice now crackled as if he were about to give up the ghost for the night. "And don't forget to dream about me, like good girls!"

"Ha! As if we had nothing better to dream about!" snapped Lotten.

"Sh! Don't talk to that nasty old fool!" advised Clara.

"You are both so—so friendly and goodnatured! I only wish I could be half as goodnatured as you," Rundquist prattled on with a sigh. "Yes, yes—God knows, when age begins to creep up on us, we dont get the things we like to get no more—and from then on life ain't worth livin'. . . . Well, goodnight now, children. . . . But look out for Carlsson—for he's got both watch and saffian boots. . . . Yes—Carlsson is a lucky fellow, he is! Well, fortune comes and fortune goes—lucky girl who has her beaux. . . . What are you tittern' about over there? . . . Say, Carlsson—how about another swig o' that there stuff? It's so terribly cold over in this corner—there's a draft from the stove!"

"No, sir, you ain't goin' to get another drop, for I mean to sleep!" snapped Carlsson, who had been interrupted in his dreams about the future, in which there was no room for either liquor or women, and where he had already settled himself in his superior position of being a peg above the common herd.

Again there came silence; and only the muffled sound of the two hunters' fish stories about their hunting exploits obtruded upon them through the closed doors of the nearby living-room. Intermittently there could be heard, too, the low rattling of the chimney damper in the gentle night wind.

Carlsson closed his eyes and, half asleep, he heard Lotten reading glibly in a whispering voice something he at first could not possibly get the hang of; but as he listened to the string of sounds and words that dragged out into one long jabber, he was gradually able to distinguish the words "andleadusnotintotemptation—butdeliverusfromevilforthineisthekingdom — andthepowerandthegloryforeverandeveramen. Goodnight, Clara! Sleep well!"

And soon after, the girls were snoring away in their bed while Rundquist sawed wood and gave out snorts and grunts in his bed with such resounding force that the windows rattled. Whether there was any conscious intent or playfulness behind this exhibition of dormant physical strength was difficult to say. Carlsson, however, lay dozing, not sure whether he was awake or asleep until he felt someone lift the comforter, and a chubby, sweaty body creep into bed with him.

"It's only me—Norman," he heard an ingratiating voice next to him say; and then it dawned on Carlsson that he was to have the farmhand as his bedfellow.

"Well, well—if it ain't the hunter come home to roost," croaked Rundquist in his rusty bass voice. "I thought it was Calle who was out shootin' tonight, it bein' Saturday."

"You're a fine one to talk about shootin'—you ain't even got a gun," hissed Norman back at him.

"You mean to say I don't know how to shoot, eh?" sizzled the old man, bent upon having the last word. "I can shoot an old starling with my backside! Yes—and that from between the sheets, too, if you want to know!"

"Did you put out the fire in the stove?" the kindly voice of the widow Flod called through the door leading from the entrance hall.

"Yes, sure!" they all answered in chorus.

"Well, then—goodnight. . . ."

"Goodnight, Auntie. . . ."

This was followed by long-drawn-out sighs, there was puffing and panting, snuffling and snorting, and soon the snoring was in full swing.

But Carlsson was still only half asleep and lay in that state for quite a while, counting the windowpanes to make sure his dreams would come true.

To the memory of Cornelius W. Wickersham

THE SCAPEGOAT
(1906)

Chief of Police Tjärne was a tall, emaciated person with a head much too small for his body. Created like a snake, it seemed as though he would have no difficulty crawling through any hole if he once managed to slither his head through it. When he rose from his chair to stretch across the table to get a match, it looked as if he crawled through the air. When his long arm swept forward between glasses and bottles without upsetting anything whatsoever, his one concern was to prevent knocking his head against the hanging lamp. This made him twist his head in such a way that his face lay on his back. Otherwise, he was considered to be a handsome man, and he was successful with women. Yet he never boasted about this. - - - - - In common with his prototype, Don Juan, he found nothing strange in this. He scarcely was conscious of his devastating power. And if he was chided about it, he acted ashamed, as of a weakness. - - - - - -

Askanius received his chief of police like a disciple who had come to hear words of wisdom. "So-o, you have already had your dinner? Well, then, sit down and have a drink with us. It's a beautiful spring evening, and the crayfish have come into the brook. . . . Soon I shall invite you to a crayfish party, yes, yes. . . ."

The chief of police intercepted with: "Really. . . . have they really. . . .?" He didn't bother to complete the sentence, for he knew it would be cut off anyhow.

The attorney offered a polite: "Why, for heaven's sake. . . ."— and all the while he was thinking of his brother and the bond he would have to furnish for him.

Askanius, however, felt the dryness from which his audience was suffering. And this evening he had an unquenchable urge to excel, to evoke their interest and admiration. Thus he began with his old *tour de force*: how he had sung before Emperor Napoleon III at Versailles. As usual, he started with a description of the fountains—which cost *thirty thousand francs* every single day they played—as an introduction. He detailed it as minutely as if his auditors heard them described for the very first time. And curiously enough, both the attorney and the police chief had been at Versailles and seen these miracles. But they had never dared to acknowledge this to Askanius for the simple reason that he would not have believed them. He would have considered them as interlopers, as thieves, bent on depriving him of property exclusively his own.

The two culprits exchanged glances now and then; and then Libotz became absorbed in calculations over the cost of the surety bond. But every time his eyes took a downward trend, he was promptly pulled back by Askanius, who forced him to pay attention with a question uttered in Danish: "Are you listening?" Then Libotz showed his face again, although his eyes were turned inward, for he was making calculations in his mind.

This evening, however, Askanius got tangled up in his fountains. It was apparent that his mind was getting foggy, and he sank into a discussion with himself. He could not remember which one of the fountains was the biggest.

"Let me see now? Did I say Diana. . . . I don't mean Diana"—and here he began to play drum on his forehead. "What *is* its name now?"

Libotz, who took it for granted that the question was directed to him, was startled out of his absentmindedness and gave him answer.

"Neptune is the biggest."

"No—Neptune is not the biggest—no. . . ." blurted out Askanius with authority.

Now the chief of police forgot himself completely and broke in: "Why, of course, it is Neptune. I have been there myself."

This was entirely too preposterous. Askanius therefore simply took it as some sort of jesting, and continued:

"You see, gentlemen, such fountains you find nowhere else in the world—except in St. Petersburg. . . . Have you gentlemen ever been in St. Petersburg? No! Well, you see there. . . . Or in Schönbrunn? Not there either! Oy,oy,oy—that is the very acme of greatness—the most gigantic experience in life. . . . But Versailles—that is one place every human being should see before he dies. . . . You gentlemen should tear yourselves loose some time. . . . Drink a little less and save. . . . save, be stingy, and say: 'I want to stint, I am going to deny myself even the necessities—but I must see Versailles before I die. . .' I'll lend you my Baedeker travel guide. . . . I have two: one in French and one in German—the trip costs two hundred francs—that's an even one hundred and fifty crowns. . . ."

"One hundred and forty!" interrupted the chief of police who found it impossible to resist Askanius's haughty airs any longer.

"May I—may I. . . ? May I finish my sentence?" demanded Askanius.

"Certainly! Certainly!" granted the police chief.

"As I was saying—we sang for the Empress, gentlemen, and believe it or not, she was dressed—in honor of the day—in the Swedish colors, in yellow and blue. . . . Now wasn't that a gracious thing to do?"

And then came the Emperor! From youth Askanius had nourished an indescribable contempt for him, the Sphinx, Badinguet, and whatever he had been called. But from the day that he had sung for the Frenchmen's emperor, he appeared to Askanius as transformed, not to say transfigured. Napoleon IIInow became a genius, the greatest political figure that ever lived; and as an army leader he was in every respect comparable to Charles the Great of Sweden. The café proprietor was lacking in voice and resonance this evening and he could not get up on his feet; therefore he rang for champagne.

His two victims were dripping from perspiration and were overwhelmed by all this grandeur which was heaped on them like a heavy blanket. Libotz, who never wished to offend anyone, tried to bolster the atmosphere again. But to attempt to speak on any other subject, or about anyone else than Askanius, would have meant death to the proprietor. And so he took up the refrain again by asking a seemingly innocent question.

"What voice did you sing then, Mr. Askanius?"

Askanius acted as if he were searching his memory, masticating a lie on his tongue like a piece of chew. At last he answered diplomatically, his words moderately cutting, but with a finality that brooked no further obtrusive or impertinent questioning on the subject.

"Gentlemen, in a well-conducted quartet for male voices, there exists only *one* voice—one for all, and all for one. . . . And anyone who has the slightest understanding of the great and difficult art of singing, knows that all four voices are equally important—whether they are called first or second tenor, or first or second bass."

Now this was just too elementary, and his manner of leaving his listeners in ignorance of his having sung merely second tenor, annoyed the police chief, who was himself an old quartet singer. The champagne had made them spirited, and now Tjärne felt he could do without further instruction. So, quite casually, he broached the intelligence that he had sung first tenor in the university quartet. This caused a grave silence. Askanius fought with his better self, his pride, his sense of justice. Ought he to stoop to pick up so dangerous a bone of contention? If he did, he would be lost, for it looked as if Libotz was prepared to step in and take the part of the college singing! No, he would not! And without losing ground, he went roundabout, without stubbing a toe.

"Gentlemen," he whispered, "there are two kinds of singing, just as there are many kinds of wines, cigars, entrées, coffees, and liqueurs. Isn't that so? Very well, we have cultivated singing, and we have natural singing, do you follow me? For my own part, I prefer professional, artistic singing; and I think every person who has a cultivated, musical background—he may belong to whatever social stratum you like—does the same, as a matter of fact. Therefore, and as a fitting and dignified answer to the somewhat unwarranted remark Police Chief Tjärne took the liberty to make a moment ago, permit me to raise my glass in a toast to this art!"

"Bravo!" came a shriek from the police chief, who was altogether too keen about debauchery and too indolent to wish to waste any effort on a quarrel. And so he drank with pleasure an old nature singer's toast to the art of singing—an expediency that always brought him an extra glass, filled to the brim.

Libotz had covered his face with the palm of his hand in order to wipe away a smile. When he noticed that Askanius now could neither see nor hear, he turned to Tjärne.

"He is precious just the same," he spoke aloud.

The time was now going on twelve.

"Say something amusing," Askanius spoke up suddenly—not because he desired to hear anything said, but merely so that he could get a moment's respite. And with this he placed himself in position as if he were waiting, patiently and resignedly, for their chatter to come to an end. Meanwhile he played with his own thoughts, reading over in his mind what to say next. Tjärne, who was well acquainted with his tactics, now turned to Libotz and commenced to speak about Paris and got his answers and a few fresh contributions of information.

No doubt any ordinary person in Askanius's position would have expressed surprise that the other two gentlemen had also been in Paris, and with a dash of self-amusement have saved himself from looking ridiculous a moment ago by passing over the episode with a smile. But Askanius was no ordinary person. In addition to his good attributes, he was as well possessed of an enormous self-esteem and ego, and he was greedy for power. He was the center of his little world of hungry and debt-ridden, who lived by his charity. Singing and Paris were his particular domains. They belonged to him, and no one else was permitted to intrude on them. As he now heard that *they* had visited Paris too—and he knew that already— he was tempted to strike a blow by interposing with remarks and corrections. But his superiority complex and vanity and megalomania got the upper hand. Puffing vigorously and snorting on his cigar, he breathed heavily under the exertion of trying to find some totally new topic of conversation which would snip off the thread of their arguments. Several guests who had just left looked in through the windowpanes; and this gave Askanius his opportunity. He rose and went over and pulled down the shades.

"I think it is better with the shade down," said he, as he seated himself again. Then he asked: "Won't you gentlemen drink up. . . ."

With this the police chief filled his glass to the brim, but he did not let go of the thread to Paris. Libotz, the altruist, felt sorry for Askanius, who was suffering the pangs of death. He interrupted Tjärne's flow of words with the proposition: "Let us drink to the health of Mr. Askanius!"

This drink became the decisive one; and now commenced a change of character such as generally occurs in the fourth act of a polite drama. The chief of police grew loud, malicious, and challenging. He promptly flew into an argument with the café proprietor. Askanius was not at a loss for words or answers. Soon the conversation turned into a cockfight over Shakespeare. The two dialogued simultaneously, trying to wear each other down and waiting for a chance—*not* in order to make reply to a question, but in order to be able to drive forward his own argument at full speed.

Askanius did not listen to his opponent. Every time he spoke, he turned away from him in utter disgust, the while making faces that carried the message: "Go ahead and finish your blabber. I'll soon pick you to pieces."

They had now stumbled onto the broad and open road of quotations and Tjärne had stored many in his memory—while Askanius knew only one. This lone card he now sat clutching in his brain, to use at the opportune moment.

"Ah," yelled Tjärne, "this is sublime! It is Macbeth who speaks it:

> Life's but a walking shadow. . . .
> It is a tale. . . . full of sound and fury,
> signifying nothing."

"Pshaw!" hissed Askanius. "This has much more spirit and nobility in it and has much more depth. . . . I think it is Othello, or Hamlet. . . . let me think. . . ." But here his memory misfired; the question remained unspoken, and the chief of police was not slow to attack the silence.

"This is what Lear says:

> Down from the waist they are Centaurs,
> though women all above;
> but to the girdle do the gods inherit,
> beneath is all the fiend's;
> there's hell, there's darkness,
> there's the sulphurous pit."

"Ugh! How can you speak such terrible things!" broke in Libotz, who was presently within the sacred and innermost temple yards of love.

"That's irony," shrieked Askanius. "You see, gentlemen, anyone who does not appreciate irony should never be allowed to discuss Shakespeare. *Par exemple,* I think it is *The Merchant of Venice.* . . . but it doesn't matter who said it. . . . who says that life is woven of the same cloth as our dreams. . . . but, of course, this should not be taken literally—he lets some fool say it—to show what a fool he is. That's why we have to be careful when we try to interpret a great poet. . . . The only ones who can interpret him as he *should* be

411

interpreted, are those whom nature has endowed with a feeling of understanding for the great, the beautiful, the true in life and nature."

This exertion proved to be too much for him. Askanius was now entering a new stage. He closed his eyes, went into a trance, and his soul drifted off to unknown spheres. His hands kept fumbling with his cigar, which he lighted continually, only to have it go out immediately. His body, however, was not fully awake, and the cigar ash kept dropping into his champagne glass.

The chief of police, who had been browbeaten, lost his sense of tact and became brutal. He grabbed the cognac bottle and filled a drinking glass half full. He took a swallow and rinsed out his mouth, downing the rest.

Askanius must have had his eyes in his fingers, for half asleep he stretched out his hands, grasping the cognac bottle by the neck and placing it close to him. He held it with a firm and miserly grip, pressing it against the waistcoat pocket in which he kept his eyeglasses.

Now Tjärne began to speak out of his beard, baring his teeth, and certain that Askanius was dead to the world.

"To have to sit and listen to his drivel! Why, it's nothing short of fantastic! Isn't it? And he has the audacity to talk about Shakespeare!"

"Ssh! Ssh!" Libotz warned him. "We must not talk like that. We must be grateful to him as our host."

"It's all very well to be grateful! But to sit and flatter him, and be licking his boots, and have to say "Yes, yes" to him in everything—that's enough to give the man illusions of grandeur. You'll see—some fine day he'll explode from arrogance! . . ."

Libotz tried to branch away and made a start with the Norwegian question. It turned out to be a long-winded discussion; and finally they got themselves so involved that they annexed each other's viewpoint and ended by arguing both against each other and themselves.

Askanius seemed to have dozed off, and now he suddenly spoke in his sleep, his eyes shut.

"The national education, gentlemen—the national education does not have its origin in the public school or in universal suffrage,

412

least of all for us Swedes—this may sound like a paradox, but it isn't. . . ."

"What's he doing? Is he correcting compositions?" interjected Tjärne.

But Askanius went on without faltering. "Nothing has so contributed to the Swedish nation's education, culturally speaking, as— as the smörgåsbord."

Hilarious laughter rang out in the pavilion, in approbation of this entertaining dialogue, even though it was not intended to be amusing but rather something deep.

"It may sound like a paradox," continued Askanius, "but, believe me, gentlemen, I can be sitting at my place behind the counter, making believe I am writing, or counting, or reading—a customer comes in, and. . . ."

Here the dramatic situation was accompanied by gestures, and the cognac bottle was set free, so that the chief of police could get himself another drink.

"A customer enters, an unknown, a stranger. . . . Now it so happens that I have a mirror underneath the clock on the wall and I can see—I have my eyes with me even when they are shut. . . ."

The police chief pushed himself back on his chair, amazed that Askanius could prove to be so false.

"A customer has, of course, the privilege to eat as much of the smörgasbord as he wishes, but a gentleman does not abuse the privilege. . . . a gentleman makes himself a sandwich, pours himself an aquavit, goes over to his table and sits down, asks for the menu and a bottle of ale. Why does he do this? Because he is well bred, because he has *savoir faire*. A German will never learn to behave like that, even if one should inform him that it is not intended that a customer should eat his fill of the smörgåsbord . . . he just is not receptive to instruction. . . . Who is that singing in the garden?"

"Let them sing!" retorted Tjärne. "But skoal to the smörgåsbord!"

413

LETTERS

LETTERS OF STRINDBERG TO HARRIET BOSSE,

[28 April, 1901.]
Beloved,

You ask if you can impart something good and beautiful to my life! And yet—what have you not already given me?

When you, my dearly beloved, my friend, stepped into my home three months ago, I was griefstricken, old and ugly—almost hardened and irreclaimable, lacking in hope.

And then you came!

What happened?

First you made me almost good! Then you gave me back my youth! And after that, you awakened in me a hope for a better life!

And you taught me that there is beauty in life—in moderation . . . and you taught me the beauty of poetic imagery—*SWANWHITE!*

I was sad and grieving—you gave me happiness!

What, then, is it you fear?

You—young, beautiful, gifted—and what is much more: wholesome and good!—There is so much you can teach me! And you are rash enough to say that you would like to learn!

You have taught me to speak with purity, to speak beautiful words. You have taught me to think loftily and with high purpose. You have taught me to forgive an enemy. You have taught me to have reverence for the fates of others and not only my own.

Beloved! Who can tear us apart, if Providence refuses to separate us?

If it is the will of Providence—well, then we shall part as friends for life; and you will remain my immortal faraway Love, while I shall be your servant Ariel, watching over you from afar! I shall warm you with my love and my benevolent thoughts. . . . I shall protect you with my prayers!

Let us wait until the sixth of May and see whether Providence desires to separate what He has joined together!

Yours

27 June, 1901.

Dearest, beloved wife,

So many tears, so many tears, and so scorching that they burn out my eyes! And why? Mostly because I am plagued by the thought of all the sufferings I involuntarily have brought upon you. . . . But at the height of my self-accusation I cry out: But I could not have acted differently! I could not. . . .

And still, when I come into the golden room, I see you—see you such as I found you that day—sitting there in agony, weeping. . . . and then my heart nearly breaks from grief and pain. . . .

I thought I had learned to resist the pain of suffering—but this—this was more than I could bear. And last night—I thought I would suffocate from weeping . . . and in the darkness I fumbled for the little hand that made me feel so secure against the horrors of the night when I held it in mine. . . .

The feeling of my loss—the grief—the uncertainty—the pangs of conscience. . . .

I never step outside the door—but remain here in my hermitage. . . .

Yet not alone—for in here you are everywhere—in your regal beauty—with your gentleness—your innocent smile. . . . Was all this necessary in order to make me realize how deeply I love you?

No—for I knew it when I said to you: You now hold my life in your hand, Harriet! If you leave me, I shall die!

If you are leaving me. . . . if you have left me—I do not know. . . .

Leaving me—having left me—without having reconciled me to humanity—and woman!

29 June.—Your telegram "I am living," a demon whispered in my ear to translate into: "I was dying while near you! Now that I am away from you, I can live!"

(The same day).—After having wept in my retreat, which I have not been outside for three days, I received your letter.

Do I not love you?—Woe—who has whispered such thoughts to

418

you? If you were here, you would see what kind of existence I lead without you! You would read how beautifully I have described our entrance into our home! "Flowers on the table—the flames of the lighted candles in the candelabra stand still in devotion—the flowers are silent in thought."

And now the lights are going out by themselves! It is growing dark in the dining-room—but still can be seen the sun-yellow, gilded shade of the brass lamp in our room—the pale-green room—green as a mid-summer meadow. . . .

He is frightened by the darkness. . . . She stretches forth her little hand, the soft, delicate, gentle hand—the little hand in the darkness! And she leads him toward the sunshine—toward the light in her pale-green room. . . .

And he thanks her who has reconciled him to mankind and woman. . . .

My dearest! Can you not feel at a distance—distance is something that does not exist for us—that I am living only in you, that I love you?

You are with me all the day long, and the incense of your being sweeps to me here through space. . . .

Are you not conscious of my longing?

Do not my tears give solace to you when you are in grief? I shall cry—cry like a child—in the belief that my tears will fall on your poor little heart!

What can be the meaning of this?—Yes—a trial. . . . I hope merely that! The self-accusations lacerate me, but I cry in my hour of need: I could not do otherwise!

I *could* not go with you—yet I had no right to seek to prevent you when you finally left. . . .

I am sitting here guarding your home, pleading with God for patience and that I may witness the day when you shall return to me.

I no longer see you in the flesh. . . . I see only your soul, its beauty and goodness—which you were beginning to forswear. I hold your inner image so pure, so chaste, lest it be soiled by even a breath of evil! I keep before me only Eleonora's Christ head. . . . Poor Eleonora, whose mission it was to help him share his suffering!

Beloved, if you should realize at last that we are united by the mighty, sacred bonds of love, then call on me! And then we can meet in Sassnitz! Only there!

Your Gusten

I stretched out my hand to you yesterday.—That generally signifies: Let all that was painful be forgotten; it carries the message: forgive and forget! But you did not accept it. May you never have to regret this!

How often during the nights. . . . have I not taken your outstretched little hand and kissed it, even though it had clawed me— merely from mischievous, childish whim to claw! I recall one night: I kissed your hand with a prayer that you would sleep well, and you reciprocated by kissing mine. And then you gave vent to a reflection. . . . which I shall never forget. . . . Do you remember what you said?

There are words that must be spoken despite one's disapproval of them, in spite of suffering from their sting. Such a word was the one you took so to heart when last we saw each other. But it was a stick of dynamite placed on the railroad track as a signal of warning before [the critical moment of] danger.

Do you recall what it was that set it off? You wanted to deprive my child of my name. I made the remark that if my child were given the name of B., it might hurt the child all through life, and that her comrades would some day get the idea that she was born out of wedlock.

But long before this you had played with the poison. When it became apparent that you were in a blessed condition, surprised at this, you uttered insulting words! You "could not grasp how it had happened!" Later you began to cast insinuations that the child was not mine, that it could not be mine, simply could not be like me— in a word, you played the rôle of poison mixer. And then go back to that other time, when we feared that you were with child, and your outburst that night at the inn at Hornbaek, when you gave thanks to God that you were not in that blessed state, and emphatically spoke of "virtuousness." Incredible!

Recall further the first weeks of our marriage. The day after we were wed, you declared that I was not a man. A week later you were eager to let the world know that you were not yet the wife of August Strindberg, and that your sisters considered you "unmarried."

Was that kind? And was it wise?

If the child is not mine, then it must be someone else's. But that was not what you meant to imply. You merely wished to poison me;

and this you did unconsciously. To bring you back to your senses, I awakened you with a shock.

Are you awake now? And can you resolve not to play with crime and madness in future?

You write that you have not had a happy life. What do you think I have lived through? Having seen what I considered sacred treated as buffoonery, having seen the love between husband and wife after so short a time exposed to public view—I came to regret that I had ever taken anything seriously, was driven to believe everything in life to be colossal farce and fakery! I well-nigh lost my faith—in everything!—and came very near to falling back into malignity, decided to write farcical plays, colossal ones, farces about love, about mother-love, about world history, and about sacred things. I had thought of writing a parody on *SWANWHITE* for Anna Hoffman—but when I came to the *EASTER* girl I stopped.

You once asked God to give me His blessing for having written *EASTER*. Did you speak honestly that time? If you did, how could you—eight days after our marriage—exalt Lindelin as your womanly ideal . . . and say that you could not be an artist without being first a harlot?

And you glorified adultery, threatened to take a lover, bragged that you could acquire one whenever you desired. . . . It was in this manner you sought to give me back my faith in woman—and in humanity!

And now you ask: How can I, in spite of all this, still love you? You see: Such is love! It suffers all—but it will not tolerate humiliation and debasement!

And at the very moment that our marriage was to be cleansed and ennobled through our child—you take leave of me!

Where do you desire to have your belongings sent? To Grev-Magnigatan or to Blasieholmen?

[August Strindberg]

* * *

[2 or 3 September, 1901.]

My life, my thoughts, and my pen! I wished to lay all at your feet, for I loved you! But I had no desire to descend again into the ugly and the vile!

And we were settled in a home, a home given us by God, you

said. . . . And the pigeons built their nests under our cornice, and the swallows, too. . . . And you thought our home more beautiful than any other. But then the gold in your ring of faithfulness turned black and you found it in turn dull and ugly. . . . But the yellow room still had the clean fragrance of my true, strong, pure love—and then I was driven out by your hate. . . . And behold, the yellow room became malodorous. It was your selfish hatred that gave out the stench—it was not I. . . .

How long do you think I can wander here among the dead? Not for long, for then I shall soon find myself in the grave—and I have nothing against that; yet I have duties to perform in life.

Tell me therefore whether I shall expect you or not. . . . Every hour is an hour of pain, and I must get out of here if you are not coming back!

What is it you demand of me, what terms do you set up?

Yesterday I was on the point of breaking up our home, destroying all our memories—all. . . . and—as I cannot travel—again putting up with other people's furniture in a furnished room!

Then I shall ask God that I may be given the grace to forget you, forget your name and that you ever existed—you, whom I once spoke of as my "first wife."

I have cherished a hope: your letter from Denmark, when you departed the previous time without leavetaking. I read from it "Beloved! What is this? Our hearts, which have been welded together by a kiss of God. . . ."

And it ends—with this cry of distress: "Oh, my beloved friend!"—I have now wept outwardly until my eyes have paled, and inwardly until my soul has been cleansed!

I have kissed your image and called out to you, and if you had been dead I would have sorrowed for you until you had risen from the grave!

For the last time: Come back to your yellow room! There alone you will find tenderness and care, and there alone shall our child see the light of day!

Come, whatever moment of the day you choose. Call upon Lovisa and she will accompany you past my door, which will not open until you give the word!

You need not reply to my last two letters! They constitute answers in themselves, and they contained no questions!

* * * * * *

When you told me last Saturday that you were engaged, I almost knew it beforehand. But I could not wish you happiness, as that is something I cannot believe in, for it does not exist. I felt no anxiety for the child, for I believe in God.

I would, however, have liked to bid you goodbye. And now I wish to thank you—despite all—for everything, for the months of spring seven years ago. . . . when I, after twenty years of misery, was allowed to see a little of the bright side of life. But I could not bring myself to write. . . . I received apprehensions that made me hesitant. Sunday went by, and so did Monday, in work and quiet resignation. You noticed that I, exactly a year ago, ceased making visits, and know the reasons for that.

And yesterday Tuesday came! When I went out in the morning, I thought it was Sunday. The city had changed in appearance, and so had the rooms here in the apartment. You had died! And then began a glorification of memories for the rest of the day, twelve hours, in the space of which I lived through these past seven years.

Reproaches, pangs of conscience for all that I had failed to do, every harsh word—all, all, exactly as when someone dear to you had passed out of life. The less beautiful was obliterated, only what was lovely remained.

In view of the fact that all was over [between us], I had the definite impression: Dead! I mourned you as one who was dead, and I could not feel a desire to have you back, since you no longer existed. . . .

In my memory I saw the *Easter* girl, *To Damascus,* Djurgården with the military salute and the King's greeting, [Hotel] Rydberg and Drottningholm.

I wept—not from the pain of losing you this time, but from the happiness that these moments of you, and with you, had given me. . . .

Today is the day of *SWANWHITE!* It will be given tonight with Sibelius's music. I have received it from you—as I have said in writing—and although I sometimes have doubted it, I do believe it! That is how I see it now, Harriet, after your death, despite the fact that I always knew who you were, your nature, your inclinations. I have explained this in *CHRISTINA.* Your *SWANWHITE,* which I received from you—and you from me—and which you never came to act. . . .

Today I have divined it as if. . . . you were not dead! . . .

My thoughts and goodwill follow you, and I am—despite everything—forever your friend and your child's.

But I feel anxiety for you—and something is happening that I cannot grasp. . . . In fact, I have not understood any part of this last incident; but as I am forbidden to write to you, perhaps there is not even any necessity for it!

If you only knew how dangerous it is to tangle with human fates and to play with thunder and lightning!

To free oneself from the tangle is such a painful undertaking. . . . you know how tedious and agonizing the process was for us! You are satisfied if you can evoke a man's interest—and then drop him. But there is more to it than turning on your heel and walking away. . . . There is much more!

Just one thing! Let me have Lillan when you marry! Or do you want me to go far away?

To be passing each other here on the streets is painful and unclean. And the child should be kept away from all this!

Do you want me to go away? I believe I am a disturbing influence and from this apartment emanate invisible threads that carry inaudible soundwaves which, nevertheless, reach their destination. . . .

Our bond is not yet broken, but it has to be severed. . . . otherwise we shall be contaminated. . . . You remember our first days [together] when the evil radiation from souls, alien to ours, played havoc with us merely through thinking of us. . . .

Tell me what you wish, but arrange it so that we are not pulled down into an abyss of darkness—of which I am fearful. . . . A telegram pertaining to your *SWANWHITE* just arrived—despite all!

Why did you not wish to be what I created you to be in my imagery? I could not have pulled you down, as you said! That I don't believe!

One word more, just one! Do not sink down, Harriet! For then I shall weep again over the transience of all that is beautiful. . . .

Your *SWANWHITE*, which I received from you, and you from me!

* * *

424

I must finish my letter and tell you plainly, in a few words, what I mean. You know I have been wanting to regain my freedom and to give yours back to you; and each time you turned away from me and gave your affection to someone else. I was free until the moment you again began to think of me. Then it grew cloudy, and I reproached myself afterwards. . . .

That is why I beg you now, when there is no chance of return: Do not think of me, neither with good will nor evil, do not speak of me ever, do not mention my name—and if others should do it, refuse [to listen], or keep silent!

I do not wish to live this double life, entrapped in others' eroticism. . . . I would rather mourn you as dead than remember you as the wife of another man. And you bring disharmony into your own life, for it is only we two who "live on an astral plane." Lightning can strike behind and in all directions, and one of us could die—perhaps [even] the one you would miss most. . . .

You know very well how often you have been ill and even felt tired of living (suicide mania). The cause? Why, all those whose feelings you have aroused, have cast back on you the currents you have evoked, and you in turn have suffered. That you were not killed one time (1901) was a miracle; and that I did not kill myself a still greater one.

Sometimes I think that you intended to do away with me. Dear child, there was nothing I could have wished for more. . . . but what would have been gained? I, like other sinners, would, I suppose, have been washed clean as a corpse. . . . my soul would live on in those of my works that will survive, my name on the billboards in the city would always remind you of me, our child would perhaps for a time torture you by the mention of my name—yet not for too long! Thus, there is no help except for me who was born with a repulsion for life and gladly would depart from it—although in a decent manner. . . .

Sometimes I think it would be altogether more right and better to part in hatred, in real hate; then that would be the end. You may answer: We have parted in hate. . . . time and time again! And then we met again! Why do you keep playing with love, you who have suffered so much because of it and spread so much misery and sorrow (I know one man who died as a result!)? I once believed

425

you had been playing with me, too, but it seemed unreasonable that a lovely young girl would give herself to an old man merely for an opportunity to murder him. And that we found it so hard to part indicated nevertheless a certain liking.

I beg you now: Leave me in peace! In my sleep I am defenseless, like the rest, irresponsible. . . . and I am ashamed of myself afterwards—now I think of it as a crime. . . .

COMMENTARIES
AND CRITIQUES

PROBING STRINDBERG'S PSYCHE

By Arvid Paulson

In recent years psychoanalysts, psychiatrists, and other professional as well as amateur investigators, have devoted themselves, in books and periodicals, to the evaluating of August Strindberg's personality. In the past also much has been written on the subject both in Europe and America; and the great Swedish author's enigmatic psyche will, for many years to come, attract the curiosity of psychologists and be a source of conflicting opinions and diagnoses. Yet I doubt that the research and investigations will result in a definitive consensus. On the contrary, I think future verdicts are likely to differ so sharply and even violently that if the propounders of the various theories and speculations should meet face to face, the encounter might very well give rise to a scene not unlike that between the faculty deans in Strindberg's *A Dream Play*.

To the psychiatrist or psychoanalyst any person with imagination, particularly one with unusual imagination, is immediately suspect. When eccentricity of behavior is an added ingredient in the make-up of such an individual, the risk of being labeled a psychopath is near at hand; and when the object of psychiatric interest happens to be a person of world renown, there will always be those who in print will take up the cudgels for their own particular viewpoint.

Strindberg's imagination knew no bounds. It reached into every branch of learning and behavior; it spanned the universe; it delved into the labyrinths of men's hearts and minds, always in search of the unknown quantity that would fit into his dramatic chess games and jigsaw puzzles of drama and bring into a focus the devastating conflicts that beset mankind through the mystery of and the great breach between the sexes. Because Strindberg became principally known for his dramas of marital strife and has been labeled a misogynist because of his involvement with the universal problem of relations between man and wife, his dramas, novels, short stories and other writings of a brighter hue and in gentler vein have been lost sight of . . .

Ever since Alfred Storch wrote his book *August Strindberg im Lichte seiner Selbstbiographie* in 1921 and Professor Karl Jaspers his *Strindberg und Van Gogh* and *Allgemeine Psychopathologie,* the notion that Strindberg was mentally deranged—based on their analyses of the Swedish author's psyche, with the common diagnosis that he suffered from schizophrenia—has become so firmly entrenched in the minds of psychoanalysts as well as the public that the German assumption has been accepted even by some noted Strindberg scholars in his native Sweden.

Not until recently, when the distinguished psychiatrist and physician Dr. Sven Hedenberg published the results of his investigations into the subject under the title *Strindberg i skärselden* ("Strindberg in Purgatory"; Akademiförlaget-Gumperts, Göteborg, 1961) has the Storch-Jaspers myth been examined by a psychiatric authority in so thorough-going and believable a manner. Dr. Hedenberg furnishes authentic and convincing proof of the irresponsibility and fallaciousness of the two German psychoanalysts' conclusions, which were based upon inadequate research and knowledge both of Strindberg the man and of his literary production. . . .

In his expressionistic dramas Strindberg not only created a new dramatic form but as well added new spheres of thought and emotion, despair and tragedy—yet brought into them a note of sublime inspiration and a hope for a better mankind, a hope for liberation from the enchainment by the materialism, vanities and the destructive traditions handed down to us as yardstick for our behavior and morals, our very existence, from birth to the end of our life. As he in *A Dream Play* uses Indra's Daughter and the Poet as human catalysts and pathfinders to point the way to freedom and redemption, painting his dramatic canvas with a blending of realistic and mystical colors, so—with equal power and incomparable ingeniousness and individuality—he paints drama and character into his extensive gallery of portraits and scenes of life's struggles, no matter what he chooses to depict, with equal facility and mastery.

No person devoid of self-criticism could possibly, as Dr. Hedenberg points out, analyze himself so uncompromisingly, so unsparingly as Strindberg does in his writings, if he were a victim of schizophrenia.

This, in my estimation, is proved convincingly, not to say conclusively, by Dr. Hedenberg, who—as a practicing psychiatrist in Sweden and with the facilities there for sources of research and contacts unavailable elsewhere—has during the years painstakingly pursued his subject and, to my mind, penetrated more deeply into Strindberg's psyche than anyone heretofore.

To enter into details regarding Jaspers' and Storch's lack of knowledge about many facts and facets of August Strindberg's character, marriages, and episodes in his life would necessitate a more protracted review. It would also require a knowledge of psychiatry, with which I as a layman have only a superficial acquaintance. I am therefore basing my views upon what I have gained from reading Dr. Hedenberg's analytical work, but as well upon my own conviction, arrived at from my life-long acquaintance with Strindberg's works.

What the German psychoanalysts and others have failed to take into account or even fathom, are the many different grounds that were at the root of the mental disturbance and strangeness of behavior which periodically characterized Strindberg: his difficult childhood years; his inherited hypersensitivity; his hardships at school and during his university years; his puritanical conscience, always at odds with his extreme sense of logic and justice, and his urgent desire to be free from the restraint and shackles which society and the moral code of that era imposed upon men; his youthful intolerance and rebellion against dogmatic religion; the persecution and vituperation he endured for his religious views in his early days; his frustrations as a teacher and as an embryo actor in the theater and as a struggling young author; the devastating, malicious critique that met his primary efforts; his marital difficulties and perennial economic troubles, and numerous other obstacles with which he met during the course of his tormented life.

Added to this, Dr. Hedenberg points out that Strindberg himself had confided to his friend Dr. C. L. Schleich the fear that he had at one time imbibed absinthe to excess, especially during the culmination period of his Inferno crisis (1894-97), and that his aberrations and hallucinations may have derived from this. Other friends of Strindberg's have witnessed that he upon occasions, particularly in Copenhagen and Lund, had drunk freely of alcohol and then brought about situations which were embarrassing to both himself and his

431

companions. Green absinthe liqueur contains the poisonous element [oil of] thuja. Because the manufacturing of absinthe was forbidden by law in France in 1913, as it was rapidly becoming a threat to the nation's health, relatively little is written in modern textbooks about the dangers of poisoning from it. In a description of the illness, Dr. M. Lancereaux noted in 1880 that in chronic absinthe poisoning the victims no longer exhibit the convulsions which frequently occur in cases of acute poisoning. Instead, mental disturbances take place; and Dr. Lancereaux notes—after having examined and treated thirty patients—that such disturbances become apparent after a few months of drinking this cordial. He describes the symptoms typical of chronic absinthe poisoning, and these are the very same that Strindberg experienced during his Inferno period, including hallucinations of a terrifying nature, a prickling sensation, as of crawling ants, burning and cramplike pains, the seeing of lustrous, shifting lights, ringing in the ears, and the hearing of strange and plaintive outcries.[1] Jaspers mentions some of these symptoms in his books, but ascribes them in Strindberg to schizophrenia. While Dr. Hedenberg does not draw any decisive conclusions as to whether Strindberg owed his psychosis during these years to the use of absinthe, this possibility can not be excluded. Dr. Gösta Harding has also brought out the remarkable similarity in symptoms between schizophrenia and chronic absinthe poisoning.

* * * * * * *

In *Affect-Imagery-Consciousness,* Vol. 2: *The Negative Affects* (Springer Publishing Company, New York, 1963) Professor Silvan S. Tomkins of Princeton University argues that psychology has "lost its heart and mind" from, among other things, excessive reliance on primary drives as motivations and from attention to behavior rather than to the complex transformations that make behavior possible. He urges that psychology return to three critical problems now abandoned to neurophysiology and biochemistry. These three are affect, imagery, and consciousness. Using this method he has arrived at the conclusion that August Strindberg was a paranoid schizophrenic, as—according to Professor Tomkins' theory—Freud was also. In a chapter entitled:

---

[1] Dr. Lancereaux's article appeared in *Bulletin de l'Académie de Médecine,* Série 2, Tome IX, Séance 19.10. Paris, 1880, under the title: "Absinthisme chronique et absinthisme héréditaire."

"The Paranoid Posture and Mutual Admiration among Men of Genius" the author makes this statement: "Shaw, Nietzsche, Strindberg, O'Neill among others constitute a mutual admiration society." In the September, 1963, issue of *Bonniers Litterära Magasin* (Stockholm) Professor Theodor Lidz of Yale University has analyzed Strindberg's psychic personality. He maintains that Strindberg was "lacking in a well integrated ego and sought an identity in the images which emanated from his loosely integrated partial identifications." Basing his analysis on what he has learned of Strindberg's personality from reading his autobiographical novels (which Strindberg often embroidered upon, weaving in imaginary and fanciful details), Professor Lidz, like Storch and Jaspers in the early 1920's, and lately Professor Tomkins and others, ranges him within the same category as these German psychologists had done: paranoid schizophrenia. But in the same issue of BLM Dr. Gösta Harding enters a rebuttal to Dr. Lidz's arguments, in which he primarily points out the difference between European and American analytical methods in psychiatric investigations. The author presents as his view that Strindberg did not suffer from a progressive biochemical destructive process—which is generally the denotation of the term schizophrenia in Europe; while in America the malady is looked upon as a narcissistic neurosis. He regrets that Professor Sven Hedenberg in his excellent work *Strindberg i skärselden* does not take into account psychoanalytical viewpoints, although he accentuates the dynamic to a greater extent than do Storch and Jaspers. Erik Hedén in his superb biography *Strindberg* (Tidens Förlag, Stockholm, 1921) was one of the first to call attention to the fact that Strindberg's Inferno period was not only a period of destructive psychosis but, above all, a crisis which had the effect of renewing Strindberg's literary creativity. Dr. Harding notes that he already in 1950, after having consulted Dr. Curt Åmark concerning the typical symptoms of absinthe poisoning, had mentioned this in his doctoral thesis as a more probable cause of Strindberg's Inferno-period hallucinations than schizophrenia. Dr. Harding gives his diagnosis of the nature of Strindberg's psychic condition as oral and oedipal conflicts, rivalry between him and his brothers and sisters, sadistic-masochistic traits in his psyche (shown by the struggle between the sexes in his dramas), and points to the animalistic descriptions which frequently occur in his writings, especially in his letters to friends. Dr. Harding also stresses

433

his feelings of guilt and need of punishment, his tendencies toward self-torment from early childhood and throughout life, and mentions how pleased Strindberg was at discovering that Rousseau in his *Confessions* speaks of having had similar tendencies. Dr. Harding finds the psycho-dynamic side of Strindberg's personality still more interesting and speaks of it as "a symphony for many instruments and with a variety of themes which are ingeniously interwoven with one another." All through his life, Dr. Harding says, something of the neurotic child's candidness remains with him: his neurotic disturbances show the remains of child neurosis. Nothing is benumbed or static; all through his life there are sharp, unpredictable changes, and his search for identity continues to the end, much as with Faust and Peer Gynt. The Swedish psychiatrist also emphasizes Strindberg's repeatedly expressed desire to lose his wits (e.g. *The Great Highway:* "I begged, and do so still, that I go mad. . . . and wine became my friend").[2]

Strindberg dramatized himself and his marital vicissitudes and dissensions, his mental and spiritual fears, peculiarities and shortcomings with histrionic mastery and brilliant imagination. Despite his many human faults and phobias, there is nothing in his voluminous list of writings to indicate that he was not consciously in control of his mind and actions. In *Soul Murder (Vivisektioner: Själamord,* 1887) Strindberg makes some interesting observations pertaining to human frailties and paradoxical behavior. He writes: "Even if there are no absolute truths, there is, on the other hand, always the average truth of a specific era, the normal common sense of that period, the intuitive manner of viewing things—in other words, what is commonly called public opinion. A person ·who is either above or below the normal average is considered 'not quite sane.' Accordingly, Galileo was mentally deranged when he, in opposition to the public opinion of his day, broached his assumption that the earth revolved around the sun. The average person will, when he hears a new thought put forward, stand in doubt for a moment as to whether it is he or the one who propounds the new idea who is mad. In general he assumes it is the other person who is less than sane; for an individual who does not think for himself has—because of this very fact—a vigorous belief in himself. For this very reason one can very easily be taken for a

---

[2] In *Strindberg's Expressionist Plays* (Bantam Books, April, 1965).

434

madman. Everything that deviates from what is accepted as normal is lunacy in the view of the less intelligent and cultured. . . ."[3] Strindberg had an extraordinary gift for analyzing psychic aberrations and conditions. Having just read Ibsen's *Rosmersholm* Strindberg continues: "Another form of insanity, less known perhaps because of having only recently been recognized, is what I should like to call modern soul murder and psychic suicide. Ibsen, it seems, has unconsciously dealt with the first mentioned phenomenon. . . . *Rosmersholm* is incomprehensible to the average theater-goer, a mystery to the half-educated, but completely understandable to anyone who has a knowledge of modern psychology. Rebekka seems to be an unconscious cannibal who has devoured the soul of Rosmer's late wife. Her behavior has been highly suspicious as she has gone about with unconscious plans for acquiring authority in the household. Mrs. Rosmer harbors suspicions against her; in other words, sees through her scheming. But Rebekka conceals her intentions and saves herself by mentally suggesting to Mrs. Rosmer that she suffers from 'suspiciousness'. Quite naturally her suspiciousness increases when she makes further observations, yet finds it impossible to obtain concrete proof. In this manner it is an easy matter for Rebekka to drive her out of her mind. . . . How Rebekka went about committing the murder is not told in *Rosmersholm*. This very point might have been the core of the dramatic action in the play, which now moves in a different direction. She has no doubt used the well-known ancient method of forcing the weaker brain to imagine it was sick; and after that she has 'proved' to the wife, or made her believe, that death would mean happiness for her. . . . But doubtless Rebekka has unconsciously proceeded in the belief that hers was a righteous cause, or she may have imagined it to be so. For the as yet inexplicable power of self-deception is enormous. And I am convinced that many cases of insanity have their origin in self-deception or are actually soul suicides."

One remarkable quality in Strindberg was his ability to analyze his own shortcomings and to discover and pinpoint the hiatuses in his psychic makeup. This trait of his acted as a safety valve for his

---

[3] Translated by Arvid Paulson from *Vivisektioner* (1887). His translation of *Rosmersholm* appears in *Last Plays of Henrik Ibsen* (Bantam Books, 1962).

behavior and prevented him from crossing the borderline to insanity. That those close to him would resent his being called a schizophrenic or psychopath is only natural. But Harriet Bosse, his third wife, was an uncommonly frank, outspoken woman who would not be likely to make statements she did not herself believe. And she averred, both personally and in letters to this writer, that she had at no time seen any sign whatever of anything that might be called insanity in Strindberg. Strindberg, she declared emphatically, was an eccentric with definite and individual ideas, but always open to new ideas, and with a peculiarly clear, imaginative mind.

In *The Theater in our Times* (Crown Publishers, Inc., 1954) John Gassner pays tribute to the great Swedish dramatist with these words: "Both by choice and inner compulsion Strindberg became an uncanny exponent of our century. He is the dramatist of our division. . . . An artist may be a species of neurotic who cures himself through externalizing and understanding his conflicts while he is creating, and Strindberg's naturalistic plays are surely products of his lucidity. There are in them no evidence of a clouded mind, but only of a penetrating clarity and a remorseless logic. The difference between himself and less intense writers is that his clarity happens to be surcharged lucidity."

Strindberg was by turns a pessimist, a cynic, a sceptic, yet deep down in his heart he was hopeful for humanity. Ever querulous, probing, doubting, he could not make peace with his environment or with his era. He was generations ahead of his time. When his emotions took precedence over his common sense or over his conscience (his superego, as Freud called it), he suffered and tried to atone for the injury he had done to a fellow being. But this he could do only if he was convinced he had been in the wrong; for compromise with what he saw as the truth was to him unthinkable. He often erred, but he was perhaps more often right in his over-all judgment of humanity.

The Father: *A Survey of Critical Opinion of August Strindberg's Tragedy and Leading American Performances of It During the Past Half Century*

ARVID PAULSON

It is a strangely ironic fact that many of the world's greatest literary masterpieces, both of an epic and a dramatic nature, have been
corned or downright damned by either the critics or the public—
d frequently by both—when first published, or presented on the
e. Not only has this been true in literature but also in music,
era, and in art. Among modern dramatists, it is doubtful
any have been more viciously, maliciously, and ruthlessly
nd vilified than Henrik Ibsen and August Strindberg. In
sence of Ibsenism Shaw furnishes us with ample proof
ss of such attacks and how utterly devoid of under-
ingrained in a tradition of narrow, stagnant, prejudiced
oughts and ideas both the public and the critics were
Ibsen began the writing of his social dramas: *Pillars
's House, Ghosts, An Enemy of the People,* and
vever, found some staunch and formidable de-
even in Victorian England—notably William
, Justin Huntly, McCarthy, and, not least,
When Strindberg came on the scene in Eng-
d Shaw realized his stature as a dramatist,
blic did not react in the same way. Un-
duction in England was made through
ritish, forbidding) plays, without the
*Per's Journey, Swanwhite, Playing
ck Glove.*

7

From the time that *The Father* by August Strindberg was first
presented in Copenhagen on November 14, 1887, European critics
and public alike have debated, fought over, and discussed its position
and worth, both as theatrical fare and as literature. The pattern was
repeated in America.

1912

The Father was the first Strindberg play publicly to be performed
in English in America. It was presented in a translation by Edith
and Warner Oland at the Berkeley Lyceum, an intimate theater
situated just west of Fifth Avenue on Forty-third Street, and now
replaced by a commercial skyscraper. The critics were divided as to
the merits of the play and the acting of it, although most of them
were agreed that the drama was the work of genius. During the fifty
years that this play has been presented on the American stage, it has
generally failed because of having been produced as a melodrama
instead of as a furious tragedy, and because of having been acted
inadequately. That most of the critics quite profusely acknowledged
Strindberg's dramaturgical genius may, to some extent, have been
prompted by the glowing accounts of the Swedish author by one of
the leading critics of that day, James Huneker, who in 1905 wrote
in the *Theatre Magazine*:

Strindberg is born to the theatre; it holds no secrets from him. . . . H
gripping pathos and bitterness, his technical mastery, his command of chara
ter, have made him a unique figure among European dramatists. He
handle the lighter moods of comedy, and his touch is exquisite in such fa
like pieces as *The Crown Bride* and *Swanwhite*.

The feared, often sardonic, Alan Dale of the *New York Ame*
paid tribute to the play in surprisingly favorable terms:

At the end of Act II, Ibsen was out-Ibsened! *Ghosts* was but a mer
freak, and *Hedda Gabler,* compared with the sinister, awe-inspirin
some Laura of *The Father,* merely a laughing, prattling lass. . .
Father it was possible to avoid the thrall of the horrible that
compelled admiration. No more sinister picture of malevolent w
has ever been staged.

Another critic wrote:

The Father is strong meat. It calls a spade a spade every time.
beating about the bush, no effort at circumlocution. Yet its sto

and forcefully told. Its technique is as simple and concise as that of Ibsen. It is an awful conflict between a man and a woman, with the playwright bitterly arrayed against the latter. . . . Nothing commonplace about this Strindberg play. . . . It was morbid in the extreme. . . . Mr. Warner Oland acted with remarkable power and discretion. A robust and virile picture, he nevertheless made the character of the racked and hysterical man vividly interesting. His work was extremely vital and convincing. As for Miss Rosalind Ivan, she was astonishing. Her "personality," grim and appalling, gave weird weight to the odious character. Miss Ivan triumphed. It was extraordinary.

On the other hand, *Redbook* magazine commented: "The acting of the play does not realize all its possibilities, although the interpretation of the implacable, cold, determined and relentless wife by Miss Rosalind Ivan is excellent. Mr. Warner Oland accomplished less with the rôle of the husband, a rôle which offers great dramatic possibilities." Charles Darnton of the *New York World* expressed himself as follows in his review of *The Father:* "That erratic Swedish genius August Strindberg would probably have gone mad for good and all, had he been at the Berkeley Lyceum last night to see the reception of his morbid drama. . . . Even Strindberg himself might have recognized in Miss Ivan the ideal Laura. . . ." He admits that "Mr. Oland grew better in the second act and finished the play with a fairly good performance to his credit." He takes the audience to task for laughing in the wrong places, particularly in the early part of the play—where there is every reason for it!

Still another New York critic gives voice to his admiration for *The Father* in these words: "The splendid technique and the terrific power of the drama. . . . there is no escape from, even when many of its acting possibilities remain unrealized, as was the case last night. . . . Mr. Warner Oland had neither the technique nor the emotional range to depict this character, which offers an almost unlimited scope for acting."

Several newspapers seasoned their reviews with quite peppery remarks. Here is what one of them said: "Strindberg is a cracked genius, there is no doubt about that. *The Father,* like *Countess Julie* [*Miss Julie*], is an example of brilliant lunacy reduced to dramatic action." And still another one writes: "It is unlikely . . . that the Swedish dramatist . . . will become more popular here than Ibsen, with whom he no doubt will be compared. The Swede is different from the Norwegian. He is less imaginative in the poetic qualities [*sic*!] and has a quality of bitterness which the Norwegian does not show." Another reviewer comments:

Irrepressible genius such as Strindberg's must make itself heard, even if it cannot be believed. However false may seem his doctrines to the normal mind, the gruesome fascination which he contrives to weave into his abnormal, neurotic characters, and the intense power with which he builds up the climaxes of the conflicts in which he engages them, gives his plays a peculiar, grisly interest, even though he leaves their hearers disheartened and depressed.

But the *Dramatic Mirror* confesses that *"The Father* . . . is decidedly worth the attention of thinking folk," ending with: "Strindberg has manufactured this incredible story to preach the doctrine that conjugal love is strife, and that the victory must always fall to the wife because women are craftier than men."

Another critic arbitrarily noted that "It is a bad play because it is inhuman," while another one said: ". . .one must admit the subtlety and power of its denouement." Louis Sherwin of *The Globe* found fault with Warner Oland's acting, saying "Oland as the Father acted with physical force, but without subtlety. There was not the . . . grading in his performance . . . he acted so violently that when it was time for him to really rage and fume, he had nothing in reserve." But most of the critics were lavish in their praise of the young English actress Rosalind Ivan's portrayal of Laura, "the hellwoman"—as Strindberg once called her. One critic, as mentioned, wrote that even Strindberg himself might have recognized in Miss Ivan the ideal Laura.

But despite the varied opinions of the play and the acting, *The Father* might have lasted longer than it did, had not a greater and universally felt tragedy, the sinking of the *Titanic* with a loss of over fifteen hundred lives, cast a pall over the city and the world. The impact of this harrowing disaster upon theater attendance in New York lasted for a long time, and contributed to the premature closing of many plays.

1928

When Robert Whittier produced *The Father* at the Belmont Theatre May 11, 1928, he was met with a personal critique that was not only devastating but deserved. Whittier, a megalomaniac with a profound belief in his own ability to act the most difficult and demanding classical roles, not only despoiled the role of the Father but ruined the play as well (incidentally, he presented it in his own version, without crediting the translator of the play). Yet he was surrounded by a cast of well-known and capable actors. In the New York *Times* of May 12, 1928, Brooks Atkinson rather ambiguously wrote:

Fortunately, the inferior acting of Strindberg's *The Father* last evening made it possible for most of us to sit through one of the most terrible plays of modern times. Strindberg contrived an endlessly brutal tragedy which, in a good performance, should force us to question not so much *his* sanity as our own. But Robert Whittier makes the wretched Captain such a puffing rattlepate that much of the malignant bitterness disappears from the play.

Even more sardonic was Alison Smith in the *New York World:* "We are utterly at a loss to explain why he (Robert Whittier) conceived the rôle of the husband as a sort of operatic solo, basso and most profundo, with such slidings and rumblings of the chromatic scale as we have not heard since the last performance at the Metropolitan." After speaking of his "noisy and utterly misleading interpretation," she says of the play: "Into it Strindberg poured all the force of his frenetic misogyny with a stark simplicity which is appallingly convincing." In the *New York Daily News*, Ed Sullivan —as an arbiter of dramatic playwriting—commented: "In another and fuller treatment, August Strindberg's play *The Father* might have developed into a brilliant and forceful drama, but Strindberg exhausted his pen before he had developed the character of the wife . . . and therein he blundered!"

The revival of Strindberg's terrifying tragedy [writes Wilfred J. Riley in *The Billboard* of May 19, 1928] is strong proof that "the play's the thing" and that even some rather rakish acting can fail to detract much from the power underlying the work of a genius. . . . In all dramatic literature there is no play of such bitter content, such utter madness or such innate brutality. But some of Strindberg's lashing of womanhood, love and life in general, has lost its sting through inferior playing of the present cast. [Robert] Whittier is the most flagrant offender in this way and his playing of the weakwilled husband who is lured to madness by a conniving and heartless wife, is overdone to the 'nth degree. He fumes and foams and rants and rages all over the stage, blubbering and muttering, in fact doing everything but literally foaming at the mouth, until any delicate shadings or forceful subtleties that Strindberg wove into the character, have been lost entirely. Whittier's blustering is so intensive from the first curtain that the great power of the madscene in the final act has little effect.

1931

On October 8, 1931, Robert Loraine gave *The Father* at the Forty-ninth Street Theatre in New York after having successfully played in it for many months in London. Again the critique was both black and white in the evaluating of the play. Brooks Atkinson writes in the *New York Times*: "By this time Strindberg's *The Father* . . . is not a new play but it is modern. In the completeness of its expression and passion of an idea it is, in fact, one of the great works of modern drama. . . . Being a genius, he turns his drama into a hurricane of the furies. It is a dance of death of the evil forces of the world." Percy Hammond of the *New York Herald Tribune,* on the other hand, approaches the subject differently. "Strindberg—'the dramatist of pain,'" he labels him, and he continues cynically in his review of October 9: "Thanks to the cunning incantations of Mr. Loraine, you may be blinded to the fact that *The Father* is just another superstition—a bad play with a good reputation." In the *New York American,* Gilbert W. Gabriel states that

Bright-lighted Broadway dares Strindberg—and daring Strindberg, any Strindberg at all, in America, has always been daring indeed. . . . No finer play has been written for a century, no stronger—and no dismaller. No play ever deserved more honor, and no play can blame audiences less for backing away from it. . . . The terribly brilliant technique of the conflict of the play sweeps all possible swank and bunk away.

In the *Christian Science Monitor,* Edwin F. Maelvin evaluates the Strindberg work as follows: "The play itself, somber though it may be, is dramatic. It holds an audience. . . . The play, moreover, is well constructed." John Mason Brown gives vent to his feelings in the *New York Post* as follows: "Though it is probably as good as any production of *The Father* could be, it still offers a miserable evening in the theatre. It is interesting to have seen this play of Strindberg's, particularly in a production that preserves its shuddering power. But the pleasantest thing about the evening is, having seen the play, not seeing it."

Robert Garland's criticism in the *New York World-Telegram* is in much the same curious vein:

The Father leaves me cold. It leaves me cold and a wee bit irked at its workmanlike mechanics, its grim determination to be tragic. Perhaps, as a wiser man than I has said, the piece represents "Strindberg's highwater mark in dramatic technique and has successfully maintained its claim to a permanent place not only in dramatic literature but as an acting play." Perhaps, but I don't think so.

Richard Lockridge, in reviewing the play for the *New York Sun,* states:

Strindberg's insanely bitter diatribe against women, *The Father,* was offered at the Forty-ninth Street Theatre last evening with all the fury—at least all the fury—intrinsic in what is one of the strangest dramatic curiosities ever written. With Robert Loraine in the leading rôle, it piles on its agony almost unbearably, until in preoccupation with it one forgets all the faults of the play, both structural and philosophical, and even ceases to be concerned with the technique of Mr. Loraine.

After these condescending and facetious opinions, it is refreshing to quote John Hutchens, giving restitution to Strindberg in a lucid and scholarly critique in *Theatre Arts* of December, 1931. Hutchens writes:

The Father—there, now, is a play to be acted; a play which, being titanic in its demands, most greatly rewards the actor who can fulfill them even partially. . . . Is there a modern work more perfectly compact, more dread in the ferocity of its gathering momentum or shattering in its climax than this demoniac struggle? . . . In the tightness of this play, in its step-by-step progress of insanity growing on a man at war with a woman for dominance of will and intellect, Strindberg left no gaps for guess-work. It is all there, the life-theory and the story he deduced from it, awaiting a fire that can meet their own, the enormous problem of the performance being not only to portray madness without the obvious monotony of stage lunacy, but with the subtlety of a mind slowly breaking open and looking at itself in growing suspicion.

John Hutchens, however, was not alone in realizing the extraordinary genius of Strindberg, for Eugene Burr, reviewing *The Father* in *The Billboard* of October 17, 1931, gives praise not only to the magnificent acting of Robert Loraine but to the play, out of which such magnificent acting was born.

443

Last night a breath of the real theatre was blown into a Broadway full of personalities rather than actors. . . . The play primarily represents, bloodily and unflinchingly, the everlasting conflict that must go on between the sexes, each being forced to fight for the upper hand in order not to be beaten. To Strindberg's mind, bright with the clarity that comes only to the half-mad, no possible equality can exist.

And Burr adds that this usually ends in the defeat of the man, as Strindberg has indicated in this drama, which "has the power, the darkling force and the inner truth that is born of madness." Burr ends by saying: "It may be that a superlative display of what acting can be when it is really acting, will fail to become popular in our present-day, naturalistic-mad New York. But if ever a show [*sic*] deserved to be popular, this one does."

In contrast, John Anderson of the *New York Journal* paradoxically finds *The Father* both unpalatable and alluring. He speaks of it as "a play that is one of the most unpleasant and most fascinating of the modern classics, a cruel, obsessed, almost maniacal tirade aimed from the top of its screech at the conspiracy of women against men."

1949

When *The Father* was presented in Boston and on the Broadway stage in the year of the centenary celebration of the great Swedish author's birth, Elinor Hughes commented in the *Boston Herald* on the fact that it had taken sixty-two years for "August Strindberg's greatest play" to reach that city. She called it "a masterly work despite its grim and frightening nature." Elliot Norton of the *Boston Post* noted that

The Father depends for its success on shrewd staging and absolutely perfect acting. The play is so tightly meshed, its scenes so closely fitted one into another, its action so carefully developed from one moment to the next, that any break in the whole fabric is of far more consequence than it would be in a conventional drama. One discordant moment throws the whole machinery out of kilter.

Having made these salient observations, he confirms what critical authorities have long maintained but what some dissident critics have speciously argued, that *"The Father* is tragedy, not melodrama"; and he adds that what this means is that the actor "must act principally with his voice and with his eyes."

When the play arrived at the Cort Theatre in New York with Raymond Massey in the title role and Mady Christians acting the role of Laura, Brooks Atkinson observed that "since Broadway seldom has access to plays as vivid and provocative as *The Father,* it would be pleasant to report this performance as the equal of the playwriting. But Mr. Massey has caught only a part of the wildness of Strindberg's restless, unhappy genius. There is too much gentility in the texture of his acting." Not all New York critics agreed with Mr. Atkinson, for Robert Coleman of the *New York Daily Mirror* finds *The Father* "a classic bore," and *Variety* speaks of its "unrelieved grimness, coupled with the overwhelming pessimism of its militantly anti-feminist atmosphere" which seems to "rankle a contemporary audience." Yet its critic confesses that "there is no denying the superior dramaturgy that forms this violent battle of the sexes."

Gilbert W. Gabriel, who in 1931 had highly praised the play, becomes abstruse and frivolous in *Cue* of November 26, 1949, when he rather weirdly writes: "Myself, I'd recommend *The Father* almost singularly as a purge for those who've found the marriage-hymn of 'I know my love' a bit too honeymooney. Diabetics can safely indulge in Strindberg." Another dissident voice appears in the Catholic periodical *The Commonweal* of December 9, 1949. Kappo Phelan, speaking of Joseph's and Brandt's production of *The Father* at the Cort Theatre says: "I don't think they . . . rival the Provincetown's production of the play," and then continues: ". . . the amount of ill-logic, fake science and nonsense contained in *The Father* is not startling enough to keep the piece in the foreground of attention."

But on December 5, George Jean Nathan in the *New York Journal-American* comes with a devastating article in defense of the great Swedish dramatist and *The Father.*

It seems to be the opinion of some of the colleagues that Strindberg's *The Father,* written in 1887 and recently reproduced at the Cort, has dated, the implication obviously being that drama in the aggregate has made gigantic advances in the intervening years. If it has, they have apparently been going to theatres that don't send me reviewing seats or have been reading plays in Arabic, Lettish and Punjabi, languages unfortunately beyond my grasp. No one, of course, will deny that many admirable plays have been written since Strindberg's time but, if there has been a better one of its kind than

445

The Father, the aforesaid colleagues must have dreamed it up in their sleep, which, all things considered, isn't likely. . . . In its almost every detail —psychological, psychopathic, dialogic, dramaturgical—the play remains more modern than any of the numerous later ones it has inspired. And not only more modern, but in all respects infinitely superior. When anyone says it has dated, he probably means to say less that it has dated as drama than it has dated in a Broadway theatrical sense. . . . What makes *The Father* appear oldfashioned to the reviewers in question. . . . is surely not so much the play itself as the stage direction and the performance. . . . If anyone can think of an actor less suited than Raymond Massey to the intensely emotional rôle of the husband driven to insanity by his wife's taunts as to the paternity of their daughter, it must be Noel Coward or Zero Mostel.

A few weeks later (on December 25), Richard Watts, Jr.—while commenting on Strindberg's *Creditors,* then being given a thoroughly honest performance, under the direction of Frank Corsaro, at the Cherry Lane Theatre—notes in the *New York Post* that "it is to be doubted this unexpected box office appeal of the Swedish dramatist is due to any widespread public rejoicing over the one hundredth anniversary of his birth" but that playgoers "are currently interested in Strindberg because they find in his works a pioneer expression of attitude toward women that appears to be the most timely modern voice in our theater, and I suspect that this may indicate a significant trend."

1962

In May, 1962, New York had an opportunity to witness *The Father* presented as it should be presented by The Royal Theatre Company of Sweden. Excellently staged by Bengt Ekerot, the characters in their entirety were splendidly portrayed. Lars Hanson as the Captain, Irma Christenson as Laura, and Elsa Carlsson— who gave an unforgettable characterization of the old nurse-maid Margaret; one that I doubt could be surpassed—were outstanding in their roles. Howard Taubman of the *New York Times,* who knows his Strindberg and who has deplored the neglect of Strindberg's dramas in America, observes that "The Royal Dramatic Theatre knows how to establish a delicate pace and to give its players ample time to create full-length portraits. It is fascinating to note how subdued the performance is in its early stages and how it gradually gathers force and tension." He also speaks of "the careful development of the action, which unfolds slowly, subtly, and in the end with consuming ferocity." Walter Kerr of the *New York Herald Tribune* notes that "the company is quietly and admirably sure of itself, and impressively naturalistic," while Robert Coleman in the *New York Mirror* confines himself sparingly to saying that "it is difficult to evaluate performances in a foreign language. Therefore we can but tell you that we found the production interesting." Richard P. Cooke of the *Wall Street Journal* emphasizes that "the reality of the stage portraits heightens the emotional impact rather than distracting us. This is a sort of acting now out of favor by many of the newer playwrights and directors, but in the hands of competent practitioners such as the visiting Swedes, it is immensely effective." Jim O'Connor of the *New York Journal-American* calls *The Father* "a superior problem play," and adds: "Despite the play's impact, direction by Bengt Ekerot was largely static." And Richard Watts, Jr., of the *New York Post* evaluates the presentation as "a forthright and vigorous performance of a work that lives on through the intensity of its preoccupation with hatred." In his critique in The New York World-Telegram and The Sun Norman Nadel had the following to say: ". . . for me it was almost like encountering Strindberg for the first time. Not that there is anything particularly devious or obscure about THE FATHER. It's just that last night's performance so fully realized and justified its classic stature. . . . And if Strindberg knows women, he knows men—perhaps himself—even better. This is the ultimate torture that destroys the defenses of the cavalry captain. With only a slight push here and there, she [Laura, his wife,] robs that learned, sensitive man of his peace of mind, his freedom, and eventually his life." *Variety* observes that

. . . not until the dramatic straitjacket scene in the third act does the Royal Dramatic Theatre of Sweden's production of *The Father* come alive. The scene is so moving that language barriers cannot lessen its impact. But the third act is a long time arriving, and there is little else in the presentation to reward American audiences. . . . Despite the competent cast, this revival of *The Father* fails to overcome the linguistic barriers.

As we have seen, some critics complain that Strindberg's dramas are disagreeable, that he makes an audience feel uncomfortable—as well as the critics themselves. Yet they seem to find no such fault

447

with the tragedies of the Greeks or of Shakespeare, despite the fact that pieces such as *Medea, Oedipus, Hamlet, Macbeth, King Lear,* and others (as, for instance, *Dr. Jekyll and Mr. Hyde* and innumerable murder and so-called mystery plays with their gory details) are found to be both acceptable and palatable, and even entertaining theater fare. Is it this kind of play—where brawn rather than brain gains the so-called victory, and where vengeance brutally is wreaked in blood and physical annihilation, either from passion or hatred—that they prefer, rather than the undoing of the villain by a refined process of mental poisoning or mesmeric innuendo?

In war the victor often loses more than the defeated enemy. In Strindberg's dramas of marital strife, there are no heroic characters in the usual sense. Rather, the leading male and female adversaries are villains, each one in his own particular way. This is strikingly evident not only in *The Father* but in *The Dance of Death, Creditors, Miss Julie,* and other plays. And in the end there is no real victory for the protagonist who appears to be victorious, since conscience is the punisher—and *that* cannot be blotted out any more than the love, or the memory of the love that once existed between them, can be entirely extirpated.

The cruelties often inflicted upon each other by partners in marriage and continuously being brought to light in our family and divorce courts, more than match the violence exhibited by the Captain against Laura in a moment of insane rage. This incident, with which Strindberg ends the second act of *The Father,* was based on an actual occurrence reported in an English newspaper. Many people think the lamp-throwing scene not only shocking but unbelievably farfetched, despite the fact that crimes of passion are an everyday occurrence and often far more violent and horrible in real life. And when we look at history and contemplate the crimes perpetrated in the name of religion, could anything give us more cause to shudder than the cold-blooded, premeditated tortures inflicted by the very standard-bearers of Christianity against non-Christians during the Inquisition? Or the holocausts wreaked during the Thirty Years' War, the witch hunts in Europe and America, the French Revolution, the recent world wars with a Hitler and a Mussolini, with concentration camps and torture chambers and millions upon millions of innocent victims: all scenes which we have viewed calmly, complacently, unemotionally—though by

448

some, perhaps, with morbid interest and excitement—when depicted on the motion picture screen? Yet, when some critics view a slice of marital life that has its ending in tragedy, they find it too unbelievably horrible, unfit as fare for adult theater audiences! But when a mawkish play of saccharine sentimentality and with Pollyanna characters comes along, with every indication of being "what the public wants"—then these selfsame critics feel secure in praising it as "having audience appeal."

The time for change is near, however. The tragedies and the thought-provoking social changes and upheavals that follow in the wake of war and ceaseless world conflict, together with the individual problems that grow out of them, are helping to widen the mental horizon of the average theater-goer; and the dramatists who stir the mind and the imagination will eventually rule the theater. Then not only Strindberg but Ibsen also will be seen more frequently on the American stage. American has indeed much to learn from these two giants of the mind.

(Reprinted from *Scandinavian Studies,* edited by Carl F. Bayerschmidt and Erik J. Friis. This volume was published for the American-Scandinavian Foundation by the University of Washington Press, 1965, and dedicated to Henry Goddard Leach in honor of his 85th birthday.)

LETTERS FROM
GEORGE BERNARD SHAW
to
AUGUST STRINDBERG

My dear Strindberg,

Since we met in Stockholm in 1909 a few things have happened which may have the effect of rescuing England from its present condition of darkness concerning your works. 1. Vallentin has come to live in London, and Vallentin is the perfect modern Jew, devoted, intelligent, friendly, loyal, with no fault except excessive sentimentality—in short, everything that a Jew, according to Christian tradition, cannot and should not be. At all events, that is what Vallentin is to me—no doubt because he likes me and likes Charlotte (Charlotte is my wife, whom you may remember); and since you were kind to him in connection with our visit to you, he now includes us all in his circle of sympathy. You may trust Vallentin.

In the theatre things have also altered for the better. Last year Herbert Trench, a poet who had made a considerable reputation by a really remarkable poem called Apollo and the Seaman, was entrusted with a large sum of money by two rich patrons of the arts to found a theatre for the production of plays of literary excellence. As he knew nothing of the traditions of the theatre, he was expected to fail ignominiously. You will not be surprised to hear that what actually happened was that he was exceptionally successful. His greatest commercial triumph has been his production of Maeterlinck's Blue Bird. He was more envied for this than for any other of his exploits, for reasons which concern you.

Let me explain. A few years ago, one of our most popular authors, J. M. Barrie, wrote a sort of fairy play for children called Peter Pan, which had such an enormous success that it has since been revived every Christmas, ostensibly as a holiday entertainment for children, but really as a play for grown-up people; for, as you know, when we buy toys for children, we take care to select the ones which amuse ourselves. Ever since this happened it has been the dream of every London manager to find another Peter Pan. Sir Herbert Beerbohm Tree, the manager of His Majesty's Theatre, had one manufactured for him. It was called Pinkie and the Fairies, and was successful at its first production, but an attempt to revive it on the following Christmas showed that its attractions were exhausted. Then came the success of the Blue Bird, which Herbert Trench now expects to revive every Christmas as successfully as Peter Pan. Meanwhile Tree, with Pinkie and the Fairies languishing on his hands, is desperately anxious to find another piece like The Blue Bird.

Now you will begin to see what I am driving at. Tree knows that among your early plays is one called Lycko Per; and he also knows that there is only one name that strikes the European imagination more than Maeterlinck, and that is Strindberg. Why not let him have the play? Your later pieces are quite impossible at his theatre; not because it is a very big theatre (for I still contend, in spite of all you say, that your Intimes Teater is far too small even for Fröken Julie, and that nothing smaller than the Opera House is big enough for you); but because his theatre is a favorite with the innocent bourgeoisie and their daughters, who would fly horror-stricken at the very first of Julie. There is, however, attached to His Majesty's Theatre an enterprise called The Afternoon Theatre, appealing to the same sort of people who come to your Intimes Teater; and this Afternoon Theatre might very well handle one of your later works. In any case, the man who directs this Afternoon Theatre for Tree is a certain Frederick Whelen, who is also chairman of the Stage Society (which has produced Ibsen, Brieux, Tolstoi etc.), and who is now organizing a society for the performance of Strauss' Salome, forbidden here by the Censor. It is really Whelen who has worked Tree up to the pitch of believing that he must have Lycko Per or die. Apart from the fact that the production of Lycko Per might be pecuniarily useful to you, it would bring you into relations with Whelen, who would go to Stockholm by the next train if he thought you would entertain Tree's proposal.

Unfortunately, there are the usual impossible reports: It is said that you absolutely refuse to discuss Lycko Per because it is an early play—that you would fall on Whelen with fire and sword—in short, all the old Strindberg legends which circulate here just as they do in

454

Stockholm, in spite of my wife's assurances to everybody that you are a most friendly man, with memorable dark blue eyes and an appealing smile. As a matter of fact, it is necessary to keep a touch of brimstone for some people, and there are circumstances under which I should resent a proposal to begin a Strindberg campaign with Lycko Per as a declaration of cowardice to start with. But this consideration does not arise in Tree's case. He really does specifically need a play like Lycko Per for the purposes of his theatre; and nobody expects him to handle your later works there. It would be thoroughly understood that Lycko Per was your Midsummer Night's Dream and not your Hamlet; and the mere discussion and reiteration of this fact would create a good deal of curiosity to see your Hamlet in London. I therefore venture to advise you to consider the matter carefully and, if possible, favorably. I think it would be worth your while to enter into pourparlers on the subject—even if nothing came of it—for the sake of getting into communication with Whelen, who is at present much more likely to bring about a production of your later works than any other man in London; for the recently established Repertory Theatre of Charles Frohman has decided, for the present at least, to confine itself to works by English writers; and Herbert Trench, though as a poet and man of letters he understands your position and the importance of your work, is just at present too busy making money and enjoying the novelty of having proved himself a successful man of affairs, to attempt anything more than a comparatively mild sort of pioneering.

Excuse the length of this letter. If I had time I would pay another visit to Stockholm to tell you all this by word of mouth; but, as it is, I must content myself this Easter with a modest trip in France.

Yours ever
G. Bernard Shaw.

29 March 1910

My dear Strindberg,

If Lycko Per is what you describe it to be, you must have been inspired directly by heaven to write it for the satisfaction and delight of the British public. It will suit Sir Herbert Tree exactly, as his Theatre is so big and expensive that he must give the public what it wants or perish.

It seems to me that the best thing you can do is to let Tree have Lycko Per on condition that it is not to be produced until he has performed Svarta Handsken, or whatever other play you may select, at the Afternoon Theatre, the position of which I explained in my last letter.

Unfortunately I cannot read Swedish; but I see that a good deal of Svarta Handsken is in verse. This is a terrible difficulty. We have only one English writer for the stage who can turn foreign poetry into English poetry; and that is Gilbert Murray, who cares for nobody but Euripides. If Totentanz and Kronenbraut are in prose, perhaps it might be better to suggest them. I purposely leave out Vater, because somehow or other that nurse with the strait-waistcoat got on the nerves of London about twenty years ago; and ever since that people persist in talking as if you had written but one play, The Father Eternal. That, by the way, is another reason for letting them see Lycko Per in the fulness of time. It will help them to realize that you are not a man with only one plane.

I am just starting for the South of France for a month; but I shall send a copy of your letter and of this letter to Frederick Whelen, asking him to communicate with you if he can offer you a combined contract for Lycko Per with a prior production of a play to be chosen by yourself.

William Archer, the translator of Ibsen, might be persuaded to tackle Svarta Handsken. He would make a better job of the verse than most other translators.

Yours sincerely
G. Bernard Shaw

August Strindberg, Esq.,
Drottninggatan 85, IV
Stockholm.

EVENTS IN THE LIFE OF AUGUST STRINDBERG

(As compiled by Erik Hedén in his biography STRINDBERG, with additional events and dates by the translator.)

His birth 1849
Death of his mother 1862
Student at Uppsala University 1867
Public school substitute teacher 1868
Medical student 1868
Student at the Royal Academy of Acting 1869
Return to Uppsala 1870
His first published play (The Freethinker) 1870
His first play to be both published and produced (In Rome) .. 1870
University studies discontinued 1872
Editor of an insurance gazette 1873
Assistant librarian at the Royal Library 1874
First meeting with Siri von Essen 1875
His first journey to France 1876
His first marriage (to Siri von Essen) 1877
His first prolonged stay in France 1883
Domicile in Switzerland 1884
Prosecuted for heresy in Sweden 1884
Return to Stockholm to defend himself; his exoneration 1884
Return to Switzerland 1884
Domicile in France 1885
He moves to Switzerland 1886
Domiciled in Germany (Bavaria) 1887
He moves to Denmark 1887
Plans for a Scandinavian experimental theatre 1887-88
Return to Sweden 1889
Divorce from Siri von Essen 1891
He moves to Germany (Berlin) 1892
His second marriage (to Frida Uhl) 1893
His trip to England 1893
He moves to Paris 1893

The beginning of his "Inferno" period 1894
Journeys to Ystad (Sweden), Austria, and Lund (Sweden) .. 1896
His separation (1894) and second divorce 1897
Return to Paris 1897
Climax and end of his "Inferno" period 1897
Domicile in Lund (Sweden) 1896-1899
Return to Stockholm 1899
His third marriage (to Harriet Bosse) 1901
Divorce from Harriet Bosse 1904
Founding of the Intimate (Strindberg) Theatre 1907
Moves to his final domicile (the 'Blue Tower') in Stockholm .. 1908
Closing of the Intimate Theatre 1910
National subscription to the Swedish Strindberg Fund 1911
His death on May 14th 1912

PRINCIPAL WORKS
OF AUGUST STRINDBERG

PLAYS: *Mäster Olof* (*Master Olof*), 1872/1880; *Gillets hemlighet* (*The Secret of the Guild*), 1879–80/1880; *Lycko-Pers resa* (*Lucky Per's Journey*) 1881–2/1882; *Herr Bengts hustru* (*The Wife of Sir Bengt*), 1882; *Kamraterna* (*Comrades*), 1886–8/ 1888; *Fadren* (*The Father*), 1887; *Fröken Julie* (*Miss Julie*), 1888; *Fordringsägare* (*Creditors*), 1888/1890; *Paria* (*Pariah*), 1889/1890; *Den starkare* (*The Stronger*), 1889/1890; *Samum* (*Simoon*), 1889/1890; *Himmelrikets nycklar* (*The Keys of Heaven*), 1890–2/1892; *Debet och kredit* (*Debit and Credit*), 1892/1893; *Första varningen* (*The First Warning*), 1892/1893; *Inför döden* (*In the Face of Death*), 1892/1893; *Moderskärlek* (*Motherlove*), 1892/1893; *Bandet* (*The Bond*), 1892/1897; *Leka med elden* (*Playing with Fire*), 1892/1897; *Till Damaskus, I-II* (*To Damascus, Parts I and II*), 1898; *Advent* (*Advent*), 1898/1899; *Brott och brott* (*Crimes and Crimes*), 1898–9/1899; *Folkungasagan* (*The Saga of the Folk Kings*), 1899, *Gustaf Vasa* (*Gustav Vasa*), 1899; *Erik XIV* (*Erik XIV*), 1899; *Gustaf Adolf* (*Gustav Adolf*), 1899–1900/1900; *Dödsdansen* (*The Dance of Death*), 1900/1901; *Kronbruden* (*The Crown Bride*), 1900/1902; *Påsk* (Easter), 1900/1901; *Till Damaskus, III* (To *Damascus, Part III*), 1901/1904; *Engelbrekt* (*Engelbrekt*), 1901; *Carl XII* (*Charles XII*), 1901; *Svanevit* (*Swanwhite*), 1901/1902; *Kristina* (*Queen Christina*), 1901/1903; *Ett drömspel* (*A Dream Play*), 1901–2/1902; *Gustaf III* (*Gustav III*), 1902/ 1903; *Näktergalen i Wittenberg* (*The Nightingale of Wittenberg*), 1903/1904; *Oväder* (*Stormclouds*), 1907; *Brända tomten* (*The Burned Site*), 1907; *Spöksonaten* (*The Ghost Sonata*), 1907; *Pelikanen* (*The Pelican*), 1907; *Svarta handsken* (*The Black Glove*), 1908–9/1909; *Siste riddaren* (*The Last Knight*), 1908; *Abu Casems tofflor* (*The Slippers of Abu Casem*), 1908; *Riksföreståndaren* (*The Regent*), 1908/1909; *Bjälbo-Jarlen* (*The Earl of Bjälbo*), 1908/1909; *Stora landsvägen* (*The Great Highway*), 1909.

NOVELS: *Röda rummet* (*The Red Room*), 1879; *Hemsöborna* (*The Natives of Hemsö*), 1887; *I havsbandet* (*By the Open Sea*), 1890; *Götiska rummen* (*The Gothic Rooms*), 1904; *Svarta fanor* (*Black Banners*), 1904/1907; *Taklagsöl* (*The Rearing Feast*), 1906/ 1907.

AUTOBIOGRAPHICAL NOVELS: *Han och hon* (*He and She*), 1875–6/ 1919; *Tjänstekvinnans son* (*The Son of a Servant*), 1886; *Jäsningstiden* (*Fermentation Time*), 1886; *I röda rummet* (*In the Red Room*), 1886/1887; *Författaren* (*The Author*), 1887/1909; Le *Plaidoyer d'un Fou* (*The Confession of a Fool*), 1887–8/1895; *Inferno* (*Inferno*), 1897; *Legender* (*Legends*), 1897–8/1898; *Fagervik och Skamsund* (*Faircove and Foulgut*), 1902; *Ensam* (*Alone*), 1903; *Syndabocken* (*The Scapegoat*), 1906/1907.

SHORT STORIES: *Giftas I* (*Married, Part I*), 1884; *Giftas II* (*Married, Part II*), 1885/1886.

HISTORICAL WRITINGS: *Svenska folket i helg och söcken* (*The Swedish People in Holiday and Everday Life*), 1881–2/1882; *Svenska öden och äventyr* (*Swedish Destinies and Adventures*), 1882–1891/ 1884, 1904; *Historiska miniatyrer* (*Historical Miniatures*), 1905; *Nya svenska öden* (*New Swedish Destinies*), 1905/1906.

POETRY: *Dikter på vers och prosa* (*Poems in Verse and Prose*), 1883; *Sömngångarnätter* (*Sleepwalking Nights*), *I-IV,* 1883/ 1884; *V,* 1889/1890; 1900, *etc.*

MISCELLANEOUS: *En blå bok* (*A Blue Book*), 1907–1912/1907, 1908, 1912; *Memorandum till Intima Teatern* (*Memorandum to the Intimate Theatre*), 1908; *Tal till svenska nationen* (*Address to the Swedish Nation*), 1910.

The English translations which follow the original titles of the above works do not necessarily indicate that the works have been translated into English.

The date of writing of each work is followed, after a slash, by the date of original publication, except when the work was written and published in the same year.

Bibliography

Hedén, Erik., Strindberg. Stockholm; Tidens Förlag, 1926.

Lind-af-Hageby, L., August Strindberg. The Spirit of Revolt. London, Stanley Paul & Co., 1913.

Vinberg, Ola, Strindberg och hans kvinnohat. Stockholm, A.-B. Chelius, & Co., 1929.

Smirnoff, Karin, Strindbergs första hustru. Stockholm, Albert Bonniers Förlag, 1925.

Hellström, Victor, Strindberg och musiken. Stockholm, P. A. Norstedt & Söners Förlag, 1917.

Falck, August, Fem år med Strindberg. Stockholm, Wahlström & Widstrand, 1935.

Lindblad, Göran, August Strindberg som berättare, Stockholm, P. A. Norstedt & Söner, 19??.

Paul, Adolf, Min Strindbergsbok. Stockholm, P. A. Norstedt & Söner, 1930.

Paul, Adolf, Min Strindbergsbok. Stockholm, Åhlen & Åkerlund, 1915.

Smedmark, Carl Reinhold, Mäster Olof och Röda Rummet. Stockholm, Almqvist & Wiksell, 1952.

Ollén, Gunnar, Strindbergs dramatik. Stockholm, Sveriges Radio, 1961.

Meyer, Gustaf, Studentliv i Uppsala för sextio år sedan. Stockholm, P. A. Norstedt & Söners Förlag, 1930.

Smirnoff, Karin, Så var det i verkligheten. Stockholm, Albert Bonniers Förlag, 1956.

Holger Drachmann, Knut Hamsun, Justin Huntly McCarthy, Björnstjerne Björnson, Jonas Lie, Georg Brandes, Anton Nyström, Arne Garborg, Adolf Paul, Ad. Hansen, Gustaf Fröding, Laura Marholm: En bok om Strindberg. Karlstad, Forssells Boktryckeri, 1894.

Lamm, Martin, August Strindberg. Stockholm, Albert Bonniers Förlag, 1948.

Eklund, Torsten, Strindberg i blå tornet. Ögonvittnesskildringar 1908-1912. Stockholm.

Wirtanen, Atos, August Strindberg—liv och dikt. Stockholm, Bokförlaget Prisma, 1962.

Hedenberg, Sven, Strindberg i skärselden. Göteborg, Akademiförlaget-Gumperts, 1961.

Erdmann, Nils, August Strindberg. I. Från Klara skola till Röda rummet. Stockholm, Wahlström & Widstrand, 1920. II. Genom skärselden till korset. (1920)

Brandell, Gunnar, På Strindbergs vägar genom Frankrike. Stockholm, Wahlström & Widstrand, 1949.

Mortensen, Johan, Strindberg som jag minnes honom. Stockholm, C. E. Fritzes Bokförlags A.-B., 1931.

Mörner, Birger, Den Strindberg jag känt. Stockholm, Albert Bonniers Förlag, 1924.

Liebert, Arthur, Strindberg och nutidens andliga problem. Stockholm, Bokförlaget Natur och Kultur, 1925.

Claussen, Christian, En Digterskjaebne. Christiania-Copenhagen, Olaf Norli-M. Thuesen, 1913.

Falkner, Fanny, Strindberg i Blå tornet. Stockholm, P. A. Norstedt & söners Förlag, 1921.

Uddgren Gustaf, Boken om Strindberg. Göteborg, Åhlen & Åkerlunds Förlag, 1912.

Norrman, David, Strindbergs skilsmässa från Siri von Essen. Stockholm, Bokförlaget Natur och Kultur, 1953.

Paul, Adolf, Strindberg-Erinnerungen und -Briefe. Munich, Albert Langen Verlag, 1914.

Berendsohn, Walter A., August Strindbergs skärgårds- och Stockholms-skildringar. Stockholm, Rabén & Sjögren, 1962.

Brunius, August, Ansikten och masker. Stockholm, P. A. Norstedt & Söners Förlag, 1917. (Något om Strindbergs dramatiska figurer.) P. 147.

Esswein, Hermann, August Strindberg im Lichte seines Lebens und seiner Werke. Munich and Leipzig, Georg Müller, 1909.

Ahlström, Stellan, Strindbergs erövring av Paris. Stockholm, Almqvist & Wiksell, 1956.

Sprigge, Elizabeth, The Strange Life of August Strindberg. New York, The Macmillan Company, 1949.

Rahmer, S., August Strindberg: eine pathologische Studie. Munich, Ernst Reinhardt, 1907.

Taub, Hans, Strindberg als Traumdichter. Göteborg, Wettergren & Kerbers Förlag, 1945.

Lundegård, Axel, Några Strindbergsminnen knutna till en handfull brev. Stockholm, 1920.

Hedvall, Yngve, Strindberg på Stockholmsscenen. 1923.

Engström, Albert, Strindberg och jag. Stockholm, 1923.

Strindbergs systrar berätta. Stockholm, P. A. Norstedt & Söners Förlag, 1920.

Jolivet, Alfred, Le Théâtre de Strindberg. Paris, 1931.

Strindbergs brev till Harriet Bosse. Stockholm, Natur och Kultur 1932.

De återfunna breven. Stockholm, Albert Bonniers Förlag, 1955.

Paulson, Arvid, Letters of Strindberg to Harriet Bosse. New York, Thomas Nelson and Sons, 1959 (out of print).

Paulson, Arvid, Letters of Strindberg to Harriet Bosse, New York, Grosset and Dunlap, 1961.

Strindberg, Frida, Strindberg och hans andra hustru, I-II. Stockholm, 1933-34.

Lamm, Martin, Strindberg och makterna. Stockholm, 1936.

Ollén, Gunnar, Strindbergs 1900-talslyrik. Stockholm, 1941.

Jacobsen, Harry, Strindberg och hans första hustru. 1946.

Eklund, Torsten, Från Fjärdingen till Blå tornet. Stockholm, 1946.

Jacobsen, Harry, Strindberg i Firsernes København. Copenhagen, 1948.

Eklund, Torsten, Tjänstekvinnans son. En psykologisk Strindbergsstudie. Stockholm, 1948.

August Strindberg (1849-1949). Ett minnesalbum. Stockholm, Åhlen & Åkerlund, 1948.

Björck, Albert, Emanuel Swedenborg, August Strindberg och det ondas problem. Stockholm, Albert Bonniers Förlag, 1898.

Berendsohn, Walter A., Strindbergs Schauspiele aus der Schwedischen Geschichte. Berlin, W. Hilke.

Berendsohn, Walter A., August Strindbergs Parisschilderungen. Dortmund, Dortmunder Vorträge, 19??.

Berendsohn, Walter A., August Strindbergs skådespel ur svenska historien. In: Värld och vetande (Stockholm), 1959.

Berendsohn, Walter A., August Strindberg: Ein geborener Dramatiker. Munich, Langen-Müller, 1956.

Berendsohn, Walter A., Goethe och Strindberg. In: Samlaren (Stockholm), 1949.

Berendsohn, Walter A., Studier i manuskriptet till Strindbergs Karantänsmästarens andra berättelse. In: Samlaren (Stockholm), 1951.

Berendsohn, Walter A., Strindberg och Bach. In: Musiklivet—Vår sång (Stockholm), 19??.

Landquist, John, Strindbergs lyrik. In: Bonniers Månadshäften (Stockholm), June, 1912.

Hedén, Erik, Strindberg och nutidens sociala strider. In: Bonniers Månadshäften. June, 1912.

Söderblom, Nathan, Till frågan om Strindberg och religionen. In: Bonniers Månadshäften, June, 1912.

Andersson, Elis, August Strindberg. In: Göteborgsposten, 20-21 January, 1949.

Berendsohn, Walter A., Ett besök i Blå tornet. In: Värld och vetande. (Stockholm), 1961.

Strindbergs Dramen, Essays by Maximilian Harden, Richard Wendriner, Theodor Schur, Fontana, Michel, Polgar, Lindner, Widmann, Strecker, Block, Zifferer, and Elchinger. Munich and Leipzig, Georg Müller, 1911.

Uppvall, A. J., August Strindberg. A psychoanalytical study with special reference to the Oedipus complex. Boston, 1920.

Bachler, Karl, August Strindberg, Eine psychoanalytische Studie. Vienna, 1931.

Peukert, Ester, Strindbergs religiöse Dramatik. Hamburg, 1929.

Jacobsen, Harry, Digteren og Fantasten. Copenhagen, 1945.

Hagsten, Allan, Den unge Strindberg. 1951.

Norman, Nils, Den unge Strindberg och väckelserörelsen. Malmö, 1953.

Brandell, Gunnar, Strindbergs Infernokris. 1950.

Lindström, Hans, Hjärnornas kamp. Uppsala, 1952.

Borland, Harold H., Nietzsche's Influence on Swedish literature with special reference to Strindberg, Ola Hansson, Heidenstam, and Fröding. Göteborg, 1957.

Børge, Vagn, Strindbergs mystiske Teater. Copenhagen, 1942.

Elmquist, C. J., Strindbergs Kammerspil. Copenhagen, 1949.

A Touch of the Artist. In: Industria International 1962. Stockholm. (On Strindberg as the originator of abstract painting.)

Campbell, G. A., Strindberg. New York, Macmillan, 1933.

Gravier, Maurice, Strindberg et le Théâtre Moderne, In: L'Allemagne. Lyon, 1949.

Lewis, Allan, Contemporary Theatre. New York, 1962.

Liebert, Arthur, Strindberg. Seine Weltanschauung und seine Kunst. Berlin, 1920.

McGill, V. J., August Strindberg: The Bedevilled Viking. London, 1930.

Gassner, John, A Treasury of the Theatre: From Ibsen to Ionescu. New York, 1961. (See Introductions to *There are Crimes and Crimes* and *A Dream Play*. Arvid Paulson's Strindberg translations, Bantam.)

Dahlström, Carl E. W. L., Situation and Character in *Till Damaskus*. In: Publications of the Modern Languages Association, September, 1938. Pp. 886-902.

Marcus, Carl David, August Strindbergs Dramatik, Munich, 1918.

Erdmann, Nils, August Strindberg: Die Geschichte einer kämpfenden und leidenden Seele. Leipzig, 1924.

Bentley, Eric, The Playwright as Thinker. New York, Reynal, 1946.

Clark, Barrett H. and George Freedley, A History of the Modern Theatre, New York, Appleton, 1947.

von Aster, Ernest, Ibsen und Strindberg. Munich, 1921.

Marcuse, Leopold, Strindberg, das Leben der tragischen Seele. Berlin-Leipzig, 1922.

Kraus, Otto, Strindberg: Eine Kritik. Munich, 1918.

Jolivet, Alfred, Le Théâtre de Strindberg. Paris, 1931.

Mortensen, Brita M. E. and Brian W. Downs, Strindberg: An Introduction to his Life and Work. Cambridge, 1949.

von Wiese, Leopold, Strindberg: Ein Beitrag zur Soziologie der Geschlechter, Munich, 1918.

Ulanov, Barry, Makers of the Modern Theatre, McGraw-Hill, New York, 1961.

Gravier, Maurice, Strindberg, père du théâtre moderne. Stockholm, Institut suédois, 1962.

Gravier, Maurice, La dramaturgie de Strindberg. In: Les Langues Modernes, 1947.

Gravier, Maurice, Strindberg et le théâtre français contemporain. In: Les Langues Modernes, 1949.

Gravier, Maurice, Strindberg, Traducteur de lui-même. In *Mélanges,* Michaelsson, Göteborg, 1952.

Translations of Arvid Paulson

Eyes that cannot see by Albert Gnudtzmann ⎫ (Appleton)
In Confidence by Alvilde Prydz   ⎬ Out of
Poverty by Hans Alin   ⎭ print
Letters of Strindberg to Harriet Bosse (Universal Library—Grosset
and Dunlap)

Hedda Gabler ⎫
Rosmersholm ⎪
The Master Builder ⎬ By Henrik Ibsen (Bantam)
John Gabriel Borkman ⎪
When We Dead Awaken ⎭

Easter ⎫
The Father ⎪
Miss Julie ⎪
The Stronger ⎪
The Bond ⎪
Comrades ⎪
Crimes and Crimes ⎬ By August Strindberg (Bantam)
Lucky Per's Journey ⎪
The Keys of Heaven ⎪
To Damascus, Parts I-III ⎪
A Dream Play ⎪
The Great Highway ⎪
The Ghost Sonata ⎭

13 One-act Prose Plays—to be published by the Washington Square Press in the spring of 1969.

And others, including:

The Dance of Death, Parts I-II
Swanwhite
Stormclouds
The Black Glove

In: The Strindberg Reader
(Phaedra)

—and—

The Novels:
The Natives of Hemsö—The Scapegoat
By August Strindberg (Bantam)

Arvid Paulson's Ibsen translations are published by Bantam under the title "Last Plays of Henrik Ibsen." His Strindberg translations published by Bantam are: "Seven Plays by August Strindberg"; "Eight Expressionist Plays by August Strindberg"; "The Natives of Hemsö" and "The Scapegoat", two novels (in one volume). These novels have also been published separately in hardcover by Paul S. Eriksson, Inc., New York. In England "The Scapegoat" has been published by W. H. Allen & Company, London.

Strindberg, August, 1849–1912.

The Strindberg reader; a selection of writings of August Strindberg. Compiled, translated, and edited by Arvid Paulson. New York, Phaedra [1968]

467 p.   23 cm.   7.95

Includes bibliographies.

I. Paulson, Arvid, ed.   II. Title.

PT9804.P3   839.7′2′6   67–30031
                                                          MARC

Library of Congress   [2]